CR
AN ... CT 1998

SEC

CRIMINAL JUSTICE AND THE HUMAN RIGHTS ACT 1998

SECOND EDITION

Deborah Cheney
Lecturer in Law
University of Kent at Canterbury

Lisa Dickson
Lecturer in Law
University of Kent at Canterbury

Rupert Skilbeck
Barrister
36 Bedford Row

Steve Uglow
Director of Kent Criminal Justice Centre
University of Kent at Canterbury

with

John Fitzpatrick
Director of Kent Law Clinic
University of Kent at Canterbury

JORDANS
2001

Published by
Jordan Publishing Limited
21 St Thomas Street
Bristol BS1 6JS

British Library Cataloguing-in-Publication Data
A catalogue record for this book is available from the British Library.

ISBN 0 85308 724 5

Typeset by Mendip Communications Ltd, Frome, Somerset
Printed by Henry Ling Ltd, The Dorset Press, Dorchester UK

PREFACE

The preface to the first edition of this book stated that the subject was a dynamic area and readers should be aware that Convention jurisprudence was developing at a rapid rate. The production of a second edition within 2 years has proved us right. The Human Rights Act 1998 has had a major impact on the English common law where courts and judges now must address issues of fundamental rights. Those working or researching in criminal justice agencies will attest to the fact that issues of human rights are high on the agenda. Perhaps we are witnessing a sea change in the culture of public life. For example, the new referral orders under the Youth Justice and Criminal Evidence Act 1999 are enforced by community volunteers who form the Youth Offender Panels – it is noteworthy that those volunteers were critical of the lack of attention to human rights issues in their training, such as the right to legal representation. Three years earlier such matters may have been raised by specialist counsel but never would have crossed the mind of ordinary members of the local community. Debate over principles such as privacy and fairness still come second best to football at the pub but such issues now possess a prominence and importance as a result of the 1998 Act which would not otherwise have been achieved.

It must be remembered that the Act does not make the provisions of the European Convention on Human Rights part of English law. Judges must interpret existing law to be compatible with the Convention, if that is possible; legislators must legislate with the Convention in mind. Even this limited approach will have a major effect on all branches of law and especially the criminal justice system. The jurisprudence built up by the European Court of Human Rights will affect not only the substantive law but also police investigation, trial procedures, evidence, sentencing and the penal system. Not only lawyers and judges but police and prison officers and all criminal justice professionals will need to become versed in the techniques and principles of the Convention.

This second edition follows the pattern of its ancestor. Chapters 1 and 2 consider the detailed provisions of the Act and its impact on the criminal law. Chapter 3 examines pre-trial procedure, especially in relation to police investigation and police powers. Chapter 4 concentrates on the elements which are necessary to ensure the right to a fair trial. Chapter 5 looks at the effect of Convention rights on the sentencing process and Chapter 6 on the rights of prisoners. In all these areas, there is a range of common law and statutory rules which may become the subject of challenge as being incompatible with Convention principles.

The book has in many ways been a collaborative effort but Rupert Skilbeck has taken over responsibility for Chapters 1 and 2 from John Fitzpatrick. The other authors remain the same: Steve Uglow for Chapters 3 and 4, Lisa Dickson for Chapter 5 and Deborah Cheney for Chapter 6. We would like to acknowledge the considerable research help of Laura Jayne Smith and the even greater patience of our publishers. The law is stated as at 1 August 2001.

Deborah Cheney
Lisa Dickson
Rupert Skilbeck
Steve Uglow

August 2001

CONTENTS

TABLE OF CASES

References are to paragraph numbers.

TABLE OF STATUTES

References are to paragraph numbers.

TABLE OF STATUTORY INSTRUMENTS AND CODES

References are to paragraph numbers.

TABLE OF EUROPEAN AND INTERNATIONAL MATERIALS

References are to paragraph numbers.

TABLE OF FOREIGN ENACTMENTS

References are to paragraph numbers.

TABLE OF ABBREVIATIONS

AG	Attorney-General
CCRC	Criminal Cases Review Commission
the Convention	Convention for the Protection of Human Rights and Fundamental Freedoms 1950 (European Convention on Human Rights)
CPT	Council of Europe Committee for the Prevention of Torture
CRO	Criminal Records Office
CSC	close supervision centre
DG	Director General of the Prison Service
DLP	discretionary lifer panel
DPP	Director of Public Prosecutions
The European Court or the Court	the European Court of Human Rights
HMCIP	Her Majesty's Chief Inspector of Prisons
HMPS or PS	Her Majesty's Prison Service or Prison Service
PACE 1984	Police and Criminal Evidence Act 1984
PII	public interest immunity

Chapter 1

THE EUROPEAN CONVENTION ON HUMAN RIGHTS

1.1 INTRODUCTION

The arrival of the Human Rights Act 1998 is a momentous development, not only in terms of the legal pursuit of human rights, but also in terms of its wider constitutional and juridical significance. Whilst the courts have initially been anxious to control claims under the Act so as to maintain continuity, the Act sets out a new constitutional order for the country. It gives a new place to human rights in the UK. It also adjusts the relationship between Parliament, the executive and the judiciary, and it introduces a new body of law and a new approach to interpreting and developing the law for our judges. British lawyers who engage with the Act at any level will need a sound understanding of, and feel for, the history and the jurisprudence of its source – the European Convention on Human Rights. The UK remains a party to the Convention, and subject to the jurisdiction of the European Court of Human Rights (the European Court).

1.2 BACKGROUND TO THE CONVENTION[1]

On 5 May 1949, the instrument creating the Council of Europe was signed in London on behalf of 10 European countries. The new organisation was a manifestation not only of the post-Second World War desire to promote European unity, but also of the Cold War. The signatories wished to distance their countries not only from the atrocities of the previous conflict, but also from the influence of the Soviet Union, especially in Central and Eastern Europe. They sought to promote these aims by giving specific regional effect to the Universal Declaration of Human Rights which was issued by the United Nations in 1948.

Article 1 of the Council's Statute stated its aim to be 'greater unity between its members for the purpose of safeguarding and realising the ideals and principles which are their common heritage and facilitating their economic and social progress'. Article 3 declared that members 'must accept the principles of the rule of law, and of the enjoyment of all persons within its jurisdiction of human rights and fundamental freedoms'. To ensure adherence to that commitment, 12 members of the Council signed the Convention

---

1   See MW Janis, RS Kay and AW Bradley *European Human Rights Law: Text and Materials* (Clarendon Press, 1995), ch 1; DJ Harris, M O'Boyle and C Warbrick *Law of the European Convention on Human Rights* (Butterworths, 1995), ch 1.

for the Protection of Human Rights and Fundamental Freedoms (the Convention) in Rome on 4 November 1950.[2] It came into force on 3 September 1953.

Under the Convention, the Member States undertook to secure for everyone within their jurisdiction the various rights and freedoms set out in the text of the Convention. A Commission of Human Rights was established to investigate alleged breaches of the Convention and to conciliate where possible, and a Court of Human Rights was established to adjudicate in the absence of a friendly settlement. The Committee of Ministers, the executive of the Council of Europe, and therefore a political body, was constituted under the Convention to hear certain cases not referred to the Court, and to supervise the execution of the judgments of the Court. The institutions are based in Strasbourg.

British lawyers played a prominent role in the drafting of the Convention but in the discussions leading up to the final agreement the UK opposed both the right of individual petition to the Commission and the creation of the European Court. In the event, recognising the right of individual petition (former Art 25) and acknowledging the jurisdiction of the Court (former Art 46) were both made optional for the contracting parties. With time, attitudes changed, and on 14 January 1966 the UK became the tenth country to have ratified both Arts 25 and 46 of the Convention.

1.3   SUCCESS OF THE CONVENTION

The authority and the caseload of the Commission and the Court have increased very gradually. In the 1950s, the Court did not give judgment in any case; in the 1960s there were 10 judgments; in the 1970s, 26; and in the 1980s, 169. In the 1990s (to June 1998) there were more than 750 judgments. From its inception up to the end of 1997, the Commission has registered over 39,000 applications (up to 1991, the figure was just over 17,000) and made over 33,000 decisions – nearly 29,000 cases were declared inadmissible and over 4,000 admissible. It should be noted that up to 1998, only 13 inter-State applications had been registered by the Commission; the remainder came from individuals.

By October 1998, the UK had seen 135 cases against it referred to the Court, and a violation of the Convention was found in 52 cases. In comparison, Denmark, which had ratified Arts 25 and 46 by 1953, had seven cases referred to the Court, with a violation found in three cases; France (ratified by 1981), had 118 referrals and 59 violation cases; Germany (1955), had 35 referrals and 15 violation cases; Italy (1973), had 155 referrals and 101 violation cases; and the Netherlands (1960), had 50 referrals and 30 violation cases. In 1999 and 2000 the Court found violations in a further 28 cases.

---

2   Belgium, Denmark, France, Germany, Iceland, Ireland, Italy, Luxembourg, the
       Netherlands, Norway, Turkey and the UK. Sweden and Greece signed on 28 November
       1950.

The response of the UK Government to adverse judgments has been overwhelmingly to accept them, and over time to make consequential changes to domestic law and practice where appropriate.[3] For example, the Interception of Communications Act 1985, which regulates such interception and establishes a tribunal to hear complaints about it, flowed from the decision in *Malone v UK*,[4] in which the Court found that telephone tapping amounted to an infringement of the applicant's right under Art 8 of the Convention to respect for his private life.

When the European Court found, in the case of *Brogan v UK*,[5] that the extended powers of detention under the Prevention of Terrorism (Temporary Provisions) Act 1984 abrogated the prisoner's right, under Art 5, to be brought promptly before a judge, the Government decided not to amend the law. The UK remained within the terms of the Convention, however, by availing itself of the right, under Art 15, to derogate from Art 5 to the extent necessary to preserve the domestic legislation, on the grounds that a public emergency existed in this country, although that derogation has now been removed.

It is widely acknowledged that detainees, criminal suspects, prisoners, the mentally ill, homosexuals, schoolchildren, journalists and many others in the UK can trace the strengthening or clarification of their rights and protections to decisions of the European Commission and the European Court. The other European countries which are party to the Convention have also accepted and applied the decisions of the Convention bodies. For a supra-national legal institution to have established such authority, and to have had such a specific impact on the lives of individuals in so many countries, is a remarkable achievement.

1.4 THE CONVENTION TODAY

The Convention has been in danger of becoming a victim of its own success. Not only has the flow of cases from existing members swollen rapidly, but so too has the list of members. By 2001, 43 countries had signed up and ratified former Arts 25 and 46.[6] For a number of years there has been a substantial backlog in cases awaiting a decision. Undoubtedly, the most significant development for the Council and the Convention has been the extension of its

---

3   See C Gearty 'The United Kingdom and the European Court of Human Rights' in C Gearty (ed) *European Civil Liberties and the European Convention on Human Rights* (Martinus Nijhoff Publishers, 1997).
4   (1984) Series A/82.
5   (1988) Series A/145-B.
6   Albania, Andorra, Armenia, Austria, Azerbaijan, Belgium, Bulgaria, Croatia, Cyprus, Czech Republic, Denmark, Estonia, Finland, France, Georgia, Germany, Greece, Hungary, Iceland, Ireland, Italy, Latvia, Liechtenstein, Lithuania, Luxembourg, Malta, Moldova, the Netherlands, Norway, Poland, Portugal, Romania, Russia, San Marino, Slovakia, Slovenia, Spain, Sweden, Switzerland, the Former Yugoslav Republic of Macedonia, Turkey, Ukraine and the UK.

authority to the countries of Central and Eastern Europe in the wake of the end of the Cold War.

As a result of these changes, the institutions of the Convention were reformed. As of 1 November 1998 a new single Plenary Court replaced the old Commission and Court.[7] The new Court sits in: Committees (of three judges), which consider applications and may, unanimously, and with finality, reject them; Chambers (of seven judges) to which cases are referred for a decision on admissibility, the pursuit of a friendly settlement and a judgment on the merits; and a Grand Chamber (of 17 judges) which hears appeals (or takes references) from a Chamber on serious issues either concerning the interpretation of the Convention, or of general importance. Its judgments are final. The changes are designed to speed up the hearing of cases, and to that end the judges (one from each Member State) who are elected to the Court now sit full time. The role of the Committee of Ministers is now largely confined to supervising the execution of judgments of the Court under the new Art 46. Under the new Art 34 the right of individual application is now non-negotiable.

1.5   LAW OF THE CONVENTION

The Convention is one of many global and regional treaties on human rights which have been agreed since the Second World War.[8] It derives immediately from the work of the United Nations. The Preamble to the United Nations Charter 1945 reaffirmed 'faith in fundamental human rights', and Article 5 of the Charter stressed the need to promote 'universal respect for the observance of human rights and fundamental freedoms'. The traditional division of the relevant rights and freedoms into two categories was expressed in the eventual emergence of the two separate treaties promoted by the United Nations: the International Covenant on Civil and Political Rights 1966 and the International Covenant on Economic and Social Rights 1966. The Convention mirrors the first of those Covenants, and the substantive rights it protects, in Arts 2 to 14 and the Protocols, are mainly civil and political rights. The right to education in Art 2 of the First Protocol is one example of a 'social' right.

The general scheme of the Convention is to set out the general right or freedom to be protected, for example, 'Everyone's right to life shall be protected by law' (Art 2), or 'Everyone has the right to freedom of expression' (Art 10), and then to set out the different exceptions, limitations, restrictions and qualifications which might apply in each case. They will vary in application depending upon the nature of the right. For example, Art 3, 'No one shall be subjected to torture or inhuman or degrading treatment or punishment', is absolute. Article 7 (which provides that nobody can be convicted of a criminal offence until it was a criminal offence under national or international law when it was committed) is subject only to the proviso that such a conviction can be justified if the relevant act 'was criminal according to the general principles of

---

7   See Arts 19–56 of the Convention as replaced by the Eleventh Protocol.
8   See S Davidson *Human Rights* (Open University Press, 1993), chs 1 and 4–7.

law recognised by civilised nations'. Article 14 provides that the rights and freedoms set out in the Convention shall be secured without discrimination on any of a number of familiar grounds. This is also absolute, but this anti-discrimination provision relates only to the enjoyment of rights set out in the Convention. Discrimination in respect of a matter not protected by the Convention (such as a right to employment) is not a breach of the Convention.[9]

In addition to the articles of the Convention there are four Protocols relating to substantive rights. The UK has ratified the First Protocol (property, education (with a reservation) and free elections), and the Sixth Protocol (abolition of the death penalty). It has not, as yet, ratified the Fourth Protocol (imprisonment for debt, freedom of movement, expulsion of nationals and aliens), or the Seventh Protocol (expulsion of aliens, criminal appeals, wrongful conviction, double jeopardy, equality between spouses). The Government has indicated its intention to ratify the Seventh Protocol.[10]

Under Art 57, a Member State may:

> 'make a reservation in respect of any particular provision of the Convention to the extent that any law then in force in its territory is not in conformity with the provision. Reservations of a general character shall not be permitted.'[11]

Under Art 15, a State may derogate from most, but not all, of the articles of the Convention 'in time of war or other public emergency threatening the life of the nation'.[12] No derogation is possible under Art 2 (the right to life), except in respect of deaths resulting from lawful acts of war, Art 3 (torture, inhuman or degrading treatment or punishment), Art 4(1) (slavery or servitude), or Art 7 (retroactive criminal liability and punishment).

1.6   RELATIONSHIP TO MEMBER STATES

The Convention is based upon the 'ideals and principles' which are the 'common heritage' of the Member States. It is therefore unsurprising that its legal standards are closely based on the national law of those States, and that the Court further draws on those standards in interpreting and applying the terms of the Convention. Nevertheless, the Convention exists in international law to regulate national law in order to ensure that its own standards prevail. So far as possible, this is left to the Member States themselves. Most of the early signatories incorporated the Convention into their domestic law.

---

9   The Twelfth Protocol to the Convention, open for signature since 4 November 2000, provides for a free-standing prohibition against discrimination *on any ground* by a public authority. It enters into force once 25 States have ratified it.

10   In the White Paper *Rights Brought Home: The Human Rights Bill*, Cm 3782 (1997).

11   The UK entered a reservation in respect of Art 2, First Protocol (right to education) on 20 March 1952 to the effect that it would 'respect the right of parents to ensure such education and teaching in conformity with their own religious and philosophical convictions' only 'so far as it is compatible with the provision of efficient instruction and training, and the avoidance of unreasonable public expenditure'.

12   The UK previously had a derogation to Art 5 in respect of the terrorist legislation in Northern Ireland, but this was withdrawn in March 2001.

Furthermore, Art 13 provides that effective remedies must exist in national law in respect of violations of the rights set out in the Convention, irrespective of domestic incorporation. The role of the Convention, therefore, is primarily supervisory. Under Art 35, applications under the Convention may be dealt with only 'after all domestic remedies have been exhausted', and within six months of the decision complained of. Given this background, it is unsurprising that some 88% of applications to the Commission have been declared inadmissible.

If the Court does find a violation of the Convention, it 'shall, if necessary, afford just satisfaction to the injured party' (Art 41). The Committee of Ministers is empowered by Art 46 to supervise the execution of the judgments of the Court. Those judgments are essentially declaratory in nature, although the authority to afford just satisfaction extends to ordering financial compensation for legal costs and damages for pecuniary and non-pecuniary loss. The levels of compensation and damages have been criticised as being too low, rarely amounting to more than £10,000.[13] However, more recently the Court has been awarding larger sums in damages. In the recent case of *Z and Others v UK*,[14] the Court made awards of up to £50,000 for future medical costs, up to £50,000 for loss of employment opportunities and £32,000 for non-pecuniary loss for cases involving long-term abuse. The Committee of Ministers communicates with relevant Member States to ensure compliance with judgments, for example by proposing amendments to the domestic law. As noted above, the level of State compliance is very high.

It should be noted that the Convention is a treaty between States, and imposes a duty on States only to secure to everyone within their jurisdiction the various rights and freedoms set out. It imposes no direct duties on individuals, and no application can be brought against a private person. This is not to say that relations between private individuals may not be affected, particularly via the imposition of positive obligations on States (see **1.7.5** below).

Finally, it is of great significance for the relationship between the UK and Strasbourg that any application to the Court can be made only after the new domestic remedies have been exhausted. With the arrival of the Human Rights Act 1998, for the first time the Court in Strasbourg will now be dealing only with claims that have already been subject to a thorough and reasoned judicial decision in the UK. The Court has, of course, already considered several cases which have been dealt with in the higher courts in the UK. British courts have not, however, previously interpreted and applied the Convention rights in the way that they will now be required to do.

---

13   See AR Mowbray 'The European Court of Human Rights' Approach to Just Satisfaction' in *Public Law* (Sweet & Maxwell, 1997), pp 647–660; and see **2.4.8**, fn 49 below.

14   [2001] 2 FLR 612.

1.7 INTERPRETATION OF THE CONVENTION[15]

The interpretation of the Convention has been the property of the Commission and the Court and is now the sole property of the single Court. The existing jurisprudence of the Court is, of course, more authoritative, and the Commission has followed the Court in cases of disagreement. Neither the Court nor the Commission has adopted a doctrine of binding precedent, and neither has considered itself bound by its previous decisions. However, the Court stated in *Cossey v UK* that 'it usually follows and applies its own precedents, such a course being in the interests of legal certainty and the orderly development of the Convention case law'.[16]

British judges who have to decide any question arising under the Human Rights Act 1998 in connection with the 'Convention rights' set out in the Act must take into account the judgments and decisions of the Court and Commission. Taking into account those judgments and decisions will also involve taking into account the interpretative principles which the Commission and Court have evolved in order to reach those judgments and decisions. Some of these principles will be of particular importance.

1.7.1 Effect should be given to the object and purpose of the Convention

As an international treaty, the Convention falls to be interpreted (by the European Court) according to the rules of international law, and in particular the Vienna Convention on the Law of Treaties 1969. Article 31 of the Vienna Convention provides that an international treaty shall be interpreted 'in good faith in accordance with the ordinary meaning to be given to the terms of the treaty in their context and in the light of its object and purpose'. The object and purpose of the Convention has been said by the European Court to be, amongst other things, the protection of 'individual human rights',[17] the promotion of 'the ideals and values of a democratic society'[18] and the rule of law.

The Court has, in fact, adopted a strong teleological emphasis in its approach to interpreting the Convention, and has given the broad formulation of the substantive rights themselves in the text of the Convention. It follows that the Court has enjoyed a certain scope in their application, whilst remaining, of course, bound by the clear meaning of the text. For example, in *Golder v UK* the Court had to consider whether Art 6(1), in addition to guaranteeing a fair trial, was also guaranteeing a right of access to the Court in the first place. The latter was by no means spelt out in the Article. Specifically invoking, inter alia, Art 31

---

15   See DJ Harris, M O'Boyle and C Warbrick *Law of the European Convention on Human Rights* (Butterworths, 1995), pp 5–28. *NB*: There are two equally authentic texts, in English and in French, and these are the official languages for Convention proceedings.

16   (1990) Series A/184, para 35.

17   In *Soering v UK* (1989) Series A/161, para 87.

18   In *Kjeldsen, Busk Madsen and Pedersen v Denmark* (1976) Series A/23, para 53.

of the Vienna Convention, and the 'context' of Art 6, the Court decided that it did.[19]

1.7.2 The Convention should be seen as a 'living instrument'

The Court followed its declaration in *Cossey* (above) that it would usually follow its own decisions with the proviso that it would depart from them for 'cogent reasons', for example to 'ensure that the interpretation of the Convention reflects societal changes and remains in line with present day conditions'.[20] In *Tyrer v UK* the Court stated that the Convention 'is a living instrument which ... must be interpreted in the light of present-day conditions'.[21] In holding that judicial corporal punishment (a 15-year-old on the Isle of Man was sentenced to three strokes of the birch by a juvenile court) was a violation of Art 3 (degrading punishment), the Court stated that it was not applying the standards which might have been accepted when the Convention was drafted but was 'influenced by the developments and commonly accepted standards' in Member States.

The importance of this is that UK courts, in interpreting older case-law of the Court and the Commission, should be aware that Strasbourg would not necessarily decide the case in the same way if it were confronted with it today, and neither should UK courts feel so bound. Domestic tribunals can be encouraged to accept changes in society and to decide cases differently to their predecessors.

1.7.3 The Convention should deliver practical and effective rights

One of the other reasons advanced by the Court for its decision in *Golder* (above) serves to illustrate another interpretative principle adopted by the Court, which was clearly stated in *Artico v Italy*, that 'the Convention is intended to guarantee not rights that are theoretical or illusory but rights that are practical and effective'.[22] In *Golder*, a prisoner in the UK had been denied permission to consult a solicitor. He wanted to take a civil action for libel. The Court stated:

> 'It would be inconceivable ... that Article 6(1) should describe in detail the procedural guarantees afforded to parties in a pending lawsuit and should not first protect that which alone makes it in fact possible to benefit from such guarantees, that is, access to a court.'

Neither did it make any difference that there was no formal legal impediment to the prisoner bringing the libel action. The Court considered the actual hindrance sufficient to constitute a violation.[23]

---

19   (1975) Series A/18.
20   (1990) Series A/184, para 35.
21   (1978) Series A/26, para 31.
22   (1980) Series A/37, para 33.
23   (1975) Series A/18, paras 26, 35. See **2.4.8**, fn 49 below, on the *Osman* case.

1.7.4 Proportionality should be observed

In many different contexts the Court must, in interpreting the Convention, strike a fair balance between individual rights and the general interests of the community. This particularly concerns, but is by no means limited to, decisions under Arts 8 to 11, as to whether a restriction on a substantive right, while permissible in principle to protect specified other interests, is in fact 'proportionate to the legitimate aim pursued'.[24] In *Steel and Others v UK*,[25] for example, the Court found that the arrest, detention for seven hours and release without charge of three of the applicants, who had been handing out leaflets and holding up banners outside an arms conference in London, had not only been a breach of Art 5(1) (lawful arrest and detention), but also a breach of Art 10 (freedom of expression) as it 'had been disproportionate to the aim of preventing disorder or of protection of the rights of others' (two of the interests which might justify, under Art 10(2), restrictions being placed on freedom of expression).

1.7.5 Positive obligations

Because the Convention deals primarily with civil and political rights, and because it imposes obligations only on States, the predominant character of those obligations is negative, for example not to subject persons to torture (Art 3), and not to interfere with freedom of expression (Art 10). To secure many of the rights, however, States are implicitly obliged to take positive steps. For example, Art 6 provides that 'everyone is entitled to a fair and public hearing within a reasonable time by an independent and impartial tribunal established by law'. Member States are therefore obliged not only to provide courts, but also legal aid in appropriate cases, to give individuals adequate resources in order to prevent breaches of the Convention.

In *X and Y v Netherlands*, a 16-year-old mentally handicapped girl was sexually assaulted by an adult male of sound mind. He could not be prosecuted because of a loophole in Dutch law, although he could be sued. The Court found that the absence of a criminal procedure was a violation by the State of its duty to secure respect for her private life under Art 8. The Court said that the article:

> '. . . does not merely compel the state to abstain from . . . interference: in addition to
> this primarily negative undertaking, there may be positive obligations inherent in
> an effective respect for private and family life . . . These obligations may involve the
> adoption of measures designed to secure respect for private life even in the sphere
> of the relations of individuals between themselves.'[26]

This positive obligation can be expressed in a number of different ways. States may be required to have proper policing in order to allow for demonstrations to take place[27] and thus prevent breaches of the right to freedom of assembly or

---

24   *Handyside v UK* (1976) Series A/24, para 49.
25   (1999) 28 EHRR 603.
26   (1985) Series A/91, para 23.
27   *Platform Ärzte für das Leben v Austria* (1988) Series A/139, (1991) 13 EHRR 204.

of expression. There is also a duty to provide information to prevent breaches of Convention rights, for example information regarding environmental pollution.[28]

This also makes clear how the Convention may have a 'horizontal effect', that is to say, on the legal relations between private individuals. States, and by extension the courts, must ensure that those who appear before them are treated in accordance with the Convention. Therefore, they cannot uphold a claim that would violate the human rights of one of the parties. Consequently, litigants are bound to be able to use the Convention against one another.

1.7.6   Convention legal terms may have an autonomous Convention meaning

When the Court, for example, considers terms such as 'criminal charge', 'tribunal' and 'witness' in an Art 6 (right to a fair trial) case, those terms are by no means confined to their meaning in the national law of the relevant State. Not only would that allow Member States to avoid the application of the article by choosing appropriate definitions, but domestic definitions might distract the Court from the principle at stake. For example, Art 6 applies to persons 'charged', and guarantees them a hearing 'within a reasonable time'. When are they charged? In *Deweer v Belgium* the Court found it necessary to look 'behind the appearances and investigate the realities of the procedure in question' and concluded that the applicant was charged when he was 'substantially affected' by the process.[29] In a UK case an applicant has been held to have been charged in the Convention sense from the moment of arrest. In the definition of the term 'criminal', the Court has developed specific guidelines (the *Engel* criteria)[30] in order to assess the nature of the charge against an individual. To make that decision it is necessary to look at: (a) the classification of the offence in domestic law; (b) the nature of the offence itself; and (c) the nature and severity of any possible penalty.

1.7.7   States should be allowed a 'margin of appreciation'

The doctrine of the 'margin of appreciation' is a very important principle of interpretation adopted by the Court, but the domestic application of this doctrine promises to be problematic. The British judge is not in the same position as a European Court judge to concede a 'margin of appreciation' to certain public authorities, or in respect of certain legislative provisions. The margin has been granted by the Strasbourg bodies to Member States, in recognition of differences between those States. Nevertheless, in terms of their general interpretation and application of Convention rights, British judges will no doubt be mindful of any margin they might be granted if challenged in Strasbourg.

---

28   *Lopez Ostra v Spain* (1998) 26 EHRR 357.
29   (1980) Series A/35, paras 44, 46.
30   *Engel v The Netherlands* (1978–80) 1 EHRR 647.

The doctrine was first fully explained in *Handyside v UK*.[31] In this case, the publisher of *The Little Red Schoolbook* was convicted and fined under the Obscene Publications Act 1959, and confiscated copies of his books were destroyed. The Court had to decide whether such interference with the right to freedom of expression under Art 10(1) was necessary in a democratic society for the protection of morals under Art 10(2). The Court stated that:

> 'In particular it is not possible to find in the domestic law of the various Contracting States a uniform European conception of morals. The view taken by their respective laws of the requirements of morals varies from time to time and from place to place, especially in our era which is characterised by a rapid and far-reaching evolution of opinions on the subject. By reason of their direct and continuous contact with the vital forces of their countries, State authorities are in a better position than the international judge to give an opinion upon the exact contents of these requirements as well as on the "necessity" of a "restriction" or "penalty" intended to meet them. . . . Consequently, Art 10(2) leaves to the Contracting States a margin of appreciation. This margin of appreciation is given both to the domestic legislator ("prescribed by law") and to the bodies, judicial amongst others, that are called upon to interpret and apply the laws in force. . . . Nevertheless, Art 10(2) does not give the Contracting States an unlimited power of appreciation. The Court, which, with the Commission, is responsible for ensuring the observance of those States' engagements, is empowered to give the final ruling on whether a "restriction" or "penalty" is reconcilable with freedom of expression as protected by Art 10. The domestic margin of appreciation thus goes hand in hand with a European supervision.'[32]

This margin of appreciation (some prefer the rendition 'evaluation') which is allowed to Member States is, again, more commonly exercised under Arts 8 to 11, but has by no means been limited to them. For an institution purporting to apply common standards this has been one of the more controversial principles adopted by the Court, but has been accepted on the basis that it enables States with very different standards to retain confidence in the Convention.

The UK courts have grasped this issue immediately. In the case of *R v DPP ex parte Kebilene*,[33] Lord Hope discussed the issue of the margin of appreciation, pointing out that it is an international legal concept by which Strasbourg defers to the domestic courts:

> 'This technique is not available to the national courts when they are considering Convention issues arising within their own countries. But in the hands of the national courts also the Convention would be seen as an expression of fundamental principles rather than as a set of mere rules.'

He then goes on to point out that there may be difficult choices to be made between the rights of the individual and the needs of society, and states that 'In some circumstances it will be appropriate for the courts to recognise that there is an area of judgment within which the judiciary will defer, on democratic

---

31   (1976) Series A/24.
32   Ibid, paras 48–50.
33   [1999] 3 WLR 972 at 994.

grounds, to the considered opinion of the elected body or person whose act or decision is said to be incompatible with the Convention'. In the case of *Kebilene*, the Court was considering terrorist legislation, which Strasbourg has recognised as being of a 'special nature'. Consequently, in this case, which was heard prior to the enactment of the Human Rights Act 1998, but which considered it in depth, the House of Lords suggested that there is an internal 'margin of appreciation' whereby the courts may defer to the executive on certain issues.

It is important to remember that in coming to its decisions, Strasbourg has to make a comparison between 43 different countries, comparing common law, civil and Stalinist legal systems from a wide variety of societies. It is essentially applying a lowest common denominator below which standards may not fall. It will often use the 'margin of appreciation' in order to avoid having to set a higher standard on a matter that is not fundamental. Consequently, Strasbourg frequently will find no violation of a particular right, and much of the case-law will express that. However, despite the comments of Lord Hope, which should only affect a minority of cases, the UK judges considering the Human Rights Act 1998 and Strasbourg case-law do not apply such a judgment. Consequently, they can be invited to ignore previously reported cases from the European Court which did not find a violation due to the application of the margin of appreciation.

Chapter 2
THE HUMAN RIGHTS ACT 1998[1]

2.1 INTRODUCTION

According to its long title, the Human Rights Act 1998[2] is intended 'to give further effect to the rights and freedoms guaranteed under the European Convention on Human Rights ...'. It is a formulation that deserves close attention. The Act is not, it should be noted, intended to incorporate in a strict sense the European Convention on Human Rights (the Convention), or even the rights secured by the articles of the Convention, into domestic law. It does not declare those provisions to be the law of the land, justiciable in the normal way.[3]

If incorporation had been simply effected in this way, it would have severely undermined parliamentary sovereignty. Such an Act would, given the positive and general statement of the Convention rights, have allowed the judges unprecedented scope to declare any earlier Act impliedly repealed to the extent that they found it to be inconsistent with those general provisions. The Human Rights Act 1998 in fact provides what has frequently been described as an 'ingenious' attempt to avoid this potential conflict between the principle of parliamentary sovereignty and the desire to make human rights claims based on the Convention justiciable in the UK.

Such bare incorporation would also have given individuals the right to sue one another in respect of the new rights, for example degrading treatment (Art 3), or invasions of privacy (Art 8). The Act is not intended to have this 'horizontal'

---

1   The Act received Royal Assent on 9 November 1998. Section 18 (the appointment of judges to the European Court of Human Rights), s 20 (the making of orders under the Act) and s 21(5) (the abolition of the death penalty) came into force on that day; s 19 (statements of compatibility) came into force on 24 November 1998 (under the Human Rights Act 1998 (Commencement) Order 1998, SI 1998/2882); the remaining provisions came into force on 2 October 2000.

2   Note: the Human Rights Act 1998 is a short, tightly drafted piece of legislation with very wide-ranging implications. There was a full debate on the Bill in both Houses of Parliament. The Lord Chancellor, Lord Irvine of Lairg, who introduced the Bill in the House of Lords, commented extensively on the intention behind many of the provisions, and on their implications. His comments (and those of other ministers and others) are fully drawn on in this account.

3   The word 'further' is used because 'our courts already apply the convention in many different circumstances': the Lord Chancellor, Lord Irvine of Lairg *Hansard* (HL) vol 583, col 478 (18 November 1997). On the subject of incorporation, the Lord Chancellor said, 'I have to make this point absolutely plain. The European Convention on Human Rights under this Bill is not made part of our law' *Hansard* (HL) vol 585, col 421 (29 January 1998). Further, on the distinction between 'full incorporation' and the approach of the Act, see the Lord Chancellor's comment, *Hansard* (HL) vol 585, col 840 (5 February 1998).

effect, but to reserve the institution of proceedings in respect of any breach of these rights, consistently with the Convention itself, to the 'vertical' relationship between the individual, on the one hand, and the State and public authorities, on the other.[4] As we shall see, however, relations between private individuals are by no means excluded from the operation of the Act.

2.2   OVERVIEW OF THE ACT

How, then, does the Act give further effect to the rights and freedoms of the Convention? In the first place, it declares that certain articles of the Convention, to be called 'the Convention rights', are 'to have effect for the purposes of the Act' (s 1(2)).

The 'purposes of the Act' are essentially twofold. They flow as two distinct, although connected, strands throughout the Act. The first strand concerns the compatibility of domestic legislation (and of its application) with Convention rights, and the means of amending domestic legislation in a way which is sensitive to the relationship between the judiciary and Parliament. The second concerns the right of individuals to pursue and rely upon their Convention rights in domestic courts, and the impact that might have on the rights of others.

2.2.1   Compatibility of legislation

(a) The Act provides that all primary and subordinate legislation must, so far as it is possible to do so, be read and given effect to in a way which is compatible with the Convention rights, and that any court or tribunal determining any question which arises in connection with a Convention right must take into account the judgments and decisions of the Strasbourg bodies (ss 2, 3).

(b) When a superior court (High Court or above) is satisfied that a provision of primary legislation is incompatible with a Convention right, that court may make a 'declaration of that incompatibility'. Such a declaration does not affect the validity, continuing operation or enforcement of any incompatible primary legislation (s 4).

(c) A minister of the Crown 'may' respond to such a 'declaration of incompatibility', if the minister considers that there are compelling reasons for doing so, by making such amendments to primary legislation by statutory instrument, called a 'remedial order', as the minister considers necessary to remove the incompatibility (s 10). This has been called the 'fast-track' route to amending legislation.

(d) A minister bringing a Bill before Parliament must in future make a

---

4   The Lord Chancellor, Lord Irving of Lairg: '... we have not provided for the convention rights to be directly justiciable in actions between private individuals. We have sought to protect the human rights of individuals against the abuse of power by the state, broadly defined, rather than to protect them from each other' *Hansard* (HL) vol 585, col 840 (5 February 1998).

'statement of compatibility' to accompany the Bill to the effect that in the minister's view the Bill is compatible with the Convention rights, or to the effect that the minister is unable to make such a statement, but that the Government wishes to proceed with the Bill (s 19).

2.2.2   Remedies for breaches of human rights by public authorities

(a) The Act provides that it is unlawful for a public authority to act in a way which is incompatible with a Convention right; it states that public authorities include courts and tribunals, and any other persons whose functions are of a public nature, but does not include those persons in respect of their private acts (s 6).

(b) It enables an individual to bring proceedings against public authorities which are alleged to have acted unlawfully, but only if that individual is (or would be) a victim of that unlawful act; and if the complaint is against a court or tribunal only by way of appeal, judicial review or in such other forum as may be prescribed (ss 7(1)(a), 9).

(c) It enables an individual to rely on a Convention right in 'any legal proceedings', again subject to being a (potential) victim of any unlawful act by a public authority (s 7(1)(b)).

(d) It empowers a court or tribunal to grant such relief or remedy, or make such order within its powers as it considers just and appropriate, including the award of damages (but only if the court or tribunal has the power to award damages or compensation in civil proceedings); and if damages are to be awarded it must take into account the principles applied by the European Court of Human Rights (the European Court) in awarding them (s 8).

(e) Where a court is considering the grant of relief which might affect the respondent's exercise of the Convention right to freedom of expression (Art 10), it must have particular regard to the importance of that right, and be satisfied as to a number of additional matters. Similarly, if a court is determining any question which might affect the exercise by a religious organisation of its right to freedom of thought, conscience or religion (Art 9), the court must have particular regard to the importance of that right (ss 12, 13).

2.3   KEY ISSUES

–   Compatible legislation and parliamentary sovereignty.
–   Bringing rights home to individuals.
–   Public authorities.
–   The application of the Convention rights between individuals.
–   The development of the common law.
–   The operation of the Act in the criminal justice system.
–   No Human Rights Commission.

2.3.1   Compatible legislation and parliamentary sovereignty

There are various mechanisms to ensure that legislation is compatible with the Convention. These mechanisms are designed to ensure that the courts constantly consider the application, and proper construction, of the Convention rights. They are also designed to preserve parliamentary sovereignty, in a formal sense at least, in that the judiciary is given no power to strike down, amend or impede the operation of primary legislation which it believes is incompatible with the Convention rights. Amendment in such cases is left up to a minister who 'may' (not 'shall') make a (draft) 'remedial order', but only if the minister considers there are 'compelling reasons' for doing so.

It is then up to Parliament, through the strongest affirmative resolution procedure for statutory instruments, to approve the order. It is open to the minister not to make a remedial order, and open to Parliament not to approve it, as indeed it remains open to Parliament to pass legislation which is incompatible with the Convention rights. Parliament may also, of course, pass amending legislation in the ordinary way. So Convention rights are considered by the judges, but parliamentary sovereignty remains intact.[5]

On the other hand, the courts are given the power to make an unprecedented declaration of incompatibility which may, and is certainly expected to,[6] trigger a very speedy amendment of primary legislation by statutory instrument. The very existence of these arrangements will put pressure on a minister to use the powers that are available. Any draft order will lie in Parliament for only 60 days (preceded by a 60-day period for representations), may not be amended and, in the normal practice of Parliament, would not be debated for more than 90 minutes. In 'urgent cases', the minister can make an order with immediate effect, which is only later approved by Parliament, or lapses after 120 days. Important primary legislation may be amended without any of the full debates among elected representatives that take place on the various stages of a Bill. On this account it would appear that the role of Parliament has been diminished in relation to both that of the judiciary and the executive.[7]

It should be noted here that the Act certainly gives the judiciary a new role quite beyond having the bare power to prompt new legislation in such a formal and effective manner. As the Lord Chancellor, Lord Irvine, put it in a passage approvingly quoted by the Lord Chief Justice, Lord Bingham:

---

5   'That is achieved by a partnership, if I may put it like that, between Parliament and the judges. The judges do not strike down primary legislation; they merely indicate their opinion, without fuss, that certain matters are incompatible and leave it at that. When there is incompatibility between a primary statute and the European Convention on Human Rights, there will be a fast-track Parliamentary procedure': Lord Scarman *Hansard* (HL) vol 582, col 1256 (3 November 1997).

6   'Parliament may, not must, and generally will, legislate': The Lord Chancellor, Lord Irvine of Lairg *Hansard* (HL) vol 582, col 1229 (3 November 1997). It should be noted that the Lord Chancellor said this before the Bill was amended to provide that a minister must consider there are 'compelling reasons' (see s 10(2)) for making a remedial order.

7   For a thoughtful note on this and related issues, see S Fredman 'Bringing Rights Home' (1998) 114 LQR 538.

'The Courts' decisions will in future be based on a more overtly principled, and perhaps moral basis. The Court will look at the positive right. It will only accept an interference with that right where a justification, allowed under the Convention is made out. The scrutiny will not be limited to seeing if the words of an exception can be satisfied. The Court will need to be satisfied that the spirit of this exception is made out. It will need to be satisfied that the interference with the protected right is justified in the public interest in a free democratic society. Moreover, the Courts will in this area have to apply the Convention principle of proportionality. This means the Court will be looking substantively at that question. It will not be limited to a secondary review of the decision making process but at the primary question of the merits of the decision itself. In reaching its judgment, therefore, the Court will need to expand and explain its own view of whether the conduct is legitimate. It will produce in short a decision on the morality of the conduct and not simply its compliance with the bare letter of the law.'[8]

Such an approach will not only give judges a new prominence in the determination of public policy, it will also require them to develop a new approach to the construction of the law. With the provisions of the Human Rights Act 1998 they will no longer be addressing tightly defined legal provisions with the aid of tightly defined rules of interpretation. Most importantly, rights, in our common law tradition, have generally found expression in an implied and negative way: 'everything is permitted except that which is expressly prohibited'. Now they are positively stated, and in broad terms, for the judges to construe and apply.

This will undoubtedly cause conflict between the executive and the judiciary. In the case of *R v Secretary of State for Home Department ex parte Javed; R v Same ex parte Zulfiquar Ali; R v Same ex parte Abid Ali*[9] the court was considering the designation, by the Home Secretary, of Pakistan as being a 'safe country' to which he could return asylum seekers under a fast-track procedure. Counsel for the Home Secretary argued that the decision to designate Pakistan a safe country was not something that the court was competent to interfere with, particularly as the decision was subsequently laid before Parliament. That there was no error of law, but merely a different view as to his final decision. The Court found that there was a positive obligation to uphold human rights, which included the prohibition on inhuman or degrading treatment, and that on the evidence the decision was clearly wrong. Quite properly, the niceties of parliamentary procedure, where a document may have been formally 'laid before the house', but clearly with no proper debate or consideration, was not sufficient to stop the protection of the fundamental rights in Art 3.

---

8   The Lord Chancellor, Lord Irvine of Lairg 'The Development of Human Rights in Britain under an Incorporated Convention on Human Rights', The Tom Sargant Memorial Lecture (The Law Society Hall, 16 December 1997); quoted by Lord Bingham of Cornhill, The Lord Chief Justice in 'The Way We Live Now: Human Rights in the New Millennium', The Earl Grey Memorial Lecture (University of Newcastle upon Tyne, 29 January 1998) [1998] 1 Web JCLI.
9   [2001] TLR 104, QBD.

In contrast, the Court of Appeal in *The Queen on the application of Mahmood v Secretary of State for the Home Department*[10] was more concerned not to trespass into the territory of Parliament in considering another immigration case. Laws LJ commented that:

> 'The Human Rights Act 1998 does not authorise the judges to stand in the shoes of Parliament's delegates, who are decision-makers given their responsibilities by the democratic arm of the state. The arrogation of such a power to the judges would usurp those functions of government which are controlled and distributed by powers whose authority is derived from the ballot box. It follows that there must be a principled distance between the court's adjudication in a case such as this, and the Secretary of State's decision, based on his perception of the case's merits.'

More recently, the Lord Chief Justice has discussed the 'due deference' to be given to Parliament in a case involving housing law. In *Donoghue v Poplar Housing and Regeneration Community Association Ltd*,[11] the Court held that Parliament had given the courts limited involvement under the Housing Act 1988 to interfere with certain types of tenancies, and that as economic policy in this area was complex, the decision of Parliament should be given particular deference. The Human Rights Act 1998 did not require the Courts to disregard such decisions of Parliament, and it was perfectly understandable that possession could be obtained expeditiously against people with low housing priority. Here, even in an area that one might consider to be of particular importance in the human rights field, public housing, the courts are reluctant to interfere with a debate in Parliament some 13 years previously.

2.3.2   Bringing rights home to individuals

Remedies for breach of human rights are created by providing individuals with direct access to the courts in this country, through the right to bring proceedings under s 7(1)(a) in respect of the acts of public authorities. At present, according to the Government, it takes, on average, five years for an individual to get a case into the European Court of Human Rights once all domestic remedies have been exhausted, and costs an average of £30,000.[12]

The definition of public authority has been broadly drawn but will no doubt cause some difficulties (see **2.3.3** below). The definition of those individuals who can apply to the court is restricted to those who are either victims or potential victims of the unlawful acts of public authorities, and does not include those who have a 'sufficient interest', as in domestic public law (see **2.4.7** below). The obligation on the court to take into account the Strasbourg jurisprudence on 'just satisfaction' indicates that damages are likely to be as low as they have been in that jurisdiction.

Some of the most controversial discussions surrounding the passage of the Human Rights Bill concerned the effect of judicial decisions under these provisions on the freedom of the press, and the freedom of the churches. The

---

10   [2001] UKHRR 307, para 33.
11   [2001] 2 FLR 284.
12   White Paper *Rights Brought Home: The Human Rights Bill*, Cm 3782 (1997), p 6.

press was concerned that the judiciary would use Art 8 in particular to strengthen privacy laws in the UK. The churches, some of which wanted to be excluded altogether from the operation of the Act, were concerned that individuals would, for example, seek to challenge their arrangements with respect to the administration of marriages or church schools. Sections 12 and 13 provide some safeguards in both respects, but in no way exempt those bodies.

Individuals are intended to benefit from the Act in other ways. Most significantly, individuals may rely on their Convention rights not only in proceedings which they bring under s 7(1)(a), but also in any proceedings provided they are (potential) victims of an unlawful act by a public authority (s 7(1)(b)). Furthermore, and illustrating an important link between the two strands, all courts and tribunals must, so far as it is possible to do so, read and give effect to primary and secondary legislation in a way which is compatible with the Convention rights (s 3(1)), whether or not a party is a (potential) victim of a public authority.[13] Indeed, it seems likely that many Convention right points will be raised and tested in proceedings not brought under s 7(1)(a).

2.3.3 Public authorities

A public authority is not defined in the Act. Section 6(1) states simply that 'It is unlawful for a public authority to act in a way which is incompatible with a Convention right'. Various references to this were made in Parliament, meaning public authorities in the 'obvious' sense, such as government departments and police officers. Section 6(3) states that the term 'includes' (a) a court or tribunal (including the House of Lords in its judicial capacity under s 6(4)), and (b) 'any person certain of whose functions are functions of a public nature'. Section 6(5) exempts those public authorities as defined by s 6(3)(b) only in respect of their private acts, but not any other public authorities in respect of their private acts.

Once again, the Lord Chancellor shed light in Parliament on the intention behind these provisions. The passage is worth quoting in full:

> '[Section 6(1)] refers to a "public authority" without defining the term. In many cases it will be obvious to the courts that they will be dealing with a public authority. In respect of government departments, for example, or police officers, or prison officers, or immigration officers, or local authorities, there can be no doubt that the body in question is a public authority. Any clear case of that kind comes in under [s 6(1)]; and it is then unlawful for the authority to act in a way which is incompatible with one or more of the convention rights. In such cases, the prohibition applies in respect of all their acts, public and private. There is no

---

13   Lord Lester of Herne Hill took the view that '[s 11(b)] specifically reserves the right to rely on the convention in cases where a person is not seeking a right against a public authority': *Hansard* (HL) vol 583, col 782 (24 November 1997). (Section 11(b) provides 'A person's reliance on a Convention right does not restrict ... (b) his right to make any claim or bring any proceedings which he could make or bring apart from sections 7 to 9'.)

exemption for private acts such as is conferred by [s 6(5)] in relation to [s 6(3)(b)].

[Section 6(3)(b)] provides further assistance on the meaning of public authority. It provides that "public authority" includes, "any person certain of whose functions are functions of a public nature". That provision is there to include bodies which are not manifestly public authorities, but some of whose functions only are functions of a public nature. It is relevant to cases where the courts are not sure whether they are looking at a public authority in the full-blooded [s 6(1)] sense with regard to those bodies which fall into the grey area between public and private. The Bill reflects the decision to include as "public authorities" bodies which have some public functions and some private functions.

Perhaps I may give an example that I have cited previously. Railtrack would fall into that category because it exercises public functions in its role as a safety regulator, but it is acting privately in its role as a property developer. A private security company would be exercising public functions in relation to the management of a contracted-out prison but would be acting privately when, for example, guarding commercial premises. Doctors in general practice would be public authorities in relation to their National Health Service functions, but not in relation to their private patients.'[14]

It follows that the courts will first have to determine whether they are dealing with an (obvious or full-blooded) 'public authority', looking at the body as a whole; secondly, if it is not, whether certain functions of that body include 'functions of a public nature'; and, thirdly, if they do, whether the particular act complained of is 'private' in nature, looking at the act itself.

Some assistance in the definition of a public authority may come from other areas of law. For example, in judicial review there is authority as to when a body is exercising a public function and is thus susceptible to judicial review. A number of guidelines can be ascertained from the case-law:

- an agreement defined by contract is likely to be private in nature, such as a contract of employment;[15]
- a function derived from statute or Royal Charter is likely to be public in nature;
- some public interest in the decisions made should be present, probably governmental;[16]
- self-regulatory bodies whose functions have been ceded by government are likely to be public.

Under the Freedom of Information Act 2000, public authorities are defined in Sch 1. These include a magistrates' court committee, the Post Office, the Metropolitan Police Authority and the Judicial Studies Board, as well as less obvious bodies such as the Sir John Soane's Museum and the Zoos Forum!

---

14   The Lord Chancellor, Lord Irvine of Lairg *Hansard* (HL) vol 583, col 811 (24 November 1997). The Lord Chancellor had previously stated that 'the press might well be held to be a "function of a public nature", so that the PCC [Press Complaints Commission] would be a "public authority" under the Human Rights Act': ibid, col 784.
15   *R v Post Office ex parte Byrne* [1975] ICR 221.
16   *R v Chief Rabbi ex parte Wachmann* [1992] 1 WLR 1036.

There has been little dispute in actions under the Human Rights Act 1998, as the majority of authorities involved in criminal law are obviously public authorities. Most of the cases involved the challenge of a decision by the judge during the course of the trial, and consequently have to be challenged by way of exercising the right of appeal, as required under s 9. The Director of Public Prosecutions is clearly a public authority, and his decisions may be challenged in the courts, although there may well be other considerations which will make such a challenge difficult.

In other areas the decision is not so simple. In the case of *Donoghue v Poplar Housing and Regeneration Community Association Ltd*,[17] the Court decided that the definition of 'public authority' in s 6 of the Act should be given a general interpretation. Factors that might be relevant included the acquisition of the duties from a local authority, control by that authority and how close the activities were to the body. The fact that the body was a charity was not such an indicator. The Court held that decisions made by the Administrative Court as to whether bodies were subject to judicial review were useful.

2.3.4 Application of the Convention rights between private individuals

It follows from s 3(1) and s 7(1)(b) that the Act allows a person to rely on their Convention rights, where appropriate, in ordinary private actions between individuals. For example, the Convention right to freedom of expression might be prayed in aid of a particular construction of the Defamation Act 1952 in proceedings between private individuals, even though neither of them could bring proceedings against the other under the Human Rights Act 1998.

The lower courts will not be able to make declarations of incompatibility, but their decisions may now be challenged in the higher courts on the basis that an incompatibility exists, or that they have misconstrued the application of Convention rights.

It is also, of course, the case that decisions in respect of public authorities often affect relations generally between private persons. For example, a case brought under the Act under Art 8 (privacy) against the Press Complaints Commission is clearly capable of resulting in a change in the future relationship between the applicant (and others) and the journalists who are supervised by that body, even though the journalists, or indeed newspapers, as private persons, could not be made the respondents in proceedings under s 7 of the Act. The approach to be adopted in such cases was outlined in the case of *Mills v News Group Newspapers Ltd*,[18] in particular dealing with the relevance of the PCC Code of Conduct.

More obviously, a court may not allow the proceedings which occur in front of it, nor the decisions it finally makes, to be a breach of Convention rights. Consequently, even in cases between individuals the court will have to ensure

---

17   [2001] 2 FLR 284.
18   (Unreported) 4 June 2001, ChD.

compatibility with the Convention. If someone sees fit to plead this fact in a case, the court will no doubt have to follow that suggestion. Thus, courts will be enforcing Convention rights as between individuals.

2.3.5　Development of the common law

The courts have already grappled with the question of how far the Act will enable or encourage the judiciary to develop the common law in new ways, so as to affect legal relations, either between private individuals or between individuals and public authorities. Even though there is no provision in terms requiring the courts to read and give effect to the common law in a way which is compatible with the Convention rights (s 3 applies only to legislation), as public authorities (under s 6) the courts must not act in a way which is incompatible with those rights. The Lord Chancellor stated in Parliament that the judges were obliged to develop the common law consistently with the Act:

> 'We also believe that it is right as a matter of principle for the courts to have the duty of acting compatibly with the convention not only in cases involving other public authorities but also in developing the common law in deciding cases between individuals ... the courts already bring convention considerations to bear and I have no doubt that they will continue to do so in developing the common law ... [s 3] requires the courts to interpret legislation compatibly with the convention rights and to the fullest extent possible in all cases coming before them.'[19]

The courts, in developing the common law, already apply and have regard to the Convention, as an international instrument, in an appropriate case. Courts developing the common law must now also have regard to the Human Rights Act 1998 to the extent that it now forms part of the general legislative background to the common law.

One obvious example of the development of the common law, where the courts have not held back from breaking new ground, is in the right to privacy under Art 8 of the Convention. In the case of *Douglas and Others v Hello! Ltd*[20] the Court of Appeal did just that. Lord Justice Sedley, in discussing the development of the common law, stated that 'we have reached a point at which it can be said with confidence that the law recognises and will appropriately protect a right of personal privacy' (para 110). This right he found to be grounded in the equitable doctrine of breach of confidence, which would protect people from unwarranted intrusions into their private lives. Article 8 establishes the basic right of privacy as a legal principle from which the common law may grow.

This development may not have been entirely intended by Parliament. Article 13 of the Convention, the requirement for there to be an effective remedy in national law for breaches of the Convention, together with Art 1, the requirement to give effect to the rights in the Convention, were not included in the Act. It was suggested that as the entire Act was for the purpose of giving effect to the rights, they were otiose.

19　The Lord Chancellor, Lord Irvine of Lairg *Hansard* (HL) vol 583, col 783 (24 November 1997).
20　[2001] 2 WLR 992.

However, the Lord Chancellor clearly thought that the inclusion of Art 13 might have provided too much encouragement to the courts to develop new remedies:

> 'The Courts would be bound to ask themselves what was intended beyond the existing scheme of remedies set out in the Bill. It might lead them to fashion remedies other than the [s 8] remedies, which we regard as sufficient and clear.'

The Lord Chancellor made clear that the Act was not intended to have this effect:

> 'I would not agree with any proposition that the courts as public authorities will be obliged to fashion a law on privacy because of the terms of the Bill. That is simply not so. If it were so, whenever a law cannot be found either in the statute book or as a rule of common law to protect a convention right, the courts would in effect be obliged to legislate by way of judicial decision and to make one. That is not the true position. ... In my opinion, the court is not obliged to remedy the failure by legislating via the common law either where a convention right is infringed by incompatible legislation or where, because of the absence of legislation – say, privacy legislation – a convention right is left unprotected. In my view, the courts may not act as legislators and grant new remedies for infringement of convention rights unless the common law itself enables them to develop new rights or remedies.'[21]

It follows from the above that the Act, whilst formally restraining the judiciary, does in fact strongly encourage it to develop the common law vigorously. That is the logic of including courts within the definition of public authorities for the purposes of s 6, and of requiring courts to interpret all legislation compatibly with Convention rights, so far as is possible, irrespective of its application to the acts of public authorities (s 3(1)). That is also the logic of introducing into the law, for the courts to construe, rights which are positively and broadly stated. It should also be noted that the corollary to the courts not being given the power to make a declaration of incompatibility in respect of the common law is that there is no specific injunction within the Act on the courts not to affect the 'validity, continuing operation or enforcement' of the existing common law.

Furthermore, whilst s 6(3) exempts Parliament from the definition of public authority, it specifically includes courts; and whilst s 6(6), which defines the act of a public authority to include its failure to act, specifically exempts any failure to legislate (either by primary legislation or remedial order), it does not exempt the courts from failing to develop the common law within their powers.

Any court faced with the prospect of concluding that the common law is incompatible with these new rights will feel under great pressure to find a way of properly developing the common law to avoid that embarrassment. That is, of course, entirely consistent with the radical, purposive thrust of the Act as a whole. The Lord Chancellor, earlier in the speech quoted above, also made this clear:

---

21   The Lord Chancellor, Lord Irvine of Lairg *Hansard* (HL) vol 583, col 785 (24 November 1997).

'It must be emphasised that the judges are free to develop the common law in their own independent judicial sphere. What I say positively is that it will be a better law if the judges develop it after incorporation because they will have regard to Articles 8 and 10, giving Article 10 its due high value ...'[22]

2.3.6　Operation of the Act in the criminal justice system

The Act applies to criminal courts in much the same way as it does to civil courts. Magistrates' courts, the Crown Court and the superior courts with criminal jurisdiction will all be subject to the duty to read and give effect to all legislation compatibly with the Convention so far as it is possible to do so (s 3). When determining any question which has arisen under the Act in connection with a Convention right, they must take into account the judgments and decisions of the Strasbourg bodies (s 2).

The criminal courts are also public bodies for the purpose of s 6, and will act unlawfully if they act in a way which is incompatible with a Convention right. Proceedings under s 7(1)(a) may be brought against them in respect of any such unlawful acts, but see below as to how those proceedings may be brought. A party to criminal proceedings may rely upon a Convention right in criminal proceedings if that person is (or would be) a victim of a breach of that right by a public authority (s 7(1)(b)).

The police, prison, probation, social service and other bodies concerned with the criminal justice system will also be public authorities in the 'full-blooded' sense, and be required to act accordingly (s 6).

There are several points of particular significance for the criminal justice system.

-   A minister joined in criminal proceedings may, with leave, appeal to the House of Lords against a declaration of incompatibility made in those proceedings (s 5(4)).
-   Nothing in the Act creates a criminal offence (s 7(8)).
-   A court is not able to make any award of damages in granting relief for a breach by a public authority of a Convention right unless that court has the power to award damages or compensation in civil proceedings (will the Court of Appeal Criminal Division transfer an appropriate case to the Civil Division?) (s 8(2)).
-   The decisions of criminal courts, like those of civil courts, but unlike those of other public authorities, may be challenged only by way of appeal (within the existing procedures) or by judicial review (s 9(1)).
-   The only damages payable in respect of a judicial act in good faith which is a breach of a Convention right are to the victims of arrest or detention in contravention of Art 5 (right to liberty and security) (s 9(3) and Art 5(5)).
-   The provisions in s 12 requiring particular regard being given by courts to the importance of freedom of expression do not apply to criminal proceedings (s 12(5)).

22　The Lord Chancellor, Lord Irvine of Lairg *Hansard* (HL) vol 583, col 784 (24 November 1997).

–   The death penalty is abolished from the day the Act received Royal Assent (ss 1, 21(5), 22, Sch 1, Pt III).
–   No person is to be found guilty of an offence solely as a result of the retrospective effect of a remedial order (Sch 2, para 1(4)).
–   All criminal courts can challenge and refuse to apply most forms of subordinate legislation which are incompatible with a Convention right.

The Act must first, however, be approached in terms of the principles and mechanisms which are at its core, and they are mostly of general application. A quick understanding of its significance and usefulness in any particular area will depend upon a sound grasp of the implications and ramifications of those interlocking principles and mechanisms.

2.3.7   No human rights commission

The Government declined to provide for the establishment of a human rights commission, a body which would supplement the impact of the Act by promoting human rights generally by public education and consultation, and by advising individuals as to how to proceed if they felt that their rights were infringed. The Lord Chancellor cited unresolved issues as to how such a body would coexist with the Equal Opportunities Commission and the Commission for Racial Equality. A Joint Committee on Human Rights has been set up by the House of Commons and House of Lords, whose terms of reference are:

> 'To consider and report on:
>
> (a) matters relating to human rights in the United Kingdom (but excluding consideration of individual cases);
> (b) proposals for remedial orders, draft remedial orders and remedial orders made under section 10 of and laid under Schedule 2 to the Human Rights Act 1998; and
> (c) in respect of draft remedial orders and remedial orders, whether the special attention of the House should be drawn to them on any of the grounds specified in Standing Order 72 (Joint Committee on Statutory Instruments).'

Furthermore, in the build-up to, and immediate aftermath of, the introduction of the Act, the Government spent over £4 million on the training of the judiciary, magistrates and chairs of tribunals through the Judicial Studies Board, the Courts Service and the magistrates' courts committees.

2.4   PROVISIONS OF THE ACT

2.4.1   Convention rights

Section 1 of the Act defines 'the Convention rights' as 'the rights and fundamental freedoms' set out in the Convention, and declares them 'to have effect for the purposes of this Act'. The rights are set out in Sch 1. All of the substantive rights which the UK has ratified are included,[23] save for Art 13 (see para **2.3.5** above).

Also excluded is any 'designated' derogation or reservation (s 1(2)). This refers to the previous derogation which the UK, under the Convention, registered in respect of Art 5(3) (relating to the detention of terrorist suspects), and to the reservation it has entered in respect of Art 2 of the First Protocol (relating to the right to education), both of which are reproduced in full in Sch 3 (ss 14, 15). On 26 February 2001 the Government lodged a notice of withdrawal with the Secretary-General of the Council of Europe, reflecting the implementation of Sch 8 to the Terrorism Act 2000, and removing the derogation with respect to Art 5. This is implemented by the Human Rights Act 1998 (Amendment) Order 2001, SI 2001/1216, which repeals the relevant parts of s 16 of the Act. This procedure is allowed for in the Act.

Sections 16 and 17 express the determination of the Government, notwith-standing the existence of the reservation above, to comply as fully as possible with the Convention. To this end, unless extended by order, future designated derogations cease to have effect for the purposes of the Act five years after they were made, and in the case of the derogation already made in respect of Art 5(3), five years after s 1(2) comes into force. An order under s 14(1)(b) (the power to designate new derogations) will lapse unless approved by both Houses of Parliament within the period for consideration (s 16). Designated reservations (including the one made in respect of Art 2 of the First Protocol) are subject to a five-yearly review and report to Parliament (s 17).

The substantive Convention rights set out in Arts 2–12 and 14, and the Protocols, are to be read with Arts 16–18 which are also set out in Sch 1. Article 16 allows for States to impose restrictions on the political activity of aliens, notwithstanding Arts 10 (freedom of expression), 11 (freedom of assembly and association) and 14 (prohibition of discrimination).

Article 17 is designed to prevent any perceived abuse of the substantive rights. In *Glimmerveen and Hagenback v Netherlands*,[24] for example, the Commission held that interference with the right to free expression (Art 10) and the right to free elections (Art 3 of the First Protocol) was justified. The applicants had been convicted for distributing racist literature and banned from participating in an election because of their racist views. Article 18 prohibits restrictions which are permitted in respect of specific rights and freedoms in the Convention from being used 'for any other purpose'.

Finally, it should be noted that the effect of the inclusion of Arts 1 and 2 of the Sixth Protocol (s 1(1)) is far reaching. Article 1 states simply, 'The death penalty shall be abolished'. Its inclusion was facilitated by the passage of the Crime and Disorder Act 1998 and, more significantly, by Government

---

23   The Convention is defined as 'the Convention for the Protection of Human Rights and Fundamental Freedoms, as agreed by the Council of Europe at Rome on 4 November 1950 *as it has effect for the time being* in relation to the United Kingdom' (s 21) (emphasis added).

24   Application Nos 8348/78 and 8406/78, (1979) 18 DR 187.

proposals to amend the Armed Forces Acts to abolish the death penalty for military offences in all circumstances, whether in peace or wartime. The subsequent ratification of the Sixth Protocol has completed the abolition of the death penalty in the international legal sphere.

2.4.2 Section 2

The use of Strasbourg case-law

Section 2 provides that 'A court in determining a question which has arisen in connection with a Convention right must take into account' the various judgments, decisions, declarations and opinions of the Strasbourg bodies (the European Court, European Commission and Committee of Ministers) whether made before or after the coming into force of the Act, 'so far as, in the opinion of the court or tribunal, it is relevant to the proceedings'. 'Tribunal' is defined as 'any tribunal in which legal proceedings may be brought' (s 21).

The use of the word 'question' indicates that the court or tribunal is not limited to taking into account the Strasbourg jurisprudence for the purpose only of determining the bare meaning of those rights, but must also take it into account to the extent that it is considered relevant to the determination of the actual question which has arisen.

The words 'a question which has arisen' might suggest that there is no duty on the court or tribunal to raise the question. In Parliament, Lord Mackay of Drumadoon made the probing point in the context of unrepresented defendants, 'If the jurisprudence is not cited, the judge is perfectly entitled to go ahead and decide the matter on the arguments advanced by the party defendant himself'. The Lord Chancellor replied, 'there is a well recognised and honourable tradition in the courts of the judge giving the defendant the maximum assistance that he can'.[25]

Clearly, the fact that a court under s 6 of the Act must act in accordance with the Convention must mean that a court must raise such a point of its own volition; it would not be permitted to stand by and allow a breach to occur. In the magistrates' courts, the duty is upon the clerk to the justices to raise any such points that are not raised by defendants, whether or not represented.[26]

The words 'must take into account' indicate that the court or tribunal is not *bound* by the Strasbourg jurisprudence. The judiciary clearly relishes the task not only of taking that jurisprudence into account, but also of developing it in its own way. The Lord Chief Justice, speaking in Parliament, said, 'British judges have a significant contribution to make in the development of the law of human rights', and urged us to remember Milton's words in Aeropagitica, 'Let not England forget her precedence of teaching nations how to live'.[27]

---

25   *Hansard* (HL) vol 583, cols 526–527 (18 November 1997). But see the discussion of ss 12 and 13 at **2.4.12** and **2.4.13** below.
26   *Practice Direction (Justices: Clerk to Court)* [2000] 1 WLR 1886.
27   Lord Bingham of Cornhill *Hansard* (HL) vol 582, cols 1245–1246 (3 November 1997).

Another eminent lawyer, Lord Lester, also gave one example of how things might be done differently once rights are brought home:

> 'I have no doubt that if the McCann case [in which the UK was found in breach of Art 2 (right to life) in respect of the killing of three IRA members in Gibraltar] could have been dealt with by our own courts, using the criteria of the Convention, it might well have led to a different outcome in Strasbourg.'

He makes two points here: first, that British judges would have applied the Convention differently; and, secondly, that had it then gone to Strasbourg, those judges would, as a result of the British decision, have reached a different conclusion themselves.

The second observation illustrates the wider point that although it will remain open to those within this jurisdiction to apply to Strasbourg, they can do so only after exhausting the domestic remedies which are now provided by the Act. This will mean that the European Court will have, with every application from the UK, a fully reasoned interpretation of the relevant Convention right and fully developed argument about its application from a British court.

It may be expected that the European Court will perhaps be more careful about overturning a fully reasoned decision from the British courts than it has been in finding against the UK for an applicant who was previously unable to obtain access to the courts in the UK. Indeed, that would be consistent with the application of the doctrine of the margin of appreciation, which may be granted by the European Court not only to Parliament in respect of substantive law, but to the British courts in their interpretation and application of it.[28]

The judgments, decisions, declarations and opinions which must be taken into account arise from the different functions of the Strasbourg bodies. Articles 31, 26 and 27(2) (s 2(1)(b) and (c)) have been replaced since they refer to the Commission, which has been abolished. Nevertheless, the decisions and opinions the Commission gave in the past must be taken into account, and there are approximately 100 volumes of decisions, mainly on the question of admissibility of cases taken to Strasbourg.

Sections 2 and 3 state that rules *may* be made as to how Strasbourg jurisprudence should be produced in proceedings. However, the Lord Chancellor's Department Consultation Paper on Rules and Practice Directions (March 2000) decided that guidance and practice directions would be a more appropriate way in which to decide how this should be done, allowing for a degree of flexibility. The paper suggests that 'Strasbourg authorities should be cited from authoritative and complete reports that are readily available'. However, the Practice Direction for the Family Courts allows for cases printed from the European Court website, and this is the practice being adopted in the criminal courts.

Those wishing to raise a human rights issue are required to do so at the plea and directions hearing for a Crown Court trial. Most judges will require full skeleton arguments, following the guidance for Abuse of Process arguments in

---

28   See *Handyside v UK* (1976) Series A/24, discussed at **1.7.7** above.

Practice Direction (Crown Court: Abuse of Process)[29] which requires written notice 14 days prior to trial, and full skeleton argument five clear days before the hearing with a response two days prior to the hearing.

This Practice Direction does not require production of the reports relied upon, unlike the similar direction for the family courts, which states that a full copy must be lodged. This has created an interesting difficulty. Any brief perusal of a judgment of the European Court will demonstrate that brevity is not a characteristic of the Court. Often, a case will be cited merely for a paragraph within it which gives a maxim of law relied upon. The consequences of copying and serving a 70-page judgment merely for that paragraph are clearly disastrous, not only for trees but also for photocopiers and delivery men. This requirement will undoubtedly not survive in any courts where it is insisted upon. However, if an advocate is relying upon some of the more obscure authorities allowed under s 2, such as a resolution of the Council of Ministers, then a copy should be provided.

Whilst all courts are able to use Strasbourg case-law in coming to their decisions, precedent clearly applies within the jurisdiction. Once the superior courts have given a decision as to the proper interpretation of a Strasbourg judgment in UK law, that must be followed by inferior courts.[30]

2.4.3   Section 3

Interpretation of legislation
Section 3(1) reads 'So far as it is possible to do so, primary legislation and subordinate legislation must be read and given effect in a way which is compatible with the Convention rights'. This applies to existing or future legislation (s 3(2)(a)).

Lord Cooke, in Parliament, said of the requirement 'So far as it is possible to do so':

> 'the Bill definitely goes further than the existing common law rules of statutory interpretation, because it enjoins a search for possible meanings as distinct from the true meaning – which has been the traditional approach in the matter of statutory interpretation in the courts.'[31]

In debate, the Government rejected the phrase 'so far as it is *reasonable* to do so', and one illustrious commentator pointed out that 'anything's possible'.[32] The White Paper, *Human Rights Brought Home*, made clear that a dramatic change from the status quo was intended, and in the House of Lords' discussion of the Bill, the Lord Chancellor commented that:

---

29   [2001] 1 WLR 1322.
30   *R v Central Criminal Court ex parte The Guardian, The Observer and Martin Bright* [2000] UKHRR 796.
31   Lord Cooke of Thorndon *Hansard* (HL) vol 583, col 533 (18 November 1997).
32   See Lord Lester of Herne Hill QC 'The Art of the Possible: Interpreting Statutes under the Human Rights Act' (1998) *Human Rights Law Review* 665.

'We want the courts to strive to find an interpretation of legislation which is consistent with Convention rights so far as the language of the legislation allows, and only in the last resort to conclude that the legislation is simply incompatible with them.'[33]

The construction of s 3 demands that the legislation is to be interpreted (bent?) so as to make it compatible with the Convention, and not the other way around. The words 'read and given effect' emphasise that the outcome of the application of the legislation must also be consistent with the Convention itself. Nevertheless, it remains the case that the Convention rights themselves can often be interpreted in quite different ways, as the cases show. Whether, in difficult cases, the strenuous effort to achieve compatibility will result in bending the legislation to the Convention rights, or the Convention rights to the legislation, remains to be seen.

Section 3(2)(b) provides that, in those rare cases where the legislation cannot be interpreted in accordance with the Convention and the courts have to make a declaration of incompatibility, they are not able to make an interpretation such as to 'affect the validity, continuing operation or enforcement of any incompatible primary legislation'. It follows that the interpretation can affect any subordinate legislation which is incompatible with a Convention right – unless primary legislation prevents the removal of the incompatibility. If the subordinate legislation is inevitably incompatible because of the terms of the parent statute then it is not affected by the interpretation, because the parent statute as primary legislation cannot be affected. The possibility that the parent statute might be revoked (for example, if the court chooses at this time to make a declaration of incompatibility) is to be disregarded; such subordinate legislation must still stand (s 3(2)(b), (c)).

These provisions simply reproduce for the purposes of the Act the principle behind the existing powers of the courts with respect to subordinate legislation. It should be noted, however, that the requirement under s 3 with respect to the interpretation of legislation is not restricted to any particular court or tribunal, or indeed to courts and tribunals. It follows that any person or body charged with reading and giving effect to legislation must do so according to the terms of the section. The position presumably remains, however, that subordinate legislation is valid until set aside by a court with the jurisdiction to do so (normally the High Court), but it should be noted, for example, that in any criminal proceedings a court may entertain a challenge to the validity of a byelaw. The power of magistrates to rule on the validity of a byelaw was confirmed in *R v Reading Crown Court ex parte Hutchinson*.[34]

The courts have considered to what extent they are entitled to interpret legislation and 'read down' the language of the statute in order to make it compatible with the Convention. Lord Woolf has commented that s 3 does not allow the courts to legislate, but merely to interpret.[35] This question has been

---

33   *Hansard*, 583 HL Official Report (Fifth Series) col 535 (18 November 1997).
34   [1988] QB 384, [1988] 1 All ER 333, DC.
35   *Donoghue v Poplar Housing and Regeneration Community Association Ltd* [2001] EWCA Civ 595, [2001] 2 FLR 284.

fully argued in the House of Lords in *R v A* [2001] UKHL 25,[36] where the House was considering the compatibility with Art 6 of s 41 of the Youth Justice and Criminal Evidence Act 1999 which prohibits the giving of evidence and cross-examination about any sexual behaviour of the complainant except with leave of the court.

Lord Steyn (at para 44) considered the different methods of interpretation, finding that:

> 'the interpretative obligation under section 3 of the 1998 Act is a strong one. It applies even if there is no ambiguity in the language in the sense of the language being capable of two different meanings. It is an emphatic adjuration by the legislature: *R v Director of Public Prosecutions, Ex p Kebilene* [2000] 2 AC 326, per Lord Cooke of Thorndon, at p 373F; and my judgment, at p 366B. The White Paper made clear that the obligation goes far beyond the rule which enabled the courts to take the Convention into account in resolving any ambiguity in a legislative provision: see "Rights Brought Home: The Human Rights Bill" (1997) (Cm 3782), para 2.7. The draftsman of the Act had before him the slightly weaker model in section 6 of the New Zealand Bill of Rights Act 1990 but preferred stronger language. Parliament specifically rejected the legislative model of requiring a reasonable interpretation. Section 3 places a duty on the court to strive to find a possible interpretation compatible with Convention rights. ... In accordance with the will of Parliament as reflected in section 3 it will sometimes be necessary to adopt an interpretation which linguistically may appear strained. The techniques to be used will not only involve the reading down of express language in a statute but also the implication of provisions. A declaration of incompatibility is a measure of last resort. It must be avoided unless it is plainly impossible to do so. If a clear limitation on Convention rights is stated in terms, such an impossibility will arise: *R v Secretary of State for the Home Department, Ex p Simms* [2000] 2 AC 115, 132A–B per Lord Hoffmann. There is, however, no limitation of such a nature in the present case.'

He concluded that there was no need for a declaration of incompatibility, and that provisions in s 41 could be read in accordance with the Convention. However, the speech of Lord Hope of Craighead should be noted for a different interpretation of the proper approach to follow.

2.4.4   Section 4

Declaration of incompatibility
Section 4(2) reads, 'If the court is satisfied that the provision is incompatible with a Convention right, it may make a declaration of that incompatibility'.

'Provision' means 'provision of primary legislation', and the declaration in respect of it can be made in any proceedings in which a court determines that the provision is incompatible with a Convention right (s 4(1)).

This power, at the core of the Act, can be made only by a superior court. For the purposes of this section, 'court' means the High Court in England and Wales and corresponding courts elsewhere in the UK, the Court of Appeal, the House of Lords, the Privy Council and the Courts Martial Appeal Court (s 4(5)).

---

36   [2001] 1 WLR 789.

Section 4(3) and (4) empowers the court to make a declaration of incompatibility in respect of incompatible subordinate legislation where the parent statute prevents removal of the incompatibility. Thus the court can deal with offending primary and subordinate legislation at the same time. Although the court is not required by the section to make a declaration in respect of the parent statute when making a declaration in respect of the subordinate legislation, it follows that it would usually do so. The courts will look at the level of consideration given to subordinate legislation by Parliament in some detail. In *R (on the Application of Javed) v Secretary of State for the Home Department*,[37] the Court looked at the facts put before Parliament in assessing whether the order made was unreasonable.

Section 4(6) is of constitutional importance, and echoes in a more crucial context the provision in s 3(2)(b). It provides that a declaration of incompatibility '(a) does not affect the validity, continuing operation or enforcement of the provision in respect of which it is given; and (b) is not binding on the parties to the proceedings in which it is made'.

Even if the court makes a declaration, the provision stands, and stands to be enforced in respect of the parties to the proceedings. It is up to the minister and to Parliament to amend the legislation, under the remedial order procedure (s 10). The words 'does not affect' would appear to leave the courts with very little scope for allowing a party any benefit from a declaration. A court could grant an adjournment or stay, for example, only if that were consistent with its existing practice and the current state of the law.

In criminal cases, a remedial order, under s 10, might lead to the Home Secretary granting a pardon or release from prison in an appropriate case. If a remedial order has retrospective effect (Sch 2, para 1(b)) that might lead to a case being referred back to the Court of Appeal. There is an interesting issue as to the status of the prisoner at this stage. For the remedial order to be made, all appeals must have finished, and therefore the court is *functus officio*, despite having found that the conviction was in breach of the Convention, and is therefore unable to bail the prisoner. Consequently, it will be up to the Home Secretary to decide whether or not to release the prisoner prior to the remedial orders taking effect.

The Lord Chancellor, referring to the strong encouragement to the judiciary to interpret legislation compatibly with the Convention rights (s 3) and to the duty on public authorities not to act in a way which is incompatible with those rights (s 6), predicted that it would be a very rare event for a court to use its powers under s 4. He stated that 'in 99 per cent of the cases that will arise, there will be no need for judicial declarations of incompatibility'.[38]

---

37   [2001] 3 WLR 323, CA.
38   *Hansard* (HL) vol 585, col 840 (5 February 1998).

2.4.5   Section 5

Right of Crown to intervene

If a court is considering whether to make a declaration of incompatibility it must give notice to the Crown. Thereafter, a minister of the Crown (or person nominated by him), member of the Scottish Executive, Northern Ireland minister or the Northern Ireland Department is entitled to be joined as a party to the proceedings. It is specifically provided that if the proceedings are criminal proceedings the joined party may, with leave, appeal to the House of Lords against any declaration of incompatibility made in those proceedings.

The logic is clear. When a court is considering making a decision that will directly affect the Crown, and will require a minister to consider whether to make a remedial order (s 10), it is appropriate for a minister to be a party to the proceedings from that stage. The Government declined to provide for any other parties, such as organisations concerned with human rights, to be joined. The court may, of course, ask an interested party to assist the court in other, established ways.

In the recent case of *R v A* (above), the issue began as a preliminary point raised in a preparatory hearing under s 29 of the Criminal Procedure and Investigations Act 1996. The judge refused leave for the victim to be cross-examined or evidence led about her alleged sexual relationship with the defendant. He gave leave for the defendant to appeal to the Court of Appeal before the trial commenced. The Court of Appeal found that the judge was wrong, in that such questions were admissible under the Act as to the defendant's knowledge or belief in consent, but not as to the actual issue of consent. However, the Court of Appeal felt that the issue needed clarifying, stating that:

> 'Whether if, following a trial with such a direction, the appellant were to be convicted, it would be possible to argue, by way of appeal, that his trial had not been fair, in the light of article 6, remains for consideration on some future occasion. Clearly, if those events occur, that will be the time, if the point has not previously been resolved following some other trial, for the Home Secretary to be joined as a party with a view to the possibility of a declaration of incompatibility between the provisions of section 41(3)(b) (in so far as they preclude reference, in relation to consent, to the complainant's prior consensual sexual activity with the defendant) and article 6.'

They certified the question as to whether the use of s 41 to limit evidence of previous sexual relationships as to the issue of consent meant that there could be a fair trial, and gave leave to appeal to the House of Lords. At this stage, Counsel for the defendant indicated that he would invite the House to 'read down' the statute, and if that was not possible, to make a declaration of incompatibility. Consequently, the Secretary of State applied for leave to intervene, and an Appeal Committee recommended that such leave be given.[39] Consequently, the Crown and the Secretary of State were fully represented at the hearing, allowing for extremely full argument.

---

39   [2001] 1 WLR 789.

In the case of *Donoghue v Poplar Housing and Regeneration Community Association Ltd* [2001] UKHRR 693,[40] the Court suggested that the formal notice to the Crown required by s 5 of the Human Rights Act 1998 and r 19.4A of the Civil Procedure Rules 1998 should be given by the Court (Court of Appeal or the High Court), which was in the best position to judge whether it was considering a declaration of incompatibility. The parties should give as much informal notice of their intention to seek such a declaration and of the issues involved. Such informal notice should also be sent to the Court.

2.4.6   Section 6

Public authorities

Section 6(1) provides that 'It is unlawful for a public authority to act in a way which is incompatible with a Convention right'.

Section 6 introduces the second vital strand in the Act which entitles individuals to take proceedings in defence of their Convention rights. It provides the basis for such proceedings by placing a clear duty on public authorities to act compatibly with the Convention rights, but in its stark clarity also clearly seeks to promote a wide observance of the principles that lie behind the Act. This, it is hoped, will minimise the need for proceedings to be taken.

The meaning of 'public authority' and the significance of private acts by some public authorities is discussed at **2.3.3** above.

If, as the result of one or more provisions of primary legislation, the public authority could not have acted differently, the act is not unlawful. If the public authority was acting to give effect to or enforce the provisions of primary legislation, or subordinate legislation made under it, which provisions cannot be read or given effect to in a way which is compatible with the Convention rights, then the act of the public authority is not unlawful (s 6(2)).

These provisions protect any public authority which is acting in accordance with primary legislation, but only if the authority 'could not have acted differently', in other words if it was left with no choice by the primary legislation. Section 6(2)(b) protects courts in enforcing provisions which are, or derive from, primary legislation, even if those provisions are incompatible with Convention rights. It protects courts therefore from the consequences of s 4(6), which provides that a declaration of incompatibility does not affect the validity, continuing operation or enforcement of the provisions which it has just declared incompatible.

As noted above, Parliament is excluded from the definition of public authority (which includes both the House of Lords and House of Commons) or a person exercising functions in connection with proceedings in Parliament, but not the House of Lords in its judicial capacity (s 6(3), (4)).

A public authority may act unlawfully by an act or a failure to act, but expressly excluded from the latter is the failure to introduce, or lay before Parliament, a proposal for legislation, and the failure to make any primary legislation or

---

40   [2001] 2 FLR 284.

remedial order (s 6(6)). This draws the line very precisely in order to protect parliamentary sovereignty from being challenged at its margins. In particular, the decision of a minister following a declaration of incompatibility cannot itself be the subject of a challenge under this Act.

2.4.7   Section 7

Proceedings

Section 7 is the key enabling section for individuals. A person who claims that a public authority has acted (or proposes to act) contrary to s 6(1), that is in a manner which is not compatible with the Convention rights, may bring proceedings against that public authority in the appropriate court or tribunal, or rely on the Convention right or rights in any legal proceedings (s 7(1)(a), (b)). It should be noted that legal proceedings include those brought by, or at the instigation of, a public authority,[41] and an appeal against the decision of a court or tribunal (s 7(5)).

The ability to rely on Convention rights as a defence is potentially important to practitioners of criminal law. Essentially it allows for the prospect of positive defences being raised to criminal charges. For example, accusations of trespassory assembly may be met with the defence of the right to freedom of assembly and association under the Convention. A charge of possession of indecent material may be met with the defence of freedom of expression. These are as yet untested in the higher courts.

With regard to bringing proceedings for breach of Convention rights, only a person who is a 'victim' (or would be a victim) of an unlawful act may sue (s 7(1)). A victim is defined as 'a victim for the purposes of Article 34 of the Convention' (s 7(7)). Article 34 provides that an applicant can be 'any person, non-governmental organisation or group of individuals claiming to be the victim of a violation by one of the High Contracting Parties of the rights set out in the Convention and the protocols thereto'. It should be noted that the article itself defines 'applicant' rather than 'victim', and that s 7 refers to a 'person' (which includes a body of persons corporate or unincorporate)[42] and draws on the article only for the definition of 'victim'.

There is very extensive Strasbourg case-law (under Art 25, which was replaced by Art 34 on 1 November 1998) on what constitutes a 'victim of a violation'.[43] The first point to make is that it clearly excludes applications from persons not claiming to be affected themselves, and to that extent is less generous than the 'sufficient interest' test in domestic judicial review. The Home Office Minister,

---

41   'The very few private prosecutions that are undertaken will also be caught by [s 7(5)] – as it is an inclusive definition, and such proceedings would be regarded as legal proceedings. In such cases, the private prosecutor would not be a public authority, although the court, as a public authority, would be required to act not incompatibly with the convention rights': M O'Brien *Hansard* (HC) vol 314, col 1057 (24 June 1998).

42   Interpretation Act 1978, ss 5, 22(1), 23(1), Sch 1, Sch 2, para 4(1)(a).

43   See DJ Harris, M O'Boyle and C Warbrick *Law of The European Convention on Human Rights* (Butterworths, 1995), pp 632–638.

Mike O'Brien, made clear in Parliament that, in the interests of those actually affected, this was intended to exclude the possibility of interest groups bringing proceedings.

Secondly, the case-law has flexibly, and variably, included not only those directly affected but also those indirectly affected. For example, in *Dudgeon v UK*,[44] the Court found that a legislative provision which made buggery a criminal offence in Northern Ireland affected the applicant so as to constitute an interference with his right to respect for his private life (Art 8). He had never been charged, but had been questioned in respect of these provisions. The Court said, 'The legal prohibitions remain and the possibility of prosecutions by either the public prosecuting authorities or private individuals is open in law'.[45]

On the other hand, the newspapers in *Leigh, Guardian Newspapers Ltd and Observer Ltd v UK*,[46] failed to convince the Commission that they were sufficiently affected by a House of Lords' ruling[47] which prohibited generally the disclosure of documents discovered in civil proceedings, and read out in open court, so as to be the victims of a violation (an interference with their right of freedom of expression (Art 10)). They had claimed that the continuing possibility of contempt proceedings under this ruling had a continuing 'chilling effect' on their work.

If a person brings proceedings under this section by way of judicial review, the applicant will be taken to have a 'sufficient interest in relation to the unlawful act only if he is, or would be, a victim of that act' (s 7(3)). It is clear therefore that a person will not be able to escape the 'victim' test by making an application under the Rules of the Supreme Court 1965, Ord 53, r 3(7).

The Act allows for rules to be made outlining the 'appropriate court or tribunal' in which a case may be brought. Essentially, the rules which have been promulgated do not allow for any new procedures in the criminal courts. The general policy is that human rights issues should be decided in the courts considering the issues in the case, as they are limited to the powers they already possess under s 8 of the Act. In the criminal courts this means the power to exclude evidence and to stay a prosecution as an abuse of the process of the court. The criminal courts have no power to award damages under the Act. The consultation paper issued by the Lord Chancellor's Department recommended that proceedings be brought either using the existing judicial review process, or in the county court or High Court where there is a claim for damages. The third procedure is in the High Court following a finding of unlawfulness in another court without the power to award damages. This will

---

44   (1981) Series A/45, paras 92, 93.
45   'The aim is to confer access to rights, not to license interest groups to clog up the court with test cases, which will delay victims access to the courts': M O'Brien *Hansard* (HC) vol 314, col 1086 (24 June 1998). And see the examples given by the minister of the decisions of the Strasbourg bodies under Art 25: ibid, cols 1085–1086.
46   Application No 10039/82, (1984) 38 DR 74.
47   *Home Office v Harman* [1981] 1 All ER 532.

include the Crown Court and magistrates' courts, amongst others. The relevant procedure is within the new r 33.9 of the Civil Procedure Rules:

'33.9 Human Rights
(1) This rule applies where a claim is –
  (a) for a remedy under section 7 of the Human Rights Act 1998 in respect of a judicial act which is alleged to have infringed the claimant's Article 5 Convention rights; and
  (b) based on a finding by a court or tribunal that the claimant's Convention rights have been infringed.
(2) The court hearing the claim –
  (a) may proceed on the basis of the finding of that other court or tribunal that there has been an infringement but it is not required to do so, and
  (b) may reach its own conclusion in the light of that finding and of the evidence heard by that other court or tribunal.'

The ability (acknowledged by s 7(3)) of applicants to bring proceedings under s 7(1)(a) by way of judicial review raises some interesting issues. Not only is that applicant deprived of the 'sufficient interest' test normally available in judicial review proceedings, but the High Court will have to construe the meanings of 'public authority', 'functions of a public nature' and 'private acts' consistently with s 6, and therefore in ways that might not always be consistent with other public law.

Furthermore, the person bringing proceedings under s 7(1)(a) by way of judicial review is not given the same time within which to commence proceedings as a person bringing an application under s 7(1)(a) in the designated 'appropriate court or tribunal'. The judicial review applicant remains subject to the requirement in Ord 53, r 4, that is to apply 'promptly and in any event within three months'. The applicant to the 'appropriate court or tribunal' may apply within one year of the act complained of, or within such longer period as the court thinks equitable (s 7(5)). Section 7(5) does not apply to s 7(3) (applications by way of judicial review) and expressly subjects its own time-limit of one year to the stricter time-limits of the procedure which the applicant employs.

One of the many different implications of these provisions is that applicants who wish, for example, to sue a public authority, in respect of the same facts, under s 7(1) for breach of a Convention right, and in judicial review for breach of natural justice, will effectively have to bring proceedings within three months on both claims.

The Crown cannot be a victim for the purposes of a complaint under Art 6, as the prosecution is not 'charged with a criminal offence'.[48]

Finally, s 7(8) simply states, for the avoidance of doubt, that 'Nothing in this Act creates a criminal offence'. It is a short but important statement that it is not the intention of the Act to impose any criminal liability on public authorities in respect of their unlawful acts. Of course, if an incompatible act by a public

---

48   *R v Weir* [2001] 1 WLR 421.

authority amounts also to a criminal offence it can be dealt with in the usual way.

2.4.8   Section 8

Judicial remedies

The court (including tribunals) can 'grant such relief or remedy, or make such order, within its powers as it considers just and appropriate' (s 8(1)). The implications of this section are discussed at **2.3.5** above. Damages can be granted, however, only by a court which has the power to award damages or order the payment of compensation in civil proceedings (s 8(2)).

It should be noted that the power to grant relief is not restricted to s 7(1)(a) proceedings, but may be exercised in any proceedings (within the powers of the court or tribunal) in which a person relies on a Convention right.

Damages are to be awarded, after taking into account all the circumstances of the case, specifically including any other relief and the consequences of any decision in respect of the unlawful act, only if the court is satisfied that the award is necessary to afford 'just satisfaction'. In determining whether to award, and the amount of the award, the court must take into account the principles applied by the European Court, under Art 41 (formerly Art 50), in relation to the award of damages.[49]

These fairly stringent provisions are clearly designed to minimise the number and amount of awards of damages. Under this article, the European Court will afford just satisfaction only 'if necessary', so there is no principle of entitlement underlying the approach of the Court, rather one of discretion (see the comments at **1.6** above). The Court often considers the finding of a violation itself to constitute 'just satisfaction'. Nevertheless, awards for pecuniary damages (eg for loss of wages), non-pecuniary damages (eg for loss of opportunity, mental anguish and distress) and for costs and expenses ('actually incurred, were necessarily incurred and reasonable as to quantum') are made.[50]

---

49   As to the amounts awarded by the European Court, see **1.6** above. See also S Farran *The UK Before The European Court of Human Rights* (Blackstone Press, 1996), pp 386–388. In two recent cases in which the UK was found in breach of the Convention, the applicants were each awarded £10,000. In *A v UK* (1999) 27 EHRR 611, a man was acquitted by an English court of assaulting (caning) his stepson due to the current state of English law on reasonable chastisement – breach of Art 3. In *Osman v UK* [1999] 1 FLR 193, a family was barred from suing the police in negligence after the murder of the husband due to the immunity conferred in English law on the police for public policy reasons – breach of Art 6. See also the comments with regard to *Z v UK* at **1.6** above.

50   See, eg, *Young, James and Webster v UK* (1981) Series A/44; *Gillow v UK* (1986) Series A/109; *Dudgeon v UK* (1981) Series A/45, respectively; and comments on *Z v UK* at **1.6** above.

2.4.9   Section 9

Judicial acts

If proceedings under s 7(1)(a) are brought in respect of a 'judicial act' (the judicial act of a court or tribunal, or the act of a judge or a person acting on behalf or on the instruction of a judge (or tribunal member, justice of the peace or clerk or officer entitled to exercise the jurisdiction of a court or tribunal)), then those proceedings may only be brought by exercising a right of appeal or by judicial review (s 9(1), (5)).

The rules allowed in s 9(5) are brief and to the point. They appear in r 19.4A(3) and (4) of the Civil Procedure Rules 1998:

> **'Section 9 of the Human Rights Act 1998**
>
> . . .
>
> (3)   Where a claim is made under that Act for damages in respect of a judicial act –
>   (a)   that claim must be set out in the statement of case or the appeal notice; and
>   (b)   notice must be given to the Crown.
> (4)   Where paragraph (3) applies and the appropriate person has not applied to be joined as a party within 21 days, or such other period as the court directs, after the notice is served, the court may join the appropriate person as a party.
>
> (A practice direction makes provision for these notices).'

Section 9(1) does not affect any rule of law which prevents a court from being the subject of judicial review (s 9(2)). For example, the rule that mandamus will not lie to the Crown Court in the exercise of its jurisdiction relating to a trial on indictment is unaffected by this section.

Section 9 restricts applicants in these cases to appealing within the process in which the unlawful act is said to have occurred, or to judicial review, and restricts them therefore to the procedures, including time-limits, set down in those jurisdictions. It also prevents them from applying to the 'appropriate court or tribunal' established to hear applications under s 7(1)(a), unless such a course is later prescribed by rules.

Damages are not available in respect of a judicial act done in good faith except for the purposes of Art 5(5) of the Convention (which provides: 'Everyone who has been the victim of arrest or detention in contravention of the provisions of this Article shall have an enforceable right to compensation') (s 9(3)). The award is made against the Crown, after a minister is joined as a party (s 9(4)).

2.4.10   Section 10 and Schedule 2

Remedial action

Section 10 confers the crucial and very considerable power on a minister to amend[51] primary and subordinate legislation by order. That power can be

---

51   '"Amend" includes repeal and apply (with or without modification)' (s 21(1)).

triggered in two ways: first, when a court makes a declaration of incompatibility, under s 4, between domestic legislation and a Convention right; and, secondly, when the European Court makes a finding (after this section comes into force) which leads a minister to believe that a provision of domestic legislation is incompatible with UK obligations under the Convention.

The declaration of incompatibility will not trigger the procedure until all persons who may appeal have stated in writing that they do not intend to do so, or the time-limit for an appeal has expired and no appeal has been brought, or any appeal brought has been abandoned or determined. This clearly means that the process can be long-winded. Most cases will be appealed to the highest court by one side or the other. In the meantime, the offending legislation remains unamended, and the defendant remains in detention.

However, it should be noted that the incompatibility referred to in s 10(1)(b) is not an incompatibility between domestic legislation and the Convention rights in the Act (which are the subject of judicial declarations), but extends to an incompatibility between domestic legislation and any obligation of the UK arising from the Convention.

Section 10(2) is the key provision. It states 'If a Minister of the Crown considers that there are compelling reasons for proceedings under this section, he may by order make such amendments to the legislation as he considers necessary to remove the incompatibility'. Such an order is called a 'remedial order' (Sch 2).

The clause relating to 'compelling reasons' was added during the passage of the Bill to remove the implication that a remedial order would be the usual response to a declaration of incompatibility. Home Office Minister, Mike O'Brien, said in Parliament:

> 'The requirement for compelling reasons in [s 10(2)] is itself a response to concern expressed here and in another place about the remedial order provisions. It is there to make it absolutely clear that a remedial order is not a routine response in preference to fresh primary legislation.'[52]

It is the minister, however, who 'considers' this matter, just as it is the minister who can amend the legislation to the extent that he 'considers' is necessary to remove the incompatibility.[53] For an order not to be approved (it cannot be amended) by Parliament itself on the grounds that there are no compelling reasons for the use of this procedure would, while possible, imply something of a political crisis.

---

52   *Hansard* (HC) vol 317, col 1330 (21 October 1998).

53   Failure to make an order cannot be the subject of s 7(1)(a) proceedings (see s 6(6)).
      Strictly speaking, the acts of the minister under this section are amenable to judicial
      review, but given the discretion conferred at both stages here, a successful action seems
      most unlikely. See *R v Secretary of State for the Home Department ex parte Fire Brigades Union*
      [1995] 2 AC 513; and the comments of Lord Ackner in *R v Secretary of State for the Home
      Department ex parte Brind* [1991] 1 All ER 720 at 730–733. But see **2.4.15**, fn 65 below.

So far as the relationship with the judiciary is concerned, the word 'may' in s 10(2) is of constitutional importance. As the Lord Chancellor succinctly put it, 'may, not must'.[54]

If the declaration of incompatibility relates to subordinate legislation and the minister considers that it is necessary to amend the parent statute in order to remove the incompatibility, then the minister may amend the primary legislation (even if no declaration of incompatibility has been made in respect of that provision) (s 10(3)).

Where the declaration of incompatibility relates to a provision in subordinate legislation which has been quashed or declared invalid by reason of incompatibility with a Convention right, the question arises as to whether a remedial order is appropriate (or even, perhaps, 'necessary to remove the incompatibility'). Given that the incompatibility is no longer effective, the matter could be dealt with in the normal way. The power to use a remedial order in such cases is explicitly reserved, however, but in respect of urgent cases only (s 10(3), Sch 2, para 2(b)).

A measure of the Church Assembly or of the General Synod of the Church of England does not count as legislation for the purposes of this section (s 10(6)(b)). The Act generally applies to such legislation, but for reasons relating to the special procedures which exist for amending such legislation it is excluded from the scope of remedial orders.

Schedule 2 – Remedial orders
The remedial order may 'contain such incidental, supplemental, consequential or transitional provisions' as the minister considers appropriate, and may have the same extent as the legislation which it affects. It may therefore amend, repeal or revoke primary and subordinate legislation other than that which contains the incompatible provisions (para 1(1)(a), (2), (3)).

It may have retrospective effect (para 1(1)(b)), but no person is to be guilty of an offence solely as the result of the retrospective effect of a remedial order (para 1(4)). Nothing in the Act itself creates a criminal offence (s 7(8)), but the amendment of domestic law so as to make it compatible with the Convention rights could extend criminal liability in many areas. If it does so, it will not have retrospective effect.

The remedial order is subject to the strongest affirmative resolution procedure for statutory instruments. A draft is laid in Parliament but not made effective until approved. The draft lapses after 60 days unless approved. This is supplemented by a requirement that a document containing the proposed draft be laid for a 60-day period, before the draft itself is laid, accompanied by 'required information' (explaining the incompatibility, particularising the declaration, giving reasons for using a remedial order and for its terms). If representations are made during this initial period, the draft itself must be

---

54 See **2.3.1**, fn 6 above.

accompanied by a further statement summarising those representations and giving details of any resulting changes to the draft (paras 2(a), 3, 5).

This process has been elaborated to allow a little more parliamentary scrutiny and to avoid any difficulties which might arise from the fact that Parliament may only approve (or not) any order, but may not amend it.

If the minister considers, however, that because of the urgency of the matter an amendment ought to be made immediately, then an order may be made which has immediate effect (para 2(b)). It must be laid in Parliament and will lapse after 120 days unless approved. Similar arrangements are made with respect to required information and representations (para 4(2), (3)). Time does not run when Parliament is dissolved, prorogued or both Houses are adjourned for more than 4 days (para 6).

2.4.11   Section 11

Safeguard for existing human rights
Section 11 provides that reliance on a Convention right does not restrict the application of any other right or freedom in domestic law, nor the right to bring any claim or proceedings which a person could make or bring apart from ss 7–9 (s 11). The section makes clear that the Act is to supplement and improve a person's rights, and not to replace or diminish them in any way.

2.4.12   Section 12

Freedom of expression
A number of safeguards are introduced under s 12 in respect of the exercise of the Convention right to freedom of expression. The section is clearly intended to address concerns raised by the press during the passage of the Bill, but applies to publication and expression generally. Concerns focused in particular on applications that might be made in respect of any breach of the Convention right to respect for private and family life (Art 8), and the fear that relief granted in support of that right would infringe the right to freedom of expression.

It should be noted, however, that the safeguards are not restricted to proceedings taken under the Act. In defamation proceedings, for example, the court is under a duty, whether or not the point is raised, to apply these safeguards. They do not, however, apply in criminal proceedings, because '"relief" includes any remedy or order (other than in criminal proceedings)' (s 12(5)). Criminal courts are, of course, subject to s 3 (interpretation of legislation).

If a court (or tribunal) is considering whether to grant relief which affects the exercise of the Convention right to freedom of expression, it must have regard to, and be satisfied about, a number of matters. A general duty is imposed on the court in these circumstances to 'have particular regard to the importance of the Convention right to freedom of expression' (s 10(4)). It should be remembered that the Convention right to freedom of expression is not itself unqualified. On the contrary, the freedom set out in Art 10(1) is accompanied by all the limitations which are permitted in Art 10(2), and they are also part of the Convention right to which the court must have regard.

The use of the words 'particular regard' and 'importance' with respect to Art 10 must import some weight onto the scales when it is balanced against Art 8 and other rights. In the case of *Richmond upon Thames London Borough Council v Holmes and Others*,[55] the court was balancing the rights of the press to publish a story about the fostering policies of the local council and the need not to identify the children concerned. Bracewell J held that s 1 of the Children Act 1989, which would have required the welfare of the child to be paramount, did not apply and, as such, Art 10, giving freedom of expression to the press, had to apply.

Certain safeguards are introduced where any such relief (which might affect freedom of expression) is applied for in the absence of the respondent. This will apply to ex parte injunction applications. The court must be satisfied that the applicant has taken all reasonable steps to notify the respondent or that there are compelling reasons why the respondent should not be notified (s 12(3)). However, these 'safeguards' go no further than to codify the common law as it previously existed.

The court must not grant such relief as would restrain publication before trial unless satisfied that the applicant is likely to establish at trial that publication should not be allowed (s 12). The general starting point for the grant of any interlocutory relief of this sort is that the applicant must show that there is a serious issue to be tried (not a likelihood of succeeding), and then the balance of convenience is considered.[56] In various different contexts and ways, however, the courts already tread very carefully in cases in which free expression might be compromised by prior restraint.[57] Section 12 establishes a bottom line for that caution.

In the case of *Douglas v Hello! Ltd*[58] the court considered the process for injunctions following the commencement of the Act. The court held that in determining whether publication would be allowed at trial, it had to consider all Convention rights, and balance them equally, rather than giving more weight to Art 10, since that would be the balance made at trial.

Where the proceedings relate to material which appears to the court, or which the respondent claims, to be journalistic, literary or artistic material, the court must have particular regard to the extent to which:

(a) the material is already, or is about to be, in the public domain; or
(b) it is in the public interest for the material to be published,

---

55 [2000] TLR 731, FD.
56 *American Cyanamid Co v Ethicon* [1975] AC 396, [1975] 1 All ER 504, HL.
57 See, eg, *Attorney General v News Group Newspapers Ltd* [1987] QB 1, [1986] 2 All ER 833.
58 [2001] 2 WLR 992, CA.

and the court must also have particular regard to any relevant privacy code. This provision incorporates the approach of the House of Lords in the *Spycatcher* case[59] (broadening it to allow public availability and public interest to stand as separate factors, and also extending it to literary and artistic material), but also allows the court to weigh in the scales any breach by a newspaper, for example of any privacy code to which it subscribes.

In criminal cases, the Court of Appeal has issued guidance in the case of *R v Sherwood ex parte The Telegraph Group plc and Others* [2001] EWCA Crim 1075.[60] This arose out of reporting restrictions imposed during the course of a trial of a police officer for murder until the conclusion of the follow-on trial of three co-defendants. A number of newspapers appealed against the order on the basis that it was a violation of the freedom of expression guaranteed under Art 10. The Court stated that the right to freedom of expression had to balanced with the right to a fair trial in Art 6, and that no order should be made unless a ban was necessary, in the light of the facts, to avoid the perceived risk of prejudice. Following that, the Court must decide whether an order was a 'necessary interference' with the right of freedom of expression. This was assessed by considering, first, whether the reporting would give rise to a not insubstantial risk of prejudice to the administration of justice. Secondly, if there was such a risk, would the order eliminate it, or could the objective be achieved by some less restrictive order (a proportionality test). If not, the third question was that even if there was a risk of prejudice, did the public interest in reporting outweigh the interests of fair trial.

In *Mills v News Group Newspapers Ltd*,[61] the Court considered the correct approach to be adopted on an application for an injunction to prevent publication of private information, and in particular the relevance of the PCC Code of Conduct. See also *Thompson and Venables v News Group Newspapers Ltd, Associated Newspapers Ltd and MGN Ltd*,[62] with regard to the rare example of the court having to balance the rights of Art 10 against the right to life and the right to freedom from inhuman or degrading treatment or punishment.

2.4.13   Section 13

Freedom of thought, conscience and religion
Section 13 provides a similar safeguard for the exercise of the Convention right to freedom of thought, conscience and religion (Art 9), but only in general terms. In this case, the safeguard applies in all proceedings before a court or tribunal, not only in respect of relief, but also in respect of the 'determination of any question arising under this Act'.

If the determination of the question might affect the exercise 'by a religious organisation (itself or its members collectively)' of the Convention right to

---

59   *Attorney General v Guardian Newspapers (No 2)* [1990] AC 109, [1989] 3 All ER 545.
60   [2001] TLR 380.
61   (Unreported), 4 June 2001, ChD.
62   [2001] UKHRR 628.

thought, conscience and religion, the court (or tribunal) must have particular regard to the importance of that right (s 13).

Section 13 addresses concerns raised by the churches during the passage of the Bill about applications under the Act which might compromise their conduct, for example in relation to admission to the clergy, the administration of marriage or church schools. The problem partly derives from the fact that many churches will be held to be 'public authorities' under s 6(3)(b) because certain of their functions are functions of a public nature. The question then becomes which of their acts are not private acts so as to render them open to challenge under s 7(1)(a).

The Home Secretary, Jack Straw, sought to reassure them:

> 'In the debate of 20 May this year, I stated: "the regulation of divine worship" – and I mean regulation – "the administration of the sacrament, admission to Church membership or to the priesthood" – obviously the term "admission" covers non-admission and exclusion – "are in our judgment, all private matters" – [Official Report vol 312, col 1015 (20 May 1998)].'[63]

In any event, s 13 provides a blanket safeguard with respect to all decisions a court makes which affect Art 9 rights, to the extent that the court must have particular regard to their importance to the church as a body and as a whole. However, that will not stop the courts interfering in other church matters where there is an incompatibility.[64]

2.4.14   Section 18 and Schedule 4

Appointment to the European Court of Human Rights
Section 18 provides for the appointment of senior judges to the European Court of Human Rights. Lords of Appeal in Ordinary are not included. Schedule 4 makes provisions concerning judicial pensions, not least to ensure that no disadvantage accrues in this respect from sitting for a 6-year term in Strasbourg.

2.4.15   Section 19

Parliamentary procedure
To minimise the opportunity for conflict between the judiciary and Parliament, and to reinforce the desirability of bringing the consideration of human rights into all aspects of British life, s 19 requires a minister in charge of a Bill, if

---

63   *Hansard* (HC) vol 317, col 1368 (21 October 1998).
64   In *Aston Cantlow and Wilmcote with Billesley Parochial Church Council v Wallbank and Another* [2001] TLR 389, the Court of Appeal found that an ancient rule making particular landowners responsible for the upkeep of the church roof was a violation of Art 14 together with the right to property. See also *Couloris v Trustees of The Saint Sophias Greek Cathedral* (unreported) 5 July 2001, ChD and *Re Crawley Green Road Cemetery, Luton* [2001] Fam 308, Consistery Court.

possible, to confirm to Parliament that it conforms with the Convention rights. The section came into force on 24 November 1998.

The minister must make a written statement, before the second reading of the Bill, to the effect that the provisions of the Bill are consistent with the Convention rights. This is called 'a statement of compatibility'. If the minister is unable to do so, a written statement must be made to that effect, and state that the Government nevertheless wishes the House to proceed with the Bill (s 19).[65]

2.4.16   Section 20

Section 20 is a supplemental provision relating to the making of orders under the Act. A minister may make any such order by statutory instrument. The Lord Chancellor and Secretary of State may make rules by statutory instrument under s 2(3) (for evidence to be given of judgments, decisions, etc, of the Strasbourg bodies) and s 7(9) (for the determination of the appropriate court or tribunal to hear proceedings against public authorities), other than rules of court.

Orders under s 1(4) (amendments to reflect new protocols to the Convention), s 7(11) (powers of tribunals to provide appropriate remedies) and s 16(2) (extension of designated derogations from the Convention) may be made only after a draft order has been laid before, and approved by, each House of Parliament.

Statutory instruments made under s 18(7) (transitional provisions for judges serving on the European Court) and Sch 4 (judicial pensions) are subject to annulment by resolution of either House of Parliament.

2.4.17   Section 21

Section 21 is the interpretation section.

2.4.18   Section 22

Retrospective nature of the Act
Section 22 is the short title (the Human Rights Act 1998), commencement, application and extent section. Section 22(4) provides that s 7(1)(b) (the ability of individuals to rely on Convention rights in any proceedings) applies to proceedings brought by public authorities whenever the act in question (the alleged unlawful act of a public authority) took place; but otherwise does not apply to an act taking place before the coming into force of that section.

This is of obvious importance for criminal proceedings, in that it appears to suggest that the effects of the Act are retrospective. A criminal trial is clearly a

---

65   See the Lord Chancellor, Lord Irvine of Lairg, 'If a minister's prior assessment of compatibility (under [s 19]) is subsequently found by the courts to have been mistaken, it is hard to see how a minister could withhold remedial action': *Hansard* (HL) vol 582, col 1229 (3 November 1997).

proceeding 'brought by public authorities' no matter that it may have occurred many years before. If, as a result of a decision of the higher courts, it becomes clear that the original trial was unfair, it would be possible for it to be reconsidered. Of course, one would have to pass the burden of appealing out of time, or of getting the Criminal Cases Review Commission to refer the case to the Court of Appeal. However, if the point of law which has subsequently changed is a significant one, it will be more important to have the case reopened. The courts have held that a contract made prior to the commencement of the Act (2 October 2000) is not open to review under the Act,[66] but that would not involve an action brought by a public authority.

Judicial authorities have been divided as to the retrospective nature of s 22(4) of the Human Rights Act 1998, which states that right to rely on Convention rights in s 7(1)(b) of the Act 'applies to proceedings brought by or at the instigation of a public authority whenever the act in question took place'. In the case of *R v DPP ex parte Kebilene*,[67] the majority had found that a criminal prosecution was clearly 'proceedings brought by . . . a public authority' and that consequently one can rely on a breach of the Convention. However, in *R v Kansal* [2001] EWCA Crim 1260,[68] the Court of Appeal considered the issue with regard to references from the Criminal Cases Review Commission (CCRC). The Court found that the practice of the Court of Appeal was that it was not appropriate to re-open convictions following a subsequent change in the law. The practical operation of that policy was not to allow leave to appeal out of time.

On references to the Court by the CCRC, however, such a policy could not be operated; the Court had no choice but to consider the conviction. Where the case referred to the Court involved a subsequent change in the common law, or the retrospective application of the European Convention on Human Rights through s 22(4) of the Human Rights Act 1998, this created a particular problem.

Under the Criminal Appeal Act 1995, the CCRC could refer a conviction to the Court of Appeal whenever it took place. If the conviction would now be considered to have been obtained in breach of Art 6, the Court had no option but to declare the conviction unsafe. Their Lordships noted that Guy Fawkes, Sir Thomas More and Charles I were all convicted in violation of the Fair Trial provisions of Art 6.

The pragmatic approach adopted by the Court of Appeal up until now was in the public interest of achieving finality in litigation, and to concentrate resources on more meritorious claims. Parliament appeared to have laid down no limit to such appeals in either the Criminal Appeal Act 1985 or the Human Rights Act 1998. The effect of the workload of the Court of Appeal could be dramatic.

The Court requested guidance from either Parliament or the House of Lords. It came shortly thereafter, although not in response to that call, from the House

66   *Ashworth Hospital Authority v MGN Ltd* [2001] 1 WLR 515, CA.
67   [2000] 2 AC 326.
68   [2001] TLR 374.

of Lords considering the case of *R v Lambert* [2001] UKHL 37,[69] Their Lordships found that Parliament had not intended that a trial prior to October 2000 could be appealed after that date on the basis of the Convention. If that were to occur, there would be potential for confusion and uncertainty. However, in the opinion of Lord Steyn, a court which upheld a conviction in breach of a Convention right must surely be acting in a way that was incompatible with a Convention right, and therefore would be unlawful under s 6 of the Human Rights Act 1998; the issue of retrospectivity did not alter this.

See also *R (on the Application of Ben-Abdelaziz) v Haringey London Borough Council and Another*,[70] where the Court found that proceedings for judicial review were not brought 'by or at the instigation of a public authority', namely the Crown, in terms of s 22(4) of the Human Rights Act 1998. Therefore, it could not be relied upon in proceedings for judicial review.

Application
The Act binds the Crown, extends to Northern Ireland and also extends the effect of s 21(5) (abolition of death penalty – see **2.4.1** above) to any place to which a relevant provision of the Army Act 1955, the Air Force Act 1955 and the Naval Discipline Act 1957 extends.

---

69 [2001] 3 WLR 206.
70 [2001] TLR 397, CA.

Chapter 3

THE INVESTIGATION OF CRIME

3.1 INTRODUCTION

This chapter examines the key stages of pre-trial investigation and procedure in order to see the extent to which the common law complies with the requirements of the European Convention on Human Rights (the Convention). It is not a comprehensive coverage of every nook and cranny of criminal procedure, and the purpose is to illustrate the principles underlying the Convention by an examination of the more important decisions by the police and the courts. At the stage of investigation, those principles are:

- *legality*: the exercise of police powers should be in accordance with statutory or common law which is clear and accessible and the powers themselves must not be ordered haphazardly, irregularly or without due and proper care;
- *necessity*: the interference should be necessary and likely to produce results or material to aid an investigation;
- *proportionality*: the exercise of police powers must bear an appropriate relationship to the seriousness of the event. In any case, the interference must be balanced and due weight and consideration given to individual rights;
- *accountability*: the exercise of police powers should be subject to the supervisory control of a judge in accordance with the rule of law, but other safeguards might suffice if they are independent and vested with sufficient powers to exercise an effective and continuous control.[1]

These core principles can be applied to all aspects of police investigation and criminal procedure.

Traditionally the investigation of serious crime involves the police in the examination of the crime scene and the analysis of forensic evidence, the use of house-to-house inquiries, questioning witnesses and suspects, stopping and searching persons and vehicles, mounting road blocks, and arresting, detaining and interviewing suspects. The basic powers of a police constable to undertake such actions are contained mainly within the Police and Criminal Evidence Act 1984 (PACE 1984) which has codified the law on police powers.[2] Where the investigation is more covert in nature, the powers are likely to be governed by the Police Act 1997 or the Regulation of Investigatory Powers Act 2000.

---

1   These are identified by Justice, *Under Surveillance: Covert Policing and Human Rights Standards* (Justice, 1998).
2   K Lidstone and C Palmer *Bevan and Lidstone's The Investigation of Crime* 2nd edn (Butterworths, 1996).

Police investigation invariably interferes with fundamental freedoms protected under the Convention: being subjected to an intimate body search under s 55 of PACE 1984 may be seen as degrading treatment under Art 3; an officer stopping and searching a person in the street under s 1 of that Act is impinging on that person's right to liberty and security under Art 5; installing a surveillance device in a suspect's house under Part III of the Police Act 1997 breaches that person's right to privacy under Art 8. However, the existence of such powers is, in certain circumstances, necessary in a democratic society. Thus, although the statutory and common law powers of the police must comply with Convention requirements, a person's freedom from police interference is never absolute and must be balanced alongside other social interests, especially the public interest in the detection and prevention of crime.

During a normal police investigation, it is likely that any interference with Convention rights will be with those protected under Art 5. Article 5(1) provides that 'Everyone has the right to liberty and security of person'. However, this is not an absolute right. Article 5(1) details six situations where the State may be justified in deprivation of that liberty:

> 'No one shall be deprived of his liberty save in the following cases and in accordance with a procedure prescribed by law:
>
> (a)   the lawful detention of a person after conviction by a competent court;
>
> (b)   the lawful arrest or detention of a person for non-compliance with the lawful order of a court or in order to secure the fulfilment of any obligation prescribed by law;
>
> (c)   the lawful arrest or detention of a person effected for the purpose of bringing him before the competent legal authority on reasonable suspicion of having committed an offence or when it is reasonably considered necessary to prevent his committing an offence or fleeing after having done so;
>
> (d)   the detention of a minor by lawful order for the purpose of educational supervision or his lawful detention for the purpose of bringing him before the competent legal authority;
>
> (e)   the lawful detention of persons for the prevention of the spreading of infectious diseases, of persons of unsound mind, alcoholics or drug addicts or vagrants;
>
> (f)   the lawful arrest or detention of a person to prevent his effecting an unauthorised entry into the country or of a person against whom action is being taken with a view to deportation or extradition.'

Article 5(2)–(5) refers to rights which apply whether or not that detention is justified:

> '(2) Everyone who is arrested shall be informed promptly, in a language which he understands, of the reasons for his arrest and of any charge against him.
>
> (3) Everyone arrested or detained in accordance with the provisions of paragraph 1(c) of this article shall be brought promptly before a judge or other officer authorised by law to exercise judicial power and shall be entitled to trial within a reasonable time or to release pending trial. Release may be conditioned by guarantees to appear for trial.

(4) Everyone who is deprived of his liberty by arrest or detention shall be entitled to take proceedings by which the lawfulness of his detention shall be decided speedily by a court and his release ordered if the detention is not lawful.

(5) Everyone who has been the victim of arrest or detention in contravention of the provisions of this article shall have an enforceable right to compensation.'

Article 5 protects the physical freedom of the individual, ensuring that any deprivation of liberty must occur only in accordance with a 'procedure prescribed by law', for one of the reasons specified in Art 5(1)(a)–(f) and accompanied by the rights laid out in Art 5(2)–(5). These are important safeguards against the powers of the State and especially in the context of police investigation and their powers of arrest and detention.

However, police investigation can infringe Convention rights in different ways, and Article 5 must also be read in conjunction with other articles. Article 3 will also have an impact on aspects of police investigation. It provides that 'No one shall be subjected to torture or to inhuman or degrading treatment or punishment'. Article 3 is relevant, for example, to police powers to search persons or to conditions of detention. Another significant right in the context of investigatory methods is guaranteed under Art 8, which provides that 'Everyone has the right to respect for his private and family life, his home and his correspondence'. This will place certain constraints, for example, on police techniques of covert surveillance.

A police investigation is designed to produce evidence in subsequent proceedings, and the most significant reason to attack the conduct of that investigation is to seek to exclude that evidence in the course of any subsequent trial. Consequently, it is not possible to draw a sharp distinction between rights which arise under Arts 5 or 8 relating to pre-trial process and rights arising under Art 6 relating to a right to a fair hearing. Pre-trial issues impact on the trial as 'investigative evidence only becomes an issue in the context of its use or treatment in the conduct of the prosecution case before the court'.[3] Such issues about the conduct of the investigation, the conditions of detention, the right of security to person or the right to privacy can become transposed to issues about the right to a fair hearing under Art 6(1), which provides that 'In the determination of ... any criminal charge against him, everyone is entitled to a fair and public hearing within a reasonable time by an independent and impartial tribunal established by law'. Article 6 guarantees the general right to a fair trial as well as certain specific rights for the accused during the trial. These are discussed fully in Chapter 4 below. This article is relevant to police investigation since rights are not restricted to events in the courtroom, and it is clear that actions by the police or prosecuting authorities prior to the court hearing can prejudice that right. The European Court of Human Rights (the European Court) has stated:

'Article 6 – especially paragraph 3 – may be relevant before a case is sent for trial if and so far as the fairness of the trial is likely to be seriously prejudiced by an initial failure to comply with its provisions.'[4]

3   S Sharpe 'The European Convention: A Suspects' Charter?' [1997] Crim LR 848.
4   *Magee v UK* Application No 28135/95, para 41, [2000] Crim LR 681.

The passage of the Human Rights Act 1998 means that criminal investigative procedure will need to comply with all these articles. In normal cases, police pre-trial procedures are routine and transparent. Much of the domestic law on police powers in these situations is contained in PACE 1984 and the associated codes of practice. However, these powers have been widened in specific instances, such as the investigation of serious fraud under the Criminal Justice Act 1987 or under the Terrorism Act 2000. Furthermore, in contrast to overt policing techniques, in recent years more emphasis has been placed on covert, intelligence-led policing.[5] This entails a greater use of informants, the gathering of intelligence, crime pattern analysis and the surveillance of those suspected of continuing involvement in criminal activity, both intrusive but lawful (eg visual observations from public spaces or with the consent of the landholder) and intrusive but unlawful (eg through the interception of mail, telephone tapping or bugging premises involving tortious trespass). Statutes such as the Wireless Telegraphy Act 1949, the Police Act 1997 and the Regulation of Investigatory Powers Act 2000 regulate such police activity to an extent. Techniques of proactive and intelligence-led policing raise significant questions about Art 8, which provides for the right to respect for private and family life, home and correspondence, and its relationship with Art 6.

The Human Rights Act 1998 will not mean wholesale changes to these laws and procedures but there has been some refining.[6] Convention jurisprudence is not aimed at developing a pan-European criminal procedure – the concept of a 'margin of appreciation' allows for a wide variation in the pre-trial and trial rules and procedures adopted by States. It is clear, for example, that the 1984 legislation, together with its codes, create a regime which in routine cases complies with the Convention, although there are many specific areas where that compliance may be questioned. It is now necessary for national courts to ensure that the domestic law on police powers is interpreted so that the legislation complies with the Convention[7] and its related jurisprudence[8] or, if this is not possible, to issue a certificate of incompatibility.[9] We must expect that trial judges will become more accustomed to adopting a principle-led approach to issues, especially issues of admissibility of evidence. Convention jurisprudence directs courts to approach these questions through concepts such as fairness or respect for privacy, and normally will not interfere with the outcome provided the trial court frames the issue to be decided in the correct terms.

---

5   S Uglow and V Telford *The Police Act 1997* (Jordans, 1997), p 2.
6   For example, s 25 of the Criminal Justice and Public Order Act 1994 was amended by s 56 of the Crime and Disorder Act 1998, ss 58 and 59 of the Youth Justice and Criminal Evidence Act 1999.
7   Human Rights Act 1998, s 3(1).
8   Ibid, s 2(1).
9   Ibid, s 4(1).

3.2 RESTRICTIONS ON LIBERTY AND TEMPORARY DETENTION

Once the State is seen as depriving a person of his or her liberty, that has to be justified by one of the paragraphs in Art 5(1). This permits restrictions on liberty after conviction, on suspicion of committing criminal offences, of minors for educational supervision, of those of unsound mind or carrying an infectious disease, as well as of those facing extradition or deportation. Without such a justification, the detention violates the Convention.

What constitutes a 'detention' where these safeguards apply? Do the safeguards come into play whenever there is any form of restriction on movement, or do they apply only to extreme forms of detention such as at a police station or prison? The Court has held that Art 5 safeguards apply to restricted residence orders,[10] detention in a mental hospital[11] and military detention.[12] The criteria to be considered are the intensity, duration and nature of the restriction. In *Nielsen v Denmark*,[13] a mother placed her 12-year-old son in a closed psychiatric ward. This was held to be an exercise of parental rights and did not have to be justified under Art 5.

Limited restrictions attract the safeguards under the Convention. In *McVeigh v UK*[14] the applications involved the obligation under the Prevention of Terrorism Act 1976 for all persons entering the country to submit to examination at the point of entry to determine whether they had been involved in terrorism. The applicants were questioned, searched and detained for 45 hours, but released without charge. The Court held that this detention was sufficient to require the State to observe its obligations under Art 5 although detention is permitted by Art 5(1)(b) 'in order to secure the fulfilment of any obligation prescribed by law'. Not only was the obligation to submit to border checks legitimate, but so also were extended examination and detention. A balance had to be drawn between the importance of such obligations in a democratic society and the right to liberty of the person.

In English law, there are several examples of limited restrictions on liberty, such as the child curfew scheme under s 14 of the Crime and Disorder Act 1998,[15] or the electronic monitoring of released offenders under s 100 of that Act. There may be an analogy here with jurisdictions that employ house imprisonment or restrictions to particular localities, albeit curfews and taggings are of a lesser intensity. Although curfews and taggings might well be treated as 'detention' by the State, they would be covered by Art 5(1)(a) which permits 'the lawful detention of a person after conviction by a competent court'. In other words, curfew is legitimate detention following conviction in the same way as a prison sentence.

---

10   *Guzzardi v Italy* (1980) 3 EHRR 333.
11   *Ashingdane v UK* (1985) 7 EHRR 528.
12   *Engel v The Netherlands* (1976) 1 EHRR 706.
13   (1988) 11 EHRR 175.
14   (1981) 5 EHRR 71.
15   Now extended by s 48 of the Criminal Justice and Police Act 2001.

Would even more limited restrictions be seen as 'detention' and require such justification? Examples might include bail conditions by which the accused has to report daily to the police or observe a curfew. In some areas, objection has been taken to the police practice of turning up at a defendant's house and requiring a defendant under curfew to appear at the door. Although the 'deprivation of liberty' imposed by such bail conditions appear to fall well below any threshold of 'detention' so far considered by the Court, such an arrangement may be interpreted as State detention as a defendant may be on bail for several months and the restrictions on movement may be for many hours a day. If this is a 'detention', such pre-trial procedures are not covered by Art 5(1)(a) but may be covered by Art 5(1)(b) as the bail conditions are 'obligations prescribed by law', breach of which can lead to arrest and appearance before a court.

Such 'doorstep' bail conditions may also show a State's interference with the accused's right to respect for private and family life guaranteed under Art 8(1), but this right may also be derogated from under Art 8(2) which permits such interference when it is in accordance with the law and is necessary in a democratic society in the interests of the prevention of disorder or crime. Such bail conditions would meet both these criteria.

A further form of temporary detention in the preliminary stages of criminal investigation is the police power to stop and question a person on the street. The human rights aspects of such powers has been brought into sharp relief by the MacPherson Report.[16] This inquiry emphasised minority ethnic communities' lack of trust and confidence in the police, particularly because of their long-standing concerns about the use by police of stops and searches. Those concerns are about the perception that there is a lack of reasonable suspicion in making stops, indicated by the low level of arrests following stops and the sense that the police use of this power is discriminatory, if not overtly racist.

Stop and search was introduced in 1984. Prior to this, over most of the country[17] the police had no power to stop pedestrians in order to question or to search them. The police argued before the Royal Commission on Criminal Procedure[18] in 1981 that a power of temporary detention was important for crime detection since possession of prohibited articles could only be detected by such a measure.[19] Section 1 of PACE 1984 provided a general power that the police could, on reasonable suspicion that any person or vehicle was carrying stolen goods or other prohibited items, stop that person or vehicle and conduct a desultory search (checking pockets, searching bags, etc). There are analogous powers under PACE 1984 for road blocks, as well as under other statutes such as the Road Traffic Act 1988, the Sporting Events Act 1985, s 60 of the Criminal

---

16   *Report of the Inquiry into the Matters Arising from the Death of Stephen Lawrence* (Home Office, 1999).
17   In London there was such a power under s 66 of the Metropolitan Police Act 1839.
18   Cmnd 8092 (1981) paras 3.11–3.33.
19   The effectiveness of such measures was discussed in C Willis *The Use, Effectiveness and Impact of Police Stop and Search Powers* (HMSO, 1983); Home Office Research and Planning Unit Paper No 15.

Justice and Public Order Act 1994 and s 15(3) of the Prevention of Terrorism Act 1989.[20] Research data shows that s 1 powers are still widely used – over 1 million stops and searches were recorded by the police in 1998/99. Of these, disproportionately, 9% were of black suspects and 5% of Asian suspects. Only 12% of stops resulted in an arrest.[21]

Does such short-term detention require justification under the Convention? The decision by the Court in *McVeigh v UK* (above) suggests that it does – that the obligation for all persons entering the country to submit to examination at the point of entry to determine whether they have been involved in terrorism is analogous to the obligation to submit to a search in the street. If that is the case, Art 5(1)(b) would permit such detention 'in order to secure the fulfilment of any obligation prescribed by law'. The citizen is legally obliged to submit to the stop and search, and a refusal would constitute the offence of obstructing an officer in the execution of his duty.[22] The Court will always consider the balance between the importance of such obligations and the right to liberty of the person; in *McVeigh*, the interest in the prevention of terrorist activities was sufficient to outweigh the limited interference with the applicant's liberty of the person. It is probable that the public interest in the prevention of crime outweighs the interference with the applicant's rights brought about by a short-term stop. Section 1 and the Code of Practice[23] regulating it imposes an obligation on an individual to submit to a limited search for items, possession of which would be a criminal offence. The procedure meets the basic criteria of fairness, openness and workability, specifying the grounds for stopping and searching and requiring proper documentation.

Although *McVeigh* must be understood in the context of the emergency in Northern Ireland, it also provides a principle which justifies the State in its use of stop and search powers, breath tests and road blocks. It would probably also justify identity checks, were such to be introduced. But a stop is lawful only if it is based on reasonable suspicion that the person may be in possession of prohibited articles. This concept is the key element in the exercise of these powers.[24] The Code outlining how these powers should be exercised does not define them positively, but does seek to prevent officers from exercising their powers on the basis of ethnicity, age or clothing. An officer should be able to identify an objective basis for the stop, which should not include a person's refusal to answer questions, but would include his attempting to run away. Research findings (supported by the low incidence of arrests following stops) question whether individual officers who carry out stops do in fact have 'reasonable suspicion'. Sanders and Young suggest that the vagueness of this

---

20   For a full list, see PACE 1984 Code of Practice A, Annex.

21   *Statistics on Race and the Criminal Justice System* (Home Office, 1999), p 10, Table 3.2; *cf* D Brown *PACE 10 Years On: a Review of the Research* (Home Office Research Study 150, 1997).

22   Police Act 1996, s 89.

23   PACE 1984, Code of Practice A – the exercise by police officers of statutory powers of stop and search.

24   See Lidstone and Palmer (n 2 above), ch 2; A Sanders and R Young *Criminal Justice* (Butterworths, 1994), pp 38ff.

test rules out the possibility of strict adherence to the formal criteria and permits unjustified invasions of personal liberty and privacy.[25]

This argument is supported by cases such as *Lodwick v Sanders*[26] where the court agreed that an officer was still acting in the execution of his duty in detaining a driver and his lorry to ascertain whether the vehicle was stolen, despite having no evidence on which suspicion of theft could be based. The decision to stop is often based not on legally relevant criteria but on the officer's own informal norms, the three most important of which are, first, previous convictions known to the officer, secondly, the maintenance of order and of police authority and, thirdly, general suspiciousness, ie being in the wrong place at the wrong time.[27] Officers rely on instinct, and this can lead to class and race bias[28] in making stops which, in turn, can lead to a group's perception that it is being harassed. This reluctance of the English courts to inquire into the basis of police beliefs may well have to change. Unsurprisingly, the judgments in *Lodwick v Sanders* did not refer to the Convention, but future courts may require that officers should act with increasing care, and that 'suspicion' is founded on objective grounds that will satisfy the court and which are also significant.

A thought-provoking parallel is to be found in *McLeod v UK*.[29] In the course of an acrimonious divorce, the husband obtained a court order that certain items of furniture should be delivered to him by a set date. Before that date he went to the wife's house where he met two police officers who were given a list of the property, but not the court order. The wife was not present. Her mother was in the house but said that she knew nothing of the arrangement. The husband entered the house and removed the items. The officers also entered but took no part. The wife took action, inter alia, against the police for trespass. The defence was that the officers entered the property as they had reasonable grounds to apprehend a breach of the peace and, as a result, had the power to enter (a result of the decision in *Thomas v Sawkins*[30] and s 17(6) of PACE 1984). The High Court and the Court of Appeal accepted this defence,[31] but the wife went to the European Court, arguing that the State had breached Art 8. The Government response was that the officers' actions were lawful and in the interests of preventing disorder, and this was covered under Art 8(2). The European Court found that the officers' acts were a disproportionate response to the aim of preventing disorder since they had not checked the court order to ensure that the husband was entitled to enter and remove the property and since the fact that the wife was away meant that there was little risk of any disorder occurring, a conclusion as to the facts that went completely against that of the High Court and the Court of Appeal.

---

25   A Sanders and R Young *Criminal Justice* (Butterworths, 1994), pp 38ff.
26   [1985] 1 All ER 577.
27   A Sanders 'Controlling the Discretion of the Individual Officer' in R Reiner and S Spencer (eds) *Accountable Policing* (IPPR, 1993), p 83.
28   Smith and Gray *Police and People in London* (PSI, 1983).
29   (1998) 27 EHRR 493.
30   [1935] 2 KB 249.
31   *McLeod v Metropolitan Police Commissioner* [1994] 4 All ER 553.

The principle behind *McLeod* is that, in forming their beliefs and in exercising their powers of entry, the police must balance the necessity for their actions against the interests they are violating – in this case the wife's right to respect for her home.[32] This can also be seen in *Steel v UK*[33] where the police arrested certain demonstrators, detaining them and later releasing them without charge. The European Court held that the officers, in forming their beliefs about their apprehension of a breach of the peace, should have given due weight to the applicants' rights to freedom of expression under Art 10 and of peaceful assembly under Art 11. The cases suggest that any interference with a person's rights must be a necessary and proportionate response to the apprehension of disorder or suspicion of crime.

If we apply this reasoning to a police officer's decision to stop and search a suspect, it suggests that a constable must balance the strength of his or her suspicions against the person's rights, in particular the right to liberty under Art 5 but also, especially in the light of the MacPherson Report, the right not to be discriminated against under Art 14. Furthermore, were the issue to arise in court, the judge would have to consider not only whether the officer had well-founded reasonable suspicion, but also the balance between the import-ance of the obligations and the right to liberty.

Such street-level infringements of personal liberty also raise a further issue since Art 14 provides that rights shall be secured without discrimination. The figures suggest that the practice of stop and search infringes these provisions. Searches must be recorded[34] and, since April 1993, all police forces are required to publish annual figures on the ethnic origin of all those stopped and searched. The most recent figures are as follows.[35]

Stop and searches of persons under s 1 of PACE 1984 per 1,000 population aged 10 and over by ethnic appearance of person searched – selected forces

Force	White		Black		Asian	
	1997/8	*1998/9*	*1997/8*	*1998/9*	*1997/8*	*1998/9*
Cleveland	98	101	302	158	105	72
Greater Manchester	21	25	107	107	18	23
Leicestershire	16	19	159	190	19	24
Merseyside	37	42	312	310	31	34
Metropolitan	37	33	180	148	75	64
Surrey	14	13	122	109	36	46
England and Wales	19	20	139	118	45	42

Although this data is basic and does not take into account other factors that may account for this disparity,[36] it is obvious that Afro-Caribbeans are significantly more likely to be stopped and searched than whites or Asians. Some of the

---

32 But see the comments of Neill LJ [1994] 4 All ER 553 at 560g–j.
33 (1998) 28 EHRR 603.
34 PACE 1984, ss 3 and 5.
35 *Statistics on Race and the Criminal Justice System* (Home Office, 1999), p 10, Table 3.2.
36 M Fitzgerald and R Sibbitt: *Ethnic Monitoring in Police Forces* (Home Office Research Study 173, 1997).

discrepancy is accounted for by differences in the age and class structure of black and white populations. In addition, consensual searches are not recorded – it is possible that whites are more likely to consent to a search than blacks. Having taken such factors into consideration, such statistics still indicate clear discrimination. However, police culture is the culprit, rather than the law on police procedures. Research suggests that policing practice before and after PACE 1984 has changed little.[37] Despite the Code's prohibition on stereotyping at arriving at 'reasonable suspicion' and its specific exclusion of a person's colour, age, hairstyle or manner of dress as a basis for a stop,[38] there is little supervision of the individual officer's discretion either by police management or by the courts.[39]

3.2.1   What remedies may exist?

– If the person stopped were charged with an ancillary offence, such as assault on or obstruction of a police officer in the execution of his duty, an argument could certainly be made that the officer was not in the execution of his or her duty because there was an insufficient basis for suspicion and this infringed the defendant's rights under Art 5, and perhaps under Art 14. This is the common law position, and the impact of the Human Rights Act 1998 may merely mean that the courts will take care that they are seen to scrutinise the justifications for police conduct more thoroughly. It is possible to go further and suggest that, even were reasonable cause for the stop and search to exist, *Steel v UK* (above) suggests that the exercise of that power must be necessary when balanced alongside the person's right not to be discriminated against.

– If the person stopped were to be charged with possession of a prohibited article, arguing that the evidence should be excluded on the basis that there was no 'reasonable suspicion' would challenge the skills of the most committed advocate. It may be argued that, under s 78 of PACE 1984, the judge has discretion to exclude evidence which would have an adverse effect on the fairness of the proceedings. It might be assumed that evidence acquired in the course of a violation of the accused's right to liberty would prejudice his or her right to a fair trial under Art 6 and, consequently, be seen as within the judicial discretion under s 78. However, it is clear that the European Court does not operate a rule of automatic exclusion; evidence obtained as a result of a breach of a Convention right does not necessarily infringe the right to a fair trial and thus should not be automatically excluded. This can be seen where evidence is acquired by violating the suspect's right to privacy.[40] This was

37   Home Office Research and Statistics Directorate, 'Ethnicity and Contacts with the Police' (Research Findings No 59, 1997); Smith and Gray (n 23 above); M McConville, A Sanders and R Leng *The Case for the Prosecution* (OUP, 1992); W Skogan *The Police and Public in England and Wales* (HMSO, 1990); Home Office Research Study No 117.
38   PACE 1984, Code of Practice A, para 1.7.
39   Sanders (n 24 above), p 87 suggests that to impose more controls in an area of low visibility policing would have negative effects.
40   *Schenk v Switzerland* (1988) 13 EHRR 242.

recently confirmed in *Khan v UK*[41] where the police unlawfully bugged a house. The Court held that this was a breach of Art 8 but that the use in the trial of evidence gathered as a result of that breach did not necessarily lead to the denial of a fair trial. By analogy, a breach of Art 5 would also not lead to automatic exclusion of the evidence.

– These issues may also emerge in a civil action for false imprisonment or assault against the police, perhaps where a person has objected to being stopped and has attempted to walk away, only to be arrested and detained. An English court would have to address the level of significance of the officer's suspicions, the existence or otherwise of objective and reasonable grounds for that suspicion, and balance the necessity for the officer's actions against the claimant's rights to personal liberty and not to be discriminated against.

In other areas of police stops, the Convention might provide the basis for court action. For example, a person affected by a police officer's actions may seek judicial review to challenge them. An example may be an order under s 60 of the Criminal Justice and Public Order Act 1994, made, perhaps, in the course of an industrial dispute, where a senior officer has authorised general stops of persons and vehicles in an area where he has the belief 'that to do so would help to prevent incidents involving serious violence'. The Divisional Court would necessarily have to review the grounds for such a belief.

3.3   SEARCHING SUSPECTS

Under PACE 1984 an officer can physically search a suspect in several situations.

– Under s 1 a physical search is permitted as part of a stop and search – if this is in public, it is limited to a superficial examination of outer clothing and of anything being carried. A more thorough search has to be out of public view.[42]

– Under s 32, a constable may conduct a limited search of an arrested person at a place other than a police station if there are reasonable grounds for believing that there might be evidence or anything that might assist escape or present a danger. Under s 32(4), the search is limited to the extent that is reasonably required for discovering the article or evidence.

– Under s 53, once the suspect is at the police station, the arresting officer no longer has the power to search. Searches of detained persons, including a strip search if deemed necessary, must be carried out by an officer of the same sex and supervised by the custody officer under s 54. This procedure is regulated by the Code of Practice.[43]

---

41   Application No 35394/97, [2000] Crim LR 684.
42   The conduct of such a search is regulated by Code A, para 3.5.
43   The conduct of such a search is regulated by Code C, Annex A.

–   Under ss 55 and 62, there is a power to conduct intimate searches and also to take intimate samples (including blood, saliva or semen) from a suspect. The intimate search (of body orifices) requires the authorisation of a superintendent who must have reasonable grounds for believing that a weapon or drug is concealed. Only qualified doctors or nurses can carry out the search. Non-intimate samples, such as hair or nail clippings, can be taken from a suspect compulsorily under s 63, although it must be authorised by a superintendent in writing and recorded on the custody record. Again, this is regulated by the Code of Practice.

All these require either a lawful stop or arrest; without proper grounds, a search of a suspect would be an assault. But where there is reasonable cause for detaining the person, searches must not violate the guarantees against degrading treatment under Art 3 or the right to privacy under Art 8. PACE 1984 procedures conform to these requirements. Code A talks of the need to keep embarrassment to a minimum and, if there is more than simply surface search, this should not be in public view. Code C also talks of 'proper regard for the sensitivity and vulnerability of the person in these circumstances and every reasonable effort shall be made to secure the person's co-operation and minimise embarrassment'.

These procedures are in accordance with law, and draw a balance between the legitimate interests of the State in the gathering of evidence or prevention of crime and the individual's interest in his or her bodily integrity. This conforms to Convention requirements since the right to privacy can be derogated from in such circumstances. But there are no such exceptions under Art 3 – inhuman or degrading treatment is not permitted in any situation. In individual cases, police officers might breach the guidelines, as in *Lindley v Rutter*,[44] where the police sought to remove the bra of a women detainee. The court held that such treatment was an affront to human dignity, and quashed the conviction for assault on a constable since the officer was not acting in the execution of her duty.

In such a case, the trial court would have to consider the impact of Art 3. But does it add anything to the common law? The definition of 'degrading treatment' is that it must be significant and attain a minimum level of severity. In *Hurtado v Switzerland*[45] the applicant had been so shocked by a stun grenade that he had defecated in his trousers. He was not allowed to change them for over a day, during which time he was questioned and moved between buildings. This was degrading treatment. However, moving a prisoner in handcuffs in public was not held to be degrading treatment,[46] nor were intimate body searches in *McFeeley v UK*.[47] *Lindley v Rutter* suggests that English courts already operate on a lower threshold.

---

44   [1980] 3 WLR 661.
45   (1994) Series A No 280–A.
46   *X v Austria* Application No 2291/64, (1967) 24 CD 20.
47   Application No 8317/78, (1980) 20 DR 44 at 85–86.

Where a person is subjected to a degrading search, that search must be unlawful and thus an assault upon which a civil action might be based. If evidence is discovered as a consequence of a degrading search in breach of Art 3, the use of that evidence in the subsequent criminal trial would not necessarily amount to the denial of a fair trial under Art 6.[48]

A final question is whether the power to conduct intimate searches and also to take intimate samples under ss 55 and 62 of PACE 1984 is compatible with Art 3. Although the Commission found that intimate body searches in *McFeeley* were not sufficiently degrading, it has been suggested that this finding was in a terrorist context and that such searches in a non-terrorist context might be treated differently.[49] This is unlikely. To treat an intimate search as necessarily degrading and unlawful would have serious consequences for law enforcement, and English courts would undoubtedly find that such a search conducted in private by a doctor was neither sufficiently significant nor severe to amount to degradation under Art 3.

3.4 SEARCHING PREMISES

The freedom from search of home or business premises is protected by the right to respect for private life guaranteed in Art 8. This may be derogated from if such a derogation is in accordance with law, necessary in a democratic society and for the purposes of, inter alia, preventing disorder or crime This may be compared to the wide protection against unreasonable search and seizure position by the Fourth Amendment to the US Constitution.[50]

In England, the powers to search premises are contained mainly in Part II of PACE 1984. More detailed regulation is to be found in PACE 1984, Code B.

3.4.1 Searches under warrant

The general powers for justices of the peace to issue search warrants are contained in ss 8–16 of the Act. There will be an *ex parte* written application to the magistrate by a constable. The constable must state the grounds of the application, the premises to be searched and the articles being sought. The magistrate must act in a judicial manner and consider whether the evidence shows reasonable cause that a serious arrestable offence has been committed and that there is material[51] on the premises that is likely to be evidence in the investigation of the offence.[52] The magistrate must also be satisfied that entry by warrant is necessary to ensure access to the evidence.[53] This is a regime which

---

48   *Khan v UK* Application No 35394/97, [2000] Crim LR 684.
49   D Harris et al *Law of the European Convention on Human Rights* (Butterworths, 1995), pp 83–84.
50   *Katz v US* 389 US 347 (1967).
51   Not being items subject to legal privilege, excluded material or special procedure material: s 8(1)(c); see Lidstone and Palmer (n 2 above), 4.51–4.78.
52   Section 8(1)(a)–(e).
53   Section 8(3)(a)–(e).

conforms to Convention requirements since the interference with private space is in accordance with law, and is necessary, proportional and for the prevention of crime. There are several decisions which accept the necessity for the interception of, for example, telephone calls, provided this is regulated by legal process.[54] As such interceptions also require the intrusive violation of private space, this is analogous to the searching of premises under warrant.

Powers of seizure are increased by ss 50–70 of the Criminal Justice and Police Act 2001. These changes result from the judgment in *R v Chesterfield Justices ex parte Bramley*.[55] The court addressed the problem that the police in executing a warrant have to decide what property they are entitled to seize and what they are not entitled to seize, because, for example, it might be subject to legal privilege. *Chesterfield Justices* made it clear that PACE 1984 does not entitle the police to seize material and take it away for the purposes of sifting it. But there are circumstances where it is not practicable to establish on the premises subject to the search which material can be seized and which cannot – the sheer bulk of the material or because relevant material is contained within the same document or set of documents as material which is protected from seizure. Sections 50(3) and 51(3) grant officers enhanced powers of seizure where it would not be reasonably practicable to make these determinations on the premises or to carry out any necessary separation. The police are only able to look at it to the extent necessary to determine whether it was material they had a legal entitlement to retain. Where it was clear that it did not fall into that category, the material has to be returned under ss 53–55. Under s 53(4) there is the opportunity for interested parties to be present at any sift and the ability to object to removal of items on grounds that they fell into confidential categories and were not items the police were empowered to retain. There is a further safeguard in the possibility of an application to a Crown Court judge under s 59 where it is suggested that the police have exceeded their powers. In exercising these new powers the police will need to decide on the spot whether the seizure is necessary and proportionate if they are not to be in breach.

3.4.2   Searches without a warrant

Less clearly compliant are the several situations where an officer can search premises without recourse to a warrant. These include situations where the owner gives consent, where there is the common law power to enter premises to prevent a breach of the peace, or where statutory powers under ss 17, 18 or 32 of the Act apply.

–   Although other common law powers of search have been abolished, the power to enter and remain on premises 'to deal with or prevent a breach of the peace' was retained in the Act.[56] *Thomas v Sawkins*[57] concerned a

---

54   *Klass v Germany* (1978) 2 EHRR 214.
55   [2000] 1 All ER 411.
56   Section 17(6).
57   [1935] 2 KB 249; AL Goodhart '*Thomas v. Sawkins*: A Constitutional Innovation' (1936–38) 6 *Cambridge Law Journal* 22.

political meeting called to protest against the Incitement to Disaffection Bill. The police entered and remained in the hall, believing that there might be disorder, a belief based on their experience of previous similar meetings. The Divisional Court held that the police had a right to enter and remain on premises where they had reasonable apprehension of a breach of the peace. Whether this power was compliant with Art 8 was considered in *McLeod v UK*.[58] The Court of Appeal had held that *Thomas v Sawkins* was not limited to public meetings and that Parliament had accepted the validity of the power by accepting its retention in s 17(6).[59] Before the European Court the applicant argued that the power was 'not in accordance with law' as required by Art 8. The power is neither defined in statute nor is there judicial supervision. The Court considered the 'quality of the law' and held that the concept of breach of the peace had been clarified with sufficient precision to enable a person to foresee the consequences that a given act may entail. Although the decision itself was that the officers' acts were a disproportionate response, the overall effect was to confirm that this common law power can, if properly exercised, be compliant with the Convention.

– Under s 17 of PACE 1984, a constable has the power to enter and search premises without warrant for the following purposes: to execute a warrant of arrest; to make an arrest without warrant; to capture a person unlawfully at large; and to protect people from serious injury or prevent serious property damage. This is a wide power to search for persons and it is a search only to the extent reasonably required for the purpose. Following *McLeod*, this power is clearly in accordance with law and is necessary, despite the lack of judicial involvement. Any violation of private space is undertaken for purposes which accord with Art 8(2). There would be a breach if the officers lacked reasonable grounds for arrest or conducted a broader search than was reasonably required – the entry and search would no longer be in accordance with law and a defendant might seek to exclude any evidence found as a result under s 78. But the evidence would not be automatically excluded[60] either under s 78 or under the Convention.[61] In these circumstances, a court must consider Art 6 and whether the fairness of the trial has been affected, considering issues such as the extent of the police misconduct or whether the impugned material would be the main or central evidence against the accused.

– Under s 32 of PACE 1984, after an arrest for an arrestable offence, an officer can lawfully enter and search premises in which the person was when arrested or immediately before he or she was arrested if the constable reasonably suspects that there is evidence relating to the offence in question on the premises. As with s 17, the demands of effective law enforcement call for a power of immediate action and, following *McLeod*, s 32 is sufficiently precise as to the grounds for exercising that power. Prior

---

58   (1998) 27 EHRR 493.

59   *McLeod v Metropolitan Police Commissioner* [1994] 4 All ER 553.

60   Such an exclusionary rule was proposed in the *Report of the Commission on Criminal Justice*, Cm 2263 (1993) para 3.49, but the proposal was rejected by the Government.

61   *Schenk v Switzerland* (1988) 13 EHRR 242.

judicial involvement is not a possibility. Officers can go beyond their powers, for example, where reasonable grounds for the arrest do not exist or an officer seizes evidence of another offence which is neither relevant to the immediate offence nor connected with it. The same comments apply on exclusion of evidence as with s 17.

–   Under s 18 of PACE 1984, after an arrest for an arrestable offence, an officer can lawfully enter and search premises occupied or controlled by the suspect if he or she reasonably suspects that there is evidence of the immediate offence or other offences on the premises. This normally has to be authorised by an officer with the rank of inspector or above.[62] Unlike the situation envisaged by s 17 or s 32, here the demands of effective law enforcement call for a power of prompt rather than immediate action. The question arises whether the exercise of this power should require judicial involvement and authorisation. Covert surveillance is an analogous situation, and in *Klass v Germany*[63] the Court said that it is in principle desirable to entrust the supervisory control of surveillance to a judge in accordance with the rule of law, but other safeguards might suffice if they are independent and vested with sufficient powers to exercise an effective and continuous control. Physical searches of houses involve a similar and significant violation of a person's private space. Although police inspectors are able to control their subordinates, they lack independence. There may well be an argument that such search powers should, wherever possible, require prior judicial authorisation.

Looking at the overall structure of entry and search powers under PACE 1984, the *Klass* decision raises the question of whether the Convention would require a similar and independent system of effective and continuous control over the police powers of entry and search as it does over their powers of surveillance and interception of communications. The role of magistrates seems marginal – prior to the Act, research suggested that only a small proportion (17%) of searches were carried out under magisterial warrant,[64] and post-1984 research suggests that police more frequently rely on ss 18 and 32, and that warranted searches are now about 12% of all searches.[65] Is there a need for more effective supervision? Issues around this may well have to be decided by the courts in the future in the context, for example, of a civil action for trespass following property damage or personal injury resulting from a s 18 search.

Human rights concerns about police searches of premises are heightened by findings that there are doubts that the standard of reasonable suspicion is always being reached.[66] There has been even less research on the adherence by

---

62   Section 18(4).

63   (1978) 2 EHRR 214.

64   *Report of the Royal Commission on Criminal Procedure*, Cmnd 8092 (1981), supplementary volume entitled *Law and Procedure*, Appendix 7.

65   Brown (n 21 above); Lidstone and Palmer (n 2 above), para 4.07.

66   Ibid; there are also serious questions about the broader statutory powers of search and seizure exercised by other enforcement agencies, such as the Customs or Trading Standards.

the police to the standards laid down by the Code of Practice.[67] This states that searches should be made at a reasonable time, that only reasonable force should be used and that due consideration for the property and privacy of the occupier should be shown. The extent to which these standards are observed might be doubted by those accustomed to news footage of operations showing doors being broken down in the early morning so that the police, accompanied by TV cameras, can arrest and search a bemused youth in boxer shorts. The conduct of such searches must come close to crossing the minimum threshold of degrading treatment and thus risk infringing Art 3.

Entry and search are low-profile police operations. Effective remedies to enforce Convention rights are not easy to envisage.

– In future, the court in a civil action against the police for trespass would not only have to consider whether there were reasonable grounds for the police action (probably the only issue for the common law), but also whether infringement of individual liberty was balanced by the necessity for the action. Furthermore, a court might consider whether the lack of independent supervision renders Part II of PACE 1984 incompatible with the Convention.

– In criminal proceedings, the evidentiary product from illegal searches may be excluded under s 78 as it would adversely affect the fairness of the proceedings. But it remains open to the court to decide that the fairness of the trial has not been compromised by the police misconduct and that, although the right to privacy has been violated, there is no breach of the right to a fair trial under Art 6.[68]

– What is certain is that recourse to the Police Complaints Authority is not an effective remedy, not simply for complaints about the search of premises but also for stops under s 1, body searches and conditions in the police station. It is a system that 'does not meet the requisite standards of independence needed to provide sufficient protection against abuse of authority and thus provide a remedy within the meaning of Article 1'.[69]

3.5 POWERS OF ARREST

Arrest, 'the beginning of imprisonment', can be either under warrant from a magistrate[70] or without a warrant. Under PACE 1984, the traditional requirements for a lawful arrest still apply: first, that it requires 'reasonable suspicion' that an arrestable offence has been, is being or is about to be committed; secondly, that there is a physical touching of the person to be arrested; thirdly, that this is accompanied by words indicating an arrest, which can be colloquial (eg 'You're nicked'). Under s 28, the officer must not only inform the suspect of the fact of arrest but also the grounds for arrest either immediately or as soon

---

67 Code B, para 5.
68 *Khan v UK* Application No 35394/97, [2000] Crim LR 684.
69 Ibid, at para 47.
70 Under s 1 of the Magistrates' Courts Act 1980 for any offence.

as practicable. A failure to do this or the giving of the wrong reason can make the arrest unlawful.[71] There are now three categories of arrest without warrant.[72]

- The first or summary arrest power comes under s 24 and allows an officer to arrest where there are reasonable grounds for believing that such an offence has taken place and that the suspect has committed it. Arrestable offences in essence[73] are those for which a previously unconvicted offender aged over 21 could be sentenced to imprisonment for five years or more.
- The second or general arrest power is provided for by s 25 and gives a wider power of arrest for all criminal offences whether or not they are arrestable. A 'general arrest condition' must be satisfied as where, for example, the police officer doubts that the suspect has given his correct identification or address.
- The third category is under s 26 which preserves certain statutory powers of arrest.

A fourth category, the power to arrest for breach of the peace, still exists.[74]

The circumstances in which a person may be arrested and detained are provided for in Art 5(1)(a)–(f) but it is para (c) that is of immediate interest. This permits:

> 'the lawful arrest or detention of a person effected for the purpose of bringing him before the competent legal authority on reasonable suspicion of having committed an offence or when it is reasonably considered necessary to prevent his committing an offence or fleeing after having done so.'

Any arrest must be lawful and not arbitrary – the criteria must be clear, precise and accessible and founded in law. The criteria are to be narrowly interpreted.[75] There is no requirement that arrest requires a warrant in all cases[76] – there is an obvious necessity for police officers to take immediate action in some circumstances. The powers of arrest in ss 24 and 25 comply with these requirements. In both cases, there must be reasonable suspicion of having committed an offence. These provisions are generally precise and accessible enough for people to be able to foresee the consequences of any given action.

What is an 'offence'? In *Brogan v UK*,[77] s 12 of the Prevention of Terrorism (Temporary Provisions) Act 1984 provided a power of arrest and detention for those concerned with 'terrorism', defined as 'the use of violence for political ends' and 'the use of violence for the purpose of putting the public or any

---

71 *Christie v Leachinsky* [1947] AC 573.
72 See Lidstone and Palmer (n 2 above), paras 5.06ff for a detailed description of arrest powers.
73 Although s 24 includes some specially listed offences where the penalty is less.
74 *DPP v Orum* [1989] 1 WLR 88; see *Howell* [1982] QB 416 for a definition of breach of the peace. This power is nearly coterminous with the powers of arrest under the Public Order Act 1986, ss 4(3) and 5(4).
75 *Winterwerp v Netherlands* (1979) 2 EHRR 387.
76 *X v Austria* Application No 7755/77, (1977) 9 DR 210.
77 (1988) 13 EHRR 439.

section of the public in fear'.[78] The applicants argued that they had not been arrested on suspicion that they had committed an offence as 'terrorism' was not a criminal offence in itself although it would involve the commission of specific criminal acts. The European Court held that the statutory definition was in keeping with the idea of an offence.

Where there is an offence, Art 5(1)(c) allows arrest in three situations:

(1) when a person is reasonably suspected of having committed an offence;
(2) when the arrest was reasonably considered necessary to prevent a person committing an offence; or
(3) when the arrest was necessary to prevent a person fleeing after having committed an offence.

As well as satisfying one of these three justifications, it is also required that in all cases the purpose of the arrest was to bring a person 'before a competent legal authority'. This leads to the conclusion that the purpose of preventing an offence when it was 'reasonably considered necessary' does not justify a general power of preventive detention. In *Lawless v Ireland*,[79] internment of a suspected IRA activist was not justified as the act was not done in order to bring the person before a competent legal tribunal.

Do the second or third limbs of Art 5(1)(c) add anything to the first? If the Convention does not countenance a power of preventive detention, a person must have committed, be committing or be about to commit an offence before he or she can be detained – this would be necessary to bring that person before a competent legal authority. These are surely covered by the first limb except perhaps offences which are about to be committed, although such circum-stances should be covered by the offence of attempted crime. Article 5 does not countenance detention simply to prevent crime or answer questions.

Section 24(7)(b) of PACE 1984 permits a constable to arrest a person 'whom he has reasonable grounds for suspecting to be about to commit an arrestable offence'. Common law authority from which this section derives empowered arrest in circumstances that did not yet amount to a substantive crime or even an attempt.[80] The Human Rights Act 1998 would suggest that this section must now be interpreted to mean that the constable's purpose in the arrest is to bring the suspect before a court – in other words that the suspected conduct amounts to an attempt or at least a breach of the peace.

There are wider arrest powers in s 25. This permits arrest for less serious matters or non-arrestable offences in certain situations:

–   s 25(3)(a)–(c) cover the situation where the officer is unable to obtain the suspect's name or address. The offence is likely to be minor, but Art 5 does not appear to distinguish between arrest for serious or trivial offences provided the purpose is to bring the suspect before a court;

---

78   Prevention of Terrorism (Temporary Provisions) Act 1984, s 14.
79   *Lawless v Ireland* (1961) 1 EHRR 15.
80   Criminal Law Revision Committee Report, *Seventh Report: Felonies and Misdemeanours* Cmnd 2659 (1965).

–   s 25(3)(d)(i) and (ii) may trouble the courts since they permit arrest, inter
     alia, to prevent a person causing physical injury to himself or suffering
     physical injury. Such an arrest is clearly not to bring the person before a
     court and could be justified only under Art 5(1)(e) which permits lawful
     detention of persons of unsound mind;

–   s 25(6) preserves the common law power which permits arrest for breach
     of the peace.[81] Although no offence need have been committed, the
     person may still be brought before a magistrates' court and be bound over.
     In *Steel v UK*[82] the applicants had been involved in different demon-
     strations but in all the cases the police had arrested for breach of the
     peace. The European Court found that the conduct of some of the
     demonstrators had been entirely peaceful but that they had been arrested,
     detained for 7 hours and later released without charge. The applicants
     argued that Art 5(1)(c) requires arrest for an offence, and that 'breach of
     the peace' is not an offence, nor is the term defined in statute. Although a
     person may be bound over by magistrates to keep the peace, the police also
     have the option to 'de-arrest' a person if circumstances change. The Court
     considered the 'quality of the law' in this area and held that the concept of
     'breach of the peace' had been clarified with sufficient precision to enable
     a person to foresee the consequences that a given act may entail.[83]
     Although the Court found that the conduct of the peaceful demonstrators
     did not involve conduct that would justify the police fearing a breach of the
     peace, the overall effect was to confirm that this common law power of
     arrest for breach of the peace could, if properly exercised, be compliant
     with the Convention. This is consistent with the police power to enter and
     remain on premises where they had reasonable apprehension of a breach
     of the peace, which was considered in *McLeod v UK*.[84]

While the Court has accepted the powers of entry on premises or arrest
founded on the concept of breach of the peace, this is not extended to the
concept of conduct *contra bonos mores*. In *Hashman and Harrup v UK*[85] the
demonstrators disturbed a hunt by blowing a horn and shouting at the hounds.
Bound over by magistrates to keep the peace, they appealed to the Crown
Court, which held that there had been no breach of the peace but that they had
behaved *contra bonos mores*[86] and should be bound over for one year. The
European Court, not surprisingly, held that this was too imprecise and did not
give the applicants any guidance on how they should behave.

The framework of ss 24 and 25 requires 'reasonable grounds' before arrest. In
Art 5, this concept is termed 'reasonable suspicion' and requires facts that

---

81   *DPP v Orum* [1989] 1 WLR 88.
82   (1998) 28 EHRR 603.
83   *Chorherr v Austria* (1994) 17 EHRR 358 – the offence of 'causing a breach of the peace by
      conduct likely to cause annoyance' was also held sufficiently precise.
84   (1998) 27 EHRR 493.
85   (2000) 30 EHRR 241.
86   *Hughes v Holley* (1988) 86 Crim App Rep 130 laid down the test of conduct *contra bonos
      mores* as behaviour that was 'wrong rather than right in the judgment of the majority of
      contemporary citizens'.

would satisfy an objective observer that the person had committed an offence.[87] This generally accords with English law where the test is both subjective and objective – the officer must believe that he has reasonable grounds.[88] The grounds for arrest under PACE 1984 are thus consistent with Art 5.

This may not be the case with other legislation conferring powers of arrest. In *Fox, Campbell and Hartley v UK*[89] the applicants were arrested under s 11 of the Northern Ireland (Emergency Provisions) Act 1978 under which the arresting officer was permitted to arrest any person whom he suspected of being a terrorist. This section had been interpreted in another case by the House of Lords as requiring only a genuine, not necessarily reasonable, suspicion on the part of the arresting officer.[90] The European Court considered this to be in breach of Art 5(1)(c). The fact that two of the applicants had previous convictions for terrorist offences was not sufficient to justify their arrest 7 years later and without further material to support the reasonableness of the suspicion.[91] But the Court recognised that, in terrorist cases, the reasonableness of the suspicion cannot always be judged on the same standard as other offences as the arrest may be on the basis of information that could not be revealed to a suspect or produced as evidence in court.[92]

Can police arrest a suspect where the primary purpose is to further the investigation through questioning? Article 5(1)(c) specifies that arrest must be for the purpose of bringing the person before a 'competent legal authority'. Historically, in England, the purpose of arrest was exactly that – it was not for the purposes of interrogation, which was not seen as the constable's function. For the modern police, the power of arrest is consistently used not as a culmination of the inquiry and a prelude to charging, but as a technique of investigation. This practice was approved by the House of Lords in *Mohammed-Holgate v Duke*,[93] when it was held that an officer was not acting unreasonably when arresting someone against whom there existed reasonable grounds for suspicion because it was more likely that the suspect would confess in the police station than elsewhere.

Does this mean that the arrest is not for the purpose of bringing the suspect before a competent legal authority as required by Art 5? In both *Fox* (above) and *Murray v UK*,[94] part of the applicant's argument was that the reason for her arrest was not to bring her before a court but to gather information. Mrs Murray had been arrested, interviewed and released within a few hours. The European Court found that her arrest itself was based on reasonable grounds, albeit by giving some credence to the Government's assertion that the arrest

---

87 *F v Austria* (1989) 11 EHRR 112.
88 *Chapman v DPP* (1988) 89 Crim App Rep 190.
89 (1991) 14 EHRR 108.
90 *McKee v Chief Constable for Northern Ireland* [1985] 1 All ER 1.
91 Section 11 was replaced by s 6 of the Northern Ireland (Emergency Provisions) Act 1987 which now requires 'reasonable suspicion' as the grounds for arrest.
92 *Murray v UK* (1994) 19 EHRR 193.
93 [1984] AC 437.
94 (1994) 19 EHRR 193.

was based on reliable but confidential information. Where reasonable grounds exist, as in *Brogan v UK*,[95] the arrest of the suspect in order to further the investigation through interview is not a violation of the Convention. The Court in *Murray* said that the fact that the interview lasted little over an hour did not mean that the arrest and detention were not for the purpose of bringing her before a court: 'the existence of a such a purpose must be considered independently of its achievement'. Her refusal to answer questions meant that the authorities could make no headway in pursuing its suspicions but that it could be assumed that, had those suspicions been confirmed, charges would have been laid. To this extent, the Convention does not exclude detention for questioning or 'helping the police with their inquiries'.

Article 5(2)–(5) provides rights for all arrested persons – a detainee must be informed of the reasons for arrest, brought promptly before a court, able to take proceedings to test the lawfulness of the detention and have an enforceable right to compensation for unlawful detention. Article 5(2) requires the provision of reasons for arrest as soon as is practicable and in a language that the suspect understands. This conforms with domestic law under s 28 of PACE 1984. The person arrested should be told in simple, non-technical language the essential legal and factual grounds for the arrest. There is no need to tell the suspect of all of the charges that may be brought against him or her provided there is enough evidence to justify the arrest.[96] To be told that you are being arrested for, say, burglary, but not that you are also under investigation for other offences, is not a violation of Art 5(2).

In *Fox* the arresting officer told the suspects that they were being arrested under s 11 of the Northern Ireland (Emergency Provisions) Act 1978 and suspected of being terrorists. Giving the bare legal basis for the arrest, on its own, was insufficient. They were questioned about involvement in specific criminal acts and their membership of a proscribed organisation. The reasons why they were suspected was brought to their attention in the course of the questioning over the next few hours. The European Court concluded that there was no breach of Art 5(2). Although the suspects were not informed of the grounds, they were expected to pick these up in the course of questioning and the Court also regarded a delay of seven hours between the arrest and the furnishing of the grounds of arrest as sufficiently prompt. This has been described as an 'unacceptable dilution of a basic guarantee'.[97]

The police rely heavily on the power of arrest, not as a culmination of the inquiry and as a prelude to charging, but as a technique of investigation. In 1997/98 just under two million people were arrested,[98] of whom about 33% were released without charge. The decision to arrest, as with stop and search powers, is low-visibility, and the law is sufficiently vague and flexible to allow an

---

95   (1988) 13 EHRR 439.

96   *X v UK* Application No 4220/69, (1971) 14 YB 250 where he was told of the burglary charge but not about other charges that were later brought.

97   D Harris, M O'Boyle and C Warbrick *Law of the European Convention on Human Rights* (Butterworths, 1995), p 130.

98   *Statistics on Race and the Criminal Justice System* (Home Office, 1999), ch 5.

officer considerable discretion using police criteria which are not necessarily legally relevant.[99] Factors such as previous involvement with the police, not recognising police authority[100] or general lifestyle will be significant. Such powers are 'not exercised randomly or representatively across society'[101] and it is the young adult working class male, frequently black, who is the most likely object of police attention. In turn, this means that young black males are more likely to be charged, prosecuted, convicted and imprisoned than other sections of society, although crime is widely spread across age, gender, class and race.

Total arrests for notifiable offences of persons per 1,000 population aged 10 and over by ethnic appearance of person searched in 1998/99[102]

Force	White	Black	Asian
Bedfordshire	23	105	62
Greater Manchester	34	126	44
Leicestershire	20	207	26
Metropolitan	58	299	58
Surrey	18	170	38
England and Wales	27	117	44

Similar considerations apply to discrimination in arrest as with discrimination in the use of stop and search powers.[103] The Human Rights Act 1998 would allow a person charged with assault on, or obstruction of, a police officer in the execution of his or her duty to argue that the arresting officer was not in the execution of his or her duty because he or she was discriminating against a particular ethnic group, especially if the grounds of arrest were tenuous. But this is the common law position in any case, and the impact of the Human Rights Act 1998 may merely mean that the courts will take care that they are seen to scrutinise the justifications for police conduct more thoroughly. It is possible to go further and suggest that, even were reasonable cause for arrest to exist, *Steel v UK*[104] suggests that the exercise of the power of arrest must be necessary when balanced alongside the person's right not to be discriminated against.

Were the person to be charged with a more substantive offence, it would be difficult to argue that any evidence found on his or her person should be excluded on the basis that the arrest was unlawful. As has been stated, breach of Art 5 rights does not lead automatically to exclusion of the evidence. Such an argument has to be made under Art 6 and the decision in *Khan v UK*[105] suggests

---

99 D McBarnett *Conviction* (Macmillan, 1983), pp 36ff; M McConville (n 37 above), ch 2; D Black *Manners and Customs of the Police* (Academic Press, 1980).
100 I Piliavin and S Briar 'Police Encounters with Juveniles' (1964) *American Journal of Sociology* 206.
101 McConville (n 37 above), p 17.
102 *Statistics on Race and the Criminal Justice System* (Home Office, 1999), p 22, Table 5.2.
103 See **3.2** above.
104 (1998) 28 EHRR 603.
105 Application No 35394/97, [2000] Crim LR 684.

that a breach of Convention rights does not lead to automatic exclusion of the evidence, even where that evidence is the main or sole prosecution evidence.

Discriminatory practices may also emerge in a civil action for false imprisonment or assault against the police. Even were reasonable cause for arrest to exist, the court as a public body would have to consider whether the exercise of the power of arrest was necessary when balanced alongside the claimant's rights to personal liberty and not to be discriminated against. An English court would have to address the level of significance of the officer's suspicions, the existence or otherwise of objective and reasonable grounds for that suspicion, and balance the necessity for actions against the claimant's rights.

3.5.1   The use of force in arrest

In making an arrest or upholding the law, the police may use force. At common law, they would be protected from prosecution because of the defence of self-defence. There is both a common law defence and a statutory defence under s 3 of the Criminal Law Act 1967, which states that 'a person may use such force as is reasonable in the circumstances in the prevention of crime'. This would operate both where an officer was under attack or where he or she was effecting an arrest. The force used must be necessary and the response proportional. The key point in domestic law is that the officer's belief as to the imminence of the attack is central – if officers make a mistake and believe that they are under attack when they are not, the defence of self-defence is still available.[106] The circumstances are as the officer might believe them to be, whether or not there are reasonable and objective grounds for that belief.

The other issue is that even if the necessity of retaliation is by reference to the beliefs of the officer, what is a reasonable and proportionate response? Is it an issue of what would be a reasonable response either for the officer or for an objective bystander? Early cases suggested that this also rested on the officer's assessment.[107] But *Owino*[108] doubts this and suggests that, although the circumstances must be taken to be those which the officer believes them to be, the response must be that which would be reasonable in those circumstances.

How does this fit with Art 2 which protects the right to life? Deprivation of life is foreseen by this provision, but only where it arises from the use of force which is no more than absolutely necessary and strictly proportionate. Such force can only be used in one of three situations:

–   in defence of any person from unlawful violence;
–   in order to effect a lawful arrest or to prevent the escape of a person lawfully detained;
–   in action lawfully taken for the purpose of quelling a riot or insurrection.

---

106   *Gladstone Williams* (1984) 78 Cr App R 276.
107   *Attorney-General's Reference (No 1 of 1974)* [1977] QB 744.
108   [1996] 2 Cr App Rep 128.

In *McCann v UK*,[109] three suspected IRA terrorists were shot dead in Gibraltar by security forces. By a majority of 10–9, the European Court held that the UK had violated their right to life. In *Andronicou v Cyprus*,[110] security forces stormed a flat where there had been a domestic assault and where a young woman was being held by a man with a shotgun. Here, by a majority of 5–4, the Court held that Art 2 was not violated. In both cases, however, the Court agreed:

> 'that the use of force by agents of the State in pursuit of one of the aims delineated in paragraph 2 of Article 2 of the Convention may be justified under this provision where it is based on an honest belief which is perceived, for good reasons, to be valid at the time but which subsequently turns out to be mistaken. To hold otherwise would be to impose an unrealistic burden on the State and its law-enforcement personnel in the execution of their duty, perhaps to the detriment of their lives and those of others.'[111]

The Court talks of the soldiers' 'honest belief . . . for good reasons'. This raises questions about the boundaries of self-defence as it suggests an objective test of the necessity criterion and runs counter to the principle stated in *Gladstone Williams*.[112] That latter decision will need to be reconsidered in relation to ordinary criminal cases where the defence is raised. When the police use force to make arrests, that force must be absolutely necessary and strictly proportionate to the threat faced, judged by what an objective observer would have seen as necessary and proportionate in such circumstances.

But the Court's main thrust was towards the State's planning, organisation and control of such operations:

> 'The Court's sole concern must be to evaluate whether in the circumstances the planning and control of the rescue operation including the decision to deploy the (security force) officers showed that the authorities had taken appropriate care to ensure that any risk to the lives of the couple had been minimised and that they were not negligent in their choice of action.'[113]

In *Andronicou* the Court held, possibly bizarrely on the facts of the case, that sufficient care had been taken and the risk minimised. In *McCann*, it came to the opposite conclusion:

> 'Although detailed investigation at the inquest into the training received by the soldiers was prevented by the public interest certificates which had been issued, it is not clear whether they had been trained or instructed to assess whether the use of firearms to wound their targets may have been warranted by the specific circumstances that confronted them at the moment of arrest. Their reflex action in this vital respect lacks the degree of caution in the use of firearms to be expected from law enforcement personnel in a democratic society, even when dealing with dangerous terrorist suspects, and stands in marked contrast to the standard of care reflected in the instructions in the use of firearms by the police which had been

---

109   (1996) 21 EHRR 97.
110   (1998) 25 EHRR 491.
111   *McCann v UK* (1996) 21 EHRR 97, para 200; quoted with approval in *Andronicou v Cyprus* (1998) 25 EHRR 491, para 192.
112   (1984) Cr App R 276.
113   *Andronicou v Cyprus* (1998) 25 EHRR 491, para 181.

drawn to their attention and which emphasised the legal responsibilities of the individual officer in the light of conditions prevailing at the moment of engagement.'[114]

This ruling contains implications for senior police management who provide guidelines for the use of force or who are responsible for training officers to deal with, for example, hostage situations or who are in charge of the policing of such incidents. For the officers immediately concerned there would be no violation of Art 2 where fatal force was used, provided the officers were acting on a belief in circumstances that they reasonably believed to exist. Information passed to them by control rooms would come within that category. However, senior management may face homicide prosecutions where the training, planning and control is deficient and there was not appropriate care to ensure that any risk to lives had been minimised. This applies in particular to public order situations. Again, Art 2 specifically refers to the justifiability of using force in a riot or insurrection. The same principles would apply, ie the individual officer who acts on reasonable, albeit mistaken, beliefs would have a defence to subsequent charges. But senior management would need to show that the correct procedures had been in place for training officers in crowd-control techniques, for planning and controlling the particular operation and for minimising the risk to life. Furthermore, in investigating a killing by the State, the proceedings must be seen to be independent, transparent and effective.[115]

3.6   POWERS OF DETENTION

Under PACE 1984 procedures, on arrest a suspect must be taken to a police station[116] where he or she is put before the custody officer.[117] In brief, the custody officer must decide whether sufficient evidence exists either to charge the person or to warrant further detention for the purpose of obtaining evidence through interview.[118] The custody officer must ensure that the person is aware of his or her rights to legal advice, to notify someone of the fact of his or her arrest, and to see the Codes of Practice. Throughout the period of detention, it is the custody officer's responsibility to monitor the conditions of the custody: how long and how often a person is interviewed; whether medical

---

114   *McCann v UK* (1996) 21 EHRR 97, para 212.
115   *Hugh Jordan v UK* Application No 24746/94 (4 May 2001).
116   This must be a designated police station under s 30 of PACE 1984. Section 35 requires chief officers to designate certain stations to be used for the purpose of detaining arrested persons, ie stations which have the necessary personnel and resources for interviews, cells for detention, etc.
117   Section 36 outlines the role of the custody officer; s 37 defines the custody officer's duties before charge; s 38 defines the custody officer's duties after charge; and s 39 outlines the custody officer's responsibilities to the arrested person. The custody officer will not be involved in the investigation.
118   In practice, detention is almost never refused: I McKenzie et al 'Helping the Police with their enquiries' (1990) Crim LR 22.

advice is required; and whether proper sleep and refreshment has been provided. All of this should be recorded on the custody record.[119]

The custody officer is initially responsible for the length of time a person is detained in a police station. That detention must be periodically reviewed.[120] Prior to the Act, the police usually had to bring a suspect before a court within 24 hours.[121] Although s 41 lays down the principle that a person should not be held without charge for more than 24 hours, this can be derogated from in certain circumstances. Continued detention for a further 12 hours can be authorised by a senior officer (superintendent or above) if the detention is necessary to secure or preserve evidence, if the offence is a serious arrestable offence[122] and if the investigation is being conducted 'diligently and expeditiously'.[123] Further periods of continued detention up to 96 hours are possible with approval from the magistrates' court.[124] Prolonged detention is rare, with approximately 5% detained for more than 18 hours and only 1% for more than 24 hours. In absolute figures, it is estimated that annually about 5,000 people will have been held for more than 1 day, and that 747 of these will have been released without charge.[125]

The regime for the detention of suspects is established, alongside the rights in PACE 1984, by Code C, the *Code of Practice for the Detention, Treatment and Questioning of Persons by Police Officers*. This generally complies with the Convention. The detention must be in accordance with law, which will depend on the legality of the original arrest (discussed above). The other issues that arise are the length of detention before being brought before a court, the conditions of the detention itself, the conditions surrounding the interview, especially the right to legal advice, and the release from detention.

3.6.1 General conditions of detention

The general conditions of detention in a police station must conform to Art 3 guarantees that no one shall be subject to torture or to inhuman or degrading treatment or punishment. This provision cannot be derogated from even in times of emergencies, such as terrorist campaigns. The guarantee is against the most serious forms of mistreatment. For example, the European Court in *Salih Tekin v Turkey*[126] held that holding the applicant blindfolded in a cold, dark cell and inflicting treatment that left wounds and bruises on his body violated the prohibition on torture, inhuman or degrading treatment or punishment.

---

119 Section 37(4). Normally there are five copies: for the station record, for the suspect, for case papers, a transit copy and finally for the local intelligence liaison officer.

120 Section 40. The extent to which such reviews are carried out is doubtful: D Dixon et al 'Safeguarding the rights of the accused ...' (1990) 1 *Policing and Society* 115.

121 Although in the 1970s there were several instances of the police holding suspects without access to legal advice for considerable periods before bringing them to court.

122 These are listed in Sch 3 to PACE 1984.

123 Ibid, s 42.

124 Ibid, s 43.

125 See M Maguire 'Effects of the PACE Provisions' (1998) 28 *Brit Jour Crim* 19; Irving and McKenzie (n 118 above); McConville et al (n 37 above).

126 [1998] HRCD 646.

Ill-treatment must attain a minimum level of severity if it is to fall within the scope of the Convention. The assessment of that minimum is relative and depends on all the circumstances of the case, such as the nature and context of the treatment, its duration, its physical and mental effect and, in some instances, the sex, age and state of health of the victim.[127] Inhuman treatment is distinguished from degrading treatment, the latter involving humiliating and debasing conduct. This might include racially discriminatory treatment, but it would not cover wearing prison uniform or appearing in public in handcuffs.[128] Intimate body searches were held not to be sufficiently humiliating in *McFeeley v UK*.[129]

Although serious mistreatment in the UK is rare, there have been allegations that suspects are assaulted, threatened with firearms and subject to coercive interrogation techniques while in police custody. Assaults must be sufficiently serious. In *Ireland v UK*[130] the European Court found a violation of Art 3 when the evidence disclosed severe beatings of four detainees by Northern Ireland security forces. However, in *Tyrer v UK*,[131] three strokes of the birch was not inhuman although it was degrading punishment. The mistreatment can be psychological as well as physical. In *Ireland* the Court designated five interrogation techniques in use in Northern Ireland as inhuman treatment, namely wall-standing for long periods, hooding, subjection to noise, sleep deprivation and deprivation of food and drink. Under English law, coercive interviewing can lead to confessions being excluded under s 78 of PACE 1984.[132]

In *A v UK*[133] the complainant was aged 9 when he was hit with a cane by his stepfather. The applicant was known to be a difficult child, but in 1993 he was found by a consultant paediatrician to have bruises and marks on his body consistent with blows from a garden cane having been administered with considerable force by his stepfather. The stepfather was charged with assault, but acquitted by a jury which found that the degree of punishment amounted to reasonable chastisement. The European Court found that this was degrading treatment and that the State had denied the applicant an effective remedy by providing the assailant with a defence of reasonable chastisement. In *Ha You Zhu v UK*[134] the applicant, an asylum seeker, alleged that during his time in prison he was locked in a cell for up to 19 hours a day, assaulted by other inmates, suffered racial abuse and for most of the time culturally isolated as there were no other Mandarin speakers in the prison. The Government disputed these allegations and pointed to efforts made by the authorities to provide interpreters and concern for Z's mental welfare. The application was declared manifestly ill-founded and inadmissible. Whilst it was clear that Z had

---

127   *Ireland v UK* (1978) 2 EHRR 25.
128   *Kaj Raninen v Finland* (1997) 26 EHRR 563.
129   Application No 8317/78, (1980) 20 DR 44.
130   (1978) 2 EHRR 25.
131   (1978) 2 EHRR 1.
132   *Paris* (1993) 97 Cr App R 99.
133   (1998) 27 EHRR 611.
134   Application No 22496/93 (2000).

been detained in prison pending removal from the UK rather than for involvement in criminal activities and that he had experienced difficulties in prison, the prison authorities had made efforts to alleviate the situation. The minimum level of severity had not been reached.

Under the Code of Practice, provisions in designated police stations for adequate heating, sanitation, sleep, recreation and food, as well as access to medical treatment, will normally conform to Art 3. In *McFeeley v UK* (above), prisoners in Northern Ireland defiled their cells as part of a 'dirty protest'. Such conditions would have violated the guarantee against inhuman treatment but they were induced by the applicants themselves and were not imputable to the State. Solitary confinement in itself is not in breach of Article 3.

3.6.2   Length of detention

Article 5(3) guarantees the right of a person to be brought before a court 'promptly'. The court must have the power to review the detention and order the release if appropriate[135] and must also be independent and impartial. Where a soldier is detained under investigation and is brought before his commanding officer, this does not satisfy the requirements of Art 5(3). The officer is not impartial as he is likely to play a role in the subsequent prosecution.[136]

'Promptly' is not 'immediately', and detention for the purpose of further investigation and questioning is acceptable, provided there were proper grounds for the arrest itself. Where such reasonable grounds for the arrest existed, as in *Brogan v UK*,[137] the European Court has held that detention in order to further the investigation through interview is not a violation of the Convention. Extended detention without judicial intervention can breach Art 5(3). In *Sirri Sakik and Others v Turkey*[138] the applicants, who were former members of the Turkish National Assembly, were arrested on suspicion of undermining the territorial integrity of the State. They were detained in police custody for 12 or, in some cases, 14 days after their arrest before there was any judicial intervention.

Do such decisions affect the provisions governing the period of detention which are contained in ss 40–43 of PACE 1984? A person may be detained for 24 hours or, in the case of serious arrestable offences, 36 hours. After that point, further extensions require the approval of a magistrate, who is a judge for the purposes of Art 5(3). In ordinary criminal cases, 'promptly' must mean a short period of time. It is likely that the procedures and safeguards which are necessary before there is any extension of the period ensure that these provisions comply with the Convention.

---

135   *TW v Malta* (1999) 29 EHRR 185.
136   *Jordan v UK* (2001) 31 EHRR 6; *Hood v UK* (1999) 29 EHRR 365.
137   (1988) 13 EHRR 439.
138   (1997) 26 EHRR 662.

Provisions for extended detention under the Prevention of Terrorism Act 1984 were considered in *Brogan v UK* (above) where the suspect had been detained for 4 days and 6 hours before being released. The Court held that although detention may be justifiably prolonged in the context of terrorist offences, the Government could not dispense with the requirement for prompt judicial control. However, since that case, the Government has issued a notice of derogation from Art 5(3) in respect of the Prevention of Terrorism Act.[139]

3.6.3   Release from detention – bail

Being brought promptly before a court does not in itself imply release from custody. Article 5(3) also requires that a person is entitled to trial within a reasonable time (also a requirement of a fair trial under Art 6(1)) or release pending trial. This implies a right to bail which has been vigorously applied by the European Court. To what extent do the procedures in the Bail Act 1976 conform with these requirements?[140] The Court's starting point is a strong belief in the presumption of innocence. There must be relevant and sufficient reasons to justify continued detention and it should not be prolonged beyond a reasonable time.[141] The prosecution must adduce persuasive[142] evidence that relevant reasons exist. These include the risk that the accused will fail to appear at trial, interference with the course of justice, the prevention of further offences, a need for further investigation, the defendant's own protection and the preservation of public order. Not only must the prosecution adduce evidence, it is likely that it will also need to make earlier and fuller disclosure than is currently the case. The Court insists on the 'equality of arms' principle at this early stage, as much as it does at the trial itself.[143] Article 5(4) requires that a person is entitled to 'take proceedings by which the lawfulness of his detention shall be decided speedily by a court', and UK procedures on disclosure in bail hearings may breach this.

The Court will then consider whether the weight of such a relevant factor is sufficient to justify continued detention. The seriousness of the offence or the likelihood of a severe sentence are not in themselves sufficient to conclude that the accused is likely to abscond. Other factors, such as character, morals, home, occupation, assets, family ties and links with the country need to be considered. In *Letellier v France*,[144] a wife was accused of complicity in her husband's murder. Initially granted bail, she was later put into custody by a higher court. The European Court held that this was a breach of Art 5(3), and that the seriousness of the charge was not in itself sufficient – here was a mother of eight children who had already been on remand and had not absconded.

---

139 This is contained in the Human Rights Act 1998, Sch 3.
140 This draws on J Burrow 'Bail and the Human Rights Act 1998' (2000) NLJ 673, 736 and 903. Also relevant is the Law Commission *Bail and the Human Rights Act 1998* (Law Commission Consultation Paper No 157).
141 *Wemhoff v FRG* (1968) 1 EHRR 55.
142 This is a high standard: *Stogmuller v Austria* (1969) 1 EHRR 155.
143 *Lamy v Belgium* (1989) 11 EHRR 529.
144 (1991) 14 EHRR 83.

The prospect of further offending is also a relevant factor, but this should not be presumed from the fact of previous convictions, which should raise only a plausible risk in the circumstances of the case. This issue is also raised by provisions such as s 25 of the Criminal Justice and Public Order Act 1994 which prohibited bail for those facing a murder, manslaughter or rape charges where the accused has previously been convicted of a similar offence. In *CC v UK*[145] the Commission held that s 25 breached Art 5(3). Any tribunal must consider the merits of the issue, a process which the Act expressly prohibited. Burrow argues that the amendment of s 25 by s 56 of the Crime and Disorder Act 1998 so that bail may be granted in 'exceptional circumstances' still breaches the Convention as it proceeds from a presumption of guilt rather than a presumption of innocence.[146] A similar difficulty arises with provisions which provide that a defendant need not be granted bail if he was already on bail at the time of the alleged offence.[147] This assumes that the first offence was in fact committed and that there is an automatic likelihood of further offending.

The continuance of detention must be kept under review at short intervals[148] as lapse of time itself is a relevant factor. This must raise the question whether s 154 of the Criminal Justice Act 1988 (which allows magistrates not to hear repeat arguments in bail applications unless there is a fresh argument of fact or law) is compliant with Art 5(3). Furthermore, at the end of the hearing, the European Court insists that reasons for the decision are given, without which it is difficult to decide whether there has been a violation of the Convention.[149] Standard form reasons such as the 'requirements of the investigation' are not sufficient.[150] This presents problems for magistrates who rarely give fully reasoned decisions in the court record; indeed, there is a pro forma decision sheet. Again, practices will need to change.[151]

Conditions may be attached to bail.[152] Examples might include bail conditions by which the accused has to report daily to the police or observe a curfew. In some areas, objection has been taken to the police practice of turning up at a defendant's house and requiring a defendant under curfew to appear at the door, presumably as degrading treatment or as an infringement of family life. Such propositions seem far-fetched; degrading treatment requires a far greater degree of severity and Art 8 may be derogated from in accordance with law and for the purposes of preventing crime.

3.6.4   Legal assistance in detention

A right to legal assistance is implied in Art 5(4) which requires that a person is entitled to 'take proceedings by which the lawfulness of his detention shall be

---

145   Application No 32819/96, [1999] Crim LR 228; and comment [1999] Crim LR 300.
146   Burrow (n 140 above), p 903.
147   Bail Act 1976, Sch 1, para 2A.
148   *Bezicheri v Italy* (1989) 12 EHRR 210.
149   *Neumeister v Austria (No 1)* (1968) 1 EHRR 91.
150   *Clooth v Belgium* (1991) 14 EHRR 717.
151   This point is taken by the Law Commission (n 140 above).
152   *Stogmuller v Austria* (1969) 1 EHRR 155; *Wemhoff v FRG* (1968) 1 EHRR 55.

decided speedily by a court'. This inference is reinforced by Art 6(3)(b) which provides that a person charged with a criminal offence should be provided with adequate time and facilities for the preparation of his or her defence, and by Art 6(3)(c) which provides a specific guarantee of the right to defend oneself or be legally represented and to be granted public funding where appropriate. A failure to allow an accused legal advice in detention will be seen as a breach of a right to a fair hearing under Art 6.[153]

In the UK, within a police station, this right is initially supported by s 56 which provides a right to have someone informed on a person's arrest. More specifically:

– s 58 of PACE 1984 gives a right to legal advice. Anyone in police detention must be told of this right and to the availability of free legal advice. This information must be given at the commencement or recommencement of any interview. Access can be delayed (but never refused altogether) under s 58(6) and (8) if the person is suspected of a serious arrestable offence and access might lead to interference with evidence, alerting of accomplices or hindering recovery of property. Similar restrictions apply to s 56;

– s 59 of PACE 1984 provides for a duty solicitor scheme. The Legal Aid Act 1988 and the Legal Aid Board Duty Solicitor Arrangements 1994 provide that a solicitor will be on call for any police station at all times. The solicitor is obliged to accept a case and must attend the station if the suspect has been arrested for an arrestable offence, if the police intend to carry out an identification parade, or if the suspect complains of serious mistreatment at the hands of the police.

A detained person will be allowed to make a telephone call to notify someone of the fact of arrest, and will be given a notice stating these rights to legal advice and the opportunity to consult Code of Practice C. Subsequently the detainee or the lawyer will receive a copy of the custody record. After release on bail or remand into custody, the accused has access to the criminal legal aid scheme under the Legal Aid Act 1988 which covers all aspects of preparation of the defence, representation and appeal.[154]

Failure to observe the correct procedure in relation to the provision of legal advice can lead to the evidence obtained from the subsequent interview being excluded. A failure to mention access to legal advice before questions were asked was fatal to the admissibility of the incriminating answers in *Absolam*.[155] Access to a duty solicitor was the issue in *Vernon*[156] where the accused nominated a solicitor who was unavailable as it was late at night. She agreed to be interviewed but was not told of the availability of the duty solicitor. The record of the interview was deemed inadmissible under s 78 of PACE 1984 as she would

153 B Emmerson 'Crime and Human Rights' (2000) 150 NLJ 13.
154 Legal Aid Act 1988, s 19.
155 (1988) 88 Cr App R 332.
156 [1988] Crim LR 445.

not have consented to be interviewed but for this breach, and the introduction of the record would have an adverse effect on the fairness of the proceedings.

The Court of Appeal has frequently concluded that lack of advice has not affected the course of the interview nor the fairness of the proceedings. In *Alladice*,[157] access to a solicitor was wrongly refused. The accused, who was 18 years old, testified that he could deal with the interviews and the court held that the presence of a lawyer would not have added to the defendant's knowledge of his rights and was therefore not unfair. Similarly, in *Dunford*,[158] access to legal advice was wrongly refused. On this occasion, the court held that the accused's previous criminal experience would not have added to his knowledge of his rights, and upheld the decision not to exclude the admissions under s 78.

Whether such an approach can survive the passage of the Human Rights Act 1998 is doubtful. In *Murray v UK*[159] the defendant was arrested under the Prevention of Terrorism (Temporary Provisions) Act 1989. Interviewed at Castlereagh Police Office, he was not given access to a lawyer for 48 hours. He refused to answer questions during this period and the trial judge drew adverse inferences from that refusal. The European Court held that where such consequences from silence exist, it is of paramount importance for the rights of the defence that an accused has access to legal advice. The concept of fairness enshrined in Art 6 requires that the accused already has the benefit of the assistance of a lawyer at the initial stages of police interrogation. To deny access to a lawyer for the first 48 hours of police questioning – whatever the justification for such denial – was incompatible with the rights of the accused under Art 6.[160] The Government had argued that in order to complain of denial of access to a lawyer it had to be clear that, had the applicant been able to consult with his solicitor earlier, he would have acted differently, and contended that the applicant had not shown this to be the case. The Court held that the Government should not speculate on what the applicant's reaction, or his lawyer's advice, would have been had access not been denied during this initial period. As matters stand, the applicant was undoubtedly directly affected by the denial of access and the ensuing interference with the rights of the defence.

A similar result was result was reached in *Magee v UK*.[161] These affirmations of the right to legal advice must be seen in context. Both *Murray* and *Magee* involved people suspected of terrorism who were being interviewed in the coercive and intimidating atmosphere of Castlereagh. Although a police station interview room is less disagreeable, in principle this factor should not distinguish these cases from those accused of ordinary criminal offences. The strong statements from the European Court on access to legal advice apply in all cases. Another distinguishing factor may be that both cases involved the

---

157 (1988) 87 Cr App R 380.
158 (1990) 91 Cr App R 150.
159 (1996) 22 EHRR 29.
160 In *Averill v UK* Application No 36408/97, (2001) 31 EHRR 36 the Court held that denial to access for the first 24 hours was also a breach.
161 Application No 28135/95, [2000] Crim LR 681.

Criminal Evidence (Northern Ireland) Order 1988[162] which allowed a trial judge to draw adverse inferences from an accused's refusal to answer police questions. Such a scheme existed in England and Wales from 1994[163] but this has now been amended so that a court cannot draw such inferences in the absence of legal advice.[164] It is suggested that the removal of this pressure to answer questions should not affect the right to legal advice. The conclusion is that *Murray* treats the right to advice as a fundamental right, attaching to all categories of suspect and which can be restricted only in extraordinary circumstances. If this is correct, it is difficult to believe that the Court of Appeal can continue to regard the refusal of legal advice to suspects as not affecting the fairness of the trial, either because they have a criminal record or because it would not have affected their behaviour in interview. In *Murray*[165] the European Court explicitly rejected such an approach.

Although the Commission and the Court have stated that the right of access to a solicitor is fundamental to an accused's defence,[166] the Court accepts that the right to legal advice may be subject to restriction for good cause. Section 58(8) of PACE 1984 entitles the police to delay access to a solicitor under the 'serious arrestable offence' exception.[167] *Murray* and *Magee* both show that the seriousness of the offence is not by itself enough to restrict the right. Relevant factors must be those that go to interference with the investigation in some way. Such factors must be in relation to the solicitor involved and would require the police to believe on reasonable grounds that the solicitor would alert other suspects, hinder the recovery of evidence or obstruct the investigation in some way, albeit inadvertently. Such a belief could only rarely be held. Furthermore, as with refusal of bail, Convention principles suggest that a police officer should document reasons for refusal of access to legal advice, perhaps on the custody record.

The relevant factors for such restriction must relate to impeding the investigation away from the station. The police cannot refuse to allow a suspect access to legal advice on the grounds that legal advice will be to remain silent.[168] Whether such access also means a right to have a lawyer present at interview is a moot question under the Convention[169] although not in the UK. Even here, under Code of Practice C, a lawyer may be asked to leave an interview if he or she is preventing the interviewer from putting questions properly.[170]

---

162   SI 1988/1987.
163   Criminal Justice and Public Order Act 1994, s 34.
164   Youth Justice and Criminal Evidence Act 1999, s 58.
165   (1996) 22 EHRR 29, paras 67–68.
166   *Bonzi v Switzerland* Application No 7854/77, (1978) 12 DR 185.
167   Lidstone and Palmer (n 2 above), para 7.49ff.
168   *Samuel* [1988] 2 All ER 135.
169   *Murray* (1996) 22 EHRR 29, para 69.
170   Code of Practice C, para 6.9.

3.7   INTERVIEWING AND THE RIGHT TO SILENCE

Article 6 guarantees a fair hearing. This right is not narrowly circumscribed. The European Court has always taken the position that events during pre-trial proceedings (such as the absence of a lawyer's advice in the police station) can affect the fairness of the subsequent trial. As a result, the conduct of the interview between the police and the suspect becomes important. Interrogation is important to the police and an essential investigative tool. Compared to other forms of acquiring evidence, it is cheap and the end result, a confession, is evidence that is seen by juries as reliable and convincing. Despite the right of silence and the privilege against self-incrimination, most suspects (especially those detained in the police station) talk to the police and many make either complete or partial, verbal or written admissions of guilt.[171] The issue for domestic law is whether these incriminating statements should be admitted into evidence against the accused. The issue for the Convention is whether the rules of admissibility infringe the defendant's right to a fair trial under Art 6.

The position in English law is regulated by ss 76–78 of PACE 1984 and Code of Practice C:

- s 76(2) requires the prosecution to prove beyond reasonable doubt that a confession was not obtained by oppression or in circumstances likely to render the confession unreliable;
- s 77 lays down special provisions for those with a mental handicap;
- s 78 allows the court to refuse evidence if it appears to the court that the admission of such evidence would have such an adverse effect on the fairness of the proceedings that the court ought not to admit it.[172]

Most other jurisdictions use an intermediary judicial official to compile the record of the interview with the defendant as well as statements from witnesses. In England and Wales, there has been a reluctance to take this step. It would probably require the development of a new category of judge, acting in a more inquisitorial role.[173] Instead, by the means of the Codes of Practice, we have placed the police in a quasi-judicial role, responsible for interviewing suspects inside the police station and for documenting the questions and answers. Tape-recording[174] of interviews, regulated by Code of Practice E, backs up this process. There are weaknesses in the scheme:

- courts still do not automatically exclude anything said by suspects when they are alleged to have made incriminating statements outside the station or the interview room where codes of practice do not run;
- the police are still responsible for taking witness statements;

---

171   B Mitchell 'Confessions and Police interrogation of Suspects' [1982] Crim LR 596.
172   Section 78 was not in the original Bill. An amendment by Lord Scarman would have excluded evidence obtained by police malpractice. The Government watered down the original with the eventual, rather obscure text.
173   Such as the juge d'instruction in France; see *Report of the Royal Commission on Criminal Procedure* (n 60 above), paras 6.25ff; any move to an inquisitorial system was also rejected by the Royal Commission on Criminal Justice: paras 1.11–1.15.
174   PACE 1984, s 60 – this is now nationwide practice.

– there is no judicial scrutiny of the police except through the trial process itself;

– even breaches of the Codes do not automatically lead to exclusion of the evidence.

A further weakness is the ambivalent attitude by judges towards the right to silence. Article 6(2) embodies the presumption of innocence which requires that the State bears the burden of proving the accused's guilt. As a corollary, this leads to the proposition that a defendant should not be expected to provide proof of guilt by means of a coerced or involuntary confession or through having his or her silence used in evidence. This is indirectly supported by the decision of the European Court in *Funke v France*[175] that legal compulsion to produce incriminating evidence infringed the right of silence. Here the State sought to compel the accused to produce bank statements that may have been relevant to customs investigations into offences committed by him.

At common law the concept of the right to silence consisted of a conglomerate of different ideas:

– there was the requirement of a caution, ie that the police warned a suspect that he or she need not say anything and that whatever was said might be used in evidence;

– there was also the evidential rule that placed a burden of proof on the prosecution that it should prove the defendant's guilt beyond reasonable doubt,[176] in other words, a presumption of innocence;

– the prosecution was not permitted to comment on the defendant's decision to remain silent in the police station[177] or not to testify;[178]

– the judge could comment[179] but had to do so in measured terms and had to warn the jury that it must not assume guilt from the defendant's silence.

This was significantly altered in 1994 by ss 34–37 of the Criminal Justice and Public Order Act 1994. For the first time, juries were allowed to use, as evidence of guilt, adverse inferences that they had drawn from the accused's silence in the face of police questions, from any failure to account for actions, or from a refusal to testify. This is very similar to legislation introduced in 1988 in Northern Ireland.[180]

– Section 34 is aimed at 'ambush defences' and forcing early disclosure of any likely defence the suspect might have. A court can 'draw such inferences as appear proper' from a failure to mention a relevant fact relied on in the defence when it might reasonably have been mentioned during police questioning.

---

175 (1993) 16 EHRR 297.

176 *Woolmington* [1935] AC 462.

177 *Hall* [1971] 1 WLR 298.

178 Criminal Evidence Act 1898, s 1(b) – the failure of any person charged with an offence to give evidence shall not be made the subject of any comment by the prosecution.

179 *Bathurst* [1968] 2 QB 99; *Sparrow* [1973] 1 WLR 488; although see Rupert Cross' forthright comments on 'gibberish' in 'A Very Wicked Animal' [1973] Crim LR 329, 333.

180 Criminal Evidence (Northern Ireland) Order 1988 (SI 1988/1987); for its impact, see J Jackson 'Curtailing the Right of Silence: Lessons from N Ireland' [1991] Crim LR 404.

– Section 35 applies where the defendant declines to testify in court and is discussed in Chapter 4 below.
– Section 36 applies where the suspect gives no explanation to police about certain specific facts such as objects, substances or marks on clothing which tend to suggest the accused's participation in the offence. A court will 'draw such inferences as appear proper' from a failure to give such an explanation.
– Section 37 applies where the suspect gives no explanation to the police of his or her presence at a particular place which, again, would tend to suggest participation in the offence. A court will also 'draw such inferences as appear proper' from a failure to give an explanation.

Sections 34, 36 and 37 have now been amended so that a court cannot draw such inferences where the accused has not had legal advice.[181] There may be challenges to this legislation as the decision in *Funke* suggests that such provisions, which place pressure on the suspect to answer police questions, infringe Art 6(2); the right to silence was an integral part of the obligation on the State to prove the guilt of the accused.

Similar Northern Ireland provisions were considered in *Murray v UK*.[182] This involved both a refusal to answer police questions and to testify. The European Court concluded that, where a prima facie case was established and the burden of proof remained on the prosecution, adverse inferences may be drawn. Although the Court saw the right to silence as a generally recognised international standard which lay at the heart of fair procedure, the require-ment placed on the defendant to answer questions or to testify was not incompatible with the Convention, although it would be if the conviction were based solely or mainly on any refusal to give evidence. As the Northern Ireland Order (and the 1994 Act) stands, the prosecution case must overcome the hurdle of a 'no case to answer' submission and produce sufficient evidence which could form the basis for conviction for a reasonable jury. It would be difficult to argue that any resultant conviction was solely or mainly based on adverse inferences drawn from the failure to answer questions or testify.

It was argued that *Murray* was unlikely to be the last word on this issue. There were several distinctive features in the case that marked it out from an ordinary criminal prosecution:

– it concerned charges of terrorism;
– the nature of the tribunal (a Diplock court in Northern Ireland) involved an experienced judge as the trier of fact;
– the independent evidence against the defendant was overwhelming.

These factors may have been especially relevant in the Court's decision. As a whole it clearly considered that the 'adverse inferences' rule significantly affected the right to a fair hearing guaranteed in Art 6(1) and, furthermore, that there was substantial dissent. It was a guarded reaction to the Northern

---

181 Youth Justice and Criminal Evidence Act 1999, s 58.
182 (1996) 22 EHRR 29.

Ireland Order which was echoed in *Averill v UK*.[183] Incriminating fibres were found on the accused who contended that he was silent, not from the lack of legal advice, but from a policy of not talking to the RUC. The Court did not find that a sufficient justification. Despite the decision that there was no breach, the Court said that the extent to which adverse inferences could be drawn must necessarily be limited and that there might be reasons why an innocent person might be unwilling to co-operate with the police.

A jury should be made aware of the accused's justifications for remaining silent and, were it to be satisfied that the reasons were cogent, should not draw adverse inferences from silence. In a non-terrorist case, *Condron v UK*,[184] the applicants complained that their right to a fair trial under Art 6 had been violated by the trial judge's decision to leave the jury with the option of drawing an adverse inference from the applicants' silence during police interviews. The applicants had been tried on counts of supplying heroin, and of possession of heroin with intent to supply. The Crown's case had relied on police surveillance of exchanges between the applicants, their co-accused and third parties. Before interview the applicants were cautioned. The applicants' solicitor had considered that the applicants were not fit to give interviews because they were suffering from heroin withdrawal. A police doctor, however, found that the applicants were fit for interview. The applicants remained silent during the interviews on the advice of their solicitor but, at trial, gave explanations for the exchanges observed by the police. The judge directed the jury in accordance with s 34 of the Criminal Justice and Public Order Act 1994. The Court of Appeal rejected the appeal, despite what it perceived as errors in the direction, because the conviction was safe given the almost overwhelming evidence against the accused.

The European Court emphasised that the accused testified and gave an explanation for silence and that the trial was before a jury, all of which was distinguishable from *Murray*. The Court held that the right to silence was not absolute but that 'particular caution' was required by domestic courts before drawing adverse inferences. Convicting solely or mainly on such evidence would infringe Art 6, but the accused's silence, in situations which clearly called for an explanation, could be taken into account in assessing the persuasiveness of the prosecution evidence. In all the circumstances of this case, the jury should have been directed that silence could be taken into account but only if it was satisfied that the applicants' silence could not sensibly be attributed to their having no answer or none that would stand up to cross-examination.

Other statutes require persons to provide information which may be used as the basis for a criminal prosecution. For example, s 2 of the Criminal Justice Act 1987 requires any person under investigation by the Serious Fraud Office to answer questions, produce documents and furnish information.[185] The

183   Application No 36408/97, (2001) 31 EHRR 36.
184   Application No 35718/97, (2001) 31 EHRR 1.
185   Other statutes compel the provision of information but where any statements made are
       inadmissible as evidence: see Theft Act 1968, s 31(1); Criminal Damage Act 1971, s 9;
       Children Act 1989, s 98.

compatibility of such legislation with Art 6 was questioned in *Saunders v UK*.[186] The defendant was convicted of fraud on the basis of answers that he had been compelled to give in the course of investigations by inspectors from the Department of Trade. The European Court concluded that this infringed his freedom from self-incrimination and was in breach of the presumption of innocence and Art 6(2). Both *Saunders* and *Funke* (above) establish that coercion to co-operate with the authorities in the pre-trial process may infringe the privilege against self-incrimination and jeopardise the fairness of any subsequent hearing, were the prosecution to use the product of that coercion as evidence. The British Government response has been to restrict the use in evidence of answers given under such circumstances.[187]

3.8   COMMON LAW AND THE RIGHT TO PRIVACY

Undercover policing, surveillance operations and interception of communications are all part and parcel of modern police work. Historically, the police have never had any general statutory authority for such actions. Such authority as there was was based upon the common law principle that whatever is not expressly forbidden by law is permissible.[188] Covert surveillance or undercover information-gathering, not involving criminal or tortious conduct, were not forbidden because they did not, in general, infringe any right to privacy recognised by the statute or the common law. Parliament has shown itself reluctant to extend those interests through the development of any law of privacy – for example, the Younger Committee, in 1972,[189] decided against creating a general right to privacy.

Common law has never recognised a right to privacy as such. In *Malone v Metropolitan Police Commissioner*[190] the plaintiff issued proceedings after the prosecution, in a criminal trial brought against him in respect of alleged handling of stolen goods, had admitted to tapping his telephone. He claimed that telephone tapping, even authorised by the warrant of the Home Secretary, was unlawful. The argument was that to intercept or monitor a person's telephone conversations without his or her consent infringed the right to property, the right to privacy and the right to confidentiality The right to privacy contained in the Convention either conferred direct rights, or provided a guide in cases of ambiguity or lack of clarity, in English law, and that tapping was unlawful in the absence of any express grant of powers to the executive either by statute or common law. Sir Robert Megarry VC held that, 'No new right in the law, fully-fledged with all the appropriate safeguards, can spring

---

186   (1996) 23 EHRR 313.
187   See the Youth Justice and Criminal Evidence Act 1999, s 59 and Sch 3 for a list of relevant statutes.
188   *Malone v Metropolitan Police Commissioner* [1979] 2 All ER 620.
189   *Report of the Committee on Privacy*, Cmnd 5012 (1972).
190   [1979] 2 All ER 620.

from the head of a judge deciding a particular case: only Parliament can create such a right'.[191]

In *Malone v UK*,[192] the applicant brought proceedings, claiming that telephone tapping by the police had breached Art 8. The European Court unanimously agreed. Although the right to privacy may be interfered with for purposes specified in the Convention, it had to be in accordance with the law, which UK telephone tapping was manifestly not. The Court ruled that the law had to be sufficiently clear in terms to give citizens an adequate indication of the circumstances in which, and the conditions under which, telephone tapping could be carried out. The law had to indicate the scope of any executive discretion and the manner of its existence in order to give citizens protection against arbitrary interference. These issues were addressed in the Interception of Communications Act 1985 which regulates interception of the post, telephone tapping and any communications sent by a public[193] telecommunications system.[194] This framework was replaced by the Regulation of Investigatory Powers Act 2000.

Away from the interception of communications, in the absence of any common law right to privacy, there have been few legal constraints on police undercover operations until the Human Rights Act 1998. There is now protection and accountability provided by recent legislation, such as the Police Act 1997 and the Regulation of Investigatory Powers Act 2000.

3.9   UNDERCOVER AGENTS AND ENTRAPMENT

Intelligence-led policing[195] can involve the targeting by the police of individuals suspected of involvement in criminal activities. The purpose is often to acquire evidence to be used in subsequent prosecution. This raises the issue of whether the investigatory technique is one which threatens the overall fairness of the proceedings against the defendant. In domestic law, s 78 of PACE 1984 allows a judge to exclude evidence in such circumstances. Under the Convention, Art 6 guarantees a fair trial, and abuse of the State's position can breach that right.

Undercover policing takes many different forms – informants, the agent provocateur, 'sting' operations, covert facilitation and, frequently, entrapment techniques.[196]

–   *'Honeypot' or manna from Heaven operations*: these involve the police establishing bogus businesses in an effort to 'trade' with criminals. Common examples of this are phoney second-hand dealerships. In

191   (1996) 23 EHRR 313.
192   *Malone v UK* (1984) 7 EHRR 14 at 39–41.
193   As defined in s 9 of the Telecommunications Act 1984.
194   As defined in s 4(1) of the Telecommunications Act 1984.
195   S Uglow and V Telford *The Police Act* (Jordans, 1997), p 2; see also ch 3.
196   C Stevens 'Covert Policing Techniques' (Police Association of South Australia, Current Issues Working Paper 10).

Christou[197] the police ran a jeweller's shop, buying stolen goods, recording transactions and ultimately trapping over 30 people. This took place over a period of time which meant that the suspects were allowed to continue their offences without immediate police action.

– *Integrity tests*: essentially, these involve placing tempting opportunities before targeted suspects. In *Williams v DPP*[198] the police left a transit van apparently loaded with cigarettes in public view, arresting the appellants when they attempted to take some of the cartons. The Court held that they had not acted as agents provocateurs and admitted the evidence, but it is clear that the police procured the commission of an offence which would not otherwise have been committed.

– *Decoy or lure operations*: these involve police acting as potential or actual victims. Male police officers might, for example, loiter around public toilet blocks to bait the advances of homosexual men.

– *'Sting' or active participation operations*: there are the most commonly used type of covert facilitation. In such operations, police are active participants or conspirators with the suspected citizens they hope to trap. A common example (perhaps the most common) is police posing as drug buyers and often completing mock purchases from unsuspecting dealers/sellers.

– *Solicitation*: there is often a fine line between the active participation of a police officer in a criminal transaction and solicitation, whereby the police officer actively encourages and coerces the commission of a crime. In *Wilson*,[199] a police informer enticed the accused into forging large quantities of American Express traveller's cheques. Although the judge refused to exclude the evidence, he merely imposed suspended sentences, a clear comment on the propriety of the proceedings.

It may be useful first to consider the 'camera on legs' operation, where the police officer acts undercover, not simply as an observer, but as a participant.[200] American law permits a substantive defence of entrapment. In *Jacobson v US*[201] the defendant was convicted of receiving child pornography through the mail, which he had ordered from a catalogue supplied to him by a government agency. The Supreme Court quashed the conviction. Although 'artifice and stratagem may be employed to catch those engaged in criminal enterprises', government agents may not originate a criminal design. The jury had to decide whether there was a reasonable doubt that the defendant possessed the requisite predisposition to commit the offences before the government intervention.

In common law, there is no such substantive defence.[202] English courts have instead attempted to exert control over sting operations, entrapment and other

---

197 [1992] 4 All ER 559.
198 [1993] 3 All ER 365.
199 *The Guardian*, 15 December 1994 – the Court of Appeal judgment was 9 May 1996 (Lawtel).
200 M Maguire and T John 'Covert and Deceptive Policing in England and Wales' (1996) *European Journal of Crime, Criminal Law and Criminal Justice* 316.
201 503 US 540 (1992); *Sorrells v US* 287 US 435 (1932); *US v Russell* 411 US 423 (1973).
202 *Sang* [1980] AC 402.

undercover police actions by the indirect means of exclusion of evidence through s 78 of PACE 1984. The test is whether the offence would have occurred but for the involvement of the police – an issue of causation rather than predisposition. *Smurthwaite*[203] involved allegations that the defendant had solicited another to murder his wife. An undercover police officer, pretending to be a contract killer, recorded incriminating conversations, which were admitted into evidence. The Court of Appeal upheld this, asking 'Was the officer acting as an agent provocateur in the sense that he was enticing the defendant to commit an offence he would not have otherwise committed?'[204]

The same issue on the extent to which undercover officers can be actively involved was raised in *Ludi v Switzerland*[205] and in *Teixeira de Castro v Portugal*,[206] in both of which undercover police officers made sample purchases of drugs. The issue was whether the admission of the testimony of the officers was in breach of the accused's right to a fair trial. The outcomes were different. In *Ludi*, the operation was part of a judicial investigation and the drugs deal was already underway when the undercover officers arrived. The operation was not seen as a violation. In *Teixeira de Castro*, there was no real judicial supervision of the operation, nor was there any pre-existing evidence to implicate the defendant. The European Court stressed the issue of whether the defendant was 'predisposed' to commit the offence. It has been suggested that this decision means that English courts will need to develop a substantive defence of entrapment.[207]

The issue here for domestic law relates to the need for judicial supervision of undercover operations. One theme of Convention jurisprudence is the need for any infringement of rights to be 'in accordance with law'. In civil law systems, this is achieved by the investigating judge ensuring that a balance is maintained between individual rights and the administration of justice, and that police undercover operations do not go beyond the proper boundaries. In common law systems, the promulgation of proper guidelines has been in the hands of senior police management.[208] The appellate courts have laid down some principles on covert operations in cases such as *Christou* and *Smurthwaite*, but these scarcely amount to a statutory framework which gives express powers to the police to undertake such operations and which establishes a proper system of supervision. For example, s 31 of the Criminal Justice and Police Act 2001 provides a legal framework to allow young persons, under 18 years of age, to make test purchases of alcohol to ensure that landlords are carrying out proper age checks. If properly regulated, these test purchases will come within Convention guidelines.

---

203 [1994] 1 All ER 898.
204 Ibid at 903a, per Lord Taylor CJ.
205 (1992) 15 EHRR 173.
206 (1998) 28 EHRR 101.
207 [1998] Crim LR 751, 753.
208 *Codes of Practice: Covert Law Enforcement Techniques* (Association of Chief Police Officers and HM Customs and Excise, 1999).

There is an obvious analogy with the search of premises under the provisions of Part II of PACE 1984 where, before the police are authorised to enter private property, they are required to go before a magistrate who assesses the evidence and issues the warrant. The Regulation of Investigatory Powers Act 2000 has introduced a framework of authorisation, which is discussed at **3.13** below. The statute distinguishes between the following:

–   directed surveillance which is undertaken for the purposes of a specific investigation, and which is likely to result in obtaining private information about a person. It does not include situations where the surveillance is an immediate response to events;
–   intrusive surveillance which is carried out on residential premises or in private vehicles and which either involves an investigator on the premises or in a vehicle, or the use of a surveillance device;
–   covert human intelligence source which involves agents who establish a personal relationship to obtain information, which is then covertly disclosed.

In all these cases, the surveillance is regarded as lawful if an authorisation under the Act is obtained and subsequent actions are in accordance with that authorisation. There is a considerable difference in the nature of the authorisation required – directed surveillance and the use of covert human intelligence sources require, by s 30, a designated police officer, probably a superintendent. Intrusive surveillance, on the other hand, requires authorisation from a commissioner. The authorisation for undercover operations will usually be given by the police themselves. It would not be unreasonable to require police officers to seek judicial approval before engaging in undercover operations, even where these are not directly intrusive, if they wish to use the evidence gathered in any subsequent prosecution. As far as the Convention is concerned, undercover work will inevitably infringe on a suspect's privacy. Article 8 allows such infringement in the interests of crime prevention if it is in accordance with law. The old ACPO Code of Practice was not law, nor was there any independent system of accountability. The new statutory scheme for operations at a lower level than intrusive surveillance seems to suffer from similar failings.

The European Court will ultimately look in individual cases not at a defect in procedure but at the overall fairness of proceedings. This is the thrust of the Court of Appeal's approach in cases such as *Smurthwaite* and, while it conducts a proper inquiry into that issue, it is unlikely that the European Court would interfere.[209]

---

209   A recent decision is *Shannon* (unreported) 14 September 2000, CA.

3.10   INTERCEPTION OF MAIL AND TELEPHONE TAPPING

The interception of communications can take place through telephone taps or by the cloning of mobile phones or pagers, as well as through the opening of mail. The practice of intercepting letters under the Home Secretary's warrant is very long standing, although the authority for doing so is obscure. The issue was considered by the Birkett Committee appointed in 1957[210] which considered that the Home Secretary's powers were recognised by a statutory exemption from criminal proceedings for post office employees who opened or delayed letters while acting under his warrant. The Committee was inconclusive as to whether the Home Secretary's powers emanated from the Royal Prerogative.

For the police, authorisation of such intercepts of post or telecommunications must be given by the Secretary of State under Part I of the Regulation of Investigatory Powers Act 2000. However, Crown Servants,[211] such as officers from Customs and Excise, have wider powers to make such intercepts under the Wireless Telegraphy Act 1949.[212]

It is now a criminal offence for a person intentionally to intercept a communication except under a warrant issued by the Secretary of State, or where there were reasonable grounds to believe that the sender or recipient of the communication consented.[213] The Secretary of State cannot issue a warrant except for the following purposes:[214]

– in the interests of national security;
– for the purpose of preventing or detecting serious crime;
– for the purpose of safeguarding the economic well-being of the UK.

In deciding whether to issue a warrant, the Secretary of State must consider whether the information could be reasonably obtained by other means.[215] Warrants are issued by the Secretary of State, although there is a special procedure for urgent cases.[216] Warrants will last for 3 months. Warrants issued on the grounds of national security or economic well-being can be renewed for up to 6 months, whereas any other warrant can be renewed for 3 months only.[217] In issuing a warrant, the Secretary of State must ensure that the extent to which the material is disclosed, the number of people to whom it is disclosed, the extent to which it is copied and the number of copies made, are kept to the

---

210   *Report of the Committee of Privy Councillors*, Cmnd 283 (1957).
211   The police are not Crown Servants: *AG for New South Wales v Perpetual Trustee Co Ltd* [1955] AC 457.
212   Such powers are unlikely to comply with the requirements of the Convention.
213   Regulation of Investigatory Powers Act 2000, s 1.
214   Ibid, s 5(3).
215   Regulation of Investigatory Powers Act 2000 s 5(4); *cf* similar provisions under s 93(2)(a) of the Police Act 1997.
216   Regulation of Investigatory Powers Act 2000, s 7(2); *cf* similar provisions in s 94(2) and s 97(3) of the Police Act 1997.
217   Regulation of Investigatory Powers Act 2000, s 9.

minimum necessary. Finally, copies of the material are to be destroyed as soon as its retention is no longer necessary for the purpose for which it was issued.[218]

In 1996, the Secretary of State authorised 1,142 telephone and mail interceptions under the Interception of Communications Act 1985. An executive power of this nature has considerable implications for individual privacy[219] and, although the Act conforms in a minimal sense with the requirements of Art 8, there are few controls, either through judicial or parliamentary scrutiny. In this sphere, the passage of the Human Rights Act 1998 will not necessarily lead to any improvement in the protection of privacy.[220] The Convention accepts that secret surveillance may be justified in order to counter threats from espionage, terrorism or serious crime. However, the European Court has recently ruled that telephone tapping carried out on the instructions and under the supervision of investigating judges in France violated Art 8 because there were inadequate safeguards against various possible abuses. In *Huvig v France*[221] and *Kruslin v France*[222] the following deficiencies were identified:

–   there had been no definition for the categories of people liable to have their telephones tapped, nor the nature of the offence which might give rise to such order;
–   the investigating judge had not been under an obligation to set a limit on the duration of the tapping;
–   the procedure for drawing up the summary reports of the intercepted conversations was unspecified;
–   the precautions to be taken with regards to the communication of the recordings intact and in their entirety for possible inspection by the judge and by the defence were unspecified;
–   the destruction of the recordings, particularly where the accused had been discharged or acquitted, were unspecified.

In *Klass v Germany*,[223] German legislation permitted the State to open and inspect mail and listen to telephone conversations in order to protect against,

---

218   Regulation of Investigatory Powers Act 2000, s 15.
219   See the complaint of Robin Cook MP *Hansard* HC Deb vol 173, cols 443–450 (24 May 1990).
220   It has been suggested that the Human Rights Act 1998 is 'to make the right of privacy somewhat akin to the traditional civil rights of the citizen which seem to carry little significance as regards the exclusion of evidence' (P Mirfield 'Regulation of Investigatory Powers Act 2000(2): Evidential Aspects' (2001) Crim LR 91).
221   (1990) 12 EHRR 528: the applicants were suspected, and subsequently convicted, of various offences of tax evasion by the use of forged invoices. In the course of the judicial investigation the investigating judge authorised a senior police officer to have the applicants' business and private telephone lines tapped. The applicants complained of a violation of Art 8 of the Convention. It was held unanimously that there had been a breach of Art 8.
222   (1990) 12 EHRR 547: the applicant was convicted of, inter alia, armed robbery. One decisive piece of evidence against him was a taped record of his telephone conversation with another person whose telephone line was tapped in relation to other proceedings. The applicant argued that the interception and recording of his telephone conversation violated Art 8 of the Convention. Again, it was held unanimously that there had been a breach of Art 8.
223   (1978) 2 EHRR 214.

inter alia, 'imminent dangers' threatening the 'free democratic constitutional order' and 'the existence or the security' of the State. The applicants, five German lawyers, claimed that the legislation infringed Arts 6, 8 and 13. They accepted the State's right to have recourse to such measures, but challenged the legislation on the grounds that it contained no absolute requirement to notify the persons after the surveillance of their mail had ceased, and that it excluded any remedy before the courts against the ordering and implementation of the measures. The European Court provided the following general guidance as to the application of Art 8 to legislation authorising surveillance:

- the legislation must be designed to ensure that surveillance is not ordered haphazardly, irregularly or without due and proper care;
- surveillance must be reviewed and must be accompanied by procedures which guarantee individual rights;
- it is in principle desirable to entrust the supervisory control to a judge in accordance with the rule of law, but other safeguards might suffice if they are independent and vested with sufficient powers to exercise an effective and continuous control;
- if the surveillance is justified under Art 8(2), the failure to inform the individual under surveillance of this fact subsequently is, in principle, justified.[224]

Even so, breach of these principles and an applicant's right to privacy does not lead to automatic exclusion. In *Schenk v Switzerland*,[225] there was no breach of a right to a fair trial even though an illegally obtained tape-recording was admitted into evidence. The European Court considered the fairness of the proceedings as a whole. The accused had had the opportunity to challenge the use and authenticity of the tape, and there was other evidence supporting the conviction.

It is clear that there must be adequate and effective safeguards against abuse and thus proper machinery for supervision. This need not be in the hands of a judge, and the machinery under the Interception of Communications Act 1985 (now under the Regulation of Investigatory Powers Act 2000) was considered adequate in *Christie v UK*.[226] Similar machinery for commissioners and tribunals established under the Security Services Act 1989 and the Intelligence Services Act 1994 has also been regarded as sufficient to provide independent scrutiny.[227]

The House of Lords has held that mobile phones are not part of the public telecommunications system and are not covered by the 1985 Act.[228] The situation in *Halford v UK*[229] is comparable since there the applicant was a senior police officer with the Merseyside Police who was pursuing an industrial tribunal claim against her employers on the grounds of sex discrimination. Her telephone calls made on the internal police network were intercepted and the

---

224 (1978) 2 EHRR 214 at 232–236.
225 (1988) 13 EHRR 242.
226 Application No 21482/93, 78A DR 119.
227 *Esbester v UK* (1993) 18 EHRR CD 72.
228 *Effik* [1995] 1 AC 309.
229 (1998) 24 EHRR 523.

European Court held that these were not covered by the 1985 Act and were in breach of Art 8 as the interference was not 'in accordance with the law'. It is clear that intercepts from mobile phones are also not regulated by statute and are in breach of the Convention.

3.11 COVERT SURVEILLANCE

Modern technology has brought in its wake sophisticated mechanisms for observing people's lives or listening in on their communications. Policing now employs a range of special investigating methods, whether these involve the use of informants, undercover agents, surveillance, computer screening or advanced technical devices. Over the past decades, however, the devices available to the police for surveillance operations have become more specialised. New technologies have enhanced the ability not only to track people through walls, overheard conversations and movement, but also through their computerised record trail. We are familiar with advanced microphones and closed circuit television cameras (CCTV), but there are other, more esoteric, examples of surveillance technology.[230]

–   BT has a system which can switch on the telephone in a person's house in order to listen to any conversations in the vicinity.
–   Massive millimetre wave detectors use a form of radar to scan beneath clothing. By monitoring the millimetre wave portion of the electromagnetic spectrum emitted by the human body, the system can detect items such as guns and drugs from a range of 12 feet or more. It can also look through building walls and detect activity.
–   Van Eck Monitoring works on the basis that every computer emits low levels of electromagnetic radiation from the monitor, processor and attached devices. Although experts disagree over whether the actual range is only a few yards or up to a mile, these signals can be recreated remotely on another computer.
–   Tracking devices of all kinds include cellular phones which transmit location information to the home system to determine call routing. This information can be used for automated tracking of the caller's movements. In 1993, fugitive Colombian drug kingpin, Pablo Escobar, was pinpointed through his cellular phone. Currently, there is an effort to develop a system that would give location information for every cellular phone.
–   In the United States, law enforcement agencies use forward looking infrared (FLIR). This was originally developed for use in fighter planes and helicopters to locate enemy aircraft. FLIR can detect a temperature differential as small as 0.18 degrees centigrade. Texas Instruments and others are marketing hand-held and automobile- and helicopter-mounted models that can metaphorically look through walls to determine activities

---

230   These are drawn from D Banisar 'Big Brother Goes High Tech' *Covert Action Quarterly* (Spring 1996); see also *Criminal Justice Matters: Surveillance No 20* (Spring 1995).

inside buildings. FLIR is used to track people and cars on the Mexican border and search for missing people and fugitives. However, law enforcement agents have also used it in residential neighbourhoods to obtain a thermal image of particular houses, because the high-pressure sodium lights used to grow marijuana indoors create huge amounts of heat. Where such surveillance has been undertaken without warrants, it raises the question whether the surveillance was an unlawful search in breach of the Fourth Amendment.[231]

Covert surveillance of one form or another is undertaken in order to obtain evidence of offences. In the UK, until 1998, such surveillance was carried out under Home Office guidelines published in 1984[232] which required the personal authority of the Chief Constable for such an operation. In 1995 there were 1,300 police authorisations in England and Wales, and 2,100 in the UK. An example of a surveillance operation which came to the courts is the case of *R v Khan*,[233] in which the appellant was suspected of importing drugs. He visited the house of another man where, unknown to both of them, the police had installed a listening device from which they subsequently obtained a tape-recording of a conversation which clearly showed the accused's involvement. There were no statutory provisions which authorised such an action, which was both a civil trespass and also a prima facie breach of the right to respect for private and family life protected by Art 8 of the Convention. The Home Office guidelines, however, had been complied with. At the trial and on appeal, the appellant argued that, nevertheless, the evidence had been improperly obtained and should be excluded. The House of Lords held that any breach of privacy or of Art 8 was relevant to, but not determinative of, the trial judge's discretion to exclude evidence under the provisions of s 78 of PACE 1984 and that in this case the facts were such that the judge had been entitled to hold that the circumstances did not require the exclusion of the evidence. Lord Nolan ended his judgment by saying:

> 'The sole cause of this case coming to your Lordships' House is the lack of a statutory system regulating the use of surveillance devices by the police. The absence of such a system seems astonishing, the more so in view of the statutory framework which has governed the use of such devices by the security service since 1989, and the interception of communications by the police as well as by other agencies since 1985.'

Although there are statutory codes of practice under PACE 1984 for normal 'overt' police investigations, in the early 1990s there was no statutory code for secret surveillance. This presented a problem since such activities constitute an interference with the right to privacy protected by the Convention. This situation was reviewed by the European Court in *Khan v UK*[234] (above) which unanimously held that there was a breach of Art 8. The key issue was whether the surveillance was 'in accordance with law'. The Court said that this phrase

---

231   S Uglow 'Covert Surveillance and the European Convention on Human Rights' [1999] Crim LR 287, 292.
232   There were similar guidelines for Scotland, Northern Ireland and Customs and Excise.
233   [1996] 3 All ER 289.
234   [2000] Crim LR 684.

required not just compliance with domestic law, but also related to the quality of that law, requiring it to be compatible with the rule of law. Domestic law must provide protection against arbitrary interference. The Home Office guidelines were not adequate and the surveillance could not be considered to be in accordance with law.

The Court also ruled that the Police Complaints Authority could not be an effective remedy for those with complaints against the police; it did not meet the requisite standards of independence needed to constitute sufficient protection against abuse of authority.

More surprisingly, the Court went on to rule that, despite the admission of the evidence obtained by the breach of Art 8, and despite the fact that this was the main evidence against the accused, there was no violation of the right to a fair trial. The applicant did not suggest that there was an 'automatic exclusion' rule where a Convention right had been breached, but argued that there must be an effective procedure to challenge admissibility of evidence, that the trial court must have regard to the nature of the violation and that conviction should not be based solely on evidence obtained by a breach of a Convention right. The Court reiterated the general principle that the essential issue was the overall fairness of the proceedings. On the issue of the significance of the evidence, the Court noted that even in *Schenk v Switzerland* (above), the evidence had 'perhaps a decisive influence'. In addition, the applicant had the opportunity to challenge the validity of the evidence (under s 78) at each stage, and the Court gave weight to the fact that the domestic courts did not feel that the admissibility of the evidence had given rise to substantive unfairness.

The weaknesses of this judgment are brought out by the one dissentient, Judge Loucaides, who defined 'fairness' as implying observance of the rule of law and, although there was no breach of domestic law, that the UK courts ought not to admit evidence obtained in breach of the Convention. Effective enforcement of the Convention is otherwise hindered since the police would not be deterred from repeating the conduct. Exclusion of the evidence is the practical and effective remedy and should be a necessary corollary to Art 8 rights.

The circumstances that gave rise to *Khan* have changed; covert surveillance is now governed by the Police Act 1997 and the Regulation of Investigatory Powers Act 2000.

– The Police Act 1997 deals with a limited but very important area of police activity, namely those forms of police surveillance which involve some form of unlawful conduct on the part of the police. Normally, the unlawfulness will involve civil trespass. Section 92 makes such conduct lawful under certain conditions. It does not provide a general scheme to regulate covert surveillance generally. The aims are more limited, namely to protect the police from civil actions on the grounds of civil trespass and the Government from high profile actions in front of the European

Court.[235] There must be some doubt over whether the Act will satisfy the requirements of Art 8, in particular because there is no requirement for prior judicial approval in all cases.

–   The Regulation of Investigatory Powers Act 2000 creates a parallel system of authorisations for undercover investigations which are not unlawful but, although the police would not face domestic civil action, they may be acting in breach of the suspect's right of privacy. To that end, authorisation will be needed for 'directed surveillance', 'intrusive surveillance' and the 'use of covert human intelligence sources'.

3.12   POLICE ACT 1997

Prior to the passage of the above Acts, UK police practices[236] of visual and aural surveillance were in breach of the right to privacy since these practices were regulated only by administrative guidelines which were not clearly formulated nor accessible for citizens. The need for a statutory system of authorisation can be seen in *Klass v Germany*[237] where the European Court acknowledged the significance of the technical advances made in surveillance, as well as the development of terrorism. Although the State must be entitled to counter terrorism with secret surveillance of mail, post and telecommunications under exceptional circumstances, this does not give it the right to adopt whatever measures it thinks it appropriate in the name of counteracting espionage, terrorism or serious crime.

In *Leander v Sweden*,[238] the applicant had been refused permanent employment as museum technician with the Naval Museum on account of certain secret information which allegedly made him a security risk. He contended that the vetting had involved an attack on his reputation and that he should have had the opportunity of defending himself before a tribunal. The European Court held that the gathering of information in a secret police register and its release to the public service, namely the applicant's prospective employer, had not violated Art 8 even though there had been an interference with the applicant's rights under Art 8(1). The Court was, however, satisfied that the Swedish personnel control system had the legitimate aim of protecting national security, and that it was 'in accordance with the law'. The Court's decision was in this case influenced by the involvement of parliamentarians, the Parliamentary Ombudsman and the Parliamentary Committee on Justice in the supervision of the system.

Part III of the Police Act 1997 establishes a system to authorise various methods of covert surveillance. Initially, the Government sought only to formalise the existing system of authorisation by chief officers, but there was considerable

---

235   Justice, *Briefing on the Police Bill 1997* (Justice, 1997).
236   See C Joubert 'Undercover Policing – A Comparative Study' (1994) *European Journal of Crime, Criminal Law and Criminal Justice* 18.
237   (1978) 2 EHRR 214.
238   (1987) 9 EHRR 433.

opposition to this from inside and outside Parliament.[239] The Act still relies on senior police officers to give the initial authority to the investigating officers, and for such authorisations to be retrospectively scrutinised by commissioners appointed under the Act. But, very significantly, where the surveillance is of a private dwelling or office, or involves acquiring knowledge of confidential information of various kinds, it is necessary for the commissioners to give prior approval.

The key argument advanced for judicial oversight of the authorisation procedure was that in a modern democracy, independent judicial scrutiny is required before interference with individual rights, and that such interference should never be left simply to executive authorisation. This argument was put in particular by Lord Browne-Wilkinson:[240]

> 'We have no written constitution. We do not enjoy special constitutional rights against the state. Our freedom depends and depends only, on the fact that no Minister, no administrator and no member of the police has any greater power than any other citizen to enter our property or to seize our person. In particular, the state and its officers have no power to enter our houses or workplaces or to seize our property. Such conduct is unlawful and the administrative action which is apparently being pursued has been ... unlawful conduct on the part of the police.
>
> The basic freedom which we enjoy because the executive does not have power over us has been established by the common law for over 200 years. It is one of the foundations of our freedoms. ... there was only one exception to immunity from police invasion of our privacy; that is, a search warrant granted by an independent court and not by the executive.'

These arguments were echoed both in Parliament[241] and the press. The point was also strongly put that proposals permitting such surveillance simply on the authorisation of a senior police officer were likely to breach the guarantees of human rights contained in the European Convention. The right of the individual to respect for his home, personal privacy and private papers is guaranteed by Art 8. This position was eventually accepted by the Government, although the argument for judicial approval of every authorisation was rejected.

Many jurisdictions possess statutory schemes where the use of listening devices to intercept private conversations can only be on the basis of a judicial warrant. One survey[242] showed that prior judicial authorisation was the norm in Australia, New Zealand, United States, Canada, France and the Netherlands before there could be lawful interception of communications. The survey concluded that such prior authorisation does not prejudice operational effectiveness of the police in combating serious crime because:

---

239 B Emmerson 'Crime and Human Rights' (2000) 150 NLJ 13.
240 *Hansard* (HL) (1997) vol 575, cols 809ff.
241 For example Lord Lester of Herne Hill QC: *Hansard* (HL) (1997) vol 576, cols 220ff.
242 Justice (n 235 above).

–   such scrutiny raises standards by improving the internal screening of applications, ensuring that applications are supported by evidence and are not simply fishing expeditions;
–   it reduces the number of surveillance operations;
–   the authorising judge is able to impose safeguards and conditions.

In the United States, judicial authorisation is required even in the highly sensitive areas of foreign intelligence gathering.[243]

The key section of the Police Act 1997 is s 92, which states:

> 'No entry on or interference with property or with wireless telegraphy shall be unlawful if it is authorised by an authorisation having effect under this Act.'

This section is very broadly drawn; it makes lawful any entry or interference with property where the necessary authorisation has been given under s 93 or s 94. A literal reading of s 92 means that it would be possible to circumvent the procedures either for a search of premises under Part II of PACE 1984 or under the Regulation of Investigatory Powers Act 2000.

There are, however, many constraints:

–   authorisation will normally be given by the chief officer of the force;
–   the criteria for interference with property are reasonably specific;
–   all authorisations will be scrutinised by the commissioners;
–   there are channels for complaint.

If the sheer breadth of s 92 has attracted disapproval, equally important is the criticism that this part of the Act is much too narrowly drafted: what was required was legislation which provided an overall scheme for regulating the use of listening devices and all forms of covert surveillance. New technologies are emerging: the police require a system of authorisation which would legitimise their operations, while individuals require assurance that fundamental freedoms are not being eroded.

Unlike those jurisdictions which require judicial scrutiny of applications, the initial authorisation under s 93 of this Act can be by a senior police or customs officer. The key criteria for authorisations are laid down in s 93(2). The authorisation should be given only where the authorising officer believes that:

–   the action is necessary as it will be of 'substantial value' in the prevention or detection of 'serious crime'; and
–   the objectives of the action cannot reasonably be achieved by other means.

Any belief that the criteria are satisfied is clearly a subjective judgment, but the interpretation does not lie solely within the untrammelled discretion of an authorising officer. If approval were needed for the authorisation, the officer would have to satisfy a commissioner that the belief was held on reasonable grounds.[244] If the officer were appealing against refusal of such approval or the

---

243   Foreign Intelligence Surveillance Act, 50 US 1801ff quoted in Justice (n 235 above).
244   Police Act 1997.

quashing of an authorisation, the Chief Commissioner would also be in a position to evaluate the reasonableness of the decision.[245]

Crime is to be treated as serious by virtue of s 93(4) if:

– it involves the use of violence, results in substantial financial gain or is conducted by a large number of persons in pursuit of a common purpose;[246] or
– it involves the commission of an offence for which a person aged over 21 without previous convictions could reasonably be expected to receive a prison sentence exceeding 3 years.[247]

Accountability is provided by the appointment of commissioners who must hold or have held high judicial office, ie High Court judges or above. They are appointed for a period of 3 years. The Chief Commissioner acts under this Act and under the Regulation of Investigatory Powers Act 2000.

Under s 101 the Secretary of State shall issue a code of practice to regulate the work of the authorising officers. Such a code should lay down the procedures and guidelines to ensure that authorising officers are aware of what is expected of them. As with the PACE codes, a breach of a provision is a factor that the trial judge may take into account in deciding whether the exclude evidence under s 78.

Where proper authorisation is given under the Act, it is possible that the statutory scheme, with its provisions for independent scrutiny by commissioners, may satisfy the requirements of Art 8. The weakness lies in the absence of prior judicial control in all cases. The position under the 1997 Act should be contrasted with the Home Secretary's approval which is for telephone tapping in the Regulation of Investigatory Powers Act 2000. In *Klass v Germany*[248] the European Court felt that it was in principle desirable to entrust the supervisory control to a judge in accordance with the rule of law. However, it also suggested that other safeguards might suffice if they are independent and vested with sufficient powers to exercise an effective and continuous control. A police officer, no matter how senior, cannot be seen as meeting the requisite standards of independence needed to constitute sufficient protection against abuse of authority.

3.13 REGULATION OF INVESTIGATORY POWERS ACT 2000

The Police Act 1997 affected only those surveillance operations which required authorisation under the Act, namely unlawful conduct. Other UK police practices of visual and aural surveillance, lawful under domestic law, did not

---

245 Police Act 1997, s 104(3) and (4).
246 Ibid, s 93(4)(a).
247 Ibid, s 93(4)(b).
248 (1978) 2 EHRR 214.

require statutory authorisation. Until 2000, there was a significant risk that such practices were in breach of the right to privacy since these practices were not regulated even by administrative guidelines until 1999. Even then the regulation consisted of national guidelines recommended by the Association of Chief Police Officers. Even when these were followed, there would have been a strong argument that any evidence gathered by such operations ought to have been excluded as a breach of Art 8. Has this position been remedied by the passage of Part II of the Regulation of Investigatory Powers Act 2000?[249]

The Act applies to directed surveillance, intrusive surveillance and the use of covert human intelligence sources.

–   Directed surveillance is undertaken for the purposes of a specific investigation, and is likely to result in obtaining private information about a person. It does not include situations where the surveillance is an immediate response to events.
–   Intrusive surveillance is carried out on residential premises or in private vehicles and involves either an investigator on the premises or in a vehicle, or the use of a surveillance device. This does not include tracking devices on vehicles, but does include interception of communications where one party consents and there is no interception warrant. A surveillance device not on premises is not intrusive unless it is providing information of the same quality and detail as would have been expected from a device on the premises. TV detector vans are specifically excluded!
–   The use of a covert human intelligence source involves agents establishing a personal relationship to obtain information, which is then covertly disclosed. This is undertaken in such a manner that the person is unaware of the surveillance or its purpose. This covers undercover officers and other informants.[250]

In all these cases, the surveillance is regarded as lawful if an authorisation under the Act is obtained and subsequent actions are in accordance with that authorisation.

For directed surveillance and the use of covert human intelligence sources, the initial authorisation required by s 30 will be by a designated police or customs officer.[251] Authorising officers will be superintendents, although this has to be specified by statutory instrument. The key criteria for authorisations are laid down in s 28(2) and (3) and s 29(2) and (3). The authorisation should be given only where the authorising officer believes that:

–   the action is necessary as it falls within one of the purposes specified in ss 28(3) and 29(3);
–   the surveillance is proportionate to the objectives;

---

249   Part II was brought into force on 25 September 2000 by the Regulation of Investigatory Powers Act 2000 (Commencement No 1 and Transitional Provisions) Order 2000, SI 2000/2543.
250   For these definitions, see s 26 of the Regulation of Investigatory Powers Act 2000.
251   Many other public authorities are included (see ibid, Sch 1).

– (in relation to human intelligence sources) proper supervision and control arrangements exist.[252]

The purposes of directed surveillance or of human intelligence sources must be one of the following: the interests of national security; the prevention and detection of crime and disorder; the economic well-being of the State; public safety; public health; or tax collection.

The authorising officer must believe that the action is necessary, proportionate and relates to one of these objectives. Any belief that the criteria are satisfied is clearly a subjective judgment, but the interpretation does not lie solely within the untrammelled discretion of an authorising officer. Although further approval is not needed for the authorisations under ss 28 and 29 to take effect, it is possible that there would be a complaint to the tribunal established under the Act,[253] in which case the officer would have to satisfy the tribunal members that the belief was held on reasonable grounds.

For intrusive surveillance, the authorisation required by s 32 will be by a senior authorising officer (for the police this will be the Chief Constable of the force).[254] In urgent cases, it will be possible for the operation to be authorised by deputies of parallel rank. Authorisation should be given only where the authorising officer believes that:

– the action is necessary as it falls within one of the purposes specified in ss 28(3) and 29(3), namely the interests of national security, the prevention and detection of serious crime or the interests of the economic well-being of the State;
– the surveillance is proportionate to the objectives.

Crime is to be treated as serious by virtue of s 81(3) if:

– it involves the use of violence, results in substantial financial gain, or is conducted by a large number of persons in pursuit of a common purpose; or
– it involves the commission of an offence for which a person over 21 without previous convictions could reasonably be expected to receive a prison sentence exceeding 3 years.

The authorisation does not take effect, except in cases of urgency, until notice of the intrusive surveillance has been given to a surveillance commissioner and has been approved. The senior authorising officer must believe that the action is necessary, proportionate and relates to one of the above objectives. Any belief that the criteria are satisfied is subjective, but not only within the discretion of an authorising officer. As commissioner approval is needed for an intrusive surveillance authorisation, the officer would have to satisfy a commissioner that

---

252 Regulation of Investigatory Powers Act 2000, s 29(5).
253 Ibid, s 65.
254 For intelligence service operations, the Secretary of State must authorise the action. Elsewhere, as with ss 28 and 29, many other public authorities, as well as the police, will need to use these provisions for their covert operations (see ibid, Sch 1).

the belief was held on reasonable grounds.[255] If the officer were appealing against the quashing of an authorisation, the Chief Commissioner would also use similar criteria to evaluate the reasonableness of the decision.[256]

Accountability is provided by the appointment of commissioners, who must hold or have held high judicial office, ie High Court judges or above.[257] The Chief Commissioner acts under the authority given both by this Act and the Police Act 1997. His functions are to oversee the whole range of surveillance activities undertaken by the police (as well as the intelligence services and Customs) and to report to the Secretary of State annually. Under s 40, the law enforcement agencies are under an obligation to co-operate and supply the Commissioner with relevant information.

The Act also establishes a new tribunal under s 65. The jurisdiction of this body, inter alia, includes complaints by any person who believes that he or she has been subject to use of the investigatory powers under Part II of the Act or under Part III of the Police Act 1997. Membership of the tribunal will consist of senior lawyers.

Under s 71 the Secretary of State shall issue a code of practice to regulate the work of the authorising officers under Part II. Such a code should lay down the procedures and guidelines to ensure that authorising officers are aware of what is expected of them. As with the PACE codes, a breach of a provision is not a criminal offence but a factor that commissioners, tribunal members or the trial judge may take into account in deciding, for example, whether to approve an authorisation or to exclude evidence under s 78.

The Act uses the Police Act 1997 as a blueprint for its scheme. However, for the first time, the whole gamut of police surveillance operations is under a form of statutory oversight. It is possible that the statutory scheme, with its provisions for independent scrutiny by commissioners and recourse to a tribunal, may satisfy the requirements of Art 8. The weakness lies in the absence of prior judicial control in all cases.

Authorisation for directed surveillance and for the use of informants and undercover agents is to be given by superintendents. This merely replicates traditional practice. There are no requirements that authorisations are made in writing, that proper records are kept or that provision is made for independent and external scrutiny, apart from that provided by the Chief Commissioner who will be in no position to evaluate whether these forms of surveillance are being abused in a police area. The scheme appears to ignore or conflict with the principles laid down in *Klass v Germany*[258] where the European Court held, in relation to phone tapping, that:

---

255   Regulation of Investigatory Powers Act 2000, s 37(2).
256   Ibid, s 38(4).
257   Ibid, s 63.
258   (1978) 2 EHRR 214.

- the law should ensure that surveillance is not ordered haphazardly, irregularly or without due and proper care. Although the criteria are clear, there are no controls over the process of authorisation;
- the surveillance must be reviewed and must be accompanied by procedures which guarantee individual rights. This scarcely exists in individual cases except for unlikely and retrospective scrutiny by the commissioners;
- where surveillance is justified under Art 8(2) the failure to inform the individual under surveillance of this fact subsequently is, in principle, justified but, by inference, where the surveillance is not justified, individuals should be informed. The Act ignores this;
- it is in principle desirable to entrust the supervisory control to a judge in accordance with the rule of law, but other safeguards might suffice if they are independent and vested with sufficient powers to exercise an effective and continuous control. A superintendent cannot be seen meeting the requisite standards of independence.

Authorisations for intrusive surveillance are, however, much more satisfactory, and an improvement on the position under the Police Act 1997. Under the 2000 Act, all authorisations for intrusive surveillance have to be approved by a commissioner. There will thus be judicial scrutiny over the whole process, which should guarantee that the authorisations are not made haphazardly, that individual cases are scrutinised to protect individual rights and that there is proper judicial control. Provisions for informing individuals of the surveillance when it turns out not to have been justified are still lacking. These provisions for the regulation of intrusive surveillance, unlike those for other forms of undercover work, should meet the requirements of the Convention.

Chapter 4

THE RIGHT TO A FAIR HEARING

4.1 THE BASICS OF A FAIR HEARING

When a person has been charged with a criminal offence, the key provision of the European Convention on Human Rights (the Convention) affecting pre-trial and trial process is Art 6, which provides for a 'fair and public hearing'. Article 6(1) states:

> 'In the determination of his civil rights and obligations or of any criminal charge against him, everyone is entitled to a fair and public hearing within a reasonable time by an independent and impartial tribunal established by law. Judgment shall be pronounced publicly but the press and public may be excluded from all or part of the trial in the interest of morals, public order or national security in a democratic society, where the interests of juveniles or the protection of the private life of the parties so require, or to the extent strictly necessary in the opinion of the court in special circumstances where publicity would prejudice the interests of justice.'

This is a strong but not an absolute right; everyone is entitled to a fair hearing in front of an independent and impartial court and a reasoned judgment. The hearing should be in public but this element of publicity can be derogated from in certain circumstances, for example for the protection of juveniles or the privacy of the parties. Article 6(1) applies to all proceedings, whereas Art 6(2) and (3) apply only to those charged with criminal offences. Article 6(2) states:

> 'Everyone charged with a criminal offence shall be presumed innocent until proved guilty according to law.'

Article 6(2) embodies the key element of a criminal trial which is the presumption of innocence. In other words, the obligation is on the State to prove each and every element of the offence charged. The accused should not be coerced into providing evidence for the prosecution. This was discussed in the previous chapter in relation to the right to silence, but here it raises issues about the reversal of the burden of proof or the imposition of strict liability as a breach of Art 6. Article 6(3) provides for certain specific rights for defendants:

> 'Everyone charged with a criminal offence has the following minimum rights:
>
> (a) to be informed promptly, in a language which he understands and in detail, of the nature and cause of the accusation against him;
> (b) to have adequate time and facilities for the preparation of his defence;
> (c) to defend himself in person or through legal assistance of his own choosing or, if he has not sufficient means to pay for legal assistance, to be given it free when the interests of justice so require;
> (d) to examine or have examined witnesses against him and to obtain the attendance and examination of witnesses on his behalf under the same conditions as witnesses against him;

(e)   to have the free assistance of an interpreter if he cannot understand or speak the language used in court.'

Although Art 6 is the central text in discussing pre-trial and trial procedure, the fairness of a hearing is not to be judged solely by what takes place within the walls of a courtroom. Events and decisions that occur at the investigation stage necessarily affect what goes on in court and hence the fairness of the hearing. For example, if the State were to lead evidence of a confession which is the result of police coercion or has been made without access to legal advice, this may mean that there has been a breach of Arts 3 or 5. This violation will be relevant to the issue whether in such circumstances a hearing can ever be fair.

Breach of other rights may constitute evidence of unfairness but the ultimate issue is the concept of a 'fair hearing'. This chapter examines the key stages leading up to the trial and the trial itself in order to see the extent to which the common law complies with the requirements of the Convention. Inevitably, this chapter will not cover every aspect, but the European Court of Human Rights (the European Court) has developed the following general themes underlying the concept of a fair hearing which may be applied generally.

–   The key constituents of fairness are the independence and impartiality of the court, the openness of the proceedings and the reasoned decision-making.
–   Article 6 does not impose a standard code of criminal procedure – different legal cultures have different needs and there is a wide margin of appreciation for States to determine their own procedural requirements.
–   The rules of evidence and procedure are a matter for individual States but it remains for the Court to assess their compatibility with the Convention.
–   Admissibility of evidence is a matter of regulation by national law and it is for the national courts to assess the evidence before them. The Court's task is not to give rulings on whether the evidence was properly admitted, but whether the proceedings, taken as a whole, were fair.
–   It is not simply a matter of whether a substantive rule is compatible and whether the trial judge has addressed the correct issue. The Court examines all the material before it and comes to a conclusion as to 'fairness', even where the domestic tribunal has addressed the same issue with, perhaps, the opposite result.
–   The fairness of a hearing can be explored only by looking at the process as a whole. Although the State has infringed some right of the defendant, that does not automatically mean that the cumulative effect of the hearing is unfair.[1]
–   The applicant should show that he or she has suffered actual detriment as a result of the infringement.
–   Although Art 6 concerns itself with the rights of the accused, victims and witnesses may well have rights that also need to be protected, and the Court may have to balance competing rights.

---

1   *Barberà, Messegué and Jabardo v Spain* (1988) 11 EHRR 360.

– Crucially, the Court judges the fairness of a hearing by the test of 'equality of arms', ie that the defendant is put, so far as is possible, on the same level in terms of access to legal advice, to information or to services. The State should not abuse its dominant position so as to gain a substantial advantage vis-à-vis the accused.

4.2 COMMON LAW AND CIVIL LAW

Article 6 reflects nothing so much as the Anglo-American common law trial with its adversarial nature, the predominance given to the day in court, the priority to oral testimony given by witnesses physically present in court, and the opportunities for examination, cross-examination and argument by the State and the defendant. This concentration on a single hearing has its strengths, particularly its public nature, the symbolic balance and apparent equality of arms between the accused and the State. There is also the clear separation not merely between prosecution and judge, but also between the functions of the judge as trier of law and the jury as trier of fact. But weaknesses also emerge from the self-contained, single hearing. Prosecutions and defences may founder by the failure of witnesses to appear or to come up to proof, and juries are under pressure to assimilate and assess complex narratives within a short space of time. Speed and fairness are rarely allies.

Civil law jurisdictions are structurally very different and the day in court is less pivotal. The trial judge in a French criminal trial will have a full *dossier* prepared by the *juge d'instruction*, who may well have conducted several hearings, taken relevant witness statements and interrogated the defendant. The trial will be on the basis of these documents and is merely the final stage of a judicial process which, to common law eyes, inevitably seems less public and where there is a significant link between the State through the prosecution, on the one hand, and the judiciary, on the other.[2] A further significant difference is that the adversarial mode of trial possesses a sophisticated jurisprudence on the rules of evidence. The investigative mode of trial, often without a lay jury or with jurors in consultation with the judge, places less emphasis on formal rules of proof.

It is the common law, rather than the law of civilian jurisdictions, that resonates through Art 6. It is not hard to find echoes of the due process requirements of Anglo-American law. For example, when para (3)(d) guarantees the right to cross-examine witnesses, this represents the right of confrontation which underlies the adversarial process. But as the Court has never sought to impose a standard code of criminal procedure, it is not irreconcilable that the common law prohibits the prosecution introducing evidence of the accused's previous convictions, whereas many civil law jurisdictions make widespread use of these.[3] Equally, it is not necessarily a breach of Art 6 for a State to allow a conviction to

---

2   New reforms for the French system are in the pipeline: see A West 'Reform of French Criminal Justice' (2000) 150 NLJ 1542.

3   *X v Austria* Application No 2676/65, (1967) 23 CD 31; see a summary of such practices in S Uglow *Evidence* (Sweet & Maxwell, 1997), p 408.

be based wholly on circumstantial evidence,[4] a practice which would be eschewed by others.

The jurisprudence reveals a process of refining State systems of criminal justice in order that they comply with the underlying principle of fairness. This concept is not to be interpreted legalistically. Even when all the general and specific guarantees of Art 6 have been met, the Court may still regard the proceedings as unfair. The results may seem bewildering. In *Teixeira de Castro v Portugal*[5] the police incited criminal activity which might not otherwise have taken place and irremediably affected the fairness of the proceedings. In *Khan v UK*[6] the police fundamentally breached the applicant's right to privacy to gather evidence, and yet this did not affect the fairness of the subsequent proceedings.

Eschewing legalism in favour of a principle-led approach is commendable, but it may mean that too many decisions stand on their own facts and fail to provide a clear guide. Perhaps judges often express belief or disbelief in the 'fairness of the proceedings' without giving reasons for such an assessment. At its worst, 'fairness' may be reduced to subjective, not to say metaphysical, values.

4.3   FAIRNESS AND THE COMMON LAW

UK judges would claim, probably rightly, that the major characteristic of the common law trial is the priority given to procedural fairness. They may well contend that national safeguards go further than the rights guaranteed by Art 6. A fight model requires rules of engagement which are necessarily based on the idea of fairness. The root values of procedural justice are encapsulated in the House of Lords' decision in *Woolmington v DPP*[7] when Lord Sankey said:

> 'Throughout the web of English criminal law one golden thread is always to be seen that it is the duty of the prosecution to prove the prisoner's guilt. . . . If, at the end of and on the whole of the case, there is a reasonable doubt, created by the evidence given by either the prosecution or the prisoner, as to whether the prisoner killed the deceased with a malicious intention, the prosecution has not made out the case and the prisoner is entitled to an acquittal. No matter what the charge or where the trial, the principle that the prosecution must prove the guilt of the prisoner is part of the common law of England and no attempt to whittle it down can be entertained.'[8]

Lord Sankey's 'golden thread' of justice is that the prosecution has to prove every element in a criminal charge beyond reasonable doubt. The defendant has to prove nothing. Other judges have voiced a wider principle, 'it must be a fundamental principle in all British criminal jurisdictions that the court is under the duty to ensure the accused a fair trial'.[9] Such ideas take precedence

---

4   *Alberti v Italy* Application No 12013/86, (1989) 59 DR 100.
5   (1998) 28 EHRR 101.
6   Application No 35394/97, [2000] Crim LR 684.
7   [1935] AC 462.
8   Ibid at 481.
9   *R v Sang* [1979] 2 All ER 1222 at 1248c, per Lord Scarman.

over the justice of the decision itself and over more pragmatic aims such as the determination of truth or law enforcement.[10] Fair procedure in common law criminal proceedings reflects the same elements as are specified in Art 6, such as the right to legal advice, the right to be brought to public trial in a neutral forum within a reasonable time, the presumption of innocence or the right to cross-examine and test the prosecution evidence. Ultimately, however, the Court of Appeal does have the power to reject an appeal if it considers that the conviction is 'safe' even where there is a significant procedural or evidential irregularity in the trial.[11]

Although common law judges have professed adherence to the concept of a fair trial, in the past they have avoided some unfortunate consequences by a narrow interpretation of the boundaries of the trial, preferring to consider only the proceedings in court. Thus, they have been able to consider merely the reliability and probative value of the evidence rather than its provenance and how that might affect the issue of fairness. The judge's power to exclude relevant, probative and otherwise admissible evidence was very limited. In *Jeffery v Black*,[12] two drugs squad officers arrested the accused for the theft of a sandwich in a pub. Having charged him with that offence, they took him to his rooms which they searched illegally, without his consent and without a warrant, discovering cannabis. The Divisional Court was willing to admit the evidence of finding the drugs, not considering that this abuse of authority made the proceedings unfair. In *R v Sang*,[13] the House of Lords was equally unwilling to take a broad view towards 'fairness of the proceedings'. The issue was whether the judge had a common law discretion to exclude evidence which was both relevant and probative but where the offence was instigated by an agent provocateur acting on the instructions of the police. The function of the judge is to ensure that the accused has a fair trial, and it is no part of that function to exercise disciplinary powers over police or prosecution as the defendant has available other civil and disciplinary remedies.

The common law was significantly affected by the passage of s 78 of the Police and Criminal Evidence Act 1984 (PACE 1984) which allowed a judge to exclude evidence:

> '... if it appears to the court that, having regard to all the circumstances, including the circumstances in which the evidence was obtained, the admission of the evidence would have such an adverse effect on the fairness of the proceedings that the court ought not to admit it ...'

This provision has meant that judges have taken a broader view of 'proceedings' and, for example, laid down guidelines for police entrapment operations.[14] In any case where the admissibility of evidence is disputed, the judge must address the issue of the fairness of the proceedings.

10 J Frank *Courts on Trial* (Princeton, 1973), pp 103–104.
11 Section 2 of the Criminal Appeal Act 1995, replacing the proviso in s 2(1) of the Criminal Appeal Act 1968; see J Smith 'The Criminal Appeal Act 1995' [1995] Crim LR 920.
12 [1978] 1 All ER 555.
13 [1979] 2 All ER 1222.
14 *R v Smurthwaite and Gill* [1994] 1 All ER 898.

Furthermore, the common law's doctrine of 'abuse of process' has recently developed to embrace a wider notion of fairness than was present in the old doctrines of *autrefois convict* or *autrefois acquit*.[15] 'Abuse of process' allows any court to stay proceedings either on the grounds that it will be impossible (usually by reason of delay) to give the accused a fair trial or because it offends the court's sense of justice and propriety to be asked to try the accused in the circumstances of a particular case.[16] Stays of prosecution have resulted from abuse of extradition procedures,[17] from reneging on pre-trial agreements between the prosecution and defence,[18] from double jeopardy,[19] and from undue delay or publicity.

Although the common law's regulation of its own procedures has by and large worked, the Human Rights Act 1998 will still have a part to play in refining the requirements of fairness. Concerns about courts-martial have been voiced by the European Court in *Findlay v UK*[20] and *Coyne v UK*.[21] The Court has also held that to try a young child, albeit for a serious offence, in an adult court and in the full glare of publicity, is a breach of Art 6.[22] The children did not have a fair trial since they were unable to understand and participate effectively in the proceedings due to their young age, the nature of the proceedings and the traumatising effect of those proceedings. Fairness requires that trial procedures for young children be modified to take their best interests as a primary consideration.

4.4   SCOPE OF ART 6

The specific guarantees of Art 6(2) and (3) apply when there has been a 'criminal charge'. Whether the proceedings are criminal depends initially on the classification of the law by the State, although this is not definitive. The European Court will also look to the nature of the offence and the possible sanction that may be imposed. The requirement of a fair hearing applies even though the proceedings may be formally classified as disciplinary or regulatory.[23] Thus courts martial[24] are subject to the requirements of Art 6. Prison disciplinary proceedings must also comply in so far as this is practical – such hearings do not have to be public.[25] The Court maintains a distinction between a disciplinary charge and a criminal charge.[26] The seriousness of the charges and the nature and degree of severity of the penalty must be considered,

---

15   *R v Errington* (1861) 1 B&S 688; see *R v Beedie* [1997] 3 WLR 758.
16   *R v Horseferry Road Magistrates' Court ex parte Bennett* [1994] 1 AC 42 at 74, per Lord Lowry. See also *R v Beckford* [1996] 1 Cr App R 94 at 102, per Neill LJ.
17   *R v Horseferry Road Magistrates' Court ex parte Bennett* [1994] 1 AC 42.
18   *R v Croydon Justices ex parte Dean* (1994) 98 Cr App R 76.
19   *R v Beedie* [1997] 3 WLR 758.
20   (1997) 24 EHRR 221.
21   (1997) *The Times*, October 24.
22   *T and V v UK* [2000] 2 All ER 1024, (1999) 30 EHRR 121.
23   *Engel v The Netherlands* (1976) 1 EHRR 706.
24   *Findlay v UK* (1997) 24 EHRR 221; *Coyne v UK* (1997) *The Times*, October 24.
25   *Campbell and Fell v UK* (1984) 7 EHRR 165; but see *Riepan v Austria* [2001] Crim LR 230.
26   *McFeeley v UK* (1980) 3 EHRR 161.

especially the possibility of imprisonment[27] as a sanction in such cases. Regulatory offences, such as road traffic crimes, would also come under the article's provisions, even when these are not classified as crime by the State.[28]

In *Benham v UK*[29] the applicant was brought before a magistrates' court for culpable non-payment of the community charge, a form of local taxation. In the absence of legal representation, he was imprisoned for 30 days. He claimed, inter alia, that this was a breach of Art 6(3)(c). For this to be the case, the proceedings had to be criminal, although in national law they were classified as civil. However, the domestic classification was only one element – the nature of the proceedings carried more weight. In this connection, the European Court noted that the law concerning liability to pay the community charge and the procedure upon non-payment was of general application to all citizens, and that the proceedings in question were brought by a public authority under statutory powers of enforcement. In addition, the proceedings had some punitive elements. For example, the magistrates could only exercise their power of committal to prison on a finding of wilful refusal to pay or of culpable neglect. Finally, the applicant faced a relatively severe maximum penalty of 3 months' imprisonment, and the Court concluded that Mr Benham was 'charged with a criminal offence' for the purposes of Art 6.

The safeguards provided by Art 6 apply from the moment a person is subject to a criminal charge, and cover the whole of the proceedings, including any appeals. The moment when a person is 'subject to a criminal charge' is the point at which there is notification by a person in authority to the suspect that he or she has committed a criminal offence. This is a substantive, not a formal, matter. In England, arrest or charge by the police would constitute such notification, as would the receipt of a summons to attend a magistrates' court. It is the point at which a person is substantially affected by the allegations.

During an investigation, these safeguards do not apply. Police conduct at this stage – for example, evidence gathered during police covert surveillance – can clearly affect the course of a trial and must be taken into account in assessing the fairness of those proceedings.

4.5   THE TRIAL FORUM

There are many aspects of a fair hearing which are characteristics of the forum in which the trial is held. The forum must be an 'independent and impartial tribunal established by law', access to that court, a public hearing, held within a reasonable time, in the presence of the accused, who will have an opportunity to present his or her case. Finally, there should be a reasoned judgment publicly pronounced.

---

27   In *Campbell and Fell v UK* (1984) 7 EHRR 165, this was loss of remission.
28   *Ozturk v FRG* (1984) 7 EHRR 251.
29   (1996) 22 EHRR 293.

4.5.1 An 'independent and impartial tribunal'

In determining whether a judge is independent, the criteria taken into account by the European Court are the manner of appointment, the length of tenure, the existence of guarantees against outside pressure and whether the tribunal has the appearance of being independent.[30] The court must be an 'independent and impartial tribunal established by law'. In *Lauko and Kadubec v Slovakia*[31] the accused were prosecuted and punished by a local administrative office for public order offences. The European Court held, first, that the characterisation of an offence as 'criminal' under Art 6 is not simply a matter for domestic law. Here the penalty showed that the offences were criminal in nature. Furthermore, the office could not be seen as independent of the executive within the meaning of Art 6. Administrative bodies could adjudicate but there had to be an opportunity to challenge before an independent and impartial tribunal. Here there was no opportunity for review.

In *Campbell and Fell v UK*[32] the board of visitors was held to be an independent tribunal since its members were, in practice, irremovable and acted independently in their adjudicatory functions. Members of boards of visitors are appointed by the Home Secretary for a 3-year term. However, hearings by boards of visitors were held in private, in the prison and in a coercive environment in which it may have been difficult to exercise independent judgment, and to the prisoner scarcely presented the appearance of independence. In the early 1990s, members of boards of visitors ceased to exercise disciplinary functions, which are now exercised by prison governors; there may well be greater problems viewing such hearings as 'independent and impartial'. Perhaps the appropriate parallel is with courts-martial, where the convening officer appointed the prosecutor and members of the panel, all of whom were subordinate to him.[33] More recently,[34] the Permanent Presidents of Courts-Martial were held to be sufficiently independent of the ordinary chain of military command and did not infringe the right to an independent and impartial hearing.

Hearings within prisons may represent the minimum threshold of independence. If so, normal hearings by circuit or High Court judges sitting in the Crown Court or by appellate judges easily satisfy this requirement. The latter two categories are appointed by the Crown on the recommendation of the Lord Chancellor, and their term of office is determined by age and proper behaviour. They can be removed only by an address presented to the monarch by both Houses of Parliament.[35] The circuit judge's position differs since he or she can be removed by the Lord Chancellor on the ground of incapacity or misbehaviour,[36] but independence is ensured in the sense that he or she cannot be sacked by the State for making politically inconvenient decisions. The State

---

30   *Campbell and Fell v UK* (1984) 7 EHRR 165.
31   [1998] HRCD 838.
32   (1984) 7 EHRR 165.
33   *Findlay v UK* (1997) 24 EHRR 221.
34   *R v Spear and Hastie; R v Boyd* [2001] Crim LR 485.
35   Supreme Court Act 1925.
36   Courts Act 1971.

can only interfere with this independence by passing legislation; thus, the Criminal Justice Act 1991 compels the sentencing judge to adopt particular principles before arriving at an appropriate sentence.

Deputy circuit judges, recorders and assistant recorders sit in the Crown Courts and are appointed by the Lord Chancellor for fixed periods. There is always the risk that an appointment might not be renewed for political reasons rather than for reasons of judicial ability. In Scotland this issue has already been addressed. Legislation was introduced in 2000 which proposed abolishing the office of temporary sheriff following *Starrs v Ruxton; Ruxton v Starrs*[37] where the High Court ruled that temporary sheriffs were not an independent and impartial tribunal in terms of Art 6 of the Convention and, hence, their use was incompatible with the Convention. In England, the Lord Chancellor has ruled that part-time appointments will be for a period of no fewer than 5 years. Removal from office can only be on one of five specified grounds and requires the assent of the Lord Chief Justice. This meets the principal objection that a probationary period of uncertain length, renewable by the executive, could not be regarded as independent.[38]

A similar problem may exist with magistrates. A justice of the peace (JP) is appointed for life or until the retiring age of 70. At that age a justice is put on a 'supplemental list' and no longer sits. Younger JPs can be also be put on the list by the Lord Chancellor for reasons of infirmity or incapacity.[39] This protects tenure and independence. However, the Lord Chancellor also has the power to remove a JP from the list altogether[40] without investigation and for any reason. The usual reason for removal is conviction for some criminal offence. However, a statutory power which allows the executive summarily to remove a magistrate must create question marks over the tribunal being seen as independent.

There are no direct pressures by the State aimed at influencing the outcome of a case. However, one factor which questions the court's independence is the vetting of jurors by the police and the security services. This is an honoured tradition[41] for the British State, but one which caused controversy in the 1970s and 1980s.[42] The issue was addressed by the Attorney-General in 1988 when a revised set of guidelines was published,[43] in which the Attorney-General reiterated the principle of random selection, and that only ineligible or disqualified jurors should be excluded. In cases of terrorists and national security, jurors' names will be checked at the Criminal Records Office (CRO), against Special Branch records and through local investigation. Such authorised checks require the personal authority of the Attorney-General acting on the advice of the Director of Public Prosecutions (DPP). CRO checks may be carried out in any case and, in an annex to the guidelines, the Attorney-General specified such cases as follows: where there is reason to believe that a juror is

---

37   2000 JC 208.
38   (2000) NLJ 568.
39   Justices of the Peace Act 1997, s 7(4).
40   Ibid, s 5.
41   EP Thompson 'The State versus its enemies' *New Society*, 19 October 1978.
42   *R v Sheffield Crown Court ex parte Brownlow* [1980] QB 530; *R v Mason* [1981] QB 881.
43   *Practice Note* [1988] 3 All ER 1086; the earlier version is in [1980] 3 All ER 785.

disqualified; where there has been an attempt to interfere with a juror in a prior and related trial; and where the DPP or Chief Constable considers it important that no disqualified person serves on this particular jury. However, random, and apparently routine, sample checks still continue. Since the essence of any check is its secrecy, and since the information is passed only to prosecution counsel, there is considerable capacity for the manipulation of the jury, which is a clear abuse of due process.

The vetting of juries calls into question both the independence and impartiality of the tribunal. Extraneous circumstances may also affect that impartiality and therefore the fairness of the hearing. Comment on a pending case and excessive pre-trial publicity may cause prejudice and undermine the presumption of innocence enshrined in Art 6. Press comment on cases which attract considerable public interest is inevitable, but at common law a judge may stay proceedings where that comment affects the fairness of the trial and a conviction may be quashed on this ground.[44] Where the trial takes place without a jury, the Commission is less likely to consider that there has been a violation of Art 6 since judges are unlikely to be affected by the publicity. Lay jurors are more vulnerable to press campaigns and, without a clear warning by the judge to ignore press comment, the possibility of a fair trial may well be prejudiced.[45]

Jurors and magistrates may be biased. The test is not one of actual bias but of apparent bias. This may be a ground for quashing the conviction if a reasonable person would consider that there was a real danger of bias on the part of the trier of fact.[46] The European Court applies a similar test, but one which would appear to place a heavy burden of proof on the applicant to displace the presumption that a tribunal has acted impartially. In *Pullar v UK*,[47] one of the jurors was an employee of the main prosecution witness and knew another of the prosecution witnesses, yet the Court held that the risk of bias was not objectively justified. The same outcome occurred in *Gregory v UK*[48] where the judge received a note from a juror suggesting that some of the jurors were racially prejudiced. The judge investigated the matter and gave a clear direction to the jury on the issue and no violation occurred. However, in *Sanders v UK*,[49] an identical situation occurred. All the jurors signed a note saying that the allegations were unfounded and the juror involved wrote admitting that he had made jokes about Asians. By a majority of 5–4 the Court found a breach. All the judges of the Court felt that subjective bias had not been established, but the majority considered that the allegations were capable of causing any objective observer legitimate doubts as to the impartiality of the court and were not prepared to place much weight on the judge's new direction to the jury.

44   *R v Taylor* (1993) 98 Cr App R 361.
45   *Allenet de Ribemot v France* (1995) 20 EHRR 557.
46   *R v Gough* [1993] 2 All ER 724.
47   (1996) 22 EHRR 39.
48   (1997) 25 EHRR 57.
49   Application No 34129/96, [2000] Crim LR 767.

A judge may appear biased through excessive interruptions of counsel or comment on the facts of the case adverse to the defendant during the summing up. This may lead to the quashing of a conviction if the summing up is fundamentally unbalanced.[50] Similarly, the right to a fair trial under Art 6 will be violated if the judge is not balanced, fair and accurate. Yet even when a judge has indicated his belief in the guilt of the accused, the European Commission has declared the application inadmissible as the trial taken as a whole was not unfair.[51] In practice, no application has succeeded on the ground that the judge gave the appearance of bias. The domestic law appears as stringent, if not more so, in this regard than the European Court. For example, if the summing up has been, as a whole, unfair, the repetition by the judge of the standard directions on burden of proof and that matters of fact are for the jury will not redeem matters.[52]

4.5.2 Access to a court

The right of access constitutes an element which is inherent in the right stated by Art 6(1). In *Golder v UK*,[53] a convicted prisoner was refused leave by the Home Secretary to write to his solicitor about instituting civil proceedings against a prison officer. The European Court held that he had been hindered in his access to the courts. This right of access normally concerns civil actions, but in criminal proceedings it is a basic right that ensures that an accused is brought before a court to answer charges. For most defendants, the problem is being brought before a court, not the opposite. But the police and the Crown Prosecution Service possess a discretion not to prosecute. Is a decision by either not to press charges or to discontinue an action once commenced a denial of access? The 'right to a court', which is a constituent element of the right to a fair trial, is no more absolute in criminal than in civil matters. It is subject to implied limitations, two examples of which are the decision not to prosecute and an order for discontinuance of the proceedings; in neither case could the accused argue that he or she had been denied a right to a hearing.[54]

The practice in English courts is to accept guilty pleas in a large majority of cases. This is not possible in jurisdictions such as France. In England around 94% of defendants in magistrates' courts plead guilty, and about 75% in crown courts. In effect, there is no substantive hearing before a judge as to guilt or innocence, but, provided the judge is satisfied that the accused understands the nature and effect of the plea, this is in compliance with Art 6.[55] There are also pre-trial agreements between the prosecution and defence which are often termed plea bargains.[56] Reneging on such agreements may well lead to a stay of

---

50   *R v Marr* (1989) 90 Cr App R 154; *R v Berrada* (1989) 91 Cr App R 131.
51   *X v UK* Application No 4991/71, (1973) 45 CD 1.
52   *R v Wood* [1996] 1 Cr App R 207.
53   (1975) 1 EHRR 524.
54   *Deweer v Belgium* (1980) 2 EHRR 439, para 49; *X v UK* (1981) 3 EHRR 271; *X v Austria* Application No 7950/77 (1980).
55   *X v UK* Application No 5076/71, (1972) 40 CD 64.
56   Regulated by the Court of Appeal in *R v Turner* [1970] 2 All ER 281.

proceedings on the grounds of abuse of process at common law.[57] This may not be the case under the Convention: in *Colak v FRG*[58] there was an informal and disputed conversation between one member of the tribunal and the defence that a lesser charge may be preferred. The European Court held that failing to act on such informal out-of-court statements does not render a hearing unfair. However, this is not conclusive: following *X v UK*[59] improper pressure to plead guilty may be contrary to Art 6(2). The pressure to plead guilty may come from one's counsel or from the realisation that the reduction in the seriousness of the charges will lead to a significant lowering of sentence. A later change of heart by a defendant who has accepted a plea bargain may well fall foul of Art 6, and the Court of Appeal may need to ensure that these agreements are brought out in open court and that the accused realises the significance of his decision.[60]

If a plea bargain may breach fair trial safeguards for the defendant, it may also affect the rights of the victim. The Court of Appeal recently held that where prosecuting counsel had been involved in reaching a plea bargain with the defendant allowing him to avoid a custodial sentence, it would be an abuse to allow the Attorney-General subsequently to reopen the sentence to the potential detriment of that defendant.[61] In that case the victims of sexual assault by a headmaster (a person in a position of trust) saw the defendant receive a suspended sentence for serious assaults. They may argue that the State had denied them an adequate and effective remedy against treatment that was degrading within the meaning of Art 3. There is an analogy here with *A v UK*[62] where a stepfather had been acquitted of assaulting a stepchild by using the defence of reasonable chastisement. The European Court held that children and other vulnerable individuals were entitled to State protection in the form of effective deterrence against serious breaches of personal integrity. By permitting the defence of reasonable chastisement, in the Court's view the law had not provided adequate protection against treatment or punishment contrary to Art 3. Such a case, unlike a plea bargain, involves a full acquittal of the defendant, but it may be argued that, in upholding the terms of a plea bargain, a court must balance the rights of the victim with those of the defendant. The current informal system has major benefits, but requires formal supervision by the judge as recommended by the Royal Commission on Criminal Justice.[63] Until this occurs, there is a risk for defendants that the bargain might be struck down as an inadequate remedy under Art 13.

Access to a court does not guarantee a right to an appeal. In *Monnell and Morris v UK*[64] the case concerned loss of time orders made on prisoners who

---

57   *R v Croydon Justices ex parte Dean* (1994) 98 Cr App Rep 76.

58   (1988) 11 EHRR 513.

59   Application No 5076/71, 40 CD 64 (1972).

60   For further discussion see P Darbyshire 'The Mischief of Plea Bargaining' [2000] Crim LR 895, esp at 908.

61   *Attorney-General's Reference (No 44 of 2000); sub nom R v Peverett* [2000] TLR 739.

62   (1998) 27 EHRR 611, [1998] 2 FLR 959.

63   Cm 2263 (1993), paras 7.48ff.

64   (1987) 10 EHRR 205.

unsuccessfully and vexatiously applied for leave to appeal and argued that there should have been a full rehearing at which they should have been present. Although Art 6 does not guarantee a right of appeal, where such mechanisms are in place, the requirements for a fair hearing continue to apply.

4.5.3 Public hearing[65]

Article 6(1) provides that 'everyone is entitled to a ... public hearing within a reasonable time'. The hearing does not have to be advertised – it is sufficient that the public and press are not excluded.[66] There are exceptions, including the interests of morals, public order, national security and the welfare of juveniles. Youth courts may have restricted access, as may prison disciplinary hearings,[67] without infringing Art 6. Similarly, at common law, it is also possible to hear evidence *in camera* on the grounds of national security or to protect the identity of a witness. In *X v Austria*[68] the European Court upheld the exclusion of the public at the trial of a person accused of sexual offences. The screening of a witness from the accused and from the public was justified in the case of a terrorist trial.[69]

In *T v UK*[70] the European Court considered the impact of a public trial on young defendants. The case involved the murder of an even younger child and generated massive publicity. Some limited special measures were taken, but these scarcely dented the formality and ritual of the Crown Court. Indeed, raising the floor level of the dock increased the defendants' discomfort as they felt exposed to the scrutiny of the press and the public. In such circumstances it was concluded that they had been denied a fair hearing. The judgment suggests that our trial procedures for young children charged with very serious offences be modified to take their best interests as a primary consideration.

4.5.4 Delay

Everyone charged with an offence is entitled to a hearing 'within a reasonable time'. The time-limits are naturally much longer than the initial need to bring an accused before a court 'promptly' as specified in Art 5(3). Although these latter provisions overlap with Art 6 in imposing a duty on the State to exercise special diligence in the course of investigation and bringing to trial, obligations under Art 5 cease once a person is convicted. Where a convicted person or prisoner is seeking to appeal, the 'reasonable time' requirement under Art 6 is the only protection.

These limits rarely trouble the common law, which has always prided itself on the speed with which it brings matters to a conclusion. However, in one

---

65 Anonymity of witnesses is discussed at **4.10** below.
66 *X v UK* Application No 8512/79, 2 *Digest* 444 (1979).
67 *Campbell and Fell v UK* (1984) 7 EHRR 165.
68 Application No 1913/63, 2 *Digest* 438 (1965); see also *X v UK* (1992) 15 EHRR CD 113 in the case of a terrorist trial.
69 *X v UK*, ibid, in the case of a terrorist trial. This is discussed further at **4.10** below.
70 [2000] 2 All ER 1024, (2000) 30 EHRR 121.

domestic case, *X v UK*,[71] a period approaching 5 years was held not to exceed the boundaries of reasonableness. The average time taken from offence to completion for defendants in indictable offences in magistrates' courts in 1998 was 127 days. In Crown Courts the average time between date of committal and the start of the hearing was 9.9 weeks for defendants who pleaded not guilty, and 18.4 weeks for those who pleaded guilty. The limits introduced by the Prosecution of Offences Act 1985 which regulate the time spent in custody before trial are certainly within these requirements. A breach of those limits so that a defendant is kept in custody, perhaps in error, might lead to the suggestion that the defence has been thereby impaired and that this is in breach of the requirement for a 'fair hearing'.

Excessive procedural delay is more of a problem with civilian jurisdictions than at common law and a significant proportion of cases before the European Court concerns this issue. A person is entitled to a public hearing within a reasonable time, a period which starts when the accused is charged, and finishes when there has been a conviction or acquittal. Reasonableness must be judged on the complexity of the issues, the conduct of the defendant and whether charges are pending or there are valid reasons for delay.[72] In *Howarth v UK*[73] the Court, in finding a violation of Art 6, held that an assessment of the reasonableness of the delay should include an assessment of the conduct of the case authorities. The requirement also affects appeals. In *B v Austria*,[74] there was almost a 3-year delay between the hearing of an appeal by a person held in prison and the judgment. In *Portington v Greece*,[75] a British subject convicted of murder waited 8 years between the start of the appeal and its conclusion, a delay which was seen as inexcusable by the European Court.

4.5.5   Presence and participation

Article 6 does not specifically provide for a hearing in the presence of the accused. This can be implied from the requirement of a public hearing, the right to defend oneself in person in Art 6(3)(c) and the right to examine and cross-examine witnesses in Art 6(3)(d). In *Colozza v Italy*[76] the defendant was accused of fraud, but the prosecutors were unable to locate him, although there was some evidence that the police knew his address. Despite this, he was sentenced to 6 years' imprisonment. This was a breach of a fair hearing. A person charged with a criminal offence should be entitled to be present at the trial, although this is not an absolute right and may be waived. Trial *in absentia* may be permitted where the State has acted diligently to ensure the presence of the accused.

At common law, the House of Lords has held that it is unacceptable to hold a trial in the absence of the accused, and this includes situations where a significant amount of argument takes place between counsel in judges'

---

71   (1981) 3 EHRR 271.
72   *Portington v Greece* [1998] HRCD 856.
73   (2001) 31 EHRR 37.
74   (1990) 13 EHRR 20.
75   [1998] HRCD 856.
76   (1985) 7 EHRR 516.

chambers in the absence of the defendant and the solicitors.[77] However, trials take place *in absentia* where the accused has absconded, created a disturbance or is absent through illness.[78] These exceptional circumstances comply with the approach taken by the Court in *Colozza* (above).

The accused must be able to participate effectively in the conduct of the case, not simply procedurally but also by the provision of a suitable courtroom with proper facilities and good acoustics. In *Stanford v UK*[79] the complainant argued that there was a breach of Art 6 because the placing of a screen in the courtroom between himself and the witnesses made it difficult to hear and follow proceedings. This was rejected. Although the screen had reduced the level of sound, speech was intelligible to a person of normal hearing standing in the dock, and the complainant had had full legal representation by solicitor and counsel who had not drawn this matter to the judge's attention at any time during the 6-day hearing.

In *T v UK*[80] the European Court considered the problems for the young defendants in understanding what was going on, comprehending the course of the proceedings and contributing to their defence. The format of the public and publicised trial hindered this. Although the youngsters were represented by experienced counsel within 'whispering distance', the Court said that it was:

> 'highly unlikely that either applicant would have felt sufficiently uninhibited. . . . to have consulted with them [their lawyers] during the trial or, indeed, given their immaturity and disturbed emotional state, they would have been capable outside the court room of co-operating with their lawyers and giving them information for the purposes of their defence.'

In reforming trial procedures for young children, the courtroom setting must facilitate their meaningful participation.

Disruptive defendants can be handcuffed or even gagged. The handcuffing of a defendant is permitted in domestic law exceptionally where there is a danger of escape or violence,[81] although this might hinder note-taking and participation. Unjustified use of restraints such as handcuffs can breach Art 5 rights and constitute degrading treatment under Art 3.[82] Furthermore, it may be argued that appearing in court under restraint will lead to certain assumptions by the jury (eg that the defendant is violent and dangerous). This may be seen as violating the presumption of innocence and prejudicing a fair trial.[83] Other security measures (searching members of the public, armed police in court) will not necessarily infringe the right to a fair hearing if they are justified by the circumstances of the offence.[84]

---

77 *R v Preston* [1994] 2 AC 130.
78 *R v Lee Kun* [1916] 1 KB 337.
79 (1994) Series A/182-A.
80 [2000] 2 All ER 1024, (2000) 30 EHRR 121.
81 *R v Vratsides* [1988] Crim LR 251.
82 *Kaj Raninen v Finland* (1997) 26 EHRR 563.
83 *Welch v UK* (1995) 20 EHRR 247 in which it was argued that handcuffs during trial infringed Art 6 rights but this was declared inadmissible by the Commission.
84 *X v FRG* 14 DR 62.

There is no such right to a hearing in one's presence with regard to appeal proceedings, although there must be the opportunity to make written representations and to be legally represented.[85]

4.5.6   Reasoned judgments

A necessary element of a fair hearing is that the court explains its reasons for a decision. A reasoned judgment gives a basis on which the right to appeal may be exercised, and although a judge need not cover every point, the judgment should deal in detail with any issues that would be decisive for the outcome of the case. Such a judgment should be pronounced publicly.

In first instance courts in England this can be a problem. Magistrates do not give reasons for decisions, but the system allows either for a re-hearing of the case before a Crown Court judge with two magistrates, or appeal on a point of law by way of 'case stated' to the Divisional Court. This latter procedure requires the magistrates' court to state the charges and the facts of the case as found by the magistrates. These appeal processes may subsume any difficulty caused by a verdict without reasons. However, there are other decisions in magistrates' courts where reasons are necessary, such as bail hearings. Without reasons it is difficult to decide whether there has been a violation of the Convention.[86] This presents problems for magistrates who rarely give fully reasoned decisions in the court record – indeed, there is a pro forma decision sheet. Again, practices will need to change.

In the Crown Court, a jury gives a general verdict of 'guilty' or 'not guilty'. No reasons are attached. Jury trials are clearly not contrary to the Convention, but this absence creates problems for the sentencing judge when there are alternative factual bases for the verdict, which is resolved by an adversarial fact-finding hearing. However, appellate courts can also be left speculating on the weight that a jury attached to an item of evidence.[87] Thus, the line becomes very fine between the appellate task of applying the law to given facts and that of deciding the facts. Indeed, s 2 of the Criminal Appeal Act 1995 requires the court only to consider the question as to whether the conviction is safe. This is decided in many cases on an assumption as to the factual basis of a jury's decision. Such a speculative exercise cannot be fair, and the impact of the Convention may well be to require a jury to be asked some straightforward questions as to the facts that it has found. A further impact must be to change the current criterion of 'safety'; it is possible that a conviction can be grotesquely unfair and yet completely safe at the same time. The European Court has already stated that a decision as to the safety of a conviction must be accompanied by an inquiry into the fairness of the proceedings.

Where the trial is not held in public, the decision itself need not be pronounced publicly but needs to be published subsequently. As a result of

---

85   *Monnell and Morris v UK* (1987) 10 EHRR 205.

86   *Neumeister v Austria (No 1)* (1968) 1 EHRR 91.

87   See the Court's strictures on the Court of Appeal's 'speculations' as to how significantly the jury viewed the defendants' refusal to answer police questions in *Condron v UK* Application No 35718/97, (2001) 31 EHRR 1.

Campbell and Fell v UK,[88] arrangements were made to publish the awards of boards of visitors in the local press. Boards no longer have disciplinary functions, which are now exercised by prison governors. Such hearings are criminal in nature and attract Art 6 safeguards. The hearings do not have to be public but the decisions should be (and are not) reported.

4.6   RIGHT TO LEGAL REPRESENTATION

On arrest, the initial right to legal assistance is implied in Art 5(4), which requires that a person is entitled to 'take proceedings by which the lawfulness of his detention shall be decided speedily by a court'. This inference is reinforced by Art 6(3)(b), which states that a person charged with a criminal offence should be provided with adequate time and facilities for the preparation of his or her defence, and Art 6(3)(c), which provides a specific guarantee of the right to defend oneself or be legally represented and to be granted public funding where appropriate. A failure to allow an accused legal advice at any time during the proceedings will be seen as a breach of a right to a fair hearing under Art 6. This issue was raised in relation to children's panels in Scotland[89] and remains an issue for Young Offender Panels sitting as part of the Referral Orders under Part I of the Youth Justice and Criminal Evidence Act 1999.

The right to legal representation extends to any appeal stage and disciplinary proceedings in prison.[90] In *Monnell and Morris v UK*[91] the applicants sought leave to appeal from the single judge. They were not entitled to make oral representations in person or to be represented. This was not a breach – they had already been advised by their lawyers that there were no grounds for appeal. The European Court felt that such an issue can be decided on written submissions alone, and the prosecution was also not represented. The rights to advice and the equality of arms principle had been satisfied.

The 'right to defend oneself' is a key element of equality of arms, but is not an absolute one. Where the charge is serious, the court may restrict the right of an accused to appear without legal representation. In *Croissant v Germany*[92] the accused was himself a lawyer, charged with involvement in the terrorist group, Red Army Faction. Lawyers were appointed for him by the court, and this was not in breach of Art 6. Lawyers may be appointed for a defendant if the original choice is unsuitable for some reason, perhaps because he or she had an interest in the case, was involved in professional misconduct or had shown lack of respect for the court.[93]

The right to represent oneself is not unlimited. In England, an accused may not cross-examine in person a complainant in a sexual case, a child who is the victim of or a witness to a sexual or violent offence, or any witness where the

---

88   (1984) 7 EHRR 165.
89   *S v Principal Reporter and Lord Advocate* (unreported) 30 March 2001,
      www.scotcourts.gov.uk
90   *Campbell and Fell v UK* (1984) 7 EHRR 165.
91   (1987) 10 EHRR 205.
92   (1992) 16 EHRR 135.
93   *X v UK* Application No 6298/73, 2 *Digest* 831 (1975).

quality of the evidence would be diminished were the accused to cross-examine in person.[94] This is unlikely to be in breach of the Convention since it is for the competent authorities to determine the manner in which the accused's rights are to be protected.[95] Furthermore, it may be argued strongly that a rape victim is entitled to the protection of Art 3 – that she should not be subject to degrading treatment, the definition of which is probably satisfied by cross-examination by the alleged rapist in a public court.

Normally, the accused's choice of a lawyer would be respected, but this is not necessarily so.[96] A lawyer may be excluded for good reason,[97] and this need not be a violation of Art 6. In *X v UK*,[98] counsel withdrew when the defendant admitted that certain incriminating statements he had previously denied were, in fact, true. The court required the accused to continue unrepresented, although with advice of his solicitors. The Commission did not consider that there had been a violation, but whether that would still be the outcome today is questionable.

In the UK, public funding is provided under the Legal Aid Act 1988. It covers advice and representation at all stages and in all courts, subject to the means of the defendant and subject to an 'interests of justice test', so that representation may not be granted where the offence is minor, involving no complexities of law, no difficulties in tracing witnesses or no special characteristics of the accused, such as lack of knowledge of English or mental or physical incapacity.[99] These provisions comply with the Convention requirements, which stipulate that free legal assistance must be provided where, first, the accused does not have sufficient means to pay for it and, secondly, the 'interests of justice' require it. It is not an absolute right. The issue of 'sufficiency of means' is not decided and requires the applicant to demonstrate lack of resources.[100]

Do the 'interests of justice' in s 22(2) of the Legal Aid Act 1988 comply with the European Court's definition? The Court has taken the view that legal aid (now public funding) for an indigent defendant is not automatic, but the State must consider the importance of the issue, the capacity of the unrepresented defendant to present legal argument, and the severity of the potential sentence. With certain caveats, the statutory legal aid scheme complies with this approach. Legal aid should be available wherever the offence carries a potential sentence of imprisonment. In *Benham v UK*,[101] failure to provide a poll tax defaulter with free representation was held to amount to a violation of the defendant's right to a fair trial. In *Granger v UK*[102] the applicant was refused legal aid for an appeal on the grounds that there were no substantial grounds.

---

94   Youth Justice and Criminal Evidence Act 1999, ss 34–36.
95   *Croissant v Germany* (1992) 16 EHRR 135; *X v Austria* Application No 1242/61 (1964).
96   Ibid.
97   *X v UK* Application No 8295/78, (1978) 15 DR 242.
98   (1978) 21 DR 126.
99   Legal Aid Act 1988, s 22(2).
100   *Pakelli v FRG* (1983) 6 EHRR 1.
101   (1996) 22 EHRR 293.
102   (1990) 12 EHRR 469.

At the appeal, one issue proved more complex, but the court did not review the refusal of legal aid, and this was in violation of Art 6. The original refusal of aid for the reason that there was no prospect of success was justified, and this was echoed in *Monnell and Morris v UK*[103] which stated that the interests of justice cannot require automatic legal aid where there is no objective likelihood of success. However, in *Boner v UK*[104] the Court took the view that there was a violation when the applicant had to represent himself, even though no complex issue of law emerged in the course of the appeal hearing and the chances of success from the outset were limited. The consequences for the appellant (8 years' imprisonment) were heavy and, significantly, Scots law granted a very wide right of appeal.

What is adequate time for the preparation of a defence will depend on the facts of the case, their complexity and other factors.[105] The Court has held that 5 days' notice is sufficient for a prison disciplinary hearing[106] and that it was also adequate in *Murphy v UK*[107] when the defendant met his barrister only 10 minutes before a trial at which he was sentenced to 7 years' imprisonment. Article 6 was interpreted in that case as requiring actual prejudice to the applicant to be shown[108] and, furthermore, although the barrister was only allocated to the case immediately before the hearing, no request for an adjournment had been made.

4.7 PRESUMPTION OF INNOCENCE

Article 6(2) embodies the presumption of innocence, that is, that the defendant is to be treated as not having committed any offence until the State, through the prosecuting authorities, adduce sufficient evidence to satisfy an independent and impartial tribunal that he or she is guilty as charged. This leads to certain propositions:

–   that the burden of proving the accused's guilt rests on the State at all times and that any doubt should benefit the accused;
–   that a defendant should be able to decline to answer any questions that might incriminate him or her;
–   that a defendant should not be expected to provide proof of guilt by being compelled to answer questions put by investigators, or to testify.

4.7.1 Burden of proof

The root values of procedural justice are encapsulated in the House of Lords' decision in *Woolmington v DPP*[109] where Lord Sankey said:

---

103   (1987) 10 EHRR 205.
104   (1994) 19 EHRR 246.
105   *Albert and Le Compte v Belgium* (1983) 13 EHRR 415.
106   *Campbell and Fell v UK* (1984) 7 EHRR 165.
107   Application No 4681/70, (1972) 43 CD 1.
108   *X v UK* Application No 4042/69, (1970) 13 YB 690.
109   [1935] AC 462.

'Throughout the web of English criminal law one golden thread is always to be seen that it is the duty of the prosecution to prove the prisoner's guilt ...'

There are situations where the prosecution may be said not to shoulder the complete burden of proof. The first situation is strict liability offences (a common part of magistrates' courts' work) ie crimes where the prosecution is simply put to proof of the *actus reus* of the offence without being required to prove that the defendant either intended to act in that way or to produce that result, or recognised that there was a risk that this might happen, or was grossly or merely negligent. Can such offences comply with the Convention requirement of the presumption of innocence where the State is exempted from proof of what ought to be an integral part of any offence? In *Salabiaku v France*,[110] customs officials forced the lock of the trunk and found a welded false bottom which concealed 10kg of herbal and seed cannabis. The applicant asserted that he was unaware of the presence of the cannabis and that he had mistaken the trunk for the parcel of whose arrival he had been advised. Under French law, anyone found in possession of prohibited articles is presumed to be guilty of smuggling them. The European Court held that, in principle, States may, under certain conditions, penalise a simple or objective fact as such, irrespective of whether it results from criminal intent or from negligence. Strict liability offences are not, in themselves, contrary to the Convention. However, there must be certain limits to this relating to the seriousness of the offence and the severity of the punishment.

The second situation is where there is a reversal of the burden of proof. This frequently occurs where the defendant has to prove some defence: does this infringe the presumption of innocence? In *Salabiaku* the accused was entitled to a defence of *force majeure* but he would have had to have shown that it was impossible for him to have known about the contents of the trunk. The Court held that presumptions of fact or of law operate in every legal system and that the Convention does not prohibit such presumptions in principle. It does, however, require the States to remain within certain limits which take into account the importance of what is at stake and maintain the rights of the defence. The Court recognised that the French Court of Appeal drew a clear distinction between the criminal offence of unlawful importation of narcotics and the customs offence of smuggling prohibited goods. On the first head, it acquitted the defendant, giving him the benefit of the doubt, and in so doing showed 'scrupulous respect' for the presumption of innocence. On the second head, it upheld the conviction without contradicting itself because the 'facts and the action incriminated' were different. The accused declared himself to be the owner of the trunk, thereby affirming his possession. The Court stated that for the more serious offence, the prosecution shouldered the burden of proof, but for the customs offence, a reversal of that burden was acceptable.[111]

---

110   (1988) 13 EHRR 379.

111   It is acceptable to place the burden on the accused to show that he was not living off the earnings of a prostitute who was living with him: *X v UK* Application No 5124/71, (1972) 42 CD 135.

In the UK there are many statutes which expressly or impliedly reverse the burden of proof. The issue in *R v DPP ex parte Kebeline*[112] was whether the DPP should give consent to a prosecution under ss 16A and 16B of the Prevention of Terrorism (Temporary Provisions) Act 1989. Those sections placed a legal burden on the accused to prove that the items found in possession were either not in their possession or not for a terrorist purpose. In the Divisional Court, Bingham LCJ argued that it might be true that, where a criminal intention was an essential ingredient of a crime, the defendant was better placed to prove his intention than the prosecution, but that did not relieve the prosecution of the need to prove a criminal intention against him in the overwhelming majority of cases. The result of the reversal of the onus of proof which ss 16A and 16B of the 1989 Act effected was to allow for the possibility that a defendant might be convicted, even where the jury entertained a reasonable doubt as to his guilt. Sections 16A and 16B therefore violated the presumption of innocence and were repugnant to Art 6(2) of the Convention. This reflects the common law's general approach to the interpretation of constitutions shown in *Attorney-General of Hong Kong v Lee Kwong-kut*[113] where the Privy Council held that the obligation on the accused to prove that money in his possession had not been stolen breached the Hong Kong Bill of Rights. The House of Lords has recently decided that reversals of the burden of proof can breach Art 6. In *R v Lambert* [2001] UKHL 37[114] the issue was whether the accused had to prove that he did not know he was in possession of a controlled drug under s 28 of the Misuse of Drugs Act 1971. The House held that the imposition of a legal burden (not evidential) on the defendant violated Art 6(2).

Basing criminal responsibility on strict liability or reversed onus is acceptable where the nature of the offence is regulatory and the punishment is not severe. This is not problematic when the reversal of the burden of proof is express, although it raises interesting questions about the status of the defences of insanity at common law and diminished responsibility under s 2 of the Homicide Act 1957 where the burden of proof is on the defendant to satisfy the jury that his or her state of mind is abnormal. Where the reversal of the burden of proof is implied through statutory interpretation, the Convention approach through principle will offer an acceptable alternative to that employed by the House of Lords in *R v Hunt*.[115]

4.7.2 Privilege against self-incrimination

The presumption of innocence may also be seen, at common law, in the privilege against self-incrimination. A witness may, if he or she so wishes, decline to answer a question where such answers might expose the witness to subsequent criminal proceedings.[116] There must be reasonable grounds on

---

112 [1999] 3 WLR 175, [1999] Crim LR 994 – the House of Lords avoided addressing this issue directly.
113 [1993] AC 951.
114 [2001] 3 WLR 206.
115 [1987] AC 352.
116 *Blunt v Park Lane Hotel Ltd* [1942] 2 All ER 187.

which to apprehend a risk of such proceedings.[117] It is a privilege that applies in any legal proceedings and relates not only to oral testimony, but would also permit a witness to refuse to produce documentary and real evidence.

The principle that a tribunal should have access to all evidence is displaced by the need for fairness to the accused and to minimise the risk that he or she will be convicted out of his or her own mouth. The instinct is that it is contrary to fairness to put witnesses in a position that they may be prosecuted if they answer, or punished in different ways if they refuse to answer. However, there are numerous statutory exceptions which require persons to provide information which may be used as the basis for a criminal prosecution.[118] Examples are: the powers given by ss 434 and 436 of the Companies Act 1985 which require company officers to answer questions put by Board of Trade inspectors appointed to investigate fraud within the company; environmental legislation requires compulsory provision of water quality information by self-monitoring which can provide evidence for subsequent prosecutions; s 2 of the Criminal Justice Act 1987 which requires any person under investigation by the Serious Fraud Office to answer questions, produce documents and furnish information. Use of this information in subsequent criminal proceedings is clearly in breach of Art 6.

The validity of such legislation was questioned in *Saunders v UK*.[119] The defendant was convicted of fraud. He had been compelled to give information in the course of investigations by inspectors from the Department of Trade acting under the Companies Act and these answers were used against him in the subsequent prosecution. The European Court concluded that this infringed his freedom from self-incrimination and was in breach of the presumption of innocence under Art 6(2). The right not to incriminate oneself, like the right to silence, was a generally recognised standard which lay at the heart of the notion of a fair procedure. It was irrelevant that the statements might not have been self-incriminating since even neutral evidence might be deployed in a way which supported the prosecution's case. The Court noted that part of the transcript of the applicant's answers to the inspectors had been read out to the jury over a 3-day period despite the applicant's objections. Accordingly, there had been an infringement of the applicant's right not to incriminate himself and the public interest in combating fraud could not be invoked to justify the use of answers compulsorily obtained in a non-judicial investigation to incriminate him at his trial.

This is consistent with the approach of the Court that any legal compulsion to produce incriminating evidence infringes the right of silence. In *Funke v France*[120] the Court held that the State infringed the applicant's right of silence when it sought to compel him to produce bank statements that may have been

---

117   *R v Boyes* (1861) 30 LJQB 301.
118   Other statutes which compel the provision of information but where any statements made are inadmissible as evidence are s 31(1) of the Theft Act 1968; s 9 of the Criminal Damage Act 1971; and s 98 of the Children Act 1989.
119   (1997) 23 EHRR 313.
120   (1993) 16 EHRR 297.

relevant to Customs investigations into suspected offences committed by him. Both *Saunders* and *Funke* appear to establish that coercion to co-operate with the authorities in the pre-trial process may infringe the privilege against self-incrimination and jeopardise the fairness of any subsequent hearing. In s 59 of and Sch 3 to the Youth Justice and Criminal Evidence Act 1999, there are now restrictions on the use of such evidence.

4.7.3 Right to silence

The protection from coercive pressure to answer an investigator's questions, whether inside or outside court, is a fundamental element of the guarantees of a fair hearing and a presumption of innocence under Art 6. The right to silence has been discussed in relation to police investigation of crime,[121] but it also applies in court where the accused should have the right not to testify and, perhaps, the right not to disclose the nature of his or her defence before trial. In the UK, there remain questions over whether the changes to these rights by s 35 of the Criminal Justice and Public Order Act 1994 and the Criminal Procedure and Investigations Act 1996 are compliant with Convention safeguards.

The common law right to silence in court is an amalgam of the following:

– the evidential rule that places a burden of proof on the prosecution that it should prove the defendant's guilt beyond reasonable doubt.[122] Such a presumption of innocence means that there is no obligation on the accused to produce evidence or to testify;
– the defendant is not a compellable witness for the prosecution;
– the prosecution was not permitted to comment on the defendant's decision to remain silent in the police station[123] or not to testify.[124] This position has now been significantly changed;
– the judge was always entitled to comment on the accused's silence[125] but he or she had to do so in measured terms and had to warn the jury that it must not assume guilt from the defendant's silence[126] (this has also now been significantly altered).

Over the past 25 years, there has been a constant debate over the right to silence. The Royal Commission on Criminal Justice in 1993 commissioned two separate reports.[127] The empirical evidence[128] put forward did not suggest that there was either an unacceptable acquittal rate or 'no further action' rate for those few defendants, charged with serious crimes, who chose to remain

---

121 At **3.7** above.
122 *Woolmington v DPP* [1935] AC 462.
123 *R v Hall* [1971] 1 All ER 322.
124 Criminal Evidence Act 1898, s 1(b): the failure of any person charged with an offence to give evidence shall not be made the subject of any comment by the prosecution.
125 *R v Bathurst* [1968] 1 All ER 1175; *R v Sparrow* [1973] 2 All ER 129.
126 *R v Martinez-Tobon* [1994] 2 All ER 90.
127 Royal Commission on Criminal Justice, Cm 2293 (1993); R Leng *The Right to Silence in Police Interrogation* (Research Study 10, 1993); M McConville and J Hodgson *Custodial Legal Advice and the Right to Silence* (Research Study 16, 1993).
128 This is summarised in Leng (n 127 above), ch 2.

silent.[129] Nor did the research studies consider that there was any serious problem of 'ambush' defences. The Royal Commission report did suggest that the defence should be under an obligation to disclose aspects of its case, but stood firm against the wholesale abolition of the right to silence.

The argument to retain the right of silence has many different facets. The privilege against self-incrimination has been recognised judicially in the House of Lords:

> 'The underlying rationale ... is, in my view, now to be found in the maxim *nemo debet prodere se ipsum*, no one can be required to be his own betrayer or in its popular English mistranslation "the right to silence".'[130]

This argument suggests that it is unfair for the State to force defendants to choose between speaking and convicting themselves out of their own mouths, or not speaking and being convicted by default. Furthermore, the denial of a right of silence undermines the right to privacy. Article 8 states that 'everyone has the right to respect for his private and family life, his home and his correspondence'. It has been argued that if the right of privacy is to have any meaning, criminal cases are those in which it should be asserted. This rationale is more fundamental than the privilege against self-incrimination and the presumption of innocence, since it is directly connected with concepts of personhood and respect for individual autonomy.[131]

Despite such arguments, the right of silence in court has been considerably modified by s 35 of the Criminal Justice and Public Order Act 1994.[132] This section applies where the prosecution has satisfied the court that there is a case to answer[133] and a defendant declines to testify in his or her own defence. The judge, in the presence of the jury, is empowered to tell the defendant that the stage has been reached at which he or she can give evidence, and to issue a warning that if he or she remains silent it will be permissible for the jury to draw whatever inferences appear to be proper from that failure to testify. As a result of s 38(3), a person should not be convicted solely on the basis of an inference drawn from this failure. However, it is probable that the consequence of a refusal to testify, in most cases, would be a general presumption of guilt by the jury. The current position is very similar to that introduced in 1988 in Northern Ireland.[134]

The impact of s 35 was considered by the Court of Appeal in *R v Cowan*,[135] where Taylor LCJ was reluctant to allow exceptions to the drawing of inferences.

---

129   M Zander 'The investigation of crime: a study of cases tried at the Old Bailey' [1979] Crim LR 203.

130   *R v Sang* [1979] 2 All ER 1222 at 1230c, per Lord Diplock.

131   A more detailed critique may be found in A Ashworth *The Criminal Process* 2nd edn (Clarendon Press, 1998), p 98.

132   I Dennis 'The Criminal Justice and Public Order Act 1994' [1995] Crim LR 4.

133   The jury must be directed that it has to be satisfied that there is a case to answer before considering whether adverse inferences should be drawn from the failure to testify: *R v Birchall* [1999] Crim LR 311.

134   Criminal Evidence (Northern Ireland) Order 1988, SI 1988/1987; for its impact, see J Jackson: 'Curtailing the Right of Silence: Lessons from N. Ireland' [1991] Crim LR 404.

135   [1995] 4 All ER 939.

'We accept that . . . it will be open to a court to decline to draw an adverse inference from silence at trial and for a judge to direct or advise a jury against drawing such inference if the circumstances of the case justify such a course. But in our view there would need either to be some evidential basis for doing so or some exceptional factors in the case making that a fair course to take. It must be stressed that the inferences permitted by the section are only such "as appear proper". The use of that phrase was no doubt intended to leave a broad discretion to a trial judge to decide in all the circumstances whether any proper inference is capable of being drawn by the jury. If not, he should tell them so; otherwise it is for the jury to decide whether in fact an inference should properly be drawn.'[136]

The Court of Appeal rejected any attempt to restrict the operation of s 35, but stressed that the nature, extent and degree of inferences to be drawn from silence lay within the discretion of the trial judge. The reluctance of judges to use that discretion to limit the impact of s 35 has already been demonstrated in *R v Friend*[137] when the Court of Appeal refused to intervene in the case of a 15-year-old accused of murder. The defendant had a mental age of 9, and yet the trial judge still directed the jury that it was open to it to draw adverse inferences from his failure to testify.

Will the courts still follow this uncompromising approach? *Funke v France*[138] suggests that where there is compulsion to answer questions, the answers should not be used in evidence against the person. Does this apply where there is indirect pressure to testify? First indications suggest that this may not be the case. Similar Northern Ireland provisions were considered in *Murray v UK*.[139] The European Court concluded that, where a prima facie case was established and the burden of proof remained on the prosecution, adverse inferences may be drawn from a failure to testify. Although the Court saw the right to silence as a generally recognised international standard which lay at the heart of fair procedure, the requirement to testify placed on the defendant was not incompatible with the Convention, although it would be if the conviction were based solely or mainly on any refusal to give evidence. As the Criminal Justice and Public Order Act 1994 stands, the prosecution case will have to overcome the hurdle of a 'no case to answer' submission, and it would be difficult to argue that any resultant conviction was based solely or mainly on adverse inferences drawn from the failure to testify.

It was argued that *Murray* was unlikely to be the last word on this issue. There were several distinctive features in the case that marked it out from an ordinary criminal prosecution:

– it concerned charges of terrorism;
– the nature of the tribunal (a Diplock court in Northern Ireland) involved an experienced judge as the trier of fact;
– the independent evidence against the defendant was overwhelming.

---

136   [1995] 4 All ER 939 at 942f–945d; see also *R v A* [1997] Crim LR 883.
137   [1997] 2 All ER 1011.
138   (1993) 16 EHRR 297.
139   (1996) 22 EHRR 29.

These factors may be especially relevant in any future applications. The Court as a whole clearly considered that the 'adverse inferences' rule significantly affected the right to a fair hearing guaranteed in Art 6(1) and, furthermore, there was substantial dissent. The Court's guarded reaction to the Northern Ireland Order may well contain sufficient ammunition for future challenges to the compatibility of the 1994 Act.

Is there an analogy in *Condron v UK*,[140] where the Court was dealing with inferences drawn from a failure to answer police questions under s 34? The Court emphasised that the accused testified and gave an explanation for silence and that the trial was before a jury, all of which were distinguishable from *Murray*. The Court held that the right to silence was not absolute but that 'particular caution' was required by domestic courts before drawing adverse inferences. Convicting solely or mainly on such evidence would infringe Art 6, but the accused's silence, in situations which clearly called for an explanation, could be taken into account in assessing the persuasiveness of the prosecution evidence. In all the circumstances of this case, the jury should have been directed that silence could be taken into account but only if it was satisfied that the applicants' silence could not sensibly be attributed to their having no answer or none that would stand up to cross-examination. A similar approach would work well for s 35.

4.8   DISCLOSURE OF EVIDENCE

Disclosure of the evidence against the accused is a major element of a fair hearing. Article 6(3)(a) requires that a person charged with a criminal offence be informed of the nature and cause of the accusation against him. Several notorious cases in England involving miscarriages of justice have emphasised the need for the accused to have access to information necessary for the proper preparation of the defence. The regulation of prosecution disclosure has been significantly altered by precedent and statute in the past 5 years. These reforms have also affected the position of the defence, and there is now a statutory requirement to disclose the defence case prior to trial.

By 1996 the common law had developed to the extent that full disclosure of prosecution information prior to trial was seen as an essential element in a fair trial.[141] In trials on indictment, the defendant is entitled to advance disclosure not only of the evidence on which the prosecution is intending to rely, but also of 'unused material'. In magistrates' courts, there is no obligation on the prosecution to disclose with regard to summary offences, but there is a statutory obligation[142] in the case of triable-either-way offences which are being tried summarily. There is, of course, a general duty on the court to ensure a fair trial, which would require the prosecution to produce all the material evidence.[143]

---

140   Application No 35718/97, (2001) 31 EHRR 1.
141   *R v Ward* [1993] 2 All ER 577; *R v Preston* [1993] 4 All ER 638.
142   Criminal Law Act 1977, s 48; and Magistrates' Courts (Advance Information) Rules 1985, SI 1985/601.
143   *R v Liverpool Crown Court ex parte Roberts* [1986] Crim LR 622.

The major problem for the police and prosecution were the decisions in *R v Maguire*[144] and *R v Ward*[145] to give the defendant access to 'unused material' collected during the investigation. They also had to disclose any matters which might have been held against prosecution witnesses, for example that the witness had been subject to police disciplinary hearings.[146]

There has never been a general common law obligation on the defendant to disclose the nature of the defence. However, this has been introduced in some circumstances by statute:

–   for alibi defences by the Criminal Justice Act 1967;
–   for expert evidence under s 81 of PACE 1984;
–   for preparatory hearings in serious fraud cases.[147]

Clearly, the shorter the notice the prosecution has of a defence witness or item of evidence, the less able it is to counter the impact of such evidence. Furthermore, the principal function of a jury is to determine the truth, and it should be entitled both to an indictment which lays out an agenda of the issues to be decided and to both parties putting forward their own evidence on those issues and how each intends to answer the other's evidence. Concealment of evidence until a late stage by either side necessarily means that the jury is unable to assess the weight or probative quality of such evidence. Such principles of proof argue for joint disclosure, and Scotland has operated such a practice for several years with little dissent.[148] Indirectly, s 34 of the Criminal Justice and Public Order Act 1994 altered the balance in England and Wales aiming at forcing disclosure of the defence by allowing a court to 'draw such inferences as appear proper' from a failure to answer police questions.

The problems of disclosure have been highlighted by issues surrounding public interest immunity and by statutory changes under the Criminal Procedure and Investigations Act 1996.

4.8.1   Disclosure and public interest immunity

Extensive disclosure was resented by the police and prosecution. It was not simply the quantity and inconvenience of the procedures, but the nature of the information that they were being required to disclose. The argument was that they were faced with the dilemma of either having to disclose sensitive and confidential material, especially the identity of informants, or having to discontinue prosecution. However, the prosecution is entitled to seek immunity from disclosure on the grounds of public interest immunity (PII) because the information would, for example, reveal the identity of informants or details of police operational practices. Normally, the defence would be aware of an application to decide on a PII claim and be entitled to make representations in

---

144   (1992) 94 Cr App R 133.
145   [1993] 2 All ER 577.
146   *R v Edwards* [1991] 2 All ER 266; see *Edwards v UK* (1992) 15 EHRR 417.
147   Criminal Justice Act 1987, s 9.
148   Glynn 'Disclosure' [1993] Crim LR 841, 842.

open court. But such decisions as *R v Keane*[149] and *R v Davis*[150] approved an *ex parte* procedure so that such material could be placed before the court for a ruling on whether it should be disclosed without compromising its confidentiality. The prosecution can approach the court for an order for immunity from disclosure without informing the defence at all.

These procedures, limiting the access of the defence to sensitive material, are not significantly affected by the Criminal Procedure and Investigations Act 1996. Section 3(6) of the Act allows the prosecutor, on application to the trial court, not to disclose information where it would not be in the public interest to do so. Where material has not been disclosed on the grounds of PII, an accused person can apply to the court for a review of this decision during the trial. Where the trial is in the Crown Court, there is a duty on the judge to keep the issue under review at all times without the need for an application.[151]

This common law position is at odds with requirements of the Convention, which takes the position that if material is relevant, it should be disclosed, and the extent to which a domestic court has discretion to withhold such evidence is questionable.[152] The significant point is that it is normally a violation for a court to hear the prosecution in the absence of the accused.[153] If this is the case, the common law rules relating to PII are open to challenge under Art 6. In *Rowe and Davis v UK* the European Court held that it is:

> '... a fundamental aspect of the right to a fair trial that criminal proceedings, including the elements of such proceedings which relate to procedure, should be adversarial and that there should be equality of arms between the prosecution and defence. The right to an adversarial trial means, in a criminal case, that both prosecution and defence must be given the opportunity to have knowledge of and comment on the observations filed and the evidence adduced by the other party. In addition Article 6(1) requires, as indeed does English law that the prosecution authorities should disclose to the defence all material evidence in their possession for or against the accused. However ... the entitlement to disclosure of relevant evidence is not an absolute right. In any criminal proceedings there may be competing interests, such as national security or the need to protect witnesses at risk of reprisals or keep secret police methods of investigation of crime, which must be weighed against the rights of the accused. In some cases it may be necessary to withhold certain evidence from the defence so as to preserve the fundamental rights of another individual or to safeguard an important public interest. However, only such measures restricting the rights of the defence which are strictly necessary are permissible. Moreover, in order to ensure that the accused receives a fair trial, any difficulties caused to the defence by a limitation on its rights must be sufficiently counterbalanced by the procedures followed by the judicial authorities.
>
> In cases where relevant evidence has been withheld from the defence on public interest grounds, it is not the role of the European Court to decide whether or not

149   [1994] 2 All ER 478.
150   [1993] 2 All ER 643; *R v Johnson and Rowe* [1993] 97 Cr App R 110. See *Rowe and Davis v UK* (2000) 30 EHRR 1.
151   Criminal Procedure and Investigations Act 1996, ss 14, 15.
152   *Jespers v Belgium* Application No 8403/78, (1981) 27 DR 61.
153   *Neumeister v Austria (No 1)* (1968) 1 EHRR 91.

such non-disclosure was strictly necessary since, as a general rule, it is for the national courts to assess the evidence before them. Instead, the European Court's task is to ascertain whether to scrutinise the decision-making procedure applied in each case to ensure that, as far as possible, it complied with the requirements of adversarial proceedings and equality of arms and incorporated adequate safe-guards to protect the interests of the accused.

During the applicants' trial at first instance the prosecution decided, without notifying the judge, to withhold certain relevant evidence on grounds of public interest. It is clear that such a procedure, whereby the prosecution itself attempts to assess the importance of concealed information to the defence and weigh this against the public interest in keeping the information secret, cannot comply with the above-mentioned requirements of Article 6. It is true that at the commence-ment of the applicants' appeal prosecution counsel notified the defence that certain information had been withheld, without however revealing the nature of this material, and that on two separate occasions the Court of Appeal reviewed the undisclosed evidence and, in ex parte hearings with the benefit of submissions from the Crown but in the absence of the defence, decided in favour of non-disclosure. However, the Court does not consider that this procedure before the appeal court was sufficient to remedy the unfairness caused at the trial by the absence of any scrutiny of the withheld information by the trial judge.'[154]

In *Fitt and Jasper v UK*[155] the Court, albeit on a majority of 9–8, drew significant differences with *Rowe and Davis*. When the prosecution made an *ex parte* application to the trial judge to withhold material in its possession on the grounds of public interest immunity, the defence was not told of the category of material. It was given the opportunity to outline the defence case to the trial judge, and to request the judge to order disclosure of any evidence relating to those alleged facts. The trial judge examined the material in question and ruled that it should not be disclosed, although the defence was not informed of the reasons for the judge's decision. The Court was satisfied that the defence was kept informed and permitted to make submissions and participate in the above decision-making process as far as was possible without revealing to it the material which the prosecution sought to keep secret on public interest grounds. The Court noted, in particular, that the material which was not disclosed in the case formed no part of the prosecution case whatever, and was never put to the jury. This position must be contrasted with the circumstances where impugned decisions are based, either in whole or to an unascertainable degree, on the non-disclosed material. The Court recognised that a lesser degree of procedural protection is appropriate where non-disclosed material plays no further role in the case. The fact that the assessment of the need for disclosure was at all times carried out by the trial judge provided a further, important safeguard in that it was his duty to monitor throughout the trial the fairness or otherwise of the evidence being withheld. He was fully versed in all the evidence and issues in the case, and in a position to monitor the relevance to the defence of the withheld information both before and during the trial. Moreover, the judge applied the principles that in weighing the public interest in concealment against the interest of the accused in disclosure, great weight

---

154   (2000) 30 EHRR 1.
155   [2000] HRCD 75.

should be attached to the interests of justice, and that the judge should continue to assess the need for disclosure throughout the progress of the trial.

These decisions should clarify the role of the judge in PII decisions. However, the European Court in *Rowe and Davis* and *Fitt and Jasper* considered the possibility of introducing special counsel with security clearance to deal with disclosure issues. There is a precedent in domestic law under s 6 of the Special Immigration Appeals Commission Act 1997 which deals with asylum cases. This procedure was introduced as a result of the decision in *Chahal v UK*.[156]

Article 6(3)(a) is intended to ensure that an accused has sufficient information to prepare his or her defence[157] and not full disclosure of all the material gathered. Where information has not been disclosed, the Criminal Procedure and Investigations Act 1996 requires the judge to keep this decision under review in the light of the nature of the defence. It is unlikely that these procedures infringe the right to a fair hearing. As has been noted, the rights guaranteed in Art 6(1) may be derogated from in the interests of public order and national security. The European Court has recognised that a police informer need not be called as a witness as such a system is necessary to the administration of justice, and to require such people to testify would undermine that system.[158]

4.8.2 Disclosure and legal professional privilege

Does a defendant have the right to adduce material in a trial which is subject to legal professional privilege? The common law position is that the judicial 'balancing of conflicting interests' which characterises PII has no place within legal professional privilege. It is not for the judge to decide whether the client's interest in maintaining confidentiality is outweighed by the interests of the administration of justice. Until recently, it was considered that the public interest in the accused's right to prove his or her innocence overrode the need for candour between lawyer and client. For example, in *R v Barton*,[159] a defendant who was employed by a firm of solicitors was charged with fraud. He sought various documents which had come into existence as a result of the firm's probate work for clients. The firm alerted the clients, and a claim to legal professional privilege was made and rejected.

When a communication was originally privileged, and this is claimed against the defendant by the client concerned, it should be for the defendant to show, on the balance of probabilities, that the claim cannot be sustained. The judge must decide whether the legitimate interest of the defendant in seeking to breach the privilege outweighs that of the client in seeking to maintain it.

Barton was overruled by the House of Lords in *R v Derby Magistrates' Court ex parte B*.[160] In 1978 the applicant was acquitted of murder, having made various

---

156   (1996) 23 EHRR 413.
157   *Bricmont v Belgium* Application No 10857/84, (1986) 48 DR 106.
158   *Kostovski v Netherlands* (1989) 12 EHRR 434.
159   [1972] 2 All ER 1192.
160   [1995] 4 All ER 526.

statements admitting the killing, but later retracting these and instead accusing his stepfather of the murder. In 1992 the stepfather was charged with murder and, at the committal proceedings, the applicant was called as a witness for the Crown. Counsel for the stepfather sought to cross-examine him about instructions he had given to his solicitors in 1978 which were inconsistent with his statements implicating his stepfather. The applicant declined to waive his privilege and this was upheld. Lord Taylor of Gosforth reviewed the history of legal professional privilege and made important points as to its status:

> 'Legal professional privilege is thus much more than an ordinary rule of evidence, limited in its application to the facts of a particular case. It is a fundamental condition on which the administration of justice as a whole rests. ...
>
> As for the analogy with public interest immunity, I accept that the various classes of case in which relevant evidence is excluded may ... be regarded as forming part of a continuous spectrum. But it by no means follows that because a balancing exercise is called for in one class of case, it may also be allowed in another.
>
> ... it is not for the sake of the appellant alone that the privilege must be upheld. It is in the wider interests of all those hereafter who might otherwise be deterred from telling the whole truth to their solicitors. For this reason I am of the opinion that no exception should be allowed to the absolute nature of legal professional privilege, once established.'[161]

The width of this judgment is extraordinary. To hold that the court is never justified in undertaking a balancing exercise to compare the public interest in the lawyer/client privilege with the public interest in, for example, the liberty of an individual seems unnecessarily wide and an approach that may well be regretted in hindsight. Lord Taylor of Gosforth called in aid the Convention to justify the assertion that legal professional privilege is a fundamental condition on which the administration of justice rests. Certainly, the European Court has recently affirmed the importance of that privilege in *Foxley v UK*.[162] But Art 5 asserts the right to liberty, which is an equally fundamental concept. If a person's liberty is dependent upon the disclosure of communications between a third party and his or her lawyer, it seems bizarre to state that legal professional privilege must, in all circumstances, outweigh the injury that would occur if an innocent person received a lengthy prison sentence.

The European Court of Justice's position would appear to differ:

> '[The applicant] submitted that the right to confidential communication between lawyer and client was a fundamental human right. I do not think it is. There is no mention of it, as such, in the European Convention ... or, seemingly, in the constitution of any member state; and your Lordships have already seen that, in England and France at least, it is acknowledged to be a right that can be overridden or modified by an appropriately worded statute. ... In my opinion it is a right that the laws of civilised countries generally recognise, a right not lightly to be denied, but not one so entrenched that, in the Community, the Council could never legislate to override or modify it.'[163]

---

161 [1995] 4 All ER 526 at 540j–542d.
162 (2001) 31 EHRR 25.
163 *AM&S Europe Ltd v Commission* [1983] 1 All ER 705 at 721d–f, per Advocate-General Warner.

4.8.3   Disclosure under the Criminal Procedure and Investigations Act 1996

The procedure for disclosure was put on a statutory basis by the Criminal Procedure and Investigations Act 1996. Article 6 of the Convention requires that the accused is entitled to more detailed and specific information than notification of the charge itself. This must be given before the trial in order to permit a reasonable period for the preparation of the defence. The amount of detail required remains unclear – the European Court has suggested that a judicial notification did not identify 'in detail ... the nature and cause of the accusation'. [164] Such phrasing does not necessarily include the evidence against the accused let alone all material uncovered during an investigation. But the Commission has suggested a broader obligation to disclose any material which may 'assist the accused in exonerating himself',[165] to ensure equality of arms. *Rowe and Davis v UK*[166] shows that this is now the position with the Court itself.

The margin of appreciation accorded to States means that the 1996 Act, in all probability, satisfies such criteria in respect of time scale and detail.[167] There is a three-stage process:[168]

–   Primary disclosure by the prosecution which is automatic. The prosecution would be under a duty to supply the defence with copies of all material relevant to the offence, the offender and the circumstances of the case. This would include material which may undermine the credibility of defence witnesses as well as those appearing for the prosecution.[169] Schedules of other information held by the police or other key participants, such as expert scientific witnesses, would be supplied at this point. The only potential problem here is the lack of formal judicial scrutiny over this procedure.

–   A statement by the defence setting out the material lines of their case. The Act provides for disclosure by the accused in the form of a defence statement. In the case of proceedings in the Crown Court, this is compulsory. Disclosure of the defence is not compulsory in the magistrates' court, but the accused may give a defence statement to the prosecution and to the court on a voluntary basis.[170] Whether the disclosure is compulsory or voluntary, flaws in the defence statement can lead to adverse consequences for the accused as the jury may draw such inferences as it thinks proper from a failure to give a defence statement, or where the defence in court differs from the one set out in the statement. As discussed above, the decision of the European Court in *Funke v France*[171]

---

164   *Brozicek v Italy* (1989) 12 EHRR 371.
165   *Jespers v Belgium* Application No 8403/78, (1981) 27 DR 61.
166   (2000) 30 EHRR 1.
167   S Sharpe 'Article 6 and the Disclosure of Evidence' [1999] Crim LR 273.
168   For the background, see Royal Commission on Criminal Justice, Cm 2263 (1993), paras 6.50ff; for comments, see J Glynn 'Disclosure' (1993) Crim LR 841.
169   *R v Brown* [1997] 3 All ER 769.
170   Criminal Procedure and Investigations Act 1996, s 6.
171   (1993) 16 EHRR 297.

suggests that these provisions may well infringe the presumption of innocence.

– Under s 7, where the accused has given a defence statement to the prosecution, the prosecutor is under a duty to make any additional disclosures that become necessary. The prosecutor remains under a continuing duty to keep under review the question whether there is prosecution material which might undermine the prosecution case and which has not been disclosed to the accused and, should such material exist, it should be disclosed to the accused as soon as reasonably practicable.[172] The defence would be obliged to establish the relevance of the material sought, relating it to its disclosed case. Where the parties disagree on this aspect, the court could rule, after weighing the potential importance of the material to the defence.

The European Court has taken into account the fact that undisclosed information has come to light by the time of the appellate stage and that the Court of Appeal has been able to assess its impact on the safety of the conviction.[173] This illustrates the general point that the European Court looks at the proceedings as a whole and that, in certain situations, defects at the trial stage are remediable at the appeal stage.

Although the failure to disclose material to the defence is a breach under Art 6, the Commission has accepted that the late introduction of previously undisclosed evidence by the prosecution under the *ex improviso* rules[174] does not infringe the Convention.[175]

4.9 CALLING AND EXAMINING WITNESSES

Article 6(3)(d) of the Convention allows an accused to call and examine witnesses. This applies to the trial and has been held not to apply to the pre-trial stage.[176] It is not a breach if the accused's lawyer is not allowed to examine people being questioned by the police or the examining judge. This is more relevant to civilian jurisdictions, and the accused is normally not present or represented during police questioning of witnesses. Under the Criminal Procedure and Investigations Act 1996, there are provisions for preparatory hearings in complex cases, which are designed not to take evidence but to make preliminary rulings.

In England, the decision to call and examine witnesses at the trial lies in the hands of the parties themselves. The judge does have an overriding discretion and could refuse to hear a witness if he or she felt that the testimony would have little or no relevance to the issues. As a general rule, it is for the national courts to assess the evidence before them as well as the relevance of the evidence

---

172 Criminal Procedure and Investigations Act 1996, s 9.
173 *Edwards v UK* (1992) 15 EHRR 417; *Hardiman v UK* [1996] EHRLR 425.
174 *R v Francis* [1991] 1 All ER 225.
175 *X v UK* Application No 5327/71, 2 *Digest* 387 (1972).
176 *Can v Austria* (1985) 8 EHRR 121.

which defendants seek to adduce[177] and leaves it to them, again as a general rule, to assess whether it is appropriate to call witnesses.[178] The attendance and examination of every witness on the accused's behalf is not required and the essential aim is a full 'equality of arms' in the matter. However, it would be necessary to give reasons for a refusal to hear a witness. In *Vidal v Belgium*[179] the accused was convicted on the basis of the evidence in the case file without hearing oral testimony, including those witnesses specifically requested by the defence. Such a course of action was a breach of the right to a fair hearing. Where the defence itself fails to call a witness or where that person fails to turn up for reasons beyond the control of the court, the State is not held responsible.[180]

At common law, all witnesses are subject to cross-examination[181] and this is generally the position under the Convention. However, the European Court has accepted that some jurisdictions exempt witnesses from testifying. The non-compellability of members of the accused's family was held acceptable in *Unterpertinger v Austria*,[182] as has been the exemption for police informers.[183] It does not follow that the Court is willing to accept written statements from absent witnesses as a substitute. The admissibility of hearsay is discussed below.

4.10 ANONYMITY OF WITNESSES

Article 6(3)(d) embraces a right of confrontation, ie that the defendant has the right to know his or her accusers and to cross-examine them. Witnesses normally testify in the full glare of publicity, and, in the UK, few proceedings are heard *in camera*.[184] There are common law and statutory powers, however, which restrict this. A trial court has 'a wide inherent jurisdiction to control its own procedure'.[185] The restrictions are as follows.

– The press are in certain circumstances unable to identify young offenders or young witnesses.[186] Vulnerable adult witnesses may also be protected.[187]

– Anonymity can be granted to witnesses through the use of letters ('Colonel B'),[188] for example, in cases of blackmail victims, national security, police informants[189] or those who permit their premises to be used as police observation posts.[190] This common law power to grant anonymity is

---

177 *Barberà, Messegué and Jabardo v Spain* (1988) 11 EHRR 360.
178 *Asch v Austria* (1991) 15 EHRR 597.
179 Application No 12351/86, (1992) Series A/235-B.
180 *F v UK* (1992) 15 EHRR CD 32.
181 *R v Hilton* [1971] 3 All ER 541.
182 (1986) 13 EHRR 175.
183 *Kostovski v Netherlands* (1989) 12 EHRR 434.
184 One example is under s 8(4) of the Official Secrets Act 1920.
185 *Attorney-General v Leveller Magazine Ltd* [1979] 1 All ER 745.
186 Youth Justice and Criminal Evidence Act 1999, ss 44, 45. Committal proceedings can only be reported in outline: Magistrates' Courts Act 1980, s 8.
187 Youth Justice and Criminal Evidence Act 1999, s 46.
188 R Munday 'Name Suppression' [1991] Crim LR 680 and 753.
189 *Rogers v Home Secretary* [1973] AC 388.
190 *R v Rankine* [1986] 2 All ER 566.

exercised only exceptionally. Where there was a case for withholding the identity of a witness, the trial judge had a duty to see that justice was done, in the sense that the system operated fairly not only to the defendant but also to the prosecution and witnesses.[191]

– Where a witness fears for his or her safety, s 23(3) of the Criminal Justice Act 1988 allows a court to admit the witness statement of a witness who is too frightened to give oral testimony. In such cases the defence would not be able to cross-examine at all, and allowing the witness to testify behind a screen and/or to withhold his or her identity is a sensible compromise.

– A measure of anonymity may be achieved by use of a screen or a television link where the witness, although known to the accused, is unwilling to face him or her directly.[192] In *R v Lynch*[193] the 18-year-old victim of an indecent assault was sufficiently distressed for the judge to allow her to testify behind a screen and with a representative of Victim Support with her in the witness box. The Court of Appeal rejected the appellant's submission that this would have prejudiced the defendant in the eyes of the jury. The judge must warn the jury not to read anything into the use of the screens but the court saw little in the argument that screens were per se prejudicial to the accused.[194] The issue of the use of screens was raised in *X v UK*[195] which involved a Diplock court in Northern Ireland. The Commission rejected the complaint, finding that the decision to screen witnesses did not interfere with the accused's rights under Art 6.

– In *Watford Magistrates' Court ex parte Lenman*[196] the identity of the witnesses was not disclosed at all to the defendants. A group of youths rampaged through a city centre, violently attacking people. Witnesses were not identified and gave evidence behind screens and had their voices disguised. There was considerable risk of prejudice to the defence, which was handicapped since it was restricted in cross-examination and unable to question the credibility of the witnesses, especially as to whether they had any personal animosity against the accused. In *R v Taylor*[197] the Court of Appeal has enumerated the factors to be considered in assessing the balance of fairness. Were there real grounds for fear if the identity were disclosed? Was the evidence sufficiently important to make it unfair on the prosecution to proceed without it? Had the prosecution satisfied the court that the creditworthiness of the witness had been fully investigated? Was the court satisfied that no undue prejudice was caused to the defendant?

These constraints on the right of confrontation must be considered in the light of *Kostovski v Netherlands*,[198] and *Doorson v Netherlands*.[199] In the former, the

---

191 *X, Y and Z* (1989) 91 Cr App R 36.
192 This is by a special measures direction for eligible witnesses under s 19 of the Youth Justice and Criminal Evidence Act 1999.
193 [1993] Crim LR 868.
194 *R v Foster* [1995] Crim LR 333.
195 (1992) 15 EHRR CD 113.
196 [1993] Crim LR 388; approved of in *R v Taylor* [1995] Crim LR 253.
197 *R v Taylor* [1995] Crim LR 253.
198 (1989) 12 EHRR 434.
199 (1996) 22 EHRR 330.

conviction for armed robbery was based on reports of statements by two anonymous witnesses interviewed in the absence of the accused and counsel by the police, and in one case by an examining magistrate at an earlier stage. The European Court stressed that it was not its task to express a view on whether statements were correctly admitted and assessed by the court of trial, but to ascertain whether the proceedings as a whole, including the way in which evidence was taken and the defence rights were honoured, was fair. The fact that the prosecution witnesses' identities had been withheld meant that the accused was not only denied the right to cross-examine, but also unable to demonstrate prejudice, hostility or unreliability. Notwithstanding the possibility of intimidation of witnesses in serious cases, there was a need to balance the use of anonymous statements with the interests of the accused, and the conviction was held to be irreconcilable with the guarantee in Art 6.[200]

More recently, the Court has adopted a more moderate approach. In *Doorson* (above) the Court undertook a balancing exercise of the rights of the accused against the rights of the witness so that even where there was no overt threat against a particular witness, the general resort to violence by drug dealers was regarded as sufficient to maintain anonymity. Article 6 does not explicitly require the interests of witnesses in general, and those of victims called upon to testify in particular, to be taken into consideration. However, their life, liberty or security of person may be at stake and such interests are in principle protected by other, substantive provisions of the Convention which imply that States should organise their criminal proceedings in such a way that those interests are not unjustifiably imperilled. Against this background, the principles of a fair trial require that in appropriate cases the interests of the defence are balanced against those of witnesses or victims called upon to testify.

No violation of Art 6 will occur if it is established that the handicaps under which the defence laboured were sufficiently counterbalanced by the procedures followed by the judicial authorities. In *Kostovski* the anonymous witnesses were questioned at the appeals stage in the presence of counsel by an investigating judge who was aware of their identity, even if the defence was not. Counsel was not only present but was put in a position to ask the witnesses whatever questions he considered to be in the interests of the defence except in so far as they might lead to the disclosure of their identity, and these questions were all answered. The European Court considered that, on balance, the interests of the applicant were in this respect outweighed by the need to ensure the safety of the witnesses.

However, there have to be safeguards, ie questioning in the presence of counsel who is able to ask relevant questions, identity known to the judge, no conviction based solely or mainly on such evidence, and evidence treated with care. The key element here is the rejection of anonymity where the testimony is decisive. As was seen in *Taylor* (above), this is precisely the situation in UK courts, where such anonymity is permitted.

---

200   C Osborne 'Hearsay and the Court of Human Rights' [1993] Crim LR 255 at 261–263.

4.11 THE HEARSAY RULE

The use of statements by anonymous witnesses leads on to consideration of the hearsay rule – where the statements are by witnesses not present at the trial. Wide use would appear to be constrained by the right to confrontation in Art 6 which provides for a witness to be called, give oral evidence and be cross-examined. At common law, the hearsay rule prevents adducing such statements as evidence. The classic statement of the rule is:

> 'an assertion other than one made by a person while giving oral evidence in the proceedings is inadmissible as evidence of any fact asserted.'[201]

The rationale for the exclusion of hearsay is often put in terms of its unreliability and because the witness is not subject to cross-examination. However, the use of hearsay also means that the trial itself can be stigmatised as unfair and an abuse of due process. One of the hallmarks of totalitarian societies is the anonymous accusation based on rumour.[202] While medieval England might have been content to hang a man who was a 'notorious thief', modern legal values require specificity both as to what acts of theft have been committed and as to those who witnessed it. The latter must be identified and not anonymous, and must be available to be confronted publicly by the defendant. It is this notion of fairness which lies behind the hearsay rule.

Despite the formal exclusionary rule, hearsay evidence is admissible through wide-ranging exceptions, both at common law, especially the concept of *res gestae*, and through statute, notably the admissibility of confessions under s 76 of PACE 1984, of documentary hearsay under ss 23 and 24 of the Criminal Justice Act 1988, and of committal statements under s 68 of, and Sch 2 to, the Criminal Procedure and Investigations Act 1996. Although the confessions provisions do not infringe the right to a fair hearing, there may well be arguments raised as to the compatibility between the other common law and statutory provisions, and Art 6.

The major statutory exception to hearsay is under ss 23 and 24 of the Criminal Justice Act 1988. Essentially, a witness statement may be used where the witness is dead or physically or mentally unfit, out of the jurisdiction, unable to be traced, or has been intimidated. The trial judge does have an exclusionary discretion, under s 25, not to admit the evidence if, in the interests of justice, it ought not to be admitted. Section 25(2), while not detracting from the generality of that discretion, directs the court to look particularly at several elements: the nature and source of the document; the extent to which other evidence on the issue is available; the relevance of the evidence; or the risk of

---

201   C Tapper *Cross and Tapper on Evidence* 9th edn (Butterworths, 1995), p 46. This formula was approved by the House of Lords in *R v Sharp* [1988] 1 All ER 65 at 68b–c, and is followed by the Civil Evidence Act 1995.

202   However, this practice is still found in Western European jurisdictions where police officers are able to testify that X, who is not named, saw the accused commit the offence. Such testimony is admitted: J Andersen 'The Anonymity of Witnesses – a Danish Development' [1985] Crim LR 363.

unfairness. It would appear that the burden of persuading the court that the document should be excluded rests on the party objecting to admission. Furthermore, if the statement is one prepared for the purposes of criminal investigation, a positive duty is placed on the trial judge by s 26 so that the party tendering the statement bears the burden of persuading the court that the admission of the statement is in the interests of justice.[203]

The common law regulates the inherent unfairness contained in ss 23 and 24 through the following principles.

– Simple loss of the right to cross-examine is not per se unfair; to hold otherwise would be to nullify these provisions.
– It is not unfair to pressure the accused into testifying or to call witnesses in order to controvert the statement.
– It is not unfair if the defendant's actions can be demonstrated to have intimidated the witness.[204]
– If there is other evidence, it is easier to conclude that admission of the statement is not unfair. Equally, it is not unfair where the absent witness is required only to be cross-examined about some collateral matter.[205] But where the disputed evidence forms the hub of the prosecution case, the potential for unfairness is much greater, even where the evidence is reliable and from an unimpeachable source. In *R v French*[206] the Court of Appeal ruled that leave should not be given in such a case, but in *R v Grafton*[207] the accused and his accountant, by then deceased, were the only substantial witnesses. The accused had himself referred the investigators from Customs and Excise to the accountant for information about his business affairs. The accountant had made a statement to them which was significantly adverse to the accused. In such circumstances, the statement was admitted.
– Fairness is to be sought through the direction to the jury. The judge must stress that the evidence has not been tested by cross-examination and should point out any weaknesses or inconsistencies in the statement.

Do these safeguards comply with the requirements of Art 6? The overall effect of the 1988 Act and, in particular, the statutory duty to consider any unfairness to the defendant before admitting documentary hearsay would appear to ensure that there is a 'fair hearing' and that these provisions are not in breach of Art 6. Article 6(3)(d) embodies the accused's right 'to examine or have examined witnesses against him and to obtain the attendance and examination of witnesses on his behalf under the same conditions as witnesses against him'. It is this paragraph which impinges upon the operation of the hearsay rule and which underlines an accused's right to be protected from anonymous accusation. The strongest view is that Art 6(3)(d) prohibits the prosecution

---

203   *R v Cole* [1990] 2 All ER 108; see also *R v Price* [1991] Crim LR 707 on the similar requirement in s 25(2)(d).
204   *R v Fairfax* [1995] Crim LR 949.
205   *R v Holman* [1995] Crim LR 80 where the written evidence of Irish bank employees was accepted.
206   (1993) 97 Cr App R 421.
207   [1995] Crim LR 61.

from adducing hearsay evidence, but the European Court has not adopted so strict an interpretation.

In *Unterpertinger v Austria*[208] the accused was charged with assault on his stepdaughter and wife. The police took witness statements from the two victims who, under Austrian law, were not compellable. At the trial both victims refused to testify and the interviews with the investigating judge were read out. The defendant applied to the Commission on the grounds that the acceptance of written evidence of interviews with the judge and the police infringed Art 6(1) and (3)(d) as he was unable to cross-examine the victims. The Court concluded that the conviction had been substantially based on those statements and therefore that there was a breach of the article. A similar result occurred in *Kostovski v Netherlands*[209] where the conviction was based on accounts by two witnesses who were allowed to remain anonymous and not to testify because of their fear of reprisals. These cases suggest that where the hearsay evidence is the main or decisive evidence against the defendant, reliance on it in court will be a breach of the Convention. Other decisions have emphasised that the hearsay evidence must not be the only item of evidence. Where a victim to an assault declined to testify at trial, the Court stressed that the statements relied on were not the only evidence.[210] The cases are not wholly consistent on this point.[211]

Such decisions suggest that the safeguards built into the Criminal Justice Act 1988 are adequate. The Commission considered the relationship between the provisions of the 1988 Act and Art 6 in *Trivedi v UK*,[212] where a doctor was charged with false accounting by claiming for more night visits to a patient than had in fact occurred. The prosecution relied on written statements by the patient, who was elderly and infirm. The Commission declared the application inadmissible as the statements were not the only evidence, the judge had conducted an inquiry into the patient's condition and evidence on the patient's reliability had been admitted. The jury had been specifically warned against attaching undue weight to the patient's evidence.

Even if the principle of a 'fair trial' is accepted as the rationale for excluding hearsay evidence adduced by the prosecution, the impact of Art 6 may require amendment to the rigid application of the rule as far as defendants are concerned. *R v Blastland*[213] was a murder case in which a third party made a statement which strongly suggested that person's involvement in the killing. This statement was held inadmissible by the House of Lords. There is an argument that the concept of a fair hearing requires an inclusionary discretion to admit hearsay statements on behalf of the accused,[214] although the common law adopts the principle that any evidence admissible for the defence must also

---

208   (1986) 13 EHRR 175.
209   (1989) 12 EHRR 434.
210   *Asch v Austria* (1991) 15 EHRR 597.
211   C Osborne 'Hearsay and the Court of Human Rights' [1993] Crim LR 255 at 261–263.
212   [1997] EHRLR 520.
213   [1985] 2 All ER 1095 – a confession to the murder by a third party was excluded; *R v Turner* [1975] 1 All ER 70; *R v Harry* (1986) 86 Cr App R 105; *R v Beckford and Daley* [1991] Crim LR 833.
214   T Allen 'Implied Assertions as Hearsay' (1992) 142 NLJ 1194.

be admissible for the prosecution. The result of the exclusion of the items of evidence involved – the third party's confession and his knowledge of the crime – was to deprive the jury of information which might have left it with a reasonable doubt about the defendant's guilt. The common law rule means that a third party's confession is often excluded. But fairness cannot be ensured without a power to admit such evidence in an appropriate case and, where the context and circumstances of a third party's confession can be fully related, it should sometimes be brought to the attention of the jury. The US Supreme Court has held that the exclusion of evidence of confessions made by a third party, in accordance with ordinary rules of evidence, deprived the defendant of a fair trial.[215] But in *Blastland v UK*[216] the Commission held the application inadmissible and that the statements could be excluded provided the accused could call the third party as a witness.

4.12   IMPROPERLY OBTAINED EVIDENCE

Is it a breach of the requirement for a fair hearing to permit the State to use evidence which has been obtained by improper means? Improper in this context means in violation by the police or the prosecution of one or more of the substantive rights under the Convention. This may involve matters such as search and seizure, interviewing techniques leading to confessions, means of identification, the use of informants, undercover agents or entrapment, and various methods of covert and intrusive surveillance. These have been considered in detail in Chapter 3 above, and the following is a summary of the Art 6 issues which arise.

The primary question is whether the means employed are in fact improper.

–   Is the exercise of State powers in accordance with law? Administrative regulation of the police is normally not sufficient,[217] although the Commission has accepted that the use of evidence from informants and accomplices[218] or from undercover agents[219] has not infringed Art 6. If there is authority by statute or precedent, there remains an issue of the 'quality of law'. Even if the police conduct conforms with domestic law, that law must also protect other substantive rights under the Convention. Thus, State power may infringe on the right to personal privacy safe-guarded by Art 8, but this is only a qualified right and the European Court would have to consider whether the infringement is action necessary (for example, that it would acquire evidence that could not be obtained by other means) and proportional (ie that the extent of the infringement is commensurate to the seriousness of the offence under investigation).

---

215   *Chambers v Mississippi* 410 US 295 (1973).
216   Application No 12045/86, (1987) 52 DR 273.
217   *Khan v UK* Application No 35394/97, [2000] Crim LR 684.
218   *X v UK* Application No 7306/75, (1976) 7 DR 115.
219   *X v FRG* (1989) 11 EHRR 88.

– Is there some form of accountability to protect citizens' rights? The telephone tapping cases such as *Klass v Germany*[220] suggest that while it is in principle desirable to entrust the supervisory control to a judge in accordance with the rule of law, other safeguards might suffice if they are independent and vested with sufficient powers to exercise an effective and continuous control. The Home Secretary is clearly sufficient under the Regulation of Investigatory Powers Act 2000, but questions must be asked as to whether a police superintendent can be seen as meeting the requisite standards of independence for authorising s 18 search warrants or 'directed surveillance' under s 28 of the Regulation of Investigatory Powers Act 2000.

If the means used to obtain the evidence are deemed improper, this is not determinative. The key principle is the question of equality of arms between the State and the defendant.

– Simple defect does not lead to automatic exclusion of evidence. The common law has never accepted this approach, although other common law jurisdictions have adopted a rule that evidence obtained in such circumstances is automatically excluded.[221] The European Court has rejected the proposition that evidence obtained through unlawful or underhand means by the State infringes the right to a fair hearing and should be automatically excluded.[222]
– The evidence will normally be excluded where it is the only or main evidence against the accused.
– There must be proper procedural safeguards and other supporting proof of guilt. The defence should be able to challenge the authenticity of the evidence, and the jury should be aware of the situation. The safeguards that exist, namely the *voir dire* procedure and the exclusionary discretion under s 78 of PACE 1984, are sufficient to comply with Art 6 requirements. For example, although the admission of confession evidence obtained under duress or in the absence of satisfactory procedures to safeguard their reliability would be in breach, the safeguards by which the prosecution must prove beyond reasonable doubt that a confession was not obtained by oppression or in circumstances that would render it unreliable under s 76 of PACE 1984 would also normally satisfy those requirements. In *G v UK*[223] the provisions of the pre-1984 common law were under scrutiny. These required that a confession was obtained 'voluntarily' and the *voir dire* procedure was held to satisfy Convention requirements.
– There must be proof of detriment to the applicant.

---

220 (1978) 2 EHRR 214.
221 *Simpson v Attorney-General* [1994] 3 NZLR 703; Canadian Charter of Rights and Freedoms 1982, s 24(1).
222 *Schenk v Switzerland* (1988) 13 EHRR 242.
223 Application No 9370/81, (1983) 35 DR 75.

–   The use of such evidence can compromise the fairness of the hearing in any particular case but not necessarily. The Court will look at proceedings as a whole and must consider, not the safety or reliability of the proceedings, but their fairness.

4.13   CHARACTER OF THE ACCUSED

The circumstances in which the previous convictions of the accused are admissible evidence vary considerably across Europe.[224] In most jurisdictions, the trial is conducted solely by a judge or, where there is a jury, the judge is involved in the deliberations. Where the jury is the sole trier of fact, there is greater risk of prejudice. As a result, at common law there is a prohibition on the use of such evidence by the prosecution either in its evidence-in-chief or cross-examination of the accused under s 1(f) of the Criminal Evidence Act 1898. But there are exceptions, notably where evidence of good character has been advanced by the defendant, where the defendant has impugned the character of a prosecution witness, where the defendant has testified against a co-accused, or under the similar fact rules. Such exceptions would appear at present not to violate the right to a fair hearing. In *X v UK*,[225] evidence was given in a rape trial of previous convictions, but the Commission rejected the application, considering the variety of practice across Europe and regarding the procedure as not violating any of the requirements of Art 6 even in a trial by jury.

Provisions also allow evidence to be given not of the accused's previous convictions, but of those of others where they are relevant to the proceedings. Although the common law[226] stated that parties were not permitted to use convictions in previous cases as evidence, this meant that the prosecution[227] would need to prove the facts anew even in related trials. The absurdity of this was shown in *R v Spinks*,[228] in which the principal offender had stabbed the victim and had been convicted of grievous bodily harm (GBH). Spinks was now being tried as an accomplice and it was held that the prosecution could not use the principal's conviction as evidence that the offence had been committed.

This position was changed by PACE 1984, s 74(1) of which states:

> 'In any proceedings the fact that a person other than the accused has been convicted of an offence by or before any court in the United Kingdom or by a Service Court outside the United Kingdom shall be admissible in evidence for the purpose of proving, where to do so is relevant to any issue in those proceedings, that that person committed that offence, whether or not any other evidence of his having committed that offence is given.'

A conviction is admissible where it is relevant to an issue in the case, for example where it is an essential element of the offence with which the accused

---

224   S Uglow *Evidence* (Sweet & Maxwell, 1997), p 408.
225   Application No 2518/65, 2 *Digest* 739.
226   *Hollington v Hewthorn* [1943] KB 587.
227   This would normally be the case, although s 74 applies equally to the defence.
228   [1982] 1 All ER 587; *R v Hassan* [1970] 1 QB 423.

is charged as in *Spinks,* or to prove the purpose of a joint enterprise as in *R v Robertson and Golder.*[229] The burden of proving the convictions wrong would normally rest on the defence and is subject to the exclusionary discretion under s 78 since it may well have an adverse effect on the fairness of the proceedings as in *R v Mattison.*[230] The dangers are that the accused may be tarred with the same brush as the other defendants, and the burden of proof is reversed.

In *MH v UK*[231] the defendant was charged with a conspiracy to cheat, and the co-conspirator pleaded guilty to charges arising from the same events. This plea was admitted into evidence under s 74, and the Commission rejected the application on the grounds that the judge had directed the jury that the admission into evidence of the plea did not prove the existence of the conspiracy and that, as it was always open to the defendant to call his co-accused, there were no grounds to consider that the trial had been unfair.

4.14 APPEALS BASED ON BREACHES OF THE CONVENTION

The domestic appeal process is able to remedy certain errors of judgment by a trial. The European Court must look at the proceedings as a whole.[232] In *Edwards v UK*[233] the defects at trial involved failure to reveal additional fingerprints (a neighbour's) at the scene or to disclose the fact that the victim, an old lady, who had a fleeting glance of the assailant, did not pick out his photograph. The Court of Appeal examined the transcript of the trial, including the applicant's alleged confession, and considered in detail the impact of the new information on the conviction. In the proceedings the applicant was represented by senior and junior counsel who had every opportunity to seek to persuade the court that the conviction should not stand in view of the evidence of non-disclosure. The police officers who had given evidence at the trial were not heard. It was, none the less, open to counsel for the applicant to make an application – which they chose not to do – that the police officers be called as witnesses. In these circumstances, the European Court held that the procedure before the Appeal Court had remedied the defects at the original trial.

However, to remedy defects in the trial, it is clear that the Court of Appeal must directly address the issue of the fairness of the proceedings. In *Condron v UK*[234] the judge allowed the jury to draw adverse inferences from the accused's failure to answer police questions. The Court of Appeal regarded this as a significant defect but held that, given the weight of the prosecution evidence, the conviction was safe.[235] The European Court stated that the question whether

---

229   [1987] 3 All ER 231.
230   [1990] Crim LR 117; see also *R v Turner* [1991] Crim LR 57.
231   [1997] EHRLR 279.
232   *Helmers v Sweden* (1991) 15 EHRR 285.
233   (1992) 15 EHRR 417.
234   Application No 35718/97, (2001) 31 EHRR 1.
235   See also *R v Francom and Others* [2000] Crim LR 1018.

the right to a fair trial had been secured in any given case could not be assimilated to a finding that the conviction was safe in the absence of any inquiry into fairness. The Court of Appeal ought not to have speculated on the effect that this crucial defect in the direction might have had on the jury's deliberations.

The Court of Appeal must address the question of the fairness of the proceedings in the lower court before upholding the conviction. The principle appears clear, but it is difficult to distinguish the Court of Appeal deciding that the impact of the old lady as a witness would not have changed things in *Edwards* from the same body deciding that a proper direction on inferences would not have changed matters in *Condron*. Failure to disclose by the prosecution is surely as critical a defect as a judge's misdirection, and speculation as to the impact of the error by the European Court seems as objectionable as speculation by the Court of Appeal.

When a defendant alleges that evidence has been obtained in the course of the investigation as a result of a violation of a Convention right, it is to be expected that the trial judge will give that breach due weight in deciding that the admission of that evidence would adversely affect the fairness of the proceedings. The judge must always ensure that the trial is fair. But the same cannot be said for the judges of the Court of Appeal. Under s 2 of the Criminal Appeal Act 1995 the Court of Appeal is directed to allow an appeal against conviction if it considers that the conviction is unsafe, and to dismiss it in any other case. If this section is read literally, it would seem to preclude the appellate courts from considering questions of fairness and to signal a retreat to the position in *R v Sang*[236] where the House of Lords abdicated from any responsibility for regulating police conduct in an investigation. This is reinforced by the judgment in *R v Chalkley*,[237] but would mean that the courts were on a collision course with Strasbourg.[238] The Court of Appeal's decision suggests that a conviction can be safe even though the trial was unfair; in such a case, s 2 requires that the court dismiss the appeal. This is a time-honoured practice in the common law – although not for Parliament which has, on occasion, prohibited the use of improperly obtained or retained material as evidence, no matter how compelling. In *Attorney-General's Reference (No 3 of 1999)*[239] the Court of Appeal upheld a trial judge's decision not to admit a DNA profile in a rape case – the sample had originally been lawfully taken on another charge on which the defendant was acquitted and thus should have been destroyed.[240] The parallel with *Chalkley* is interesting – in both situations there was evidence which was conclusive but improperly obtained. In one case, parliamentary policy was to exclude it, presumably because of the human rights implications, whereas in the other case, judges were willing to ignore such considerations.

In *Condron v UK* (above) the European Court held that in assessing the fairness of the trial, the judge must look at the fairness of the entirety of the

---

236   [1980] AC 402.
237   [1998] QB 848, [1998] 2 All ER 155.
238   A Clarke 'Safety or Supervision?' [1999] Crim LR 108.
239   [2000] 4 All ER 360.
240   PACE 1984, s 64(3B)(b).

proceedings. Single flaws in procedure did not, in themselves, make a trial unfair, but any breach must be balanced against the other circumstances of the case, not least whether the disputed evidence is the sole or main evidence against the accused. In *Condron* the weight of the rest of the evidence may easily have swayed the Court towards finding that the impugned evidence (an inference from a failure to answer police questions) was relatively minor, and that the proceedings were fair overall. This would have reflected the Court of Appeal's approach, which expressed concern about the direction but considered the conviction safe. In rejecting this option, the Court stressed that Art 6 means that both trial and appellate judges must inquire into overall fairness, and the finding that a conviction is safe is not a substitute for such an inquiry. This significant point must raise serious questions about s 2 of the Criminal Appeal Act 1995, ie that it is not compatible with the court's obligations under the Convention.

However, the Strasbourg decisions are somewhat contradictory. In contrast to the judgment in *Condron* is the Court's decision in *Khan v UK*[241] where the key issue was the fairness of proceedings, which included the admission into evidence of a recording obtained by the police entering a house as trespassers and planting a listening device. The Court had no difficulty in finding that this was a breach of Art 8, but went on to rule that despite the fact that the recording was the sole evidence against the accused, there was no violation of the right to a fair trial. The majority argued that it was necessary to take into account the strength and reliability of the disputed evidence.[242] It is difficult to follow the reasoning underlying this, but the Court appears to be swayed by the sheer probative value of this recording. As we have seen, this is strange since previous decisions have almost invariably eschewed the pragmatic position of considering the facts and deciding whether a conviction is safe. The weaknesses are brought out by the one dissentient, Judge Loucaides, who defined 'fairness' as necessarily implying observance of the rule of law. Although there was no breach of domestic law, the UK courts ought not to admit evidence obtained in breach of the Convention. Effective enforcement of the Convention is otherwise hindered since the police would not be deterred from repeating the conduct. Exclusion of the evidence is the practical and effective remedy, and should be a necessary corollary to Art 8 rights.

Khan runs counter to *Condron*, to *Schenk v Switzerland*[243] and to many cases over the years[244] where the key issue was whether the impugned evidence was the main or sole item against the accused – if so, it should be excluded but, if not, then it may be admitted without violating the overall fairness of the proceedings. This doctrine raises the 'safety' versus 'fairness' debate and questions whether the two ideas are related. Presumably, fairness is the primary value – the State has a dominant position which it must be prevented from abusing by ensuring that its agents observe the rule of law. This is an aspect of

---

241 Application No 35394/97, [2000] Crim LR 684.
242 Ibid, para 37.
243 (1988) 13 EHRR 242.
244 Compare *Doorson v Netherlands* (1996) 22 EHRR 330 where other evidence existed, with *Unterpertinger v Austria* (1986) 13 EHRR 175 where it did not.

the doctrine of equality of arms and, where the disputed evidence is the only evidence, the State, by its breach of the Convention, has irredeemably altered that equality. Parity and fairness can be achieved only by refusing to allow the State to rely on evidence obtained by abuse of power, however compelling that evidence may be.

However, where the disputed evidence merely forms part of the prosecution case and is accompanied by other (lawfully obtained) items of incriminating evidence, the admission of the disputed evidence becomes a minor unfairness, and it is possible to conclude that, as a whole, the proceedings are fair. This is not a balancing act between fairness and safety, in the sense that the more probative and reliable the evidence, the less we need to concern ourselves with fairness. Instead, *Schenk* suggests that a court should put the disputed evidence on one side and consider the strength and reliability of the surrounding evidence. If this supports the prosecution case, the admission of the impugned evidence need not be unfair. Of course, this leaves questions unanswered. How strong should the surrounding evidence be? Should it be simply a prima facie case? Should it be strong but with residual doubts that may be dispelled by the disputed evidence? Should it be enough that a reasonable jury might base a conviction upon it?

The case-law does not help us with these issues. What it does is suggest that the appellate courts cannot interpret safety as simply being sure that there is sufficient probative and reliable evidence against the accused. Before a conviction is safe, it must first and foremost have been obtained in a hearing that was fair. If the Court of Appeal cannot accept that as an article of faith, if not of logic, then s 2 of the Criminal Appeal Act 1995 cannot be compatible with the Convention.

Chapter 5
IMPACT ON SENTENCING

5.1 INTRODUCTION

In the two years since the first edition of this book the sentencing climate in England and Wales has changed. This has thus impacted on the potential areas of challenge under the Human Rights Act 1998 suggested in the first edition. Some areas of concern have now been remedied, while others remain. Further, new legislation has been enacted altering the provisions for some sentences and indeed creating new ones.[1] Section 19 of the Act took effect prior to the October 2000 date, requiring that a 'Minister of the Crown in charge of a Bill in either House of Parliament must, before Second Reading of the Bill – (a) make a statement to the effect that in his view the provisions of the Bill are compatible with the Convention Rights'.[2] The recently enacted legislation considered in this chapter has been declared compatible; however, it remains to be seen whether the application of new sentences or altered sentencing provisions provide grounds for challenge either domestically or through recourse to the European Court of Human Rights (the European Court).

This chapter will consider, first, current sentencing practice and policy, including any impact on potential areas for application that new legislation may have. This is then followed by a consideration of the articles of the European Convention on Human Rights (the Convention) themselves and possible areas of concern for domestic courts regarding sentencing, as highlighted by European Court jurisprudence and more recent consideration by the domestic courts themselves.

Prior to any consideration of sentencing and the potential avenues of challenge presented by the implementation of the Act, it may be useful to review the approaches taken by the domestic courts in the interim period between the Act receiving Royal Assent in 1998 and its implementation on 2 October 2000. The jurisprudence of the European Court has long had an effect on the policy and procedures relating to sentencing policy at a domestic level[3] and the implementation of the Act will arguably complement and extend this. Through a consideration of relevant decisions handed down by the English courts since the beginning of 1999, it may be possible to suggest how far the courts have, just subsequent to implementation of the Act, already met criticisms made by the

---

1   For example, the Criminal Justice and Courts Services Act 2000 which creates two new community sentences, the exclusion order (s 46) and the drug abstinence order (s 47).
2   Human Rights Act 1998, s 19(1)(a).
3   For example, criticism by the European Court in relation to the review of the continued detention of discretionary lifers post tariff and the independence of decisions made resulted in the creation of the Discretionary Lifer Panels of the Parole Board in 1992.

Court regarding sentences meted out. Such consideration will better inform speculation concerning how the rights guaranteed by the Convention and now enshrined in the Act could be interpreted by domestic courts with regards to sentence.

During this interim period there have been a number of domestic judgments which have sought to consider the relevance of the articles of the Convention, and indeed in some cases, apply it. As University College London's Constitution Unit notes:

> 'The Courts showed increasing willingness to apply Convention rights before the Human Rights Act came into force. But the anticipated flood of challenges after 2 October has been slow to materialise ... Few clear patterns have emerged during the first two months of operation of the Human Rights Act.'[4]

With regard specifically to sentencing, the courts have been particularly slow to consider Convention articles,[5] and since the close of 1998 a number of cases dealing with appeals against sentence have pointedly refused to consider the potential effects of implementation. In the case of *R v Secretary of State for the Home Department ex parte Mitchell*,[6] it was noted in relation to an appeal for judicial review of a recall notice that following *R v DPP ex parte Kebilene*[7] 'the Act did not give rise to any legitimate expectation that, prior to its taking full effect, its terms could be relied upon'. The judge in this case continued to comment on the matter of the applicability of the Act and arguments presented by counsel, and ended his judgment by stating:

> 'It seems to me that those are contentious and interesting matters that may arise on another occasion, but I am satisfied that the application should be refused because of the reasons I gave earlier, namely that, in effect, the applicant is seeking to rewrite the statutory provision in advance of the Human Rights Act coming into force. So permission is refused in this case. May I thank you both for your submissions on that point. I think another day and another time it might give rise to more difficult issues.'[8]

In *R v T and Others*[9] Maurice Kay J commented:

4　UCL, The Constitution Unit, *Constitutional Update: Human Rights* (November 2000). However, the Unit does estimate from government figures, that 'in England and Wales, the Human Rights Act will double, to around 600 a year, the number of applications for judicial review and will add 2,300 to 2,800 extra sitting days in cases already before the higher courts at an annual cost of £60 million (including £39 million for legal aid)' (at p 3).

5　Although see *R v Bowden* (2000) Crim LR 381 where the court, while refusing to consider Art 8 in relation to charges contrary to the Protection of Children Act 1978, allowed an appeal against sentence as there was no evidence to suggest the defendant was a risk to the public and thus a custodial sentence was not warranted.

6　[1999] QB (Crown Office List) CO/4423/99; *R v Delaney, R v Hanrahan* (unreported) 14 May 1999, CA; although see more generally *R v DPP ex parte Kebilene* [1999] Crim LR 994 for discussion of when it may be relevant to consider the implications of the Act prior to implementation.

7　[1999] Crim LR 994.

8　*R v Secretary of State for the Home Department ex parte Mitchell* [1999] QB (Crown Office List) CO/4423/99.

9　[1999] 2 Cr App R(S) 304 at 310–311.

'It is one thing to enable a judge to have regard to the Convention as a factor which may affect the exercise of his discretion. However, neither *Khan* nor any of the other authorities compel the judge to take the Convention into account when exercising his discretion. Nor do they require him to give overriding affect to the Convention when he considers it along with all other relevant matters. It is a matter for the judge to decide whether to take it into account and, if he does so how much weight to give it ... Far from the Convention possibly informing the exercise of discretion, it would be effectively removing that discretion. In our judgement, the sentences imposed in the present case cannot successfully be challenged by reference to the Convention.'

Part of this initial reluctance may be attributable in part to the way in which the Court of Appeal views its role as something separate and distinct from that of the European Court. The divergence in roles was highlighted in the 2000 case of *R v Davis; R v Rowe; R v Johnson*[10] where Mantell LJ noted:

'The duty of the [European Court] is to determine whether or not there has been a violation of the European Convention or in this case, more particularly, of Art 6(1). It is not within the remit of the [Court] to comment upon the nature and quality of any breach or upon the impact such a breach might have had ... This court is concerned with the safety of conviction.'[11]

It is arguable that this perspective may indeed cause difficulties when domestic courts begin in earnest to take account of Convention articles. If the stance taken in determining whether violations have occurred differs too greatly from that of the Court, the impact of the Act in all areas of the criminal justice process, not just sentencing, may be diminished.[12]

5.2   CURRENT SENTENCING PRACTICE

A consideration of current sentencing practice is relevant at this juncture since recent legislation and an ongoing review of the framework of sentences and policy may impact on the type of sentence meted out, the length of sentences, the reasons for the sentence[13] and, arguably, the domestic interpretation of the Act. A point incidental to this discussion, but worthy of consideration, is the additional impact any changes in sentencing policy will inevitably have on the prison system.[14] Any increases in sentence length or use of incarceration will lead to a greater number of prisoners within the penal system. This, in turn,

---

10   *R v Davis; R v Rowe; R v Johnson* [2000] TLR 560, CA. At the appeal hearing the European Court had already handed down judgment that the trial of the appellants had been unfair under Art 6(1).

11   *R v Davis; R v Rowe; R v Johnson*, ibid.

12   For further discussion of the different processes used by domestic courts and the European Court, see **5.8.1** concerning the issue of proportionality.

13   The reasoning behind the sentence has been particularly relevant to reasoning within European Court jurisprudence, for example, the reasons behind the continued detention of an offender beyond the tariff period: see discussion by the Court in *Hussain v UK* (1996) 22 EHRR 1 at 24; and *T and V v UK* (2000) Crim LR 187.

14   Figures from the Home Office state that 'The general pattern in sentencing of indictable offences has changed little between 1998 and 1999 but continued to increase in severity at

leads to a period of overcrowding and arguably a decrease in standards within prisons, possible fertile avenues of appeal both domestically under the Act or eventual recourse to the Court.[15]

Sentencing policy during the last 15 years has been characterised by a piecemeal approach and the distinct lack of a coherent rationale. A brief overview of sentencing practice in relation to custodial sentences from the late 1980s to the mid-1990s suggests that the response of the courts in relation to the choice of disposal was, to a great extent, to adopt the role of political and social tool. Sentencing policy in this jurisdiction essentially consisted of guideline decisions provided by the higher courts; sentencing was in effect a policy of judicial self-regulation.[16] While such shortcomings were recognised and attempts to address the lack of a coherent rationale were made by virtue of the Criminal Justice Act 1991,[17] it has been argued that the approach was one which sought 'a partnership in which the legislature establishes the framework and the courts develop the more detailed numerical guidance; however ... the framework established by the Criminal Justice Act 1991 is less clear than one would have hoped for'.[18]

The Home Office, in 2000, commenced *A Review of the Sentencing Framework*, recognising that:

> 'Public confidence in our system of justice is too low. There is a feeling that our sentencing framework does not work as well as it should and that it pays insufficient weight to the needs of victims ... There is insufficient consistency or progression in sentencing and sentencers receive insufficient information about whether their sentencing decisions have worked.'[19]

The Review suggests that an appropriate sentencing framework should 'deliver the twin aims of public protection and a reduction in re-offending'.[20] Interestingly, given the number of appeals lodged with the European Court in relation to sentencing options and procedures in recent years, the Review document does not mention human rights, the Court, the Convention or even the Act.[21] The Review considers that sentencing should balance notions of public protection and a reduction in reoffending. The word 'balance' is also evident in the Home Office Statement of Purpose, but, as Andrew Ashworth comments, 'The reference to "balancing" fails to address the key issues of

---

both courts. 23.4 per cent of those sentenced for indictable offences in 1999 were given a custodial sentence, the highest annual rate for over 40 years. 2,500 more persons were sentenced to custody for indictable offences': M Ayres et al, Home Office Research, Development and Statistics Directorate, Issue 19/00 (31 October 2000).
15   For detailed discussion, see Chapter 6 below.
16   A von Hirsch and A Ashworth *Principled Sentencing* (Edinburgh University Press, 1992), ch 5.3.
17   Provision was made by the Act for the introduction of statutory principles to be handed down to the courts.
18   von Hirsch and Ashworth (n 16 above), p 289.
19   Home Office Communications Directorate, CCN077828, C4000 (May 2000) 1.
20   Ibid, 2.
21   The Halliday Report 'Making punishments work: review of the sentencing framework for England and Wales' was published in July 2001.

priorities, a particularly significant failing in view of the Human Rights Act 1998'.[22]

However, while the sentencing framework remains under review and criticisms regarding its aims remain valid, there are changes being made already by virtue of legislation[23] which seek, to a certain extent, to clarify and modify sentences and practice. During the last two decades the very nature of sentencing practice in this jurisdiction ensured that sentence decisions and forms of disposal have provided a rich ground for appeal to the European Court under the Convention. It is perhaps in recognition of this that the current climate of review and legislative change with regards to sentencing has evolved. Measures which may go some way to counter such criticisms include the greater recognition of the need for thorough sentencing guidelines to magistrates, creation of the Sentencing Advisory Panel[24] and statutory provision within the Crime and Disorder Act 1998 for courts to consider the creation of sentencing guidelines. Section 80(3) of that Act states:

'Where the Court decides to frame or revise such guidelines, the Court shall have regard to –

(a)   the need to promote consistency in sentencing;
(b)   the sentences imposed by courts in England and Wales for offences of the relevant category;
(c)   the cost of different sentences and their relative effectiveness in preventing re-offending;
(d)   the need to promote public confidence in the criminal justice system; and
(e)   the views communicated to the Court, in accordance with section 81(4)(b) below, by the Sentencing Advisory Panel.'

In formulating or altering guidelines the courts shall have regard to the views of the Sentencing Advisory Panel. While this is not, perhaps, the independent sentencing body envisaged by a preceding Royal Commission report, both the creation of the Panel and the statutory recognition of the need for sentencing guidelines do go some way to addressing concerns raised by unsystematic policy. Such developments are reinforced with the enactment of the Powers of Criminal Courts (Sentencing) Act 2000, legislation designed to integrate the current sentencing framework and legislation. However, this is not to suggest that all difficulties and challenges raised due to the piecemeal nature of sentencing have disappeared, as Nicola Padfield comments:

'The Guidelines have no legal status, the justices' clerks and local liaison judges may well play a role in deciding the extent to which these guidelines are adopted in individual courts. Whilst fixed penalties for some minor offences are widely accepted, so is the need to individualise them at a more serious level. The consolidation of the law on sentencing in the Power of the Courts (Sentencing) Act 2000 will do much to iron out the anomalies.'[25]

---

22   A Ashworth *Sentencing and Criminal Justice* 3rd edn (Butterworths, 2000), p 59.
23   Criminal Justice and Courts Services Act 2000 and the Powers of Criminal Courts (Sentencing) Act 2000. Both Acts received Royal Assent in the latter part of 2000.
24   Crime and Disorder Act 1998, s 81; the Panel began work in July 1999.
25   N Padfield *Text and Materials on the Criminal Justice Process* (Butterworths, 2000), p 275.

Perhaps of greatest importance with regard to sentencing are three legislative measures, each of which seeks to address criticisms concerning sentencing policy and practice made both domestically and at a European level. These are: the Crime (Sentences) Act 1997; the Criminal Justice and Courts Services Act 2000; and the Powers of Criminal Courts (Sentencing) Act 2000. The latter seeks primarily to provide a coherent body of sentencing policy and range of disposal options and, as such, will not be considered separately. The Act provides new statutory reference for many existing sentences. While the power to impose various sentences now rests within this Act, this chapter will employ the legislation currently in use in order to avoid confusion at this early stage of the Act's operation. However, it is worthy of note that the implementation of such legislation arguably does, as Padfield suggests, go a long way to meeting criticisms concerning sentencing rationale.

5.2.1 Crime (Sentences) Act 1997

The Crime (Sentences) Act 1997 received Royal Assent on 21 March 1997, the last full day of Parliament prior to the general election on 1 May 1997, which was arguably crucial to the nature of its provisions. As one commentator noted:

> 'As far as this 1997 Act is concerned, a number of amendments were moved by the House of Lords to which the previous government had to concede in order for it to be passed in time. Were it not for this crucial timing, essential aspects of the 1997 Act may well have been very different.'[26]

That said, the Act was created to counter, in part, the criticisms levelled at sentencing policy at the time being of a piecemeal nature. It was envisaged by legislators that the Act would provide a more coherent and definitive guideline as to both when a custodial sentence is warranted, and the duration of the sentence. The catch-phrase promulgated by government was the introduction of 'Honesty in Sentencing'. Emphasis on minimum sentencing and the number of previous convictions for the same offence, are features of the Act which reflect its aim, 'namely greater certainty in the sentencing of repeat offenders who commit serious crimes, class A drug trafficking and domestic burglaries'.[27] The aim, in effect, was to provide more secure parameters within which a judge may exercise his discretion. The Act arguably also seeks potentially to minimise the criticism levelled at sentencing practice high-lighting discrepancies in sentencing between courts, whereby defendants found guilty of the same offence in similar circumstances receive disparate sentences.[28] Such provisions provide some level of safeguard and consistency for defendants and arguably also serves to reduce the areas of potential challenge against sentence under the Human Rights Act 1998.

---

26   L Jason-Lloyd (1997) 147 NLJ 1070.

27   Ibid, p 1072.

28   For examples of such disparate sentencing practice, see the Prison Reform Trust's report, *Sentencing: A Geographical Lottery* (July 1997).

However, controversy surrounding the Act focused primarily on s 2, which makes provision for imposing an automatic life sentence[29] and, in particular, s 2(2), which states:

'The court shall impose a life sentence, that is to say –

(a) where the person is 21 or over, a sentence of imprisonment for life;
(b) where he is under 21, a sentence of custody for life under section 8(2) of the Criminal Justice Act 1982

unless the court is of the opinion that there are exceptional circumstances relating to either of the offences or to the offender which justify its not doing so.'

The application and interpretation of this section has been considered at a domestic level in *R v Kelly*[30] and it was noticeable in the judgment, and indeed in subsequent cases concerning this section, that the domestic courts focused on the final clause of s 2(2). In this the courts have chosen to place great importance on the idea of 'exceptional circumstances' in determining whether an automatic life sentence should be imposed. The issues surrounding the application of such a sentence will be considered later in this chapter; at this point, however, it is interesting to note the European Court's reaction to argument relating to the Convention. The Court in *Kelly* noted with regard to the impending implementation of the Human Rights Act 1998 that it had not yet been brought into force and thus: 'we think it preferable that consideration of the conformity of s 2 with the Convention should be deferred until that issue comes before the court for authoritative decision'. At the time of writing, such a case had not yet been heard but it is possible to argue that a future court, employing the provisions of the Human Rights Act 1998, may choose to interpret s 2 in a different manner, with different emphasis on the wording.

5.2.2 Criminal Justice and Courts Services Act 2000

The Criminal Justice and Courts Services Act 2000 received Royal Assent in November 2000 and contains some sections pertinent to a discussion on sentencing and current sentencing practice, and which may affect areas of potential challenges under the Human Rights Act 1998. Worthy of particular note are the opening two sections of the Act. Section 1 states:

'(1) This Chapter has effect for the purposes of providing for –

(a) courts to be given assistance in determining the appropriate sentences to pass, and making other decisions, in respect of persons charged with or convicted of offences, and
(b) the supervision and rehabilitation of such persons.

(2) Subsection (1)(b) extends (in particular) to –

(a) giving effect to community orders,
(b) supervising persons released from prison on licence,
(c) providing accommodation in approved premises.'

---

29   The Act itself provides a list of the offences which are included in this definition and trigger the provisions of the section.
30   *R v Kelly* [2000] 1 QB 198, [1999] 2 WLR 1100.

Section 2 states:

'(1) This section applies to –

(a) the functions of the Secretary of State under this Chapter,
(b) the functions of local probation boards, and officers of local probation boards, under this Act or any other enactment so far as they may be exercised for the purposes mentioned in section 1.

(2) In exercising those functions the person concerned must have regard to the following aims –

(a) the protection of the public,
(b) the reduction of re-offending,
(c) the proper punishment of offenders,
(d) ensuring offenders' awareness of the effects of crime on the victims of crime and the public,
(e) the rehabilitation of offenders.'

These sections, like those contained in the Powers of Criminal Courts (Sentencing) Act 2000, demonstrate a willingness on the part of Parliament to form a more coherent sentencing policy and rationale. By giving legislative force in this way to the aims of sentences, and the issues to be taken into account by sentencers, it is arguable that sentencing policy is being clarified. Indeed, one example of the way in which the Act seeks to achieve this can be seen in the renaming of some community penalties.

One of the difficulties that has arisen in relation to sentencing is perhaps the perception of community-based sentences being regarded as a 'soft-option', thus leading, arguably, to a greater use of incarcerative sentences than is perhaps warranted. This, in turn, may, again arguably, have had an effect on the number of applicants seeking redress in the European Court, most notably under Arts 3 and 5, questioning the effect of the punishment as degrading treatment or continued detention after a certain period being unlawful. To this end the Criminal Justice and Courts Services Act 2000 has enacted a number of what may appear to be cosmetic changes, but which may, in fact, impact subtly on sentencing practice. Section 43 affects probation orders, renaming them 'Community Rehabilitation Orders'. Similarly, s 44 changes the name of community service orders to community punishment orders and, by virtue of s 45, combination orders become community punishment and rehabilitation orders.

5.3   ARTICLES OF THE CONVENTION RELEVANT TO SENTENCING

Neither the Convention nor the Human Rights Act 1998 provides a specific right which allows a convicted individual to challenge the sentence which has been imposed. Case-law from the European Court dealing with sentencing therefore concerns applications which have been made under a number of articles. Of primary interest is Art 5, which sets down the right to liberty and security, and elucidates the circumstances in which a State can deprive an individual of his or her liberty. However, a number of other articles have also been invoked by those seeking to challenge the legitimacy of their sentence. The most important of these are Arts 3, 6, 7 and 8 which will be considered, together with Art 5. Article 14 of the Convention sets out a right against discrimination which is also included in the rights laid out in the Schedule to the Human Rights Act 1998. This article operates solely in conjunction with the other articles of the Convention, and applications cannot be lodged alleging only a breach of Art 14.[31] As such, it is not considered within this chapter as a separate issue. However, it is entirely possible that applications will be made before a domestic court in relation to sentencing which allege a breach of this article in conjunction with an allegation of violation of another right.

For many years the Convention has provided a final avenue of recourse for individuals who believe that some protected right has been infringed by a domestic court of law. However, with regard to the question of sentence and possible infringement of rights, an individual will have to overcome even greater obstacles than usual.[32] As stated previously, no one article of the Convention offers a specific right to challenge a sentence which an individual regards as unfair. As such, potential appeals must be lodged firmly within the ambits of other articles in order to succeed. It has been noted in relation to the European Court that:

> 'although the Commission predictably receives a number of applications from individuals who consider that their conviction or sentence was based on an error of fact or law, in the absence of any breach of one of the specific convention guarantees, such applications are declared inadmissible as manifestly ill founded.'[33]

The Human Rights Act 1998 affords individuals certain rights which can, in fact, be applied to the question of the sentence to be awarded on conviction. It is arguable that most of the applications made under the new domestic human rights legislation will, like their European counterparts, involve challenges made against custodial sanctions, and most probably custodial sentences of a long duration. This is probably due, in part at least, to the length of the appeal process from exhausting domestic remedies to judgment in the European Court. It is arguable that the element of the cost of bringing such a prolonged action, if financial assistance is not available, adds to this. It is to be hoped that the implementation of the Human Rights Act 1998 will allow more challenges, perhaps not relating to custodial sentences, to be made and deliberated on in a shorter period of time.

---

31   Interestingly, measures to create a new form of Art 14, which is capable of being the sole subject of an application, have been widely acceded to by signatories of the Convention. However, the UK has, as yet, refused to become a signatory to the new provision.

32   Chapter 6 below provides an illustration of this premise through case-law relating to prisoners.

33   C Ovey 'The European Convention on Human Rights and the Criminal Lawyer: An Introduction' (1998) Crim LR 4, 8.

5.4   ARTICLE 3: INHUMAN OR DEGRADING TREATMENT OR PUNISHMENT

While it is generally accepted that incarceration in itself does not constitute grounds for appeal under Art 3,[34] it has proved possible to challenge some sentences in this way. The European Court has recently declared admissible an application[35] by Adele Price claiming breach of Art 3 in relation to her detention in prison for contempt of court. Ms Price was a victim of Thalidomide and was affected by phocomelia which had resulted in her being without limbs. She also suffered from serious kidney problems. She had been sentenced to 1 week's imprisonment following being held in contempt of court. The European Court, in considering her application and deeming it admissible, noted:

> 'The applicant submitted that the sentencing judge was well aware of her health problems but decided to commit her to prison without first ensuring that there would be adequate facilities. At the police station she was detained in cold conditions which provoked a kidney infection. Her cell in the prison health centre was unadapted to her needs, as was recognised by the prison doctor who examined her on admission, and the nurses and prison officers who cared for her were unsympathetic and did little to help. Throughout the period of her detention she had been subjected to inhuman and degrading treatment which had left her with physical and psychological scars.'[36]

While this is only a decision as to the admissibility of the complaint and not a judgment of the court, it is interesting in that the European Court demonstrates its willingness to consider, in effect, the appropriateness of a decision to incarcerate an individual, and the idea that incarceration itself may be, in certain instances, potentially inhuman and degrading treatment. Although it is arguable that the facts of this case are extreme, it does potentially suggest that courts may have to consider a decision to impose a custodial sentence not only in terms of whether it is warranted by the seriousness of the offence committed, and the dangerousness of the offender, but also whether the circumstances of the offender mean that such incarceration may result in inhumane and degrading treatment.

One of the primary difficulties arising for applicants seeking to challenge a sentence under Art 3 is the need to demonstrate that the ill treatment alleged attains a minimum level of severity. In one application,[37] declared inadmissible, the European Court elucidated on the necessary criteria to demonstrate either a minimum level of ill treatment or inhuman treatment. The Court stated, 'The assessment of that minimum is relative and depends on all the circumstances of the case, such as the duration of the treatment as well as the physical or mental

---

34   Although, see *Weeks v UK* (1987) 10 EHRR 293, paras 46–50, whereby the Court expressed the opinion that if an indeterminate sentence were imposed on a defendant on purely punishment ground, rather than in the interests of protecting the public, questions of compatibility with Art 3 could be raised.

35   *Adele Price v UK* Application No 33394/96 (2000).

36   Ibid, p 7.

37   *Prithpal Singh Sehmi v UK* Application No 43470/98 (2000).

effects'.[38] This statement echoes the findings of the Court in *T v UK* and *V v UK*,[39] whereby it was found that the detention of two offenders during Her Majesty's pleasure, with processes of release determined by a tariff system, did not in and of itself give rise to a breach of Art 3. In these two judgments the Court found that the detention did not amount to a breach of Art 3. However, while the decisions of the Court in *T v UK* and *V v UK* did not accept that such a breach had occurred, it is in cases of the detention of juveniles that many Art 3 claims are concerned and, as such, the development of European Court jurisprudence in this area will be considered separately.

5.4.1 Juveniles[40]

The detention and punishment of juveniles in this jurisdiction has long been a subject of controversial debate. Should young people be detained for long periods of time, and are their best interests and the interests of society best served by a sentence of incarceration? What form of punishment could be substituted if incarceration is deemed inappropriate? Discussions and criticisms of juvenile sentencing policy proceed unabated as policy alters in response to political and public concern.[41]

The issue of corporal punishment, as opposed to detention, has been dealt with by the European Court in one interesting case[42] which involved a boy who had been sentenced by a juvenile court in the Isle of Man to three strokes with a birch, awarded on his conviction for assault occasioning actual bodily harm. The applicant sought to rely on Art 3, claiming that his punishment breached the article as it was 'inhuman or degrading treatment or punishment'. Worthy of note is the fact that, prior to the hearing by the European Court, the applicant sought to withdraw his complaint. As such, when the Court came to consider the case, which it had refused to strike out, it was observed that any claims for compensation under Art 50 need not be considered.[43]

The Court found that such punishment did indeed constitute a breach of Art 3 as, in the Court's opinion, the punishment was 'degrading', especially in view of the age of the applicant:[44]

> 'The very nature of judicial corporal punishment is that it involves one human being inflicting physical violence on another human being. Furthermore, it is institutionalised violence, that is in the present case violence permitted by the law,

---

38   *Prithpal Singh Sehmi v UK* Application No 43470/98 (2000), p 3; see also *Keenan v UK* Application No 27229/95 (date of judgment 3 April 2001).

39   For judgment and reasoning of the Court, see *T v UK* (1999) 30 EHRR 121.

40   The term 'juvenile' for the purposes of this chapter includes both children and young people. Defendants aged between 10–13 are classed as 'children', and those aged between 14–17 as 'young people' (Criminal Justice Act 1991, s 68, Sch 8).

41   See T Newburn 'Youth, Crime and Justice' in M Maguire, R Morgan and R Reiner *The Oxford Handbook of Criminology* (Clarendon Press, 1997), p 648; and also, for more recent developments concerning the detention of such young people, see the Crime and Disorder Act 1998, Powers of Criminal Courts (Sentencing) Act 2000 and A Ashworth *Sentencing and Criminal Justice* (Butterworths, 2000).

42   *Tyrer v UK* (1978) 2 EHRR 1.

43   Ibid, para 45.

44   He was 15 years old at the time of sentence.

ordered by the judicial authorities of the State and carried out by the police authorities of the State. Thus, although the applicant did not suffer any severe or long-lasting physical effects, his punishment – whereby he was treated as an object in the power of the authorities – constituted an assault on precisely that which it is one of the main purposes of Article 3 to protect, namely a person's dignity and physical integrity. Neither can it be excluded that the punishment may have had adverse psychological effects.'[45]

While this case may not seem of direct relevance at this juncture in a discussion concerning detention of juveniles, it is important because of the reasoning of the Court. The Court was concerned that the offender had been treated as 'an object in the power of the authorities'. Arguably, if such reasoning and interpretation were to be employed by a domestic court considering an alleged breach of Art 3, imposition of a custodial sentence on a young offender could, in extreme circumstances, fall foul of the article, in a similar manner to that in the application of *Price v UK*.[46] However, such argument would be successful only in extreme circumstances dependent on the nature of the sentence, especially in light of the findings of the European Court on this matter in the cases of *T v UK* and *V v UK* (above). The applicants in both cases alleged a breach of Art 3 in this way, but the Court found that no violation of the Convention had occurred in respect of this part of the application. Of importance to the Court was the fact that no allegations had been made concerning the conditions of detention or treatment of the two applicants.

5.5   ARTICLE 5: RIGHT TO LIBERTY AND SECURITY

Article 5 has previously provided one of the more common avenues of recourse to individuals in the UK who wish to challenge the validity of their sentence. The article, in essence, guarantees that a person has a right to liberty and security, with certain exceptions. Those exceptions, listed in Art 5(1), generally provide for instances when a person has either been detained in pursuit of criminal investigations or has been lawfully convicted by a competent court. Of perhaps greater interest to possible claimants under the Human Rights Act 1998 is Art 5(4) which allows for sentence review. Article 5(4) provides that:

'Everyone who is deprived of their liberty by arrest or detention shall be entitled to take proceedings by which the lawfulness of his detention shall be decided speedily by a court and his release ordered if the detention is not lawful.'

The implementation of the Human Rights Act 1998 may indeed have an impact on the sentencing practice in this jurisdiction after reflection on a number of cases[47] which have been brought before the European Court. A number of

---

45   *Tyrer v UK* (1978) 2 EHRR 1, para 33.
46   Application No 33394/96 (2000). Although, at the time of writing, this application has only been deemed admissible and no judgment as to the merits of the application have been made. Such argument will be more difficult to sustain should the Court find that no breach of Art 3 exists.
47   The discussion focuses on judgments made against the UK in order to see how the implementation of the Human Rights Act 1998 will impact at a domestic level.

these cases have already resulted in changes to domestic sentencing practice.[48] Cases from the UK which have been brought before the European Court under Art 5(4) have involved the cases of individuals serving both discretionary and mandatory life sentences, detention during Her Majesty's pleasure and sentences which are claimed to be too long. Both discretionary and mandatory life sentences have been the subject of claims made under Art 5(4) with differing outcomes.

5.5.1 Discretionary life sentences

Discretionary life sentences are imposed as the highest tariff level for a particular crime, for example where the aggravating circumstances involved in the particular case, or the dangerousness of the defendant, warrant such a disposal. As such, the tariff imposed does not relate directly to the crime committed, but to the nature of the offender or the aggravated way in which the offender committed the offence. At trial, a judge must give an indication of the minimum length of time the defendant must serve before release can be considered.[49] Once this minimum period of time has expired (the tariff period) the European Court has determined that an offender has a right to have his continued detention reviewed, in order to determine whether the features of his character, such as his dangerousness, which gave rise to the discretionary life sentence, still exist and warrant continued detention.[50] However, the mechanisms in place for effecting such a review have, in this jurisdiction, been subjected to challenge before the European Court.

In *Weeks v UK*[51] the European Court allowed that Art 5(4) could be applied to the question of the lawfulness of continued detention in a discretionary life sentence. In this particular case, Mr Weeks had been released on licence after serving 10 years of a discretionary life sentence for the offence of armed robbery. He was subsequently recalled to prison and his licence revoked by order of the Home Secretary on two separate occasions. The issues before the European Court fell under two separate heads. First, whether the continued detention in prison after the first recall was 'justified' under Art 5(1) and, secondly, whether the review procedures in place were such that the lawfulness of the continued detention had been reviewed in accordance with Art 5(4).

The Court ultimately rejected Mr Weeks' application under Art 5(1) but recognised the application of Art 5(4) to the question of indeterminate sentences of this nature, noting that:

---

48   See the decision in *Thynne, Wilson and Gunnell v UK* (1990) 13 EHRR 666 which contributed to the enactment of s 34 of the Criminal Justice Act 1991. Section 34 introduced the procedures for review of discretionary life sentences once the tariff period imposed by the judge had expired.

49   This has been usual practice for a number of years but was formalised in s 34(1) and (2) of the Criminal Justice Act 1991, which provide that a judge should specify the minimum period of time to be served in order to satisfy the demands of societal retribution and both individual and general deterrence. The Act notes that only exceptionally should a judge decide that such an indication is not warranted.

50   Applications under Art 5(4); see *Van Droogenbroeck v Belgium* (1982) 4 EHRR 443.

51   (1987) 10 EHRR 293.

'Article 5(4) does not guarantee a right to judicial control of such scope as to empower the "court", on all aspects of the case, including questions of expediency, to substitute its own discretion for that of the decision-making authority. The review should, however, be wide enough to bear on those conditions which, according to the Convention, are essential for the lawful detention of a person subject to the special kind of deprivation of liberty ordered against Mr Weeks.'[52]

Furthermore, the Court was critical of the procedures in place for review of the sentence of a recalled prisoner, while accepting that a parole board was a competent 'court' within the ambit of the article, commenting that 'there remains a certain procedural weakness in the case of a recalled prisoner'.[53] The Court was similarly critical of the UK Government's claim that the process of judicial review of a parole board decision was an adequate procedure to determine the lawfulness of continued detention as required by Art 5(4). The Court stated that:

'the scope of the control afforded is thus not wide enough to bear on the conditions essential for the "lawfulness", in the sense of Article 5(4) of the Convention, of Mr Weeks' detention, that is to say, whether it was consistent with and therefore justified by the objectives of the indeterminate sentence imposed on him. In the Court's view, having regard to the nature of control it allows, the remedy of judicial review can neither itself provide the proceedings required by Article 5(4) nor serve to remedy the inadequacy, for the purposes of that provision, of the procedure before the Parole Board.'[54]

In the later case of *Thynne, Wilson and Gunnell v UK*[55] the three applicants sought to challenge the review procedures surrounding their discretionary life sentences which had been imposed following separate trials involving various serious criminal offences, including rape and indecent assault of underage boys. The applicants sought to rely on *Weeks* and claimed that their sentences were of a similar nature to the 'special category' of sentences which are afforded protection by Art 5(4). The Commission, when considering the validity of the claim, considered the reasoning behind the sentencing as relevant to when a review procedure should be triggered and it was noted in the subsequent Court judgment that the Commission believed that:

'Unlike mandatory life sentences, a discretionary life sentence in the United Kingdom is handed down not only because the offence is a grave one, but because, in addition to the need for punishment, the accused is considered mentally unstable and a danger to the public ... While it is true that all life sentences often involve both punitive and security elements, the discretionary life sentence belongs to a separate category because the sentencing court recognises the mental instability or dangerousness of the accused may be susceptible to change over the passage of time. The Commission further observes that the domestic courts have openly stated that a discretionary life sentence is composed of a punitive element ... and a security element based on the need to protect the public ... In addition, had it not been for the presence of mental instability and dangerousness, the

---

52   (1987) 10 EHRR 293 at 315, para 59.
53   Ibid at 318, para 66.
54   Ibid at 319, para 69.
55   (1990) 13 EHRR 666.

applicants would have received a determinate sentence under the law of the United Kingdom leading to an earlier release date.'[56]

The Court concurred, observing that the applicants' sentences involved both punitive and security elements and that once the tariff period had expired each was entitled to have his continued detention reviewed. The Court determined that there was 'no reason to depart from its findings in the *Weeks* judgement that neither the Parole Board nor judicial review proceedings – no other remedy being available to the three applicants – satisfy the requirements of Article 5(4)'.[57]

These cases are interesting both for the immediate impact they have had on domestic legislation and, conversely, for the lack of changes they effected. Subsequent to the findings of the Court in *Thynne, Wilson and Gunnell*, procedures for reviewing discretionary life sentences were altered, courtesy of s 34 of the Criminal Justice Act 1991, which attempts to heed the decisions on the two cases and meet obligations under art 5(4). However, these alterations did not go as far as creating an independent sentencing review tribunal so that, notwithstanding the alterations to the mechanisms of review, judicial review effectively remained the final avenue of recourse for complainants at this time.

The situation has now been remedied with the creation of discretionary lifer panels and, to a certain extent, the creation of the Criminal Cases Review Commission (CCRC) which was established by the Criminal Appeal Act 1995. This independent authority may indeed provide the solution to the problems recognised by the European Court in *Weeks* and *Thynne, Wilson and Gunnell*, and thus limit the potential for challenge under the Human Rights Act 1998 in this particular area. However, as the CCRC role develops with the passage of time, it is possible that their procedures may also be subjected to challenge under Art 5(4).[58] As the Government noted in its publication of the then Human Rights Bill, the Act would enable 'the Convention rights to be judged by British courts [and] will also lead to closer scrutiny of the human rights implications of new legislation and new policies'.[59] Such a claim must surely be extended to new procedures, even if they are established independent of the courts. The CCRC remains a mechanism, albeit independent of the judicial process.

In relation to the discretionary lifer panels and the tightening of review procedures since the 1987 decision of the European Court in *Weeks*, it is notable that a number of applications have been declared admissible by the Court in 2000. This suggests that procedures in place for reviewing discretionary life sentences still do not meet all the requirements of Art 5.

---

56   (1990) 13 EHRR 666, para 81.
57   Ibid, para 80.
58   Statistics suggest that of 1,304 applications made to the CCRC in its first year, only 11 were referred back to the Court of Appeal (*Inside Time*, Issue 28 (Spring 1998), 1). Reasons for the low number of referrals must be adduced to determine whether the procedures currently employed by the CCRC are in fact 'speedy' and, indeed, whether they fall within the definition of Art 5(4).
59   *Rights Brought Home: The Human Rights Bill* (1997) Cm 3782, para 1.18.

As recently as September 2000 the Court found there to be a violation of Art 5(4) with respect to review. In *Oldham v UK*[60] the Court considered the requirement previously recognised in European case-law of the need for automatic reviews of lawfulness of detention to be at 'reasonable intervals'.[61] Mr Oldham had been recalled to prison in 1996, subsequent to being released on life licence three times. The review by the discretionary lifer panel (DLP), which took place 4 months after recall, considered that his continued detention was necessary and lawful and that Mr Oldham needed to carry out further work in respect of alcohol, anger and relationships. This decision was not then reviewed until December 1998, although the applicant had completed various offending behaviour courses within 8 months of his return to prison. The complained-of breach in relation to Art 5(4) pertained to this intervening period between the two DLP hearings. The UK Government made representation that the applicant:

> 'had problems to address and progress to monitor which could not realistically be done in under that period. They also argued that discretionary lifers, who are detained on grounds of risk to the public, should not be compared with cases of persons detained on grounds of mental illness.'[62]

However, the Court did not agree with such arguments, noting that:

> 'Article 5(4) was held applicable to discretionary life sentences since these were imposed on offenders due to considerations of mental instability and dangerousness which were susceptible to change over the passage of time ... [the court further stated that the Government had not] ... substantiated their assertion that mental disorder in a context of mental illness is more susceptible to change over time than mental instability posing risks of dangerousness.'[63]

The Court's findings suggest that domestic courts will receive applications for consideration under the Human Rights Act 1998 regarding the continued detention of discretionary life sentences post tariff. However, despite the number of cases in the European Court pertaining to this area of life sentence which have found for the applicant, 2-year periods between reviews should not be taken to be automatically unreasonable and thus a breach of Art 5(4). While this is approximately the time period in many of the cases in which breaches are found, the court in *Oldham* was clear in its approach that:

> 'It is not ... for this Court to attempt to rule as to the maximum period of time between reviews which should automatically apply to this category of life prisoner as a whole. It notes that the system as applied in this case has a flexibility which must reflect the realities of the situation, namely, that there are significant differences in the personal circumstances of the prisoners under review.'[64]

---

60   [2000] HRCD 505.
61   See *Herczegfalvy v Austria* (1992) Series A/244, p 24, para 75.
62   *Oldham v UK* [2000] HRCD 505. In *Herczegfalvy v Austria* (1992) Series A/244 the European Court determined that periods of 15 months and 2 years between reviews in the case of a person detained on grounds of mental illness were not reasonable.
63   *Oldham v UK* Application No 36273/97 (2000), para 34.
64   Ibid, para 31.

In terms of domestic application, therefore, any such applicants must not place too great a reliance on the time frames considered in the jurisprudence of the European Court. This statement by the Court in *Oldham* suggests that domestic courts applying the Human Rights Act 1998 will judge each application on a case-by-case basis, formulating judgment through consideration of the individual circumstances and facts of the case.

Another application declared admissible in March 2000[65] concerned delays in the review of the continued detention of a discretionary lifer post tariff. Again, on the facts, the application under Art 5(4) has been declared admissible. More interesting are the comments made by the European Court with regard to the application contending breach of Art 5 in relation to the independence and impartiality of the DLP of the Parole Board. The applicant contended that DLPs could not be regarded as independent as a result of their membership in that the entire Secretariat of the Parole Board are HM Prison Service employees and that the Secretary of State, another party to parole release decisions,[66] was in charge of HM Prison Service. The Court considered this part of his application inadmissible in that the DLP was able to, and in fact did, apply the correct statutory test to the applicants' circumstances and that the DLP satisfied the requirements of impartiality and independence envisaged by Art 5. While the decision of inadmissibility of this part of the applicant's complaint suggests that challenges at domestic level regarding membership and independence of the DLPs may be unsuccessful, Home Office research findings have raised criticisms concerning DLPs which may, in the future, lead to applications regarding DLP decisions being made under the Human Rights Act 1998. Research exploring the decision-making processes of DLPs conducted in 1999 noted that:

> 'The recall process raises particular concerns. Recall hearings were conducted in a similar way to other DLPs but the issues raised were different. In a recall case, the panel was being asked not only to assess risk, but to confirm the recall of someone who had previously been deemed safe to release if managed adequately in the community. The human rights implications of this are too easily ignored.'[67]

This criticism was made due to findings which suggested that DLPs in recall cases did not always separate these two issues and address them separately.

---

65   *John Hirst v UK* Application No 40787/98 (2000).

66   With regard to this criticism of the role of the Secretary of State and the potential for DLP members, who are arguably employed by the Secretary of State, research found that 'The Secretary of State's view on the desired outcome of the hearing was of a routine nature, sometimes out-of-date and often supplied late. However, it had two important functions. It was referred to by the panel as they finalised the written decision. When received on time, it was also useful to legal representatives as they prepared the case for the prisoner. The impact of the Secretary of State's representative at the hearing was variable and often minor': N Padfield, A Liebling and H Arnold *Discretionary Lifer Panels – an exploration of decision-making*, Research Findings No 132, Home Office Research, Development and Statistics Directorate (2000), p 3.

67   Ibid, p 4.

5.5.2   Mandatory life sentences

Decisions concerning discretionary life sentences have had further effect due to the reliance placed on them by applicants before the European Court challenging mandatory life sentences. As recently as 1994 the UK's policy of review in relation to life sentences was challenged on the basis of the judgments in *Weeks* and *Thynne, Wilson and Gunnell* (discussed at **5.5.1** above). The applicant in *Wynne v UK*[68] claimed that both types of life sentences were materially similar in that both sentences were made up of punitive and security requirements. As such, it was argued that Art 5(4) should also have application in relation to mandatory life sentences. In this instance the Court declined to recognise the applicability of Art 5(4) noting that the distinction between the two sentences lay in the fact that in the case of mandatory sentences it is the offence which attracts the sentence and not the nature of the offender, be it dangerousness or mental instability. The Court stated that, unlike discretionary life sentences which attract a right to review, release from a mandatory life sentence was a privilege and not an enforceable right.

Despite the decision in *Wynne v UK* the question of review procedures for mandatory life sentence has once again been raised before the European Court. In the decision as to admissibility the Court considered the application to be manifestly ill-founded.[69] It reaffirmed its decision in *Wynne* noting that mandatory and discretionary life sentences belonged in different categories and that in relation to mandatory life sentences Art 5(4) was satisfied by the original trial and no further right to challenge the lawfulness of continued detention existed. Further, there was no such right extended to decisions to recall an offender released on licence subsequent to a mandatory life sentence. If domestic courts seek to adopt the same reasoning under the new human rights legislation, which is arguably likely, it will be difficult to utilise the new provisions to challenge a mandatory life sentence in this way.

5.5.3   Detention during Her Majesty's pleasure

When a juvenile is convicted of murder, the usual sentence of mandatory life imprisonment does not apply. Instead, the young person is sentenced under the Children and Young Persons Act 1933[70] and is detained during Her Majesty's pleasure. Such a sentence is similar to a discretionary life sentence and has proved to be subject to challenge through the European Convention. In 1996 the European Court found that this sentence could be in violation of Art 5(4) in that young people detained in this way were entitled to have their sentence reviewed regularly, in the same manner as discretionary life sentences.

Hussain v UK[71] involved a young man who, at the time of his offence, was 16 years old. He was convicted of murdering his 2-year-old brother and sentenced

---

68   (1994) 19 EHRR 333.
69   *Robert Kerr v UK* Application No 44071/98 (1999).
70   Section 53.
71   (1996) 22 EHRR 1.

to detention during Her Majesty's Pleasure. His application to the European Court involved a challenge under Art 5(4) that the continuation of his detention should be subject to review by a court. The European Court considered the nature of the sentence and concluded that:

> '... a sentence of detention during Her Majesty's Pleasure is mandatory: it is fixed by law and is imposed automatically in all cases where persons under the age of 18 are convicted of murder, the trial judge having no discretion ... On the other hand, it is undisputed that, in its statutory origins, the expression "during Her Majesty's Pleasure" had a clear preventative purpose and that – unlike sentences of life custody or life imprisonment – the word "life" is not mentioned in the description of the sentence. ... an indeterminate term of detention for a convicted young person, which may be as long as that person's life, can only be justified by considerations based on the need to protect the public. ... A failure to have regard to the changes that inevitably occur with maturation would mean that the young persons detained under section 53 would be treated as having forfeited their liberty for the rest of their lives, a situation which ... might give rise to questions under Article 3 of the Convention. ... Accordingly, new issues of lawfulness may arise in the course of the detention and the applicant is entitled under Article 5(4) to take proceedings to have these issues decided by a court at reasonable intervals.' [72]

The Crime (Sentences) Act 1997 sought to meet criticisms made by the European Court in relation to detention of juveniles in this way. As is the case with discretionary life sentences, s 28 of the 1997 Act entitles individuals detained during Her Majesty's pleasure to have their continued detention reviewed. It would seem that the concerns and possibilities for challenge under the Human Rights Act 1998 in relation to juveniles sentenced for murder are the same as those which are raised in connection with discretionary life sentences. However, one crucial difference between the two remains. In the case of discretionary life sentences it was noted at the time that, subsequent to recent legislation, the trial judge should recommend the tariff period which should be served by the offender. After the expiry of this time the prisoner becomes entitled to a review of his detention. However, juveniles sentenced pursuant to a conviction for murder are not subject to the same procedures;[73] it is not a trial judge who ultimately determines the tariff period of their detention, but the Secretary of State. As such, the tariff period imposed is not subject to the same avenues of recourse, namely the Court of Appeal. This procedure has since been considered and found wanting in the decision of the House of Lords in *R v T* and *R v V*.[74]

In the recent judgment in the case of *Curley v UK*[75] the European Court declared there to be a breach of Art 5(4) in relation to the review of detention post tariff of an offender detained during Her Majesty's pleasure. While this judgment was delivered in March 2000, perhaps suggesting that review

---

72   (1996) 22 EHRR 1, at 24, para 51.
73   Their sentence arises pursuant to different legislation to their adult counterparts, namely the Children and Young Persons Act 1933.
74   *R v Home Secretary ex parte (1) Venables (2) Thompson* [1997] 3 All ER 97.
75   (2001) 31 EHRR 14.

procedures for such prisoners have not been improved since *Hussain*,[76] it is of limited critical value because the detention in question in *Curley* relates to the period just preceding the implementation of changes to the review of Parole Board procedures on 1 August 1996.

5.5.4   Detention under the Mental Health Act 1983

If, at the time of conviction, a defendant is found to be suffering from recognised levels of mental instability, he or she may receive an indeterminate sentence for his or her crimes, to be spent within the confines of a secure hospital, pursuant to s 37 of the Mental Health Act 1983 (which has superseded s 60 of the Mental Health Act 1959). In order that a defendant be placed in a secure hospital in this way, the court must ensure that certain procedures have been followed, the individual must have been convicted of a criminal offence for which an incarcerative sentence would be likely, or he or she would have been convicted if the trial had continued. In this way it is possible for a court to make a s 37 order prior to conviction if it is satisfied that the defendant had indeed committed the acts charged. Interestingly, if a court imposes such an order,[77] a restriction order[78] may also be imposed.[79]

Restrictions which are placed on the detention of the individual relate to conditions of release and may involve[80] the following:

–   leave for the patient during his or her detention may be granted only with the consent of the Secretary of State and Home Office;
–   transfer from the hospital requires consent from the Home Office;
–   an eventual discharge also involves obtaining consent from the Home Office.

In order that the court may specify any of the above restrictions, the court must declare itself satisfied that the conditions of restriction are required in the interest of protecting the public from serious harm. This decision is made through a consideration of a number of factors which include the nature of the offence, the previous criminal record of the defendant and the risk factor involved in relation to the possible commission of further criminal offences (involving serious harm to the public) should the defendant be freed. Restriction orders can be made for an indefinite period of time, while hospital orders generally require renewal. However, if a restriction order is in place, the hospital order to which it attaches similarly does not require renewal for the period during which the restriction order is in force.

---

76   *Hussain v UK* (1996) 22 EHRR 1.
77   The order requires certification by two medical officers.
78   Pursuant to s 41 of the Mental Health Act 1983.
79   A magistrates' court does not have the power to issue restriction orders under s 41; however, if a hospital order is made, the magistrates' court may apply to the Crown Court for a restriction order if necessary.
80   Detention under s 37 automatically attracts certain restrictions: that the nearest relative of the patient cannot discharge the patient and that a mental health review tribunal cannot consider an appeal against detention for a minimum period of 6 months.

While it is legally difficult to challenge the decision to detain an individual,[81] given that it is primarily a medical and discretionary decision, the continued detention of a person has been the subject of consideration by the European Court on a number of occasions within the ambit of Art 5(4). The report of the Commission in the case of *B v UK*[82] demonstrated a willingness, at European level, to consider this form of sentence as within the parameters of Art 5(4). The Commission was primarily concerned with the question of whether:

> 'Article 5(4) requires the possibility of further, periodic, judicial review, on request, of the lawfulness of compulsory detention of persons of unsound mind for indefinite periods. The commission has previously concluded in the aforementioned case of *X v United Kingdom*[83] that such periodic review is envisaged by Article 5(4), following the Court's judgement of 24 October 1974 in the *Winterwerp* case[84] ... The Commission finds no reason to reach a different opinion in the present case. ... The Commission finds that no periodic court procedure, satisfying the guarantees of Article 5(4), exists in the United Kingdom to have met the applicant's complaint concerning the lawfulness of his continued detention at Broadmoor. The substantive elements of his detention were within the sole responsibility of the Home Secretary, the Mental Health Review Tribunal and doctors having a mere advisory role in respect of restricted patients like the applicant.[85]

The earlier case of *X v UK*,[86] referred to in the above judgment, also involved the detention of a mental patient and a challenge to the lawfulness of his continued detention. The European Court recognised in this instance that the procedures involved in the review of this patient's continued detention were in breach of Art 5(4) and in its later judgment[87] relating to damages and costs determined that while damages were not warranted for the suffering caused by X due to the breach of Art 5(4), domestic costs of £324 should be reimbursed. This case resulted in the insertion of certain clauses to the Mental Health Act 1983 which altered the procedures under which continued detention is reviewed. The Court, in its 1982 judgment, recognised the changes in domestic legislation (which at the time was in Bill form), and the changes the legislation would encompass:

> '[A]s a direct result of the judgement of 5 November 1981, various amendments were inserted into the Mental Health (Amendment) Bill, which is now before Parliament. In brief, these amendments provide that on the coming into force of the Act, Mental Health Review Tribunals will be empowered to consider the substantive grounds for the continued detention of a restricted patient, and will be required to order discharge where appropriate. The Government have in addition given an undertaking to Parliament to provide legal representation at public

---

81 However, if a person is found not guilty by reason of insanity, redress lies with an appeal to the Court of Appeal pursuant to s 12 of the Criminal Appeal Act 1968.
82 (1983) 6 EHRR 204.
83 Application No 6998/75; paras 120–124 of the report.
84 *Winterwerp v Netherlands* (1979–80) 2 EHRR 387.
85 *B v UK* (1983) 6 EHRR 204 at 231; paras 222–224, 233 of the report.
86 (1981) 4 EHRR 188.
87 *X v UK* (1982) 5 EHRR 192.

expense for patients coming before Mental Health Review Tribunals whose own financial resources are insufficient.[88]

The changes noted in *X v UK* had not quite taken effect at the time of the judgment in *B v UK*. In October 1997,[89] a similar application successfully challenged the continued detention of an individual pursuant to a s 37 order under the Mental Health Act 1983. Mr Johnson was convicted of causing actual bodily harm in August 1984. While on remand he was diagnosed as suffering from schizophrenia and a psychopathic personality. Accordingly, on conviction he was detained in Rampton hospital by virtue of a s 37 order. The applicant appealed to the European Court under Art 5 to challenge his continued detention subsequent to a fourth review of his condition. The fourth review, which took place in June 1989, recommended that the patient be discharged, as he no longer displayed symptoms of suffering from a mental illness, provided he was released to a hostel where further rehabilitation would be facilitated. The mental health review tribunal, which delivered its judgment on 15 June 1989, agreed with the medical diagnosis and ordered the conditional discharge of Mr Johnson, on the condition that he continue to be supervised by his psychiatrist, and also that he reside in a hostel approved by his psychiatrist. As such, his release was deferred until suitable accommodation could be arranged. Despite numerous attempts to secure such accommodation, nothing was arranged between the date of the review and 1993. A subsequent mental health review tribunal ordered Mr Johnson's unconditional release in 1993 in the interests of justice, despite recommendations that only a conditional discharge was appropriate. Mr Johnson's claim at a European level was made under Art 5, in respect of the period of continued detention between June 1989 and January 1993.

The European Court again made reference to the problems inherent in the review process for the continued detention of individuals subject to the Mental Health Act 1983, especially in regard to the safeguards, suggesting that earlier criticisms concerning continued detention in this manner had not been adequately met by the changes in procedure incorporated in the 1983 Act. The Court observed that:

> 'Having regard to the situation which resulted from the decision taken by the latter Tribunal and to the lack of adequate safeguards including provisions for judicial review to ensure that the applicant's release from detention would not be unreasonably delayed, it must be considered that his continued confinement after 15 June 1989 cannot be justified on the basis of Article 5(1)(e) of the Convention. For these reasons the Court concludes that the applicant's continued detention after 15 June 1989 constituted a violation of Article 5(1) of the Convention.'[90]

Given the finding of breach under Art 5(1), the Court determined that similar claims under Art 5(4) need not be dealt with separately. Mr Johnson was further awarded compensation[91] in respect of his unlawful detention, and an

---

88   *X v UK* (1982) 5 EHRR 192 at 193, para 10.
89   *Johnson v UK* (1999) 27 EHRR 296.
90   Ibid, para 67.
91   £10,000.

amount to cover cost and expenses incurred.[92] It has proved a less common practice that the Court utilises Art 5(1) rather than Art 5(4) in applications concerning the detention of individuals under the 1983 Act, but, as this case has demonstrated, there remains a relatively wide avenue for appeal in such instances which will, in all likelihood, be mirrored by applications under the Human Rights Act 1998 and to the CCRC.

The position concerning the review by mental health review tribunals of continued detention subsequent to a hospital order after conviction was considered again by the European Court in *Kay v UK*.[93] The court determined that breach of Art 5(1) and (4) had occurred. The facts of this case are particularly confusing. The applicant had been convicted of manslaughter on the grounds of diminished responsibility in 1971 and was made the subject of a hospital order without limit of time under ss 60 and 65 of the Mental Health Act 1959. He was conditionally discharged in 1985, but a few months later was convicted of two assaults and received a 3-year prison sentence. At this time the hospital order was still extant and the applicant appealed to the mental health review tribunal for a discharge of the order which was refused, although the tribunal considered him not to be suffering from any mental disorder. The grounds given for the continuation of the order were that the tribunal considered that the applicant should remain liable to be recalled to the hospital for further treatment. Application for judicial review for this decision was refused.

While still in prison serving the sentence for the two assaults, and 6 weeks prior to the earliest prison release date, Kay was recalled for detention at Broadmoor under a warrant issued by the Home Secretary, the grounds being that of a risk to public safety. On return to Broadmoor applications were made for appeal to a new tribunal, but hearings were delayed on application by Mr Kay's solicitor. Application was finally made to the European court alleging that the delay with regard to the mental health review tribunal hearing breached Art 5(4) and that the warrant issued by the Home Secretary breached Art 5(1). The Court held that breaches had occurred under both paragraphs of Art 5. In relation to the issuing of the warrant the breach occurred because the warrant was not legally issued as no up-to-date medical report was available upon which the decision could rely. At the time of recall there was no evidence that the applicant was suffering from a psychopathic disorder, a condition confirmed only 1 month subsequent to recall. Thus, the interim period of 1 month did not constitute a lawful detention of a person of unsound mind. The Art 5(4) breach, in the Court's opinion, occurred because too long a period of time had passed between recall and review.[94] The violation existed despite the fact that it was Mr Kay who had applied for the adjournments of the tribunal, and had later displayed disinterest in the proceedings.

---

92   £25,000 less the amount received from the Council of Europe in the form of legal aid.
93   (1998) 40 BMLR 20.
94   Almost 5 months elapsed between the referral and the first adjourned hearing date.

This decision suggests that the European Court remains concerned about the review procedures concerning detention of those under the Mental Health Act 1983, although it is notable that this decision concerned reviews which had taken place more than 10 years previously. The mental health review tribunals remain, in the Court's opinion, too slow, and thus it is arguable that such procedures should be an area worthy of the interest of the domestic courts under the Human Rights Act 1998. Such criticism by the European Court, even after review procedures have been altered in an attempt to comply with Art 5, suggests that in line with s 2 of the 1998 Act the domestic courts should give attention to this form of complaint. As such, the scope for reform of the procedures may be countenanced, and indeed required, by a Court of Appeal which seeks to question the procedures' compatibility with Art 5(4).

5.5.5   Criminal Justice Act 1991, s 2(2) – disproportionate sentences

Section 1(2) of the Criminal Justice Act 1991 states that a court should not impose a custodial sentence on an individual unless certain criteria are, in the court's judgment, met.[95] However, s 2 of the Act goes on to provide how a custodial sentence should be applied. Section 2(2) states:

'The custodial sentence shall be –

   (a) for such term (not exceeding the permitted maximum) as in the opinion of the court is commensurate with the seriousness of the offence, or the combination of the offence and [one or more] offences associated with it; or

   (b) where the offence is a violent or sexual offence, for such longer term (not exceeding the maximum) as in the opinion of the court is necessary to protect the public from serious harm from the offender.'

Of interest in relation to the new human rights legislation is s 2(2)(b) whereby a sentence that is longer than the offence warrants (through the principle of proportionality, which was the ethos of the 1991 Act) is awarded in the interest of protecting the public from possible serious harm caused by the offender.

A sentence made pursuant to s 2(2)(b) was recently challenged by an applicant from the UK,[96] but failed at the first hurdle as the Commission declared the application manifestly ill founded. The applicant, Mr Mansell, sought to have his sentence reviewed through the use of Art 5(4), adopting the same line of argument that has been made in favour of those serving discretionary life sentences. Mr Mansell had received a 5-year sentence subsequent to a conviction for three counts of indecent assault. He had a previous conviction for the indecent assault and kidnapping of a man. At sentencing the judge explained that the usual sentence for this type of indecent assault would be 2½ years, but the judge, acting in accordance with the provisions of s 2(2)(b) of the 1991 Act, determined that a 5-year sentence was warranted as this would be the

---

95   For a discussion of the tests employed by the courts, see A Ashworth and A von Hirsch
    'Recognising Elephants: The Problem of the Custody Threshold' (1997) Crim LR 187.

96   *Mansell v UK* (1997) EHRLR 666.

minimum duration of sentence he believed would be 'adequate to protect the public from serious harm'.

Mr Mansell brought his challenge before the Commission after the expiry of the 2½-year period, claiming that this was the period which had been imposed in relation to the offence, thus the remainder of his sentence was due to his own characteristics, which could change over time. As such, Mr Mansell sought a declaration from the European Court that this remaining period of detention should be subject to the same levels of review as a discretionary life sentence after the tariff period has elapsed. The Commission declared the claim manifestly ill-founded, claiming that there was a distinction between the two forms of sentence which would render Art 5(4) inapplicable to longer than standard sentences awarded under s 2(2)(b). The Commission was of the opinion that, unlike discretionary life sentences where a part of the sentence was based on the nature of the individual and therefore subject to change over time, a sentence awarded under s 2(2)(b) contained only punitive and deterrent elements. As such, it was not within the ambit of Art 5(4), and a challenge could not be mounted in the European Court. It is likely that a domestic court would follow this reasoning, subject to any differences in the philosophy of a sentence. It is arguable that in this instance each case must be decided on its merits. If a judge were to state in a judgment made under s 2(2)(b) that the sentence was being given only due to the dangerousness of the individual to the public, it is possible that after the expiry of the usual sentence time, the sentence could fall within the parameters of the protection afforded by Art 5(4), and thus the case could be reviewed pursuant to Art 5(4).[97]

5.5.6 Automatic detention

Section 25 of the Criminal Justice and Public Order Act 1994 provides that no bail can be sought for defendants charged with or convicted of homicide or rape after previous conviction of such offences. In *Caballero v UK*,[98] an applicant included in his appeal against sentence at the domestic court of appeal a claim that his automatic detention by virtue of s 25 violated his right to security and liberty under Art 5(3) and (5). While his appeal against sentence was dismissed, the complaint regarding Art 5 was ultimately brought before the European Court. The UK Government conceded that there had been a breach. While detention pursuant to s 25 is not in effect a sentence, in that the detention is prior to trial, this application is worthy of note in that legislation requiring automatic detention has been declared to be a violation of Art 5. This may be relevant to current proposals being made under the Dangerous People with Severe Personality Disorder Bill (DSPD) 2000. The applicant in this case, Mr Caballero, was detained prior to trial and, on conviction, his period of remand went towards the length of his sentences. However, it was the manner in which he was remanded to custody which violated the Convention. No application for

---

97 For a discussion of sentences imposed under s 2(2)(b) in relation to possible
    infringements of Art 6, see **5.6.1** below.
98 (2000) Crim LR 587.

bail could be made because of the requirements of s 25. The DSPD Bill makes provision for the imposition of a DSPD order[99] on individuals fulfilling assessment criteria but who have not committed an offence. Arguably, such automatic detention under the DSPD Bill may be considered a breach of Art 5 in a similar manner to that of *Caballero*.

5.5.7   Costs and an enforceable right to compensation

Article 5(5) states that anyone who has suffered from a breach of Art 5 shall have an enforceable right to compensation.[100] The inclusion of this right in the Human Rights Act 1998 has been the subject of much parliamentary debate. The wording of the clause and its implementation were discussed in Parliament during debate on the Act itself. The Lord Chancellor went as far as to attempt to elucidate on how this right would operate on implementation:

> 'I indicated at Committee stage that the Government were alive to the need to make appropriate provision for the Article 5(5) requirement and that we were considering how best to give effect to this obligation in relation to judicial acts of courts and tribunals. The effect of Clauses 6, 7 and 8 of the Bill is that there is an enforceable right to compensation in relation to public authorities generally. But special provisions are needed in relation to judicial acts of courts and tribunals.
>
> Where a complaint is made that Article 5 has been breached as a result of a judicial act or omission it will be necessary first to establish whether the judicial act complained of was unlawful, then to rule on whether the aggrieved person is entitled to compensation under Article 5(5) and then to determine the amount of compensation. In determining those questions the court will take into account the Strasbourg jurisprudence on unlawful detention and on the award of damages, as required by Clauses 2 and 8 of the Bill.'[101]

The inclusion of this part of Art 5 and its future application should, it is hoped, result in a reduction in the length of time applicants whose detention has breached Art 5 must wait for compensation.

5.6   ARTICLE 6: A FAIR AND PUBLIC HEARING

Article 6 best serves those applicants who seek to challenge a particular aspect of their trial.[102] It is not generally thought to afford a right to individuals seeking to question the sentence handed down to them by a court of law, but the question arises whether the notion of a right to a fair trial incorporates a right to a fair sentence. As difficult, and unusual, as it may be to challenge a *sentence* through the provision relating to fair trial, the European Commission has long accepted that Art 6 does apply to the sentencing decision in a trial.[103]

---

99   Requiring detention in specified facilities (cl 4 of the DSPD Bill 2000).
100 See *Johnson v UK* Application No 22520/93 (1997); and *Lines v UK* Application No 24519/94 (1997) for an amount accepted under friendly settlement.
101 *Hansard* (HL) vol 585, col 389 (29 January 1998).
102 See Chapter 4 above for a discussion of the effects of Art 6.
103 See, generally, the Commission Report in Application No 4623/70 (1972).

Interestingly, this has not been a right extended to those seeking to challenge a sentence pursuant to conviction when the defendant has pleaded guilty since where a defendant pleads guilty, there is no trial per se and the evidence and procedures which dominate an actual trial, and which are afforded protection under Art 6, are not presented or followed.

Perhaps more worthy of consideration in relation to Art 6 and sentencing is the requirement in the article that judgment 'shall be pronounced publicly but the press and public may be excluded from all or part of the trial'.[104] This obligation for public report stems, in part, from the need to protect individuals from arbitrary judgment and, perhaps, also, to ensure that the belief of society in the criminal justice system is maintained. As Bentham observed:

> 'Publicity is the very soul of justice. It is the keenest spur to exertion, and the surest of all guards against improbity. It keeps the judge himself, while trying, under trial. Under the auspices of publicity, the cause in the court of law, and the appeal to the court of public opinion, are going on at the same time ... It is through publicity alone that justice becomes the mother of security.'[105]

However, Art 6 does provide some exceptions to public scrutiny of the trial process,[106] two of which are where the interests of the juvenile defendant so requires, and if the interests of justice so dictate. Could such a requirement be utilised to suggest that if the media is not excluded from a sensitive trial involving a juvenile or adult defendant, and much public interest is generated from the coverage, the sentence awarded on conviction reflects not only the seriousness of the offence and the nature of the offender, but also the public reaction?[107] Such argument, while possible, has been considered at European level in the applications made by the two boys convicted of killing the toddler James Bulger.[108] The European Court considered, as part of the application, whether Art 6 had been infringed by virtue of the trial that the two young offenders received, including the part played by the media coverage of the trial. The Court found that:

> '... it is highly unlikely that the applicant would have felt sufficiently uninhibited, in the tense courtroom and under public scrutiny, to have consulted with [counsel] during the trial or, indeed, that, given his immaturity and his disturbed emotional state, he would have been capable outside the courtroom of cooperating with his lawyers and giving them information for the purposes of his defence. In conclusion, the Court considers that the applicant was unable to participate

---

104 Article 6(1).
105 J Bentham 'Draught of a Code for the Organisation of the Judicial Establishment in France', in Ayer and Grady *Dictionary of Philosophical Quotation* (Blackwell, 1994), p 48.
106 Article 6(1) states that press and public may be excluded 'in the interest of morals, public order or national security in a democratic society, where the interests of juveniles or the protection of private life of the parties so require, or to the extent necessary in the opinion of the court in special circumstances where publicity would prejudice the interests of justice'.
107 Either in the form of vilification of the defendant or in the representation of the defendant as a 'victim' of the criminal justice system.
108 See *T v UK* [1999] Crim LR 579.

effectively in the criminal proceedings against him and was, in consequence, denied a fair hearing in breach of Article 6(1).'[109]

While the finding of breach in this respect did not relate to sentence, in so far as the sentence for murder is mandatory and therefore any claim that media coverage of the case affected sentence was moot, it is arguable that such arguments could be used in the future under the Human Rights Act 1998 with regards to discretionary sentences and the severity of sentence meted out.

5.6.1   Criminal Justice Act 1991, s 2(2)(b) – protective sentencing

Another possible of avenue of challenge lies in the terms of s 2(2)(b) of the Criminal Justice Act 1991.[110] This provision allows a court in certain instances to impose a custodial sentence of longer than usual duration if so required in the interests of protecting the public. The tests employed by the courts in determining whether such a sentence is 'necessary', as required by the legislation, have operated on the level of consideration of whether, in light of the dangerousness of the defendant, there is a 'substantial risk' of re-offending.[111] Any appeal against such a sentence would potentially fall to be considered on the ground of the 'reasonableness' of the decision. The general ethos of the Criminal Justice Act 1991 lies in the notion of proportionality, in that sentences should reflect the seriousness of the offence, and offenders should receive a sentence which reflects their 'just deserts'.[112] Section 2(2)(b) seemingly contradicts this underlying principle of proportionality.[113] The tests utilised at a domestic level, both in imposing the sentence and in a possible appeal, do not always incorporate proportionality. More often they have their basis in the terms 'reasonableness' or 'seriousness', yet these terms have very different meanings and it is in these differences that a potential application of Art 6 lies. With the advent of the Human Rights Act 1998, judges may be forced to scrutinise their decisions to impose such a sentence more carefully. Such scrutiny may be required due to the fact that the jurisprudence of the European Court has tended to favour tests of proportionality when determining the existence of a breach, and it is to this case-law that domestic judges must look in applying the Human Rights Act 1998.[114]

In considering the differences between the different terminology it is notable that 'proportionate' incorporates notions of balance and equality, in that

---

109   *T v UK* [1999] Crim LR 579. For a discussion concerning the effects of media intrusion during the trials of juveniles, see the Europan Court's comments at paras 79–89 of the judgment.

110   See **5.5.5** above.

111   See *R v Crow and Pennington* (1995) 16 Cr App R 409.

112   Equally, under the 1991 Act, the notion of 'just deserts' should also be applied to community penalties. For a general discussion of just deserts and community penalties, see S Rex 'Applying Just Desert Principles to Community Sentences: Lessons from Two Criminal Justice Acts' (1998) Crim LR 381.

113   For a general discussion of these implications of s 2(2)(b), see A von Hirsch and A Ashworth 'Protective Sentencing Under Section 2(2)(b)' (1996) Crim LR 175.

114   Section 2 of the Human Rights Act 1998 states that courts must take into account the opinions and judgments of the European Court.

the sentence must correspond to the seriousness of the offence committed, the circumstances in which it was committed and the characteristics of the offender. While the term 'reasonable' arguably also embodies these notions, it is a more vague test. 'Proportionate' is a test which can be measured solely with reference to the offence and the offender, whereas 'reasonableness' can also be analysed in terms of the actions of the judge. Consider the question 'was it reasonable that a judge imposed this length of custodial sentence?'; the answer could lie in the proposition that, 'yes, the sentence imposed was within the tariff guidelines and the judge therefore exercised his reasonable judgement to determine that this sentence was appropriate, the decision is not *ultra vires*'. If the word 'proportionate' is substituted for 'reasonable' in the question, the answer given above would not make sense. The answer given to whether the sentence was proportionate *must* involve a consideration of only the offence, circumstances and characteristics of the offender.

Perhaps the largest problem for appellate judges in England and Wales in terms of following European Court reasoning lies in the very nature of sentencing practice. As previously discussed,[115] domestic sentencing practice is discretionary, with sentencing prescriptions created by guideline decisions of the Court of Appeal and, to a more limited extent, legislation. Thus, there is no stated policy or underlying aim of sentencing practice per se. As such:

> '[p]rotective sentences ... raise serious questions of fairness. The capacity to predict dangerousness is quite limited and such assessments tend to overpredict: ... More problematically still, the protective sentence is inconsistent with notions of proportionality. Whereas the proportionate sanction chiefly reflects the gravity of the crime of conviction, predictions rely mainly on quite ulterior matters, relating to previous criminal history and social psychological factors. If the protective sentence is justifiable at all, then, it could only be in cases of such "vivid danger" as to warrant overriding in the public interest the fairness requirements which the principle of proportionality embodies.'[116]

It is entirely possible that the 'justification' of protective sentences will be called into question through recourse to the new human rights legislation.

5.6.2 Article 6 and 'reasonable time'

Of interest in relation to Art 6 is a decision of the European Court in *Howarth v UK*[117] concerning the use of s 36 of the Criminal Justice Act 1988. This section allows the Attorney-General (AG) to apply to the Court of Appeal to review a sentence which he believes has been unduly lenient.[118] In *Howarth* the defendant had been required to perform 220 hours' community service and pay compensation. On appeal by the defendant the AG also appealed against

---

115 See **5.2** above.

116 von Hirsch and Ashworth (n 113 above), 182.

117 (2001) 31 EHRR 37.

118 There are only certain circumstances in which the AG can appeal in this way and before the Court of Appeal can increase the sentence. The Court of Appeal must be convinced that there has been some error of principle in the original sentence, and leave should be granted only in exceptional cases; see *Attorney-General's Reference No 5 of 1989* (1989) 11 Cr App R(S) 489.

the sentence as being unduly lenient. There was a 2-year period between the original sentence and the eventual Court of Appeal hearing of the AG's reference in which Mr Howarth's sentence was altered to one of imprisonment. He appealed to the European Court alleging that this delay amounted to a breach of Art 6(1) in that the article guaranteed a reasonable time requirement with regard to the hearing of criminal charges. The Court found that:

> 'No convincing reasons have been given which could justify the period of two years it took to deal with the appeal; in particular, apart from a refusal to reconsider the legal aid position, there was no judicial activity in the case from the grant of leave to appeal in December 1995 until the appeal was heard in March 1997. Accordingly, in all the circumstances of the present case, the Court considers that the length of the proceedings fails to satisfy the "reasonable time" requirement.'[119]

Arguably, if such reasoning were to be followed by British judges, successful challenges may be brought concerning the length of time taken to hear an appeal unless the delay could be shown to be justifiable.

5.7   ARTICLE 7: NO PUNISHMENT WITHOUT LAW

Article 7 states that:

> '(1) No one shall be held guilty of any criminal offence on account of any act or omission which did not constitute a criminal offence under national or international law at the time when it was committed. Nor shall a heavier penalty be imposed than the one that was applicable at the time when it was committed.
> (2) This Article shall not prejudice the trial and punishment of any person for any act or omission which, at the time when it was committed, was criminal according to general principles of law recognised by civilised nations.'

It is worthy of note that, arguably, a potential challenge to a sentence under this article must be limited by the wording and provisions of Art 7(2). Even if an act or omission is not specifically prohibited by law, Art 7 cannot be invoked against a sentence or conviction if the act contravenes unspecified 'general principles' of criminal law.

Further problems arise from the very nature of sentencing practice, ie the discretionary practice involved in non-mandatory sentences. As David Thomas has commented:

> '[t]he principle prohibiting retrospective increases in penalties ... is clearly capable of causing major practical problems when it is applied to changes in sentencing law which are essentially procedural in character or which take effect through a discretionary process which allows for some mitigation of the retrospective increase.'[120]

---

119   *Howarth v UK* Application No 38081/97 (2000), paras 29, 30.
120   DA Thomas 'Sentencing Legislation: A Case for Consolidation' (1997) Crim LR 406 at 413.

Challenges have been made in the European arena with varying degrees of success which suggests that the provisions of Art 7 may be invoked at a domestic level through recourse to the Human Rights Act 1998. Two examples of how Art 7 has been invoked against sentence imposed in the UK are provided below. These illustrate how the European Court has interpreted the provisions of the article, and demonstrate the difficulties to be overcome by potential applicants seeking to claim that the sentence imposed has been made as a result of retrospective application of the law. This is followed by an example of domestic practice relating to retrospective application of the judgment through the appeal process. This domestic practice suggests that, however difficult to demonstrate, especially in light of Art 7(2), domestic courts will maintain a keen eye on Art 7 challenges.

Worthy of note is one issue that has been discussed by the European Court with regard to Art 7 and found not to be a breach of the provisions. Deemed inadmissible was an application[121] claiming that an order to register with the Sex Offenders Register violated Art 7. Of interest to potential claimants are the reasons why the European Court considered this part of the application inadmissible in that they provide further elucidation of the interpretation of the article which may be employed at a domestic level:

> 'The Court notes that the applicant has referred to newspaper reports of vigilante attacks on paedophiles following their identification by the press and television. However, there is no evidence before it to suggest that these attacks were connected in any way with the registration of the offenders in question with the police or that the requirement to register will lead to information which is not already publicly available becoming known to the media or the general public. Again, having regard to the preamble to the Act and also to the nature of the Act's requirements, the Court considers that the purpose of the measures in question is to contribute towards a lower rate of reoffending in sex offenders, since a person's knowledge that he is registered with the police may dissuade him from committing further offences and since, with the help of the register, the police may be enabled to trace suspected reoffenders faster.
>
> The Court recalls that the concept of "penalty" in Article 7 of the Convention is an autonomous concept: it is for the Court to determine whether any particular measure is a "penalty". The second sentence of Article 7(1) indicates that the starting point of such a determination is whether the measure in question was imposed following conviction for a "criminal offence". Other relevant factors are the characterisation of the measure under domestic law, its nature and purpose, the procedures involved in its making and implementation, and its severity
>
> The Court notes first, that there is a link in the present case between the conviction and the impugned measures: the registration requirements automatically apply to the applicant because, at the time of the commencement of the Act, he was serving a sentence of imprisonment following his conviction for a sexual offence.'[122]

---

121   *David Adamson v UK* Application No 42293/98.
122   Ibid.

5.7.1   The 'marital rape exemption'

SW v UK and *CR v UK*,[123] heard together by the European Court, related to the application of Art 7 in relation to a sentence imposed for marital rape. The applicants were both found guilty of different rape offences by English courts. SW was convicted of raping his wife on 18 September 1990, and CR pleaded guilty to the attempted rape of his spouse in November 1989. The application was made on the grounds that at the time of the offences, the common law presumption that a man could not rape his wife, as she was deemed to consent to conjugal relations on marriage, was still in force. This common law presumption was abolished by the case of *R v R*[124] in July 1990, after the offences involving the two applicants took place, whereby the European Court, and ultimately the House of Lords, stated that times had changed[125] and so must the common law, and so a wife is no longer deemed to have given consent to all marital intercourse on marriage.

The Court determined that although, technically, the immunity had not been abolished at the time of the offence, the evolution of case-law up to 1990 'had reached a stage where judicial recognition of the absence of the immunity had become a reasonably foreseeable development of the law'.[126] The Court further stated that:

> 'The essentially debasing character of rape is so manifest that the result of the decisions of the Court of Appeal and the House of Lords ... cannot be said to be at variance with the object and purpose of Article 7 of the Convention, namely to ensure that no-one should be subjected to arbitrary prosecution, conviction or punishment. What is more, the abandonment of the unacceptable idea of a husband being immune against prosecution for rape of his wife was in conformity not only with a civilised concept of marriage but also, and above all, with the fundamental objectives of the Convention, the very essence of which is respect for human dignity and human freedom.'[127]

5.7.2   Confiscation orders and drug trafficking offences

In contrast, a decision by the European Court involving drug trafficking offences was held to fall within the scope of Art 7. In *Welch v UK*[128] the Court considered the applicability of Art 7 to a confiscation order imposed on Mr Welch subsequent to his conviction through the Drug Trafficking Offences Act 1986, which did not come into force until January 1987. The offence for which he was convicted took place in 1986, and Mr Welch claimed that, as the provisions of the legislation were not in force at the time of the commission of the offence, a retrospective penalty had been imposed on him in the form of the confiscation order. The Court agreed and awarded him £13,562.60 for costs and expenses. The Court felt obliged to note that:

---

123   (1995) 21 EHRR 363.
124   [1991] 4 All ER 481, CA; (1992) 94 Cr App R 216, HL.
125   See the judgment of Lord Keith of Kinkel in *R v R* (1992) 94 Cr App R 216.
126   *SW v UK* and *CR v UK* (1995) 21 EHRR 363 at 402.
127   Ibid.
128   (1995) 20 EHRR 247.

'The concept of a "penalty" in this provision is, like the notions of "civil rights and obligations" and "criminal charge" in Article 6(1), an autonomous Convention concept. To render the protection offered by Article 7 effective, the Court must remain free to go behind appearances and assess for itself whether a particular measure amounts in substance to a "penalty" within the meaning of this provision.'[129]

The Court went on to consider the implications of the confiscation order and determined that it did, in fact, amount to a penalty within the meaning of Art 7. Accordingly, a breach of the article was recorded, with one *caveat*:

'The Court would stress, however, that this conclusion concerns only the retrospective application of the relevant legislation and does not call into question in any respect the powers of confiscation conferred on the courts as a weapon in the fight against the scourge of drug trafficking.'[130]

The Court also noted that the reason the confiscation order fell within the definition of the term 'penalty' under Art 7 was because the imposition of the order was punitive in nature as well as an attempt to make reparations and, as such, was protected. Interestingly, other legislative provisions which relate to confiscation orders are formulated in the same way as those in the Drug Trafficking Offences Act 1986, and as such are liable to challenge in the same way.[131] The decision in *Welch* may have an effect on judgments after incorporation of the Human Rights Act 1998. The European case was cited in a case before the domestic courts. In *R v Taylor*[132] the defendant sought to rely on the judgment in *Welch* in relation to a similar confiscation order. The court in *Taylor* noted the European judgment, but stated that since the legislation relating to the confiscation order was explicit,[133] as was the decision in *Welch*, Art 7 was not applicable. The court in *Taylor* directed itself to the comments of the European Court that its decision was made on the circumstances of the case and should not be construed as calling into question 'the powers of confiscation conferred on the courts as a weapon in the fight against the scourge of drug trafficking'. It was in reference to this reasoning that the Court of Appeal in *Taylor* determined that Art 7 did not apply. Similarly, domestic courts considered *Welch* in the appeal *R v Malik*.[134] However, the Court of Appeal in this instance considered *Welch* in relation to argument concerning Art 6(2), finding that the article was not breached by the relevant provisions of the Drug Trafficking Act 1994 since 'There was nothing unlawful with the procedures ... followed; there was nothing that conflicts with Europe at all and the submissions made were simply misconceived.'[135]

However, it is arguable that appeals against confiscation orders, in relation to the possible retroactivity of the legislation, will be made by virtue of the

---

129   (1995) 20 EHRR 247, para 27.
130   Ibid, para 36.
131   For example, s 102 of the Criminal Justice Act 1988.
132   (1996) 2 Cr App R 64.
133   Drug Trafficking Offences Act 1986, s 38.
134   *R v Malik* [2000] TLR 430.
135   Ibid, para 10.

provisions of the Human Rights Act 1998. As such, it is possible that the courts will ultimately reverse the reasoning witnessed in *Taylor* and *Malik* in order to ensure that Art 7 is complied with in all circumstances. Further, it is arguable that these concerns will apply equally to other provisions relating to confiscation orders.

5.7.3   Crime (Sentences) Act 1997, section 2

The Crime (Sentences) Act 1997 has introduced a two-tariff system pre/post commencement. The Act, while subject to controversy, has walked the fine line between acceptable change and imposition of a heavier penalty. It introduces a life sentence for defendants convicted of a second serious offence as listed in s 2 of the Act. This new sentencing guideline may have fallen foul of Art 7 had it not been for the requirement that the new provision is not triggered unless the second offence was committed after the time of commencement of the Act. It is interesting to question whether this need to refrain from imposing any legislation which could possibly be seen to be retrospective has resulted in the wording of the Act in this way and the creation of a time lag in which widely disparate sentences will be found.

The recent case of *R v Kelly*[136] involved the first application of s 2 of the Act. Mr Kelly's offence of inflicting grievous bodily harm with intent attracted a mandatory life sentence due to his conviction in 1980 for armed robbery. The judge in the case, Fabyan Evans, imposed a tariff period of 4 years, after which Mr Kelly could seek review of his sentence. Interestingly, this sentence was referred to as a 'mandatory' life sentence. The European Court, as previously discussed,[137] determined that one of the crucial differences between mandatory and discretionary life sentences is that a mandatory sentence is imposed due to the nature of the crime, whereas a discretionary life sentence is awarded by virtue of certain characteristics of the defendant – dangerousness or mental instability. It is arguable that the new 'two strikes' mandatory life sentence is also imposed due to the nature of the defendant, ie his dangerousness and his displayed propensity towards violent crimes. The sentence is not awarded with reference to his current offence.[138] While the imposing of an automatic life sentence is seen as mandatory in such '2 strikes' circumstances, a court may choose to impose a lesser sentence in 'exceptional circumstances'. The case of *R v Offen*[139] makes clear that in considering whether exceptional circumstances exist, a cause must assess the offender's potential risk to the general public.

---

136   *Daily Telegraph*, 2 May 1998.
137   See **5.5.1** and **5.5.2** above.
138   With the exception of the fact that the offence must fit within the categories of eligible offences listed within the Act.
139   [2001] 2 All ER 154.

5.7.4 Retrospectivity and the House of Lords

In *R v Governor of Brockhill Prison ex parte Evans (No 2)*[140] application was made concerning sentence calculation dates for release procedures. While this case concerned the retrospective application of a court order rather than legislation, the case arguably demonstrates how important domestic courts consider the issue of retrospective application to be. The process employed by the Governor of Brockhill prison in relation to the appellant was incorrect at the time of the appeal[141] and thus the appellant's release date was incorrectly determined as approximately 1 month later than it should have been, as confirmed by the Divisional Court. The appeal before the House of Lords concerned in part whether the order by the Divisional Court, that the appellant was entitled to release on 17 September,[142] should be considered as having determined the matter prospectively, or whether it should be deemed to have retrospective effect, given the time frames involved. Lord Hope of Craighead stated:

> 'It is difficult to see how the Divisional Court's order could be understood as having any other meaning than that it was stating retrospectively what the applicant's rights were as at 17 September 1996. Nevertheless the Solicitor-General suggested that some thought should be given to this issue in view of the importance which it might have following the coming into force of the Human Rights Act 1998. He said that there was a possibility that it might be appropriate for the technique of prospective overruling to be adopted in a limited number of cases, such as where a consistent line of authority was developed pointing one way and then reversed. But he recognised that there was a risk that the courts might be seen to be departing from the judicial function if they were to indulge in the practice of laying down the law only for the future ... As I have said, it is difficult to see how the court's order could be understood as having any application to the applicant's case other than it was to be applied to her retrospectively. If ever there was a case where the declaratory theory should be applied it must surely be one where the liberty of the subject is an issue – as it plainly is where the point relates to the entitlement of the subject to be released from custody.'[143]

5.8 ARTICLE 8: RESPECT FOR PRIVATE AND FAMILY LIFE

Article 8 provides that each person has a right to respect for private and family life. In terms of sentences, the important element of this right is whether the sentence imposed breached that right. Admittedly, many custodial sentences will seemingly interfere with this right; individuals who are incarcerated may be placed in a penal institution which is not geographically close to their family.

---

140 [2000] 3 WLR 843.
141 In between the time of calculation of release date and the eventual final appeal, procedures for calculation or earliest release date were clarified and altered.
142 As opposed to 18 November, as calculated by the Governor of Brockhill prison; the order by the Divisional Court was made on 15 November.
143 *R v Governor of Brockhill Prison ex parte Evans (No 2)* [2000] 3 WLR 843 at 855, per Lord Hope of Craighead.

However, the provisions of the article ensure that a breach is present only if the interference is not 'necessary in a democratic society'.[144] As such, it would be difficult successfully to challenge a custodial sentence merely on the grounds that it removed the defendant from his family. As custodial sentences are either mandatory and thus 'necessary', or are imposed as the highest discretionary tariff warranted in the circumstances of the case, such an argument would be very difficult to sustain. However, it has proved possible to challenge the rigor and length of a custodial sentence.

In respect of non-custodial or community penalties, recent changes in legislation have resulted in the abrogation of the previous requirement that an adult defendant's consent must be obtained prior to the imposition of a community sentence. As such, a court can impose a community sanction irrespective of any concerns or reservations expressed by the defendant. It is possible that a challenge against the interference with the right to respect for family life could be mounted in this area.

5.8.1   Custody and 'necessary in a democratic society'

In February 1997 the European Court delivered judgment in *Laskey, Jaggard and Brown v UK*.[145] The case concerned the conviction of the applicants in an English court for various offences against the person, and related offences, subsequent to the discovery of sado-masochistic practices. The applicants claimed that the application of the criminal law to their private and consenting activities was unforeseen, and contended that, as such, their prosecution 'amounted to an unlawful and unjustifiable interference with their right to respect for their private life'.[146] Similarly, the applicants contended that the custodial sentences handed down subsequent to conviction also amounted to a breach of Art 8 as the sentences were not 'necessary in a democratic society'. At their original trial the three men received custodial sentences of differing lengths,[147] which were reduced on appeal.[148]

The European Court found unanimously that there had been no violation of Art 8 in terms of the prosecution of the applicants. The interference by the State was justified as being necessary in a democratic State to protect the health of its members.[149] In relation to the sentence imposed, the Court found that the disposals were not disproportionate in the circumstances.

---

144   Article 8(2).
145   (1997) 24 EHRR 39.
146   Ibid, para 32.
147   Mr Laskey received a sentence totalling 4 years and 6 months, Mr Jaggard 3 years, and Mr Brown 2 years and 9 months.
148   The sentences were reduced by the Court of Appeal, which dismissed the appellants' appeal against conviction, but reduced the sentences on the grounds that the appellants had not realised or appreciated that their actions constituted a criminal offence contrary to the Offences Against the Person Act 1861. The sentences were reduced as follows: Mr Laskey, a total of 2 years' custody, Mr Jaggard, 6 months' custody, and Mr Brown, 3 months' custody.
149   Interestingly, while the Court's decision was unanimous, the Commission, in its report, decided that there was no violation, but the vote was 11 votes to 7.

'It remains to be ascertained whether these measures were proportionate to the legitimate aim or aims pursued.

The Court notes that the charges of assault were numerous and referred to illegal activities which had taken place over more than 10 years. However, only a few charges were selected for inclusion in the prosecution case. It further notes that, in recognition of the fact that the applicants did not appreciate their actions to be criminal, reduced sentences were imposed on appeal. In these circumstances, bearing in mind the degree of organisation involved in the offences, the measures taken against the applicants cannot be regarded as disproportionate.'[150]

This case gives rise to a number of questions which will be relevant to the sentencing practice of domestic judges following the enactment of the Human Rights Act 1998. Primarily, the question arises of whether, had the sentences not been reduced on appeal, the Court would have found a breach of Art 8 in relation to the severity of the sentence. The reasoning employed by the Court suggests that it may well have done. Reference is made to the fact that the sentences were reduced, and it was 'in these circumstances' that the finding of no breach was made. Arguably, the severity of the sentence imposed will have a bearing on whether the article is breached. In terms of the Human Rights Act 1998 this will mean that domestic judges, who must consider European Court jurisprudence, will have to consider carefully whether the sentence meted out is commensurate with both the offence committed and the infringement it places on the right to respect for private and family life.

Such arguments become especially relevant in the light of the more recent judgment handed down by the European Court in *ADT v UK*.[151] This application concerned similar activities to those pursued by the applicants in *Laskey* above. The applicant in *ADT* was convicted pursuant to s 13 of the Sexual Offences Act 1956[152] and complained to the European Court contending that such a conviction infringed Art 8 in that conviction limited his rights to a private life, especially as no corresponding statutory provisions existed regulating the activities of women or heterosexuals in a similar manner. The European Court agreed with the applicant and refused to accept the British Government's reliance on the Court's decision in *Laskey*, noting that:

'Whilst State interference might be justified in certain circumstances including the protection of morals or health, the activities had only involved a limited number of friends and it was unlikely that anyone else would have become aware of them. Moreover, although the acts were recorded on videotape, A had expressed a strong desire to remain anonymous and it was unlikely that he would have allowed the video to be publicly available. The acts were, therefore, purely private. As there were no public health issues to be considered, no interference with the right to engage in such activities was justified.'[153]

While the judgment relates in particular to the conviction of the applicants, rather than the sentence, it is worthy of note in that the European Court made

---

150   (1997) 24 EHRR 39, para 49.
151   [2000] 2 FLR 697.
152   Section 13 makes it an offence to engage in an act of gross indecency with another man.
153   [2000] 2 FLR 697.

its ruling based on whether the prosecution was necessary and reasonable, in this instance in relation to the protection of public health, again reinforcing the need for domestic courts to consider such measures when meting out sentence.

Perhaps more interesting is the terminology employed by the Court in *Laskey*. The Court addressed the question of whether the consequences faced by the applicants on prosecution were 'proportionate' to their offences.[154] As previously discussed,[155] the term 'proportionate', while advocated as a principle of sentencing by the Criminal Justice Act 1991, is not a term always employed by domestic courts. Sentencing practice is an amalgamation of precedent, guideline judgments of the Court of Appeal and statutory direction, with little evidence of an external policy rationale. Arguably:

> 'without external policy guidance, the appellate courts tend to have difficulty fashioning a principled resolution of sentencing issues. That difficulty has manifested itself in the English sentencing cases: guideline judgements issued without a clear statement of supporting rationale; claims about deterrence or treatment made with little regard for the availability of supporting evidence; proportionality among dispositions not carefully considered or maintained. Such deficiencies may be understandable ... but they do not bode well for a well-thought-through sentencing jurisprudence developed by courts alone.'[156]

However, while this argument suggests that there will be difficulties in relation to the reasoning of the European Court, it does not suggest that domestic courts pay no heed to notions of proportionality, rather that it is employed as a term in a manner different to that of the European Court. Indeed, in 2000 the Court of Appeal stated in *R v Wood*:

> 'We feel uncomfortable that a life sentence can be imposed for an offence under s 18 of the Offences Against the Person Act 1861 in respect of which an experienced judge, who has heard the evidence, is of the view that three years' imprisonment would, but for s 2, have been the appropriate sentence. The word disproportionate springs to mind.'[157]

Difficulties which arise with regard to this proportionality argument not only appear in considering the reasoning of the European Court and domestic courts. Such tensions are evident in commentary made at a purely domestic level. Indeed, as Ashworth questions in relation to the Criminal Justice Act 1991, 'Is the principle of proportionality "overriding" in current sentencing practice, as it was clearly intended to be by the framers of the 1991 Act?'[158] The answer, through his consideration of sentences being awarded for various

---

154 See also *Hoare v UK* (1997) EHRLR 678 for discussion of proportionate sentencing.
155 See **5.6.1** above.
156 A von Hirsch and A Ashworth *Principled Sentencing* (Edinburgh University Press, 1992), p 295.
157 (2000) Crim LR 599; this case involved an appeal against automatic life sentence imposed pursuant to s 2 of the Crime (Sentences) Act 1997 and whether the offence of buggery constituted a first serious crime for the purposes of the Act. Buggery is not listed as a trigger offence but can now be regarded in many instances as the offence of rape, since the definition of rape in the Criminal Justice and Public Order Act 1994 was amended.
158 A Ashworth *Sentencing and Criminal Justice* 3rd edn (Butterworths, 2000), p 130.

offences, is that such sentences as described cannot be regarded as solely reflecting commensurability. Such criticism is fuelled by comments made in the Home Office document, *A Review of the Sentencing Framework*:

> '... the current legal framework established in the Criminal Justice Act 1991 remains, and this appears now to be a contributory factor to inherent problems of sentencing – based as it is on the principles of "just deserts" by which the sentence imposed is tied to the seriousness of the offence, taking little account of offenders' propensity to re-offend. It also offers little opportunity to take into account how offenders respond to measures taken during the sentence which are designed to reduce their offending, nor the need for some form of reparation to society.
>
> The time is ripe, therefore, to review the sentencing framework and to determine, in a modern criminal justice system, what sort of framework would best deliver the twin aims of public protection and a reduction in re-offending.'[159]

Such comments suggest that the sentencing framework and rationale may move away from notions of proportionality in the future, towards a more deterrent and retributive foundation. Such a move may result in a greater conflict between the reasoning of European judgments and that of domestic courts.

As such, it is possible to argue, in this area at least, that the application of Art 8 may result in different outcomes dependent on whether the applicant is before a European or domestic court. While s 2 of the Human Rights Act 1998 states that domestic courts must take into account European jurisprudence when applying the articles, there is no requirement that domestic courts employ the tests utilised in the European Court of Human Rights. Unless domestic courts consider sentences in terms of proportion rather than employ any one of a number of factors, and develop a coherent rationale to sentencing policy, it is arguable that the potential effect of Art 8 may be diminished. The difference in the tests applied may result in some appellants being compelled to challenge the domestic interpretation of the reasonableness of their sentence in a European Court. It remains to be seen, through application, what tests the appellate courts will employ, and how they apply Art 8 and European jurisprudence.

5.8.2 Community penalties

The right to respect for private and family life may have an application in relation to community penalties, although it is more difficult to assess exactly in what area domestic challenges may be successful. With regard to juveniles, any community sentence[160] meted out is done so only after pre-sentence reports have been conducted, and the opinion and advice of various concerned parties has been sought.[161] As such, it is likely that the potential for breach of Art 8 will be considered at this stage, prior to the imposition of a custodial sentence.

---

159 Home Office Communications Directorate, CCN077828, C4000 (May 2000), p 2.
160 For a range of community sentences which can be imposed, see the Powers of the Criminal Courts (Sentencing) Act 2000 and the Criminal Justice and Courts Services Act 2000.
161 For example, s 38 of the Crime (Sentences) Act 1997 requires that should a court wish to impose any form of supervision order on a young person aged 16 or under, the court

Possible successful challenges of such sentences by juvenile offenders will arguably arise only when Art 8 and its implications have not been considered at all in the determination of the sentence warranted.

With regard to adult offenders no such requirements exist and the court may, if it is deemed appropriate, impose a non-custodial sentence without the agreement of the offender. However, while it is possible to suggest that challenges may be possible, it will be difficult for a complainant to demonstrate that the sanction was not 'in accordance with law' and 'necessary in a democratic society' or, indeed, that the sanction was not proportionate to the offence or harm caused. It is unlikely that a community sentence in and of itself will be deemed to violate Art 8, and any such applications will have to demonstrate that the particular circumstances of the case were such that Art 8 had been breached by virtue of those extenuating and unusual circumstances.

One area that has been considered, both at European and domestic level, is that of registration on the Sex Offenders Register.[162] The decision of the European Court declaring the application inadmissible demonstrates how difficult such challenges may be. The application alleged that compulsory registration on release from custody infringes the rights protected by Art 8. In its decision recognising the inadmissibility of the application the Court noted that:

> '... the requirement on the applicant to provide the information in question to the police amounts to an interference with his private life within the meaning of Article 8(1). It is therefore necessary for the court to examine whether it is justified under the terms of the second paragraph of Article 8. Since the measures in question are set out in clear terms under the Act, it cannot be doubted, that they are "in accordance with the law". Furthermore the court considers that the measures pursue legitimate aims, namely prevention of crime and the protection of the rights and freedoms of others. It remains to be decided whether they are "necessary in a democratic society", that is, proportionate to the aims pursued. In this connection the court [finds] that there is no evidence before it to suggest that the applicant is at particular risk of public humiliation or attack as a result of his obligations under the Act.'

In this way it is arguable that any potential arguments made at domestic level with regard to registration under the Sex Offenders Act 1997 will fail. Indeed, this argument was considered at domestic level in the case of *R v Chief Constable of Avon and Somerset Constabulary ex parte B*[163] prior to implementation of the Human Rights Act 1998. The domestic court, while not directly considering the reasoning of the European Court in the previous admissibility decision, came to the same conclusion, noting that the orders had legitimate objects as required by Art 8.

---

must first obtain and consider information concerning the offender's family
circumstances, and the likely effect of those circumstances, before passing sentence.
162 *David Adamson v UK* Application No 42293/98 (date of judgment 26 January 1999).
163 (Unreported) 5 April 2000.

Chapter 6

PRISONERS' RIGHTS

'I flatly reject the cynical view that, because we cannot make the world perfect, we should give up on trying to make it better. The obligation on us is not to put everything right, but to do what we can to make a difference.'[1]

6.1 INTRODUCTION

At the time of writing there are 64,960 prisoners, remanded or sentenced, within the custody of Her Majesty's Prison Service (HMPS).[2] Apart from circa 24 prisoners who have been told by the Home Secretary that they will die in prison, the remainder will be returned to the community.[3] HMPS efforts to work towards 'building bridges with the community', thereby effectively acknowledging that prisoners are part of a community, is itself linked directly to the Human Rights Act 1998 field. As the Director General (DG) of the Service, Martin Narey, has stated, such 'bridges' 'open up prisons to innovation and to outside scrutiny, each of which are essential to the humanity of the sort of prison service which I want to lead'.[4] Given his statement, and the figures

---

1 Speech by the Foreign Secretary, Robin Cook, to the Royal Institute of International Affairs (London, 28 January 2000); quoted in *Human Rights, Foreign and Commonwealth Office Annual Report 2000*, Cm 4774 (2000), 135.

2 Prison population by age, sex, type of prisoner and establishment, as of 8 November 2000: *Occupation of Prisons, Remand Centres, Young Offender Institutions and Police Cells, England and Wales 31 October 2000* (Home Office Research, Development and Statistics Directorate, Offenders and Corrections Unit (10 November 2000), pp 6–8), Table M3. See also, M Elkins, C Gray and B Hidkyar *Prison Population Brief England and Wales: September 2000* (Home Office Research, Development and Statistics Directorate).

3 'Law chief gives Hindley new hope of release' *The Times*, 7 June 2000. It is worthy of note that, in the same article Lord Woolf hinted at challenges under the Human Rights Act 1998 even by prisoners who have been told that they would end their lives in prison. He confirmed his own reservations by saying 'any given case is so lacking in aspects of redemption that one can anticipate that throughout the natural life of the individual concerned, it will never be proper to release that person'. However, in 'Ministers may defy rights Act over Hindley' *The Times*, 21 September 2000, the Lord Chancellor Lord Irvine of Lairg stated, 'I can envisage that in one or two cases they [Ministers and Government] would take the view that there was some overriding reason why they would not want to make it [the law] compliant'. This latter stance is one of the instances envisaged in this chapter in the first edition of this publication when it was stated, 'as long as prisoners had recourse to judgment outside the UK, there was a greater chance that changes could be effected. That is to say, the European Court judgments, being such that the British Government was not obliged to follow them, lent them the characteristics of tools to be selectively adopted in suiting political ends': D Cheney et al *Criminal Justice and the Human Rights Act 1998* (Jordans, 1999), p 143.

4 M Narey, quoted in 'Partnerships Inside' *Prison Service Journal* No 131 (September 2000), p 5.

themselves, it would be untenable to consider that human rights should be suspended at the gates of every prison and reactivated only when a prisoner takes that first step back to freedom. Prisoners have rights.

HMPS has acknowledged this position for some time, not least as a result of the fact that the European Court of Human Rights (the European Court) has, in recent years, taken the lead ahead of the domestic courts in advancing the rights of prisoners in England and Wales. Many policies have been shaped bearing in mind the litigation that has proceeded to Strasbourg. That said, it is clear that the lengthy procedures for taking a case to Strasbourg have, in effect, ruled out any satisfactory facility for relief for prisoners other than lifers, and certainly for short-term prisoners. With the coming into effect of the Human Rights Act 1998 on 2 October 2000, HMPS must face a potential barrage of legal demands under every right of the new legislation, from the whole spectrum of the prison population. Expectation of challenges from the general population has certainly been acknowledged;[5] as such, with 1,950 prisoners at any one time engaged in legal action against it, HMPS must realistically expect that prisoners themselves will seek to test the human rights field.[6]

But is HMPS acknowledging this and, more importantly, is HMPS culture such that it lends itself to facilitating challenge for prisoners?

There is evidence of reluctance by HMPS in the past to accept 'rights issues'. In 1980, when a conference focusing on prison discipline was organised by the British Institute of Human Rights, HMPS circulated an instruction to staff not to attend.[7] However, there is no doubt that in the immediate 'run-up' to the coming into force of the Human Rights Act 1998, an uncharacteristic proactive stance has been taken by HMPS. Whereas the policy and practices of HMPS have been characterised by piecemeal development for many years,[8] the heralding of the Act seems to have prompted proactive considerations and behaviour. Prison Service Instruction (PSI) 60/2000, issued on the authority of HMPS Management Board on 28 September 2000, stated, 'We have reviewed policies and practices in advance of 2 October and believe that they are broadly compliant with ECHR [the Convention] ... it is important that ECHR [the Convention] becomes an explicit part of the Service's approach to policy formulation and decision making and that its rights inform both processes'.[9] A

---

5   Some £60 million has been set aside by the Lord Chancellor's Department to cope with legal costs, £39 million for public funding and £21 million for extra court sittings. Parliament has been granted the powers for eight more High Court judges, and the number of judicial review courts have been doubled. See *The Times*, 12 September 2000.
6   See 'Prison Chiefs are in the front line' *The Times*, 12 September 2000.
7   P Quinn, 'Thirty years on: a rights polemic' *Prison Service Journal* No 131 (September 2000), pp 38, 39.
8   Examples of widespread policy changes on such a basis are epitomised by the effects of the Woodcock Enquiry following the escape from HMP Whitemoor, and the Learmont Enquiry following the escape from HMP Parkhurst. See Sir John Woodcock, CBE, QPM *Report of the Enquiry into the escape of six prisoners from the special security unit at Whitemoor prison, Cambridgeshire, on Friday 9 September 1994*, Cm 2741 (1994); and General Sir John Learmont, KCB, CBE *Review of Prison Service security in England and Wales and the escape from Parkhurst Prison*, Cm 3020 (1995).
9   *The Human Rights Act and the ECHR* PSI 60/2000.

direct example of such reviews has been the discontinuance of the strip-searching of prisoners identified at risk of suicide and self-injury by PSI 27/2000, on the grounds that it was regarded as 'Likely to be challenged under Article 3'. Yet there have been other innovations, arguably initiated in the light of foreseeable challenges. These include: the focus on child protection measures; the appointment of both a Race Equality Advisor and Muslim Advisor; the launch of RESPOND;[10] new procedures for mother and baby units; and the individualising of the under 18 and women's estates. These are all to be welcomed as positive moves which will, by their very essence, ensure that rights concerns are at the forefront, by individualising persons in the prison estate, and that HMPS has a positive obligation to act in a way which reinforces the principles of the Act. We must not make light of the changes introduced, and thus I would seek qualification in the borrowed words of Her Majesty's Chief Inspector of Prisons (HMCIP), 'It may seem churlish therefore to be suggesting yet more improvements, but they are made in the spirit of maintaining momentum, not suggesting that nothing is happening'.[11]

Such momentum is necessary to give effect to one of the greatest potential benefits of the Act – a more proactive and responsive Prison Service. In March 2000 the DG, Martin Narey, pledged a more transparent and accountable Service.[12] The existence of an expanded route to challenge for prisoners, which the Act affords, will ensure that this is so. A move towards a culture of openness by the Service has already begun, not least seen in such as the partnerships embraced with both the Probation Service and voluntary sector,[13] the latter resulting in the appointment of a voluntary and community sector co-ordinator. However, responsivity to prisoners also includes, or at least should, a change in prison culture itself. That such a change is effected is more crucial in terms of prisoners benefiting from the Act, not least because, as stated by Coyle, 'the environment does not lend itself to respect for the person'.[14] Indeed, the DG effectively reiterated this statement himself, speaking at a conference at Huntercombe YOI, when he said:

> 'Prisons are of their very nature inward looking. Sometimes that inwardness makes them bleak and dangerous. Closed from outside influence they can degenerate and, at worst, prisoners can be abused and brutalised. This is a real and constant danger because for perfectly good reasons prisons are not easy to penetrate.'[15]

If blinded by their own culture in their everyday management, prisons can lose sight of functions they are expected to perform for society, which functions now include recognising the rights and responsibilities of a prisoner, properly

10   Racial Equality for Staff and Prisoners.

11   *Annual Report of HM Inspector of Prisons 1998–1999.*

12   Martin Narey, speaking to the annual conference of the Prison Governors' Association: 'Director General pledges a more transparent and accountable Service' *PS Press Release* (29 March 2000).

13   See Home Office *Compact on Relations between Government and the Voluntary and Community Sector in England* (HMSO, 1998); and Home Office *Prisons/Probation Review: Final Report* (1998).

14   A Coyle *The Prisons We Deserve* (HarperCollins, 1994) 215.

15   M Narey; quoted in 'Partnerships Inside' *Prison Service Journal* No 131 (September 2000), pp 3, 5.

balanced with those of other prisoners, prison staff, victims and the public. It cannot be taken for granted that staff will magically acknowledge prisoners' rights as if the Act had cast some spell over them. As Quinn states:

> 'Human Rights is an attitude of mind ... not something to be mugged up in half a day for the purpose of ticking the "done that" box. In the end an attitudinal shift must come about if rights considerations are to be internalised on landings.'[16]

As part of this internalisation, it is surely the case that HMPS must begin to stop measuring 'improvements' by quantitative fact (not least of this criteria being key performance standards), and start measuring them by qualitative judgment.

The areas of proactivity and prison culture are intertwined, the latter having considerable effect upon what is seen as an area needing attention, and thereby what is seen as a necessary policy change. That this is so has been demonstrated by recent PS statements which suggest that PS management consider that all that needs to be done has been effected. The DG himself has confirmed 'We are not going to panic and the Scottish experience, where the Act is already law, has shown that we are right not to do so', referring to how in Scotland there have been only three out of 460 applications under the Act involving prisons.[17] This is an unrealistic comparison from which to draw conclusions about the number of complaints that can be expected from the English prison population. Consider, for example, that the average number of prisoners held within the Scottish Prison Service (SPS) estate on any particular day in 1999/2000 was 5,974 (maximum 6,273, with the highest number recorded in 1999 being 6,311 on 23 March 1999).[18] Consider also that over the period 1998–1999 the Scottish Prisons Complaints Commissioner made 12 recommendations to the SPS arising from prisoners' complaints,[19] whereas over the same period the Prisons Ombudsman received, 1,937 complaints, of which 491 investigations were completed, and in which 252 recommendations were made.[20] It is difficult to see how the two can be compared.

Yet it could be said that it is less how the SPS has fared on the human rights front that appears to be at the root of the PS stance, than arguably a case of prison culture. It was reported that the Home Secretary felt it necessary to take a stance of having 'strongly rejected the idea that the Act would be a charter for prisoners ... to challenge every aspect of their detention'.[21] This is reinforced by consistent claims on the part of HMPS that policies have been made 'ECHR-proof'. Pickering, of Prison Administration Group, notes, in an

---

16   P Quinn, 'Thirty years on: a rights polemic' *Prison Service Journal* No 131 (September 2000), pp 38, 41.

17   See M Narey 'We know our Rights' *The Guardian*, 12 May 2000, and 'Prison chiefs are in the front line' *The Times*, 12 September 2000.

18   *Scottish Prison Service Annual Report and Accounts 1999–2000*, Appendix 2 and 'Prison Statistics Scotland 1999', SPS *News Release* (16 November 2000).

19   *Scottish Prison Service Annual Report and Accounts 1998–1999*, Custody Directorate.

20   *Prisons Ombudsman Annual Report 1999–2000*, Cm 4730 (2000), p 7. The first three-quarters of the last year averaged 454 complaints, with the last quarter receiving 573 new complaints.

21   'Judges face torrent of human rights claims' *The Times*, 12 September 2000.

administrative response to legal issues, 'our policies have been devised to be ECHR proof and will be defended rigorously in the event of any challenge'.[22] This approach detracts from the emphasis the Act places on 'responsibilities' and the essence of the Act being a 'living document', there to mould and shape. It is again worth quoting Quinn, this time at the Perrie Lectures in 1998 that, 'In the wider society the little person who stands up for their rights against the excesses of bureaucracy of the State is seen as something of a hero. If that person is a prisoner, they are likely to be seen as a nuisance, a subversive or a troublemaker'. Prison staff, understandably, want certainty and a quiet prison. However, this leads to anyone pursuing his or her entitlements often being deemed 'litigious' or – even more derogatory – 'difficult' or 'eccentric'.[23] The vocabulary used by the Prison Administration Group reflects this. It sees the duty of ensuring someone's human rights as a threat ('defended vigorously at any challenge') which HMPS needs to be armoured against ('ECHR-proof'). This seems to be a static approach, and a potential waste of the opportunity the Act affords both prisoner and Service. The vocabulary shows how prison culture continues to posit the prisoner, not as someone legitimately pursuing and genuinely seeking their rights, but as a 'nuisance, subversive or trouble maker'.[24] It suggests the PS approach to be one of 'winning and losing', rather than what it actually should be: working toward respect for human rights. As long as this attitude remains, and 'prison culture' takes precedence over a new 'human rights culture', prisons remain a very fertile ground for challenges to be made.

Such concerns are fuelled not least by proposed changes to two mechanisms of PS accountability, and sources of complaint for prisoners: the offices of HMCIP and the Prisons' Ombudsman. The Home Secretary announced in April 2000 that the remit of the Prisons' Ombudsman would be extended, and the post would become that of Prisons' and Probation Ombudsman. Whilst extending the opportunity for complaint to those serving non-custodial sentences, it is nonetheless a role which, by expanding the current brief, could potentially give rise to a workload resulting in delays in dealing with prisoners' complaints. In a similar vein it was announced that the offices of HM Chief Inspectors of Prisons and Probation would be merged, an amalgamation seen as potentially more worrying by many, despite being premised ostensibly as a move towards greater accountability. The serving HMCIP, Sir David Ramsbotham, and the former

---

22   R Pickering, 'What's all this about Human Rights?' *Prison Service Journal* No 131 (September 2000), pp 47, 49.

23   Although it is worthy of note that the Home Secretary has gone on record to state that an eccentric lifestyle did not mean that a person did not have human rights: 'Judges face torrent of human rights claims' *The Times*, 12 September 2000.

24   This is equally the stance taken if complaints are made to a board of visitors, area manager, governor or Prisons Ombudsman, rather than these complaints procedures being facilitated as the legitimate means prisoners have available to them to seek to better their lot.

HMCIP, Sir Stephen Tumim, have both stated on record that the change is a downgrading of the HMCIP role.[25]

6.2   RELEVANCE TO PRISONERS

'Without justice and the rule of law, people cannot be sure of claiming any of the other rights to which they are entitled and which they need to live their lives with dignity.'[26]

The UK Government has adopted an international profile of consideration for human rights overseas, not least the rights of prisoners. Leaving aside submissions to the European Community both on the part of the UK itself and in respect of the behaviour of other nations, this stance is nowhere more evident than in the Annual Human Rights Reports of the Foreign and Commonwealth Office (FCO). Since 1997 these annual publications have recorded the work of the FCO to promote human rights abroad. As such, they contain a strong government line on how prisoners should be treated.

In the report of the FCO in 1999 the Government stated its belief in a need for a new approach to rights and justice. This approach was to embrace the rights of people detained or imprisoned, as:

'Accessible justice means that individuals are able to obtain redress through an honest and effective legal system which also provides suspects and convicted persons with all the protections stipulated in international human rights instruments.'[27]

---

25   Speaking at the Annual Conference of UNLOCK, the national association of ex-offenders, in August 2000, both Sir David and Sir Stephen stressed the importance of an independent Prisons Inspectorate and the threat which was posed both to the number of inspections which could be carried out, and to the peripheral duties undertaken, such as dedicated thematic reviews. See also 'New right for criminals' *The Times*, 17 April 2000; 'Inspector of Prisons faces job merger' *The Times*, 17 May 2000; 'Prison inspector defends his role' *The Times*, 14 June 2000. On 28 March 2000 the then President of the Prison Governors Association (PGA), Christopher Scott OBE, spoke in support of the role of HMCIP when stating that 'The country requires a strong independent Chief inspector of HM Prison Service not just of prisons. I know that the present Chief Inspector is of the same view. In my opinion Sir David has been an outstanding Chief inspector. He so often appears to be a thorn in the flesh of the Prisons Board and for that matter governors. So he should be. This country has much that is envied by other nations not least our record of independently minded people who are not afraid to upset the status quo when things need putting right. No one could ever accuse Sir David of courting popularity and neither should he. The country needs his independence, his tenacity, and even his occasional gaffes if it is to continue to strive for a civilised, ethical, fair, just and caring penal system . . . It would be a travesty should his very independent views and his independent outspoken comments, so often off message and without the Government seal of approval, prevent him carrying on with his exacting but necessary work of raising conditions within our penal system': Chairman's Annual Address, PGA 2000 Annual Conference (28 March 2000).

26   *Human Rights and Justice, Human Rights: Foreign and Commonwealth Office Annual Report 2000* (Cm 4774).

27   *Rights and Justice, Human Rights: Foreign and Commonwealth Office and Department for International Development Annual Report 1999* (Cm 4404).

Under the heading of the Government-supported 'New Models of Accessible Justice and Penal Reform project', one of the three key areas to be addressed by six countries in Africa, South Asia and the Caribbean was that of improving the human rights and conditions of prisoners.[28]

By the year 2000 the report, covering the period June 1999 to June 2000, was providing a comprehensive overview of challenges to human rights around the world and activities by the Government to integrate human rights into foreign policy and address those challenges. As stated by the Foreign Secretary in January 2000, 'We support human rights and democracy for other people because these are the values we demand for ourselves'.[29]

Within the Human Rights Act 1998 nothing is stated directly about the particular situation of prisoners per se; rather, any rights must be inferred from those rights that are available to the community at large. Does the UK therefore reflect in home policy the pledge made by the Foreign Secretary, held to be so important to uphold overseas, not least in the importance in which prisoners rights are held? How much of the Act will be held to be relevant to prisoners? The rights contained in the Act are a combination of absolute, limited and qualified rights. Where subject to exceptions, these are: 'as is in accordance with the law and is necessary in a democratic society in the interests of national security, public safety or the economic well-being of the country, for the prevention of disorder or crime, for the protection of health or morals, or for the protection of the rights and freedoms of others'. Is it then the case that even some very basic rights, when claimed violated by a prisoner, can be held not so; that any interference infringing a right has been necessary and proportionate, purely by virtue of their status as a prisoner?

That this might be the case is forecast to some extent where public opinion is taken into account. It has already been recorded in the introduction to this chapter that 'defiance' is a possibility where courts rule that laws are in breach of the Act.[30] Not least of the possible reasons for this will be public opinion. How prisoners are dealt with has a tenuous and intangible relationship with public opinion; how prisoners are treated by virtue of the resources allocated to their care and management bears some relationship to media reported public opinion. Yet what is enshrined in law has a symbolic significance. The Act forces people to think of the humanity of others, to meet a duty/responsibility and to support a positive attitude to human rights within the community. As the introduction to this chapter has shown, all but a handful of those imprisoned will be returning to their communities, something not in the forefront of the minds of the majority of the community. People cannot be blamed; dehumanising prisoners acts in the manner of all myths, to make us feel better about ourselves. Thus, that myth must pose prisoners as 'different'. But the Act tells us that they are not different in that they also have rights.

---

28   *Rights and Justice, Human Rights: Foreign and Commonwealth Office and Department for International Development Annual Report 1999* (Cm 4404).

29   Speech by the Foreign Secretary, Robin Cook, to The Royal Institute of International Affairs, Chatham House, London (28 January 2000), in *Human Rights: Foreign and Commonwealth Office Annual Report 2000*, Cm 4774 (2000), Annex 1: Key Speeches, p 132.

30   See 'Ministers may defy rights Act over Hindley' *The Times*, 21 September 2000.

Long term, the mere existence of the Act, described as a 'living instrument', may counter the feelings of social exclusion that surround prisoners, and build bridges for them within the community. This, in turn, has the capacity to change 'prison culture', which has been suggested as so problematic in the introduction to this chapter. That is to say, it is difficult to change the culture within prisons when the staff (members of the public merely there to do a job) go out into a climate which may reinforce negative attitudes to prisoners which diminish their status as people with rights. If the Act is to prove a truly 'living instrument', such changes are no exaggerated claim.

As for the potential for the Act to make significant inroads with regard to prisoners, this matter will be discussed under the individual rights enshrined in the Act.

6.3   RIGHTS

'The Human Rights Act contains powerful provisions with powerful consequences.'[31]

6.3.1   Article 2: Right to life

Under Art 2 of the European Convention on Human Rights (the Convention) a public authority must not cause death intentionally and must take steps to protect and prolong life.[32] Issues relevant here are deaths in custody, the handling of documentation in respect of the suicidal, care for the vulnerable and measures in respect of their safety in areas such as reception, supply of healthcare within the prison setting[33] and balancing risk to the public in respect of release decisions.

Self-harm and suicide
The DG, Martin Narey, stated in December 1999 that 'Everyday in prisons in England and Wales around 1000 prisoners, out of a population of nearly 66,000

---

31   Home Secretary's address to the Legal Affairs and Human Rights Committee of the
     Parliamentary Assembly, Strasbourg (27 January 1999) *Policy Statements, News Releases,
     Parliamentary Questions, Speeches* Home Office Human Rights Unit, available from
     www.homeoffice.gov.uk.
32   *X v UK* Application No 7154/75, (1978) 14 DR 31; as quoted by R English *Analysis of The
     Convention and the Human Rights Act 1998* (One Crown Row, Human Rights Interactive).
     For a briefing on the area of deaths in custody, see H Arnott, D Coles and S Creighton
     'Prisoners, deaths in custody and the Human Rights Act' (Prisoners Advice Service and
     Inquest, October 2000).
33   A prisoner is entitled to the same standard of healthcare as he or she is at liberty; *Brooks v
     Home Office* [1999] 2 FLR 33. See also *Patient or Prisoner? A new strategy for health care in
     prisons: Discussion by HM Inspectorate of Prisons* (Home Office, 1996). In January 2000 an
     HMPS Working Party was established to consider the future prison nursing workforce,
     with particular reference to health care officers, and in May 2000 Paul Boateng, Prisons
     and Probation Minister, underlined the importance of the recommendations being made
     by the Working Group to develop high quality prison nursing: HMPS Press Release, 17
     May 2000. In November 2000 HMPS appointed a Chair for a new Working Group to
     consider the future needs of prison doctors.

are identified at being of extreme risk of self-harm and suicide ... every four days or so, tragically, someone will succeed'.[34] The total number of self-inflicted deaths in prison during 1998 was 82, a number exceeded before completion of the same period in 1999, when standing at 84 on 14 December[35] and rising to a total of 91 (two-thirds of those on remand) by the end of the year, the greatest number of suicides ever and the highest rate.[36] By July 2000, self-inflicted deaths during the year already numbered 48, with 53 by August, forecasting a tragic possibility that by the end of 2000 the 1999 record number will have been surpassed. This is despite the fact that in 1999 the DG made reducing suicides a priority for the Service.

These figures give rise to the question: why? However, what is central to consideration of that 'why?' are two questions: first, is HMPS failing in its obligation to prevent suicides, and will this present challenges under the 1998 Act?; secondly, are any potential failings in fact linked to failure under a number of rights under the Act?

Examining the evidence, it is certainly the case that some, but certainly not all, of the deaths may be related directly to the fact that prisoners are suffering from some form of mental disorder. In August 2000 the DG disclosed that '20% of men and 40% of women entering jail have attempted to kill themselves in the past'. He also said that since the introduction of care in the community the proportion of prisoners with mental illness had risen sevenfold.[37] That said, there is some suggestion that as HMPS is aware of the risk such prisoners pose, has it perhaps been failing in its obligation to protect life? If so, does this remain a failing and one that might be challenged under the Act? As the introduction to this chapter recorded, PSI 27/2000 was introduced to discontinue the strip-searching of prisoners considered at risk of self-harm and suicide, on the grounds that it would be challenged under Art 3 of the Convention (see below). Equally, HMPS introduced a programme to phase out the use of strip cells for

34   M Narey; quoted in 'Reducing suicides Top Priority for Director General' *PS Press Release* (14 December 1999).

35   The annual rate of self-inflicted deaths, per 100,000 prisoners, was calculated in December 1999 to be 129 per 100,000, the highest rate between the years 1994 and 1999, and rising at about 7% per annum. 'Reducing Suicides Top Priority for Director General' *PS Press Release* (14 December 1999); M Leech *The Prisons Handbook 1999* (Waterside Press, 1998), pp 462–468; M Leech and D Cheney *The Prisons Handbook 2000* (Waterside Press, 1999), pp 485–489; 'Consideration of Reports submitted by States parties under article 40 of the Covenant: The United Kingdom of Great Britain and Northern Ireland', *United Nations Committee on the International Covenant on Civil and Political Rights*, CCPR/C/UK/99/5 (April 2000), p 56.

36   See R Ford 'Prison suicides set a new record' *The Times*, 14 August 2000; S Wood 'Courts at fault on prison suicides', Letters to the Editor *The Times*, 23 August 2000; 'Reducing Suicides Top Priority for Director General' *PS Press Release* (14 December 2000).

37   R Ford 'Prison suicides set a new record' *The Times*, 14 August 2000.

the suicidal by April 2000.[38] This proactive response by HMPS illustrates how a violation of one right, in this case Art 3, can attend directly upon that of failure to protect under Art 2. However, even the most basic of failings in respect of managing suicidal prisoners can be potentially fatal, as Lady Sutherland wrote from her experience of 10 years as a member of a prison board of visitors, 'Documentation on potentially suicidal prisoners is not well managed and often is not available when the prisoner is moved either within the prison or to a new location'.[39] Equally, whilst there is no obligation to rescue, Rosalind English suggests that the domestic courts have some sympathy with imposition of such a positive obligation where prisoners are concerned. This is demonstrated by the case of *Sheila Reeves (Joint Administratrix of the Estate of Martin Lynch Deceased) v Commissioner of Police for the Metropolis*[40] where it was held that a breach of duty by the police facilitated suicide. She further suggests that, 'The scope of positive obligations to prevent life-threatening behaviour or accidents is likely to expand by consequence of the Strasbourg Court's judgement in *Osman v United Kingdom* (1998)'.[41] Both *Osman v UK*,[42] where the issue was one of alleged police negligence leading to murder, and *Reeves* concerned the police, but are equally appropriate to prison officers. In *Osman* the European Court held, rejecting the argument of the Government, that 'it is sufficient for an applicant to show that the authorities did not do all that could be reasonably expected of them to avoid a real and immediate risk to life of which they have or ought to have knowledge'.[43] In *Reeves*, it was held that the police had been under a duty to take reasonable care to prevent a deliberate act of self-harm and that the suicide was a foreseeable consequence of the failure of that duty. The Court stated, 'There was no difference between the duty owed to prisoners of sound and unsound mind, as that theory was inadequate to deal with the complexities of human psychology in the context of stresses caused by imprisonment'. In the

---

38   See, eg, Lady Sutherland 'Tackling the rise in prison suicides', Letters to the Editor *The Times*, 18 August 2000; and 'Reducing suicides Top Priority for DG' *PS Press Release* (14 December 2000); 'Prison suicides set a new record' *The Times*, 14 August 2000. The issue of strip-cell use raises the important point of duty in respect of members of prisons boards of visitors (who must authorise such detention in writing), as pointed out by M Leech *The Times*, 23 August 2000.

39   'Tackling the rise in prison suicides', Letters to the Editor, *The Times*, 18 August 2000.

40   [1999] 3 WLR 363.

41   R English *Analysis of the Convention and the Human Rights Act 1998* (One Crown Office Row, Human Rights Interactive), p 8. See *Osman v UK* [1999] 1 FLR 193. In this case the Government 'did not dispute that Art 2 of the Convention may imply a positive obligation on the authorities of a Contracting State to take preventive measures to protect the life of an individual from the danger posed by another individual. They emphasised, however, that this obligation could only arise in exceptional circumstances where there is a known risk of a real, direct and immediate threat to that individual's life and where the authorities have assumed responsibility for his or her safety. In addition, it had to be shown that their failure to take preventive action amounted to gross dereliction or wilful disregard of their duty to protect life. Finally, it must be established on sound and persuasive grounds that there is a causal link between the failure to take the preventive action of which the authorities are accused and that that action, judged fairly and realistically, would have been likely to have prevented the incident in question' (para 107).

42   [1999] 1 FLR 193.

43   Ibid, para 116.

light of this decision it is possible that HMPS, given the large and increasing numbers of suicides of those in its care, may face challenges on the grounds that, as suicide risks, such prisoners had not received the care they were due.

Prison conditions and mental health

To borrow the words of the court in *Reeves* above, consideration must also be given to 'the complexities of human psychology in the context of stresses caused by imprisonment'. Not least, the HMPS must also give direct attention to the actual effect of prison conditions on mental health itself. The wider prison canvas includes those whose mental distress is accentuated, possibly even engendered, by prison conditions. Not least of the concerns in this respect must focus on the conditions of close supervision centres (CSCs), which the HMCIP, Sir David Ramsbotham, has investigated in a thematic review.[44] In October 2000 the CSC at HMP Woodhill was closed after Sir David challenged conditions as 'cruel, inhumane and demoralising' and stated that the 'chronic isolation' could put the prisoners' mental health at risk.[45] This issue will be discussed further under Art 3 in relation to a human rights challenge by Rifat Mehmet.

Violations of Art 3 can certainly, on the above examples alone, be linked to the protection of life which is demanded by Art 2 (and will be examined further in discussion of Art 3 below). As Deborah Coles has stated in relation to deaths in custody:

> 'Evidence at inquests far too often seek to explain the deaths on terms of the individual's ability to cope, or their supposed personality problems, rather than look at the physical and psychological distress caused by prison regimes and conditions, isolation and lack of access to education, training and support.'[46]

The HMCIP has been forthright in his own comments of how conditions themselves in many cases do not guard against suicide. In his inspection report of HMP Exeter, speaking of the segregation unit there he remarked, 'I believe that not only are the conditions experienced by prisoners disgracefully impoverished but wholly insufficient in terms of guarding against suicide'.[47] Both HMPS and ministers are not unaware of the link. According to Liam Fox, Shadow Home Secretary, improvements in time spent on remand, overcrowding and hours confined to cell were significant in reflecting the mental health needs of inmates and that 'improving each area would improve the mental health needs of prisoners and help cut suicide rates'.[48] That regime approaches themselves are able to prevent suicides has been acknowledged by the DG in his

---

44   *Inspection of Close Supervision Centres: August–September 1999, A Thematic Inspection* (HMCIP, 2000).

45   R Ford 'Prison inquiry into "cruel" wing' *The Times*, 2 October 2000; and 'Harsh jail makes most violent inmates worse' *The Times*, 22 March 2000. See also *Inspection of Close Supervision Centres: August–September 1999, A Thematic Inspection* (HMCIP, 2000).

46   D Coles, Co-Director of Inquest 'Deaths in Custody' in M Leech and D Cheney *The Prisons Handbook 2001* (Waterside Press).

47   *Inspection Report of HMP Exeter* (HMCIP, May 1999).

48   R Watson 'Tories speak up for the mentally ill' *The Times*, 28 March 2000. Dr Fox claimed that the issue of mental health had become the 'also ran' of medical care, particularly in prisons.

applauding of the approach taken in the United States, with the employment of 24-hour mental health nurses on site, training of officers, and paid prisoner-observers.[49]

Non self-inflicted deaths

Suicides are not the only cause of deaths in prison. In 1999 non self-inflicted deaths numbered 23 and, for the year 2000, by July that number was 34, plus two homicides.[50] Performance against the Key Performance Indicator for assault, as appearing in HMPS Annual Report 1999/2000, records the target of assaults upon less than 9% of the average prison population not met, with a total assault rate of 10%.[51] Healthcare and vigilance in respect of those prisoners vulnerable to others are both relevant considerations here. As stated by the Council of Europe Committee for the Prevention of Torture (CPT), 'The duty of care which is owed by a State to persons deprived of their liberty includes the duty to protect them from others who may wish to cause them harm'.[52] Failures in seemingly unconnected elements of prison regime management can attend upon a 'cavalier' attitude to the health and well being – or even the physical safety – both of prisoners and staff. In *John Gill v The Home Office*,[53] the Home Office was held vicariously liable for the acts of a prison officer in letting an inmate with a known propensity to violence out of his cell, who then punched a prison officer, as a risk of injury to prison officers was foreseeable. In August 2000, HMCIP Sir David Ramsbotham, suggested that inmates of one particular prison were placed at risk of bullying and abuse as a result of staffing levels diminishing patrol efficiency,[54] a situation which suggests lack of the essential protection of life demanded by Art 2. That said, it is clear that HMPS is taking the problem seriously, as evidenced in its report to a United Nations Committee that:

> 'The Home Office has given approval for the trial of electronic monitoring of the occupants of cells in both police and prison services. Using the latest technology, the equipment monitors the breathing and heart rate of occupants of cells and alerts custody officers if vital signs reach a set warning threshold. If successful, the equipment could prevent a large number of deaths occurring in the future.'[55]

49   R Ford 'Prison suicides set a new record' *The Times*, 14 August 2000. This article records that in the last year there were only five suicides in US Federal prisons amongst an inmate population of 123,000.

50   'Reducing Suicides Top Priority for Director General' *PS Press Release* (14 December 1999); M Leech *The Prisons Handbook 1999* (Waterside Press, 1998), pp 462–468; M Leech and D Cheney *The Prisons Handbook 2000* (Waterside Press, 1999), pp 485–489.

51   *HM Prison Service Annual Report 1999–2000* (HMSO, 2000).

52   Council of Europe, European Committee for the Prevention of Torture and Inhuman or Degrading Treatment or Punishment *10th General Report on the CPT's activities* (CPT/Inf, 2000) 13.

53   *John Gill v The Home Office* (2000) LTL, 6 July.

54   R Ford 'Patrol shortages endanger prisoners' *The Times*, 9 August 2000. The comments by Sir David focused upon a prison in Yorkshire, and Phil Hornsby, General Secretary of the Prison Officers Union, said that one officer was often left in charge of up to 65 inmates of the prison. That bullying has in fact resulted in prison suicides has been evidenced in past years, not least in a number of suicides at HM YOI, Feltham.

55   UN Committee on the Elimination of Racial Discrimination *Reports submitted by States parties under Article 9 of the Convention* CERD/C/338/Add.12 (Part 1) (25 April 2000).

However, Inquest remains concerned about non self-inflicted deaths in custody:

> '[A] damning report by the Parliamentary Ombudsman into the death of Kenneth Severin in Belmarsh prison was published (8 March 1999) following a complaint made on behalf of his family by Inquest. Kenneth died while being restrained by prison officers in November 1995 and the inquest into his death in January 1997 recorded an open verdict with positional asphyxia following restraint as the cause of death ... The complaint highlighted issues about prison health care, the treatment of the mentally ill in prison, the use of strip cells, and the lack of communication between discipline and medical staff. It also exposed failings at a national and local level to ensure that prison officers were properly trained in the dangers of control and restraint. A further complaint was the failure of the Prison Service to disclose the internal inquiry report to the family.'[56]

In sum, the case demonstrates a number of aspects of prison regimes and procedures that could be challenged under Art 2. It is worthy of note that in his 1999/2000 Annual Report, the Prisons Ombudsman recommended that the Service 'consider the provision of guidance on the circumstances in which force other than the approved control and restraint techniques is deemed appropriate and the type of force which may be used'.[57] HMPS accepted the recommendation, confirming consideration would be given to provision of such guidance.

Investigation of deaths in custody
The manner in which HMPS facilitates investigation of deaths of prisoners in its care is another potential area of challenge, in that 'failure to provide an opportunity for effective investigations into individuals' deaths amounts itself to a breach of Article 2'.[58] Following the inquiry into the death of Christopher Edwards in HMP Chelmsford, HMPS announced action taken upon recommendations, stating that 'the efforts of Paul and Audrey Edwards have meant that the death of their son has led HM Prison Service to address many lessons. The lessons which have been learnt will benefit other prisoners'.[59] The treatment of families of prisoners who die in prison has been made a prime concern. A Prisoner Escort Record has been introduced to assist communication between agencies. Communications about prisoners within the prison have been targeted, and mental health screening of prisoners should take place on arrival at prison. Coroners and the police must be notified of every death in HMPS custody and an independent coroner's inquiry before a jury must be held in every case. A senior investigating officer from outside the prison, in which the death took place, must carry out an investigation into all unnatural

---

56   D Coles, Co-Director of Inquest 'Deaths in Custody' in M Leech and D Cheney *The Prisons Handbook 2001* (Waterside Press).

57   *Prisons Ombudsman's Annual Report 1999–2000*, Cm 4730 (2000).

58   *Esraf Yasa v Turkey* (1998) 28 EHRR 408 and *Ogur v Turkey* [1999] HRCD 107; quoted by R English in *Analysis of the Convention and the Human Rights Act 1998* (One Crown Row, Human Rights Interactive), p 7.

59   M Leech and D Cheney, *The Prisons Handbook 2000* (Waterside Press, 2000), p 486. See also P and A Edwards 'Deaths in custody: The next of kin's experience' in M Leech *The Prisons Handbook 1999* (Waterside Press, 1998), pp 463–465.

deaths. All death-in-custody cases should be reviewed again after inquest verdicts, and such cases co-ordinated at Crown Prosecution Service (CPS) headquarters. CPS lawyers review the cases before despatch to the Director of Public Prosecutions (DPP), the CPS notifying the police of the decision and the police notifying the family of the deceased.[60] According to the findings of the organisation Inquest, and communicated to HMCIP, this ideal situation leaves much to be desired: 'some Governors have even been reluctant to pass on Inquest's details to families despite this being laid down in the Prison Service Order "Follow up on deaths in custody" '.[61] Its view of the current manner in which investigations of deaths in custody are dealt with, as evidenced in the case of *Severin and Others*,[62] suggests that HMPS may indeed be facing challenges under the heading of its investigative failings.

Food provision

The matter of food provision raises other interesting issues. *R v Secretary of State for the Home Department ex parte Robb*[63] concerned an adult prisoner of sound mind who was starving himself to death, and the position of HMPS in respect of force-feeding.[64] Self-determination was held to be paramount and Thorpe J held that:

> 'an adult of sound mind was entitled to refuse all nutrition even if suicide was the intention and the result. A prisoner has the same rights as any other citizen in this respect. It does not matter whether the prisoner's reasons for wanting to die are rational or irrational. Self-determination means that individuals decide their own fate.'[65]

However, in the matter of providing food to prisoners, the law has been quite clear on the obligations of HMPS. *R v Governor of Frankland Prison ex parte Russell*

---

60   UN Human Rights Committee *Consideration of Reports submitted by States parties under Article 40 of the Covenant*, CCPR/C/UK/99/5 (11 April 2000), paras 151, 152.

61   D Coles, Co-Director of Inquest 'Deaths in Custody' in M Leech and D Cheney *The Prisons Handbook 2001* (Waterside Press, forthcoming). See also *Suicide is Everyone's Concern: a Thematic Review* (HMCIP, 1998).

62   See also *Omasase Lumumba*, unlawful killing whilst under restraint in HMP Pentonville 1990, *Inquest Annual Report* (1992); *Alton Manning*, unlawful killing after dying from asphyxiation in a neckhold at HMP Blakenhurst, D Coles 'Deaths in Custody' in M Leech and D Cheney *The Prisons Handbook 2001* (Waterside Press, forthcoming); Summary of a Report by The Parliamentary Commissioner for Administration (The Ombudsman) of the Results of my Investigation into a Complaint made through John Austin MP by Ms Deborah Coles on behalf of the Family of the late Kenneth Severin Against the Prison Service, C993/97. HMPS has reviewed control and restraint techniques, practices and procedures, taking into account new information about the effects of excited delirium and positional asphyxia, and Prison Rule 47, as amended in 1999, gives clear instructions on the definition, use and recording of control and restraint. See UN Human Rights Committee *Consideration of Reports submitted by States parties under Article 40 of the Covenant* CCPR/C/UK/99/5 (11 April 2000), para 342.

63   [1995] 1 All ER 677.

64   Different considerations attend upon those suffering from a mental disorder: see *R v Collins ex parte Brady* [2000] Lloyd's Rep Med 355.

65   See S Foster 'Force feeding, self-determination and the right to die' (2000) 150 NLJ 857; and D Pannick QC 'State should not go out of its way to keep Brady alive' *The Times*, 14 March 2000.

and Another[66] dealt with the issue of whether a prison governor, in exercising his duty to maintain order and discipline, was authorised to attach limitations or conditions to the provision of the necessities of life to prisoners who wanted them. The decision by the prison governor in this case was that those prisoners held in segregation who refused to wear prison clothes would not be permitted to collect their meals at the servery and would, instead, be given one meal a day in their cell. The court gave consideration to the fact the obligation imposed by Prison Rules 23 and 24 to clothe and feed were expressed in unconditional terms, in contrast to rules that afford rights to prisoners subject to limitations or conditions. The court held that HMPS was under an obligation to provide food to a prisoner, by virtue of Prison Rule 24,[67] and that 'the limitation of provision to one meal per day was arbitrary, applied irrespective of the impact on the health of the individual prisoner and made no provision for monitoring and safeguarding the health of the prisoner'.[68] The court further stated that the first and foremost reason the policy adopted was unlawful (not authorised by Prison Rules) was that 'it fails to give proper effect to rule 24 and (in view of the possible indefinite duration of the segregation of a prisoner in the unit) may well breach the fundamental rights protected by Article 3'.[69]

Spread of disease

One final potential area of challenge is that of prevention of spread of disease, such as life-threatening AIDS. The Prison Reform Trust has suggested that prisoners may argue that they should have access to condoms to prevent the spread of HIV/AIDS.[70] HMPS policy of providing condoms at the discretion of the medical officer was challenged in *R v Secretary of State for the Home Department ex parte Fielding*.[71] The applicant, a practising homosexual, who was at liberty on licence at the time of hearing in July 1999, was refused condoms whilst at HMP Littlehey, but able to obtain condoms when moved to the privately run prison Blakenhurst. He challenged the policy of HMPS as irrational. Evidence was

---

66 [2000] 1 WLR 2027.

67 Prison Rule 24: '(1) Subject to any directions of the Secretary of State, no prisoner shall be allowed, except as authorised by the medical officer or a medical practitioner such as is mentioned in rule 20(3), to have any food other than that ordinarily provided. (2) The food provided shall be wholesome, nutritious, well prepared and served, reasonably varied and sufficient in quantity. (3) The medical officer, a medical practitioner such as is mentioned in rule 20(3) or any person deemed by the governor to be competent, shall from time to time inspect the food both before and after it is cooked and shall report any deficiency or defect to the governor. (4) In this rule "food" includes drink'.

68 *R v Governor of Frankland Prison ex parte Russell and Wharrie* (2000) *The Times*, July 10. See S Foster 'Prison protests and the duty to provide food' (2000) 150 NLJ 1379.

69 'For it arbitrarily cuts down for an indeterminate period to one third the provision of food to the prisoners affected without any or any proper or sufficient regard to the entitlement of prisoners under rule 24 to adequate food. It is inflexible. It fails to provide the elementary health safeguards that such a reduction in provision (if otherwise lawful) would require in its train'. European cases considered by the court were: *Greek Case* (1969) 12 *Yearbook of the European Convention on Human Rights* 1; *McFeeley v UK* (1980) 3 EHRR 161; *Raninen v Finland* (1997) 26 EHRR 563; *T v UK* (1983) 409 DR 5; *T v UK* (2000) 30 EHRR 121; *Tyrer v UK* (1978) 2 EHRR 1.

70 *A Hard Act to Follow? Prisoners and the Human Rights Act* (Prison Reform Trust, 2000).

71 [1999] COD 525.

produced that current HMPS policy gave medical officers the freedom to prescribe condoms if in their clinical judgment there was a known risk of HIV infection.[72] The 1995 'Dear Doctor' letter which this evidence constituted contained the comments:

> 'Legal advice is that consenting acts between adult prisoners in a prison cell are not automatically unlawful and that a prison cell is in many circumstances capable of being deemed a "private place" under the terms of the Sexual Offences Act 1976. Even in those circumstances where homosexual behaviour is not lawful (eg if one or both the participants is under the age of 18 years[73]), neither the doctor nor the Prison Service could be liable since the demonstrable intent in making condoms available is to preserve health rather than to encourage homosexuality. The provision of condoms would not constitute "aiding and abetting". This follows on from the judgement in the case of *Gillick v West Norfolk and Wisbech Area Health Authority* [1985] 3 All ER 402 (1985).

> The burden of our legal advice is in fact that there may be a legal risk in not providing condoms in the relevant set of circumstances through failure of a duty to care. In order to meet this duty, doctors are encouraged to prescribe condoms and lubricants where in their clinical judgement there is a known risk of HIV infection as a result of HIV risk sexual behaviour.'[74]

This view was confirmed by an affidavit from Doctor Longfield,[75] dated 26 January 1999, who also acknowledged problems of consistency across prisons and that the application of policy in the current case was significantly more restrictive than a fair reading of the 'Dear Doctor' letter justified.

With regard to the suggestion that current policy was irrational, the court looked at the point that if condoms were available on demand, the message to the prison population and public would be one of HMPS encouraging homosexuality, whereas policy was designed to protect the health of prisoners (and the population at large following their release, thus a protection of the public issue). The court held that the view taken was not irrational, and that with regard to the remaining question of whether the mechanism chosen to control supply was itself irrational, it was not irrational to leave the decision to a prison medical officer. In the particular case it held that 'It follows that, although the particular decision to refuse to supply condoms about which the applicant complained was wrong, it was wrong because the policy was misinterpreted, not because the policy itself was unlawful'.[76]

---

72   Covered by advice in a 'Dear Doctor' letter (DDL(97)10) 16 August 1995, from Rosemary Wool, then Director of PS Health Care. This followed a letter on 18 May 1994 (DDL(94) 6) after the first recorded case of sexual transmission of HIV infection between prisoners.
73   At the time of writing, the age of consent for consensual homosexual activity has been lowered to 16.
74   *R v Secretary of State for the Home Department ex parte Fielding* [1999] COD 525, per Latham J.
75   Director of PS Health Care.
76   *R v Secretary of State for the Home Department ex parte Fielding* [1999] COD 525, per Latham J.

In January 2000, application was made for permission to appeal from the July 1999 decision of Latham J. Lord Woolf MR made some significant comments at that application. These were that:

> 'From the material before me, it is reasonably clear that, on this difficult and sensitive subject, the Home Office policy is being evolved, albeit (it may be said) slowly. When the applicant was seeking an extension of time, there was communication with the Treasury Solicitor, which confirmed that the policy was evolving. In addition, it is plain from the judge's judgement that he was at least encouraging that the way that the policy is expressed should be reconsidered.'

He went on to conclude:

> 'It seems to me that this would not be an appropriate case on which to challenge the Home Office policy as it is now. First, we do not know precisely what the Home Office policy is at the present time. It may have progressed further since January 1999 . . . next October the Human Rights Act will come into force and the applicant seeks to rely on the provisions of that Act. He is in difficulty in doing so at this time, but those difficulties will disappear after the Act is in force, at least in relation to events which occur thereafter.
>
> I am quite satisfied that, while there is an issue of importance underlying this application, this is not an appropriate vehicle for that issue to be tested. The matter is more appropriately looked at again if and when the new policy of the Home Office, which is apparently under consideration, has been determined and when the Act is in force.'[77]

It is clear from this judgment that the courts more than subtly hint at the need for a more coherent formulation of HMPS policy, and that the area remains one in which challenges should be expected.

It is worthy of note that the Disability Rights Task Force has suggested that people with HIV should be regarded as disabled. The Task Force has suggested that the definition of 'disability' within the Disability Discrimination Act 1995 should be extended to cover people with HIV from diagnosis (as this provides more certainty about when protection begins).[78] If this suggestion is adopted the field is widened for different challenges, of the nature of those discussed in *Fielding*, to be made.[79]

6.3.2 Article 3: Right to freedom from torture and inhuman or degrading treatment or punishment

A number of issues have been raised under Art 2 which overlap with Art 3, not least the effect of prison conditions on mental health and subsequent potential

---

77 *R v Secretary of State for the Home Department ex parte Fielding* (unreported) 12 January 2000, CA, per Lord Woolf MR.

78 *Exclusion to Inclusion: a report of the Disability Rights Task Force on Civil Rights for Disabled People* (December 1999), pp 25, 28. Estimates suggest that there are fewer than 20,000 people with asymptomatic HIV (progressive condition pre-symptoms) and their inclusion would represent an increase in 0.2% of those people protected by the Act.

79 Fielding sought to rely upon Art 8(1) in relation to respect under the Convention for his sexual orientation; if the HIV state were indeed to be designated a disability as the Task Force suggests, Art 14 would be drawn upon in respect to Art 8.

self-harm or suicidal acts. Falling firmly under Art 3 are prison conditions, living space, overcrowding, hygiene standards and 'dirty protests'. On the latter there are no national guidelines with regard to how to deal with them, despite the potential risk to health that they pose.[80] How people are treated is particularly relevant within the ambit of this freedom, procedures at visits and reception, during drug testing and strip-searching, medical treatment and adjudication, and the conditions, severity and duration of segregation. Both physical and psychological effects of ill treatment are relevant. In conjunction with Art 14, there is also cause to look at racial discrimination, and the treatment of disabled and mentally disordered offenders.

Prisoner transport

A related area of concern is that of the transport of prisoners by prisoner escort and court custody services. In 2000 the Home Office published the first survey of prisoners' experiences of these service providers, undertaken by 952 face-to-face interviews with prisoners at magistrates' courts and Crown Courts, 61% of whom had arrived at court from prison establishments.[81] Considerations explored include those relevant in respect of Art 2, ie whether prisoners felt protected from other prisoners and whether necessary paperwork was attended to. In addition, matters were covered relevant to Art 3, ie whether prisoners could be communicated with (language), treatment by escort staff, temperature and cleanliness of the vehicles, proportion of travelling time and comfort stops and access to medical facilities.[82]

Torture and inhuman or degrading treatment

Principle 1 of the UN Body of Principles for the Protection of All Persons under Any Form of Detention or Imprisonment states that 'All persons under any form of detention or imprisonment shall be treated in a humane manner and with respect for the inherent dignity of the human person'. Principle 6 of the same document declares that:

> 'cruel, inhuman or degrading treatment ... should be interpreted so as to extend the widest possible protection against abuses, whether physical or mental, including the holding of a detained or imprisoned person in conditions which deprive him, temporarily or permanently of the use of any of his natural senses, such as sight or hearing, or of his awareness of place and the passing of time.'[83]

---

80   The Prisons Ombudsman has expressed surprise about this fact and recommended that such guidelines be created. See *Prisons Ombudsman's Annual Report 1999–2000*, Cm 4730 (HMSO, 2000).

81   B Williams, C Cuthbert and G Sattar 'Prison Escort and Custody Services: Prisoners' Experiences' *Research Findings No 123* (HO Research, Development and Statistics Directorate, 2000).

82   Similar provisions arise in respect of conditions in custody suites themselves. See *A Review of Custody Arrangements in Magistrates' Courts* (HM Court Service Inspectorate, 1999); and *Casework information needs within the Criminal Justice System: June–November 1999*, a study undertaken jointly by the Crown Prosecution Service Inspectorate, HM Inspectorate of Constabulary, HM Magistrates' Courts Service Inspectorate, HM Inspectorate of Prisons, HM Inspectorate of Probation and the Social Services Inspectorate (1999).

83   United Nations Document A/43/49 (1988).

That HMPS may be challenged on the grounds of inhuman or degrading treatment or punishment is a distinct possibility, as this section will examine. What, however, of the matter of 'torture'? Is this a heading under which the general prison population will have cause for redress, or will it be the province of those prisoners seeking asylum and the halting of deportation procedures? In respect of detainees pending deportation it is worthy of note that Art 3 has been held to apply in cases where deportation to a country with inadequate healthcare has the potential to lead to illness and death, and where the deportee would be exposed to such as the 'death row phenomenon' in the United States.[84]

Torture is a word that conjures up many images, and it is therefore necessary to ascertain what constitutes torture in a legal sense. The term is defined by the UN Convention Against Torture (1984) as:

> 'any act by which severe pain or suffering, whether physical or mental, is intentionally inflicted on a person for such purposes as obtaining from him or a third person information or a confession, punishing him for an act he or a third person has committed or is suspected of having committed, or intimidating or coercing him or a third person, or for any reason based on discrimination of any kind, when such pain or suffering is inflicted by or at the instigation of or with the consent or acquiescence of a public official or other person acting in an official capacity. It does not include pain or suffering arising only from, inherent or incidental to lawful sanctions.'

Where treatment is not such as to be considered torture, it remains possible that a violation has occurred in respect of inhuman or degrading treatment.

This definition has been well clarified by the Human Rights Centre at Essex University in its publication *The Torture Reporting Handbook*.[85] The Centre identifies three essential elements which constitute torture: the infliction of severe mental or physical pain or suffering; by or with the consent or acquiescence of the State authorities; for a specific purpose, such as gaining information, punishment or intimidation. With regard to the remaining terms of Art 3, it states:

> 'Cruel treatment, and inhuman or degrading treatment or punishment are also legal terms which refer to ill treatment causing varying degrees of suffering less severe than in the case of torture. Forms of ill treatment other than torture do not have to be inflicted for a specific purpose, but there does have to be an intent to expose individuals to the conditions which amount to or result in the ill treatment.

---

84   *D v UK* (1997) 24 EHRR 423 and *Soering v UK* (1989) 11 EHRR 439; as quoted by R English *Analysis of the Convention and the Human Rights Act 1998* (One Crown Row, Human Rights Interactive). Following the case of *Chahal v UK* (1996) 23 EHRR 413, the Special Immigration Appeals Commission Act 1997 was introduced which considers the appellants' fear of torture, inhuman or degrading treatment or punishment. See UN Human Rights Committee *Consideration of Reports submitted by States parties under Article 40 of the Convenant* CCPR/C/UK/99/5 (11 April 2000), para 375.

85   *The Torture Reporting Handbook* (Essex University, 2000) was produced with a grant of over £110,000 from the Foreign and Commonwealth Office Human Rights Project Fund and launched by Foreign Secretary, Robin Cook, in March 2000. The Handbook is available in English, French, Spanish, Arabic, Russian and Chinese.

The essential elements which constitute ill treatment not amounting to torture would therefore be reduced to: Intentional exposure to significant mental or physical pain or suffering; by or with the consent or acquiescence of the state authorities.'[86]

Characteristics relevant to degree of suffering

The degree of suffering involved is subject to individual circumstances and characteristics. This is important in that severity of ill treatment may be felt more acutely by the vulnerable, for example the effect of adult prison disciplining meted out to juvenile offenders, or the effect of segregation on mentally disordered offenders or of prisoners with a particular cultural background. Equally, a gendered perspective is relevant. The Council of Europe Committee for the Prevention of Torture has drawn attention to:

'a number of hygiene and health issues in respect of which the needs of women deprived of their liberty differ significantly from those of men ... Ready access to sanitary and washing facilities, safe disposal arrangements for blood-stained articles, as well as provision of hygiene items, such as sanitary towels and tampons, are of particular importance. The failure to provide such basic necessities can amount, in itself, to degrading treatment.'[87]

Also, as the Human Rights Centre points out:

'There are examples where ill treatment has been found to amount to torture or inhuman treatment on account of the religious character of the victim e.g. devout persons subjected to religious taunts; the plucking of the beard of an Orthodox priest.'

Prison conditions

How, then, might prisoners proceed? Prison conditions themselves are certainly a potential area to be challenged, both in themselves and in respect of the psychological effect on prisoners (as raised under Art 2). That poor conditions, some to the extreme, exist is attested to by a series of damning reports following inspections by HMCIP. These are exemplified by comments in reports such as those on HMP Rochester, found to be infested with vermin and having 'filthy conditions', and Exeter, where in the segregation unit 'slopping out' had not ended and the below ground accommodation offered little ventilation or natural light, but very effective ligature points.[88] A general comment made by Sir David Ramsbotham in his 1998/1999 Annual Report sums up his feelings when he states:

'Firstly it could be said that 1998–1999 was a very bad year for the Prison Service, marked by extreme examples of unacceptable practice in prisons. Secondly, in uncovering such practice, we disclosed that responsibility for prisoners did not

---

86 *The Torture Reporting Handbook* (Essex University, 2000).
87 European Committee for the Prevention of Torture and Inhuman or Degrading Treatment or Punishment *10th General Report on the CPT's Activities* CPT/Inf (2000) 13 (Strasbourg, 18 August 2000), paras 30, 31.
88 HMCIP Inspection Reports on HMP Rochester (21 January 2000) and HMP Exeter (12 August 1999).

appear to feature as prominently in line management's list of priorities, as one could reasonably expect.'[89]

Close supervision centres

The most strident concerns of Sir David Ramsbotham have been raised through other avenues in respect of close supervision centres (CSCs), and in terms of the regime rather than conditions. The unit at HMP Woodhill was condemned by HMCIP for operating isolation practices that pose a risk to prisoners' mental health. Media reporting in March 2000 outlined how 53 prisoners had been in total isolation since the unit opened in April 1998, spending 23 hours per day in-cell with their food pushed through a hatch in the cell door. In the introduction to his thematic inspection of CSCs, Sir David commented:

'segregation, which is the standard method of control in the CSC system, should be used more judiciously than at present, and that the conditions in which prisoners are segregated should be carefully managed, to ensure that mental health, and the possibility of progress, are not therefore jeopardised.'[90]

HMPS is facing a challenge under the Human Rights Act 1998 from a former prisoner, Rifat Mehmet, who alleges that he was subjected to inhumane and degrading treatment whilst in the CSC.[91] The high profile cases of Charles Bronson and Robert Maudsley, both of whom have spent almost 25 years in solitary confinement, have echoed these issues.[92] Whilst it has been held by the European Court that segregation in and of itself does not constitute the severe ill treatment necessary to establish violation of Art 3,[93] that conditions have to be particularly severe to succeed and ill treatment must attain a minimum level of severity to fall within the scope of the article,[94] complete sensory and social isolation does meet the criteria.[95] In *Peers v Greece*,[96] a violation of Art 3 was found in respect of the conditions of detention in a segregation unit, but not in respect of conditions in a general wing. However, in *Aerts v Belgium* the court found no violation of Art 3 in circumstances which, nonetheless, fell 'below the minimum acceptable [standard] from an ethical and humanitarian point of

---

89 Annual Report of HM Inspector of Prisons 1998–1999.

90 *Inspection of Close Supervision Centres: August–September 1999* (HMCIP, 22 March 2000).

91 'Harsh jail makes violent inmates worse' *The Times*, 22 March, 2000; and 'Prison inquiry into cruel wing' *The Times*, 2 October 2000. See also *Inspection of Close Supervision Centres: August–September 1999* (HMCIP, 22 March 2000).

92 Charles Bronson is 47 and has spent almost 25 years in solitary confinement. He was jailed in 1974 for armed robbery and has been given additional sentences in prison. In February 2000 he was awarded a life sentence after a hostage situation. Robert Maudsley is 46 and was jailed in 1974 for stabbing and has since killed three fellow prisoners. See T Reid 'Bronson tells jury of living hell in jail' *The Times*, 17 February 2000; 'Out of sight, out of mind' and 'I am left to stagnate and regress' *The Times*, 23 March 2000.

93 *Delazarus v UK* (unreported) 16 February 1993; as quoted in S Creighton and V King *Prisoners and the Law* (Butterworths, 1996), p 219.

94 *Ireland v UK* (1978) Series A/25, p 162.

95 *Windsor v UK* (unreported) 6 April 1993; as quoted in S Creighton and V King *Prisoners and the Law* (Butterworths, 1996), p 220.

96 Application No 28524/95.

view'.[97] Both *Peers* and *Aerts* were considered by the European Court sitting, in September 2000, on the matter of admissibility of *Ha You Zhu v UK*.[98] The applicant was an immigration detainee held at HMP Gateside in Scotland. His period of detention there was characterised by cultural and language isolation, racial abuse from other prisoners, being locked in his cell for almost 16 hours per day and, when he attempted suicide, placed in a suicide watch cell with a sleeping bag. After consideration of the threshold of severity required to find violation of Art 3, with regard to both the *Peers* and *Aerts* cases, the Court held that the minimum level of severity proscribed by the article was not reached and declared the application inadmissible.

In sum, given the individual focus taken, it would be foolish to proscribe what 'should' qualify as the 'minimum level of severity' and this area of challenge for prisoners remains a fertile one, if difficult to predict. However, HMPS practice in such CSCs may be advanced as a necessary evil in that, as the DG has stated:

> 'We are dealing with a tiny number of prisoners. In holding them separately, we are protecting a much larger number. We are dealing with prisoners who have taken others hostage; who have murdered other prisoners. Their freedom has to be compromised if we are to run a civilised prison system.'[99]

On the other hand, he is not unaware of the serious link between treatment and conditions of prisoners, and their behaviour, and must seek a balance if he is to stand by his words in HMPS Annual Report that 'Decency is another area where I am determined to see standards driven up. I am quite sure that there is a link between our treatment of prisoners, the environment we provide and genuine rehabilitation'.[100] Yet prisoners in CSCs appear not to fall under this consideration. They are certainly treated differently, not least in respect of the fact that Rule 46 of the Prison Rules 1999 enables the Secretary of State to direct removal from association of these prisoners for up to 1 month, a period which is renewable for a like period. Prisoners in the general prison population who are removed from association must have segregation authorised by a board of visitors member if it is beyond 72 hours. It is clear that prisoners within CSCs should fall to be dealt with on an individual basis in terms of the proper balance to be struck between their rights and those of other prisoners, staff, victims and the public. However, it is worthy of note that the European Court has stated

---

97   *Aerts v Belgium* (2000) EHRR 50.
98   Third Section Decision as to the Admissibility of Application No 36790/97 by *Ha You Zhu against the United Kingdom*.
99   E-A Prentice and R Ford 'Give me a budgie or a cyanide pill, pleads serial killer' *The Times*, 23 March 2000.
100 M Narey *HM Prison Service Annual Report 1999–2000* (HMSO, 2000).

'there could be no qualification of the protection offered by Art.3, even in the case of individuals representing a threat to public order'.[101]

Such issues have also exercised the domestic courts, drawing upon European cases, as during discussion in the case of *Russell and Another*, discussed above under Art 2. On the matter of ill treatment, it was stated in that case:

'In the context of the treatment of prisoners the treatment must go beyond the usual element of humiliation associated with imprisonment after a criminal conviction: *Tyrer v United Kingdom* (1978) 2 EHRR 1, 9–10. The public nature of the treatment is relevant as is its adverse effect: *Raninen v Finland* (1997) 26 EHRR 563. But absence of publicity will not necessarily prevent a given punishment from being degrading, for it may be sufficient that the victim is humiliated in his own eyes, even if not in the eyes of others, and the punishment or treatment need not cause any severe or long lasting physical effects: *Tyrer v United Kingdom* 2 EHRR 1, 10–11. The fact that the person concerned has brought the treatment on himself may be relevant: *McFeeley v United Kingdom*, 3 EHRR 161, 198. But that fact cannot absolve the state of its obligations under article 3: *X v United Kingdom* [1982] 28 D & R 5, 32. A degrading punishment does not lose its degrading character just because it is believed to be, or actually is, an effective deterrent or aid to maintain discipline: *Tyrer v United Kingdom*, 2 EHRR 1, 10.'[102]

Overcrowding

Overcrowding may give rise to successful challenge on the grounds of inhuman and degrading treatment.[103] As the Council of Europe Committee for the Prevention of Torture (CPT) has stated:

'An overcrowded prison entails cramped and unhygienic accommodation; a constant lack of privacy (even when performing such basic tasks as using a sanitary facility); reduced out-of-cell activities, due to demand outstripping the staff and facilities available; overburdened health-care services; increased tension and hence more violence between prisoners and between prisoners and staff.'[104]

---

101 R English, quoting from *Chahal v UK* (1996) 23 EHRR 413 in *Analysis of the Convention and the Human Rights Act 1998* (One Crown Row, Human Rights Interactive). In *McFeeley v UK* (1981) 3 EHRR 161 the conditions complained of by the prisoners were as a result of their own 'dirty protest'. 'The ECHR, whilst accepting that the harsh conditions caused by the prisoners' own actions could not engage the responsibility of the government, stated that the government were not absolved from its obligations under Article 3 merely because the prisoners were engaged in an unlawful challenge to the prison administration ... they were required to exercise their custodial authority so as to safeguard the health and wellbeing of the prisoners': S Foster 'Prison protests and the duty to provide food' (2000) 150 NLJ 1379.

102 *R v Governor of Frankland Prison ex parte Russell and Another* [2000] 1 WLR 2027, QBD.

103 *Denmark, Sweden and Norway v Greece (The Greek Case)* (1969) 12 YB 499; quoted by S Livingstone and T Owen *Prison Law: Text and Materials* (Oxford University Press, 1993), p 304.

104 *Report to the United Kingdom Government on the visit to the United Kingdom and the Isle of Man carried out by the European Committee for the Prevention of Torture and Inhuman or Degrading Treatment or Punishment from 8 to 17 September 1997* CPT/Inf (2000) 1 (Strasbourg, 13 January 2000).

Overcrowding is a constant problem for HMPS, and was raised as an issue by the President of the Prison Governor's Association at its conference in March 2000, when he stated:

> 'Overcrowding continues to bedevil our local prisons despite the prison-building programme. As I know from Birmingham prison far too many inmates are locked up two to a cell designed for one and are required to eat their meals in a lavatory. This is an obscenity.'[105]

In March 1995 it was estimated that by the year 2000–2001 the prison population would average 54,300, yet it currently stands at nearly 65,000, 1,610 (3%) higher than the certified normal accommodation of 63,350[106] and is expected to increase to 68,300 by March 2002.[107] HMPS Annual Report for 1999/2000 records performance against key performance indicators (KPIs), and in respect of overcrowding the target was not met, with the average rate of doubling being 18.9% against an 18% target.[108] Whilst HMPS holds the view there is a safe level of overcrowding, the CPT believes that 'safe overcrowding' should not be allowed to become the benchmark, even in local prisons, and recorded that its visit to HMP Dorchester (designated 'safely overcrowded' by HMPS) merely confirmed its misgivings. It concluded:

> 'It is a fundamental requirement that those committed to prison by the courts be held in safe and decent conditions. For so long as overcrowding persists, the risk of prisoners being held in inhuman and degrading conditions of detention will remain. To return to the example of HMP Dorchester, even if conditions there are "safe" according to Prison Service criteria, in the view of the CPT they can hardly be qualified as decent.'[109]

Looking at the HMCIP inspection report published on HMP Dorchester 3 years after the CPT visit, it is hard to find fault with its earlier findings with the report recording that, 'Impoverishment is obvious from the moment a prisoner

---

105   Chairman's Annual Address, PGA Conference, Christopher Scott OBE, President (28 March 2000).

106   As of September 2000, around 12,000 prisoners shared overcrowded cells.

107   *Response of the United Kingdom Government to the report of the European Committee for the prevention of Torture and Inhuman or Degrading Treatment or Punishment on its visit to the United Kingdom and the Isle of Man* CPT/Inf (2000) 7 (Strasbourg, 11 May 2000), paras 55 and 58. See also M Elkins, C Gray and B Hidkyar *Prison Population Brief: September 2000* HO Research, Development and Statistics Directorate (2000). The estimate in 2007 is of 80,300 prisoners; see P White and C Cullen *Projections of long term trends in the prison population to 2007* HO Research, Development and Statistics Directorate (10 February 2000). The number of prisoners in England and Wales, expressed as a rate per 100,000 population, was the second highest in Western Europe in 1999: C Cullen and M Minchin 'The Prison Population in 1999: a statistical review *Research Findings No 118*, HO Research, Development and Statistics Directorate (2000).

108   *HM Prison Service Annual Report 1999–2000* (HMSO, 2000).

109   *Response of the United Kingdom Government to the report of the European Committee for the prevention of Torture and Inhuman or Degrading Treatment or Punishment on its visit to the United Kingdom and the Isle of Man* CPT/Inf (2000) 7 (Strasbourg, 11 May 2000), para 59. *Report to the United Kingdom Government on the visit to the United Kingdom and the Isle of Man carried out by the European Committee for the Prevention of Torture and Inhuman or Degrading Treatment or Punishment from 8 to 17 September 1997* CPT/Inf (2000) 1 (Strasbourg, 13 January 2000), paras 72 and 76.

is received into the prison', and that lack of activity places resulted in the majority spending their days locked up.[110]

Intimidation

Attitudes and behaviour towards prisoners may amount to degrading treatment, but that treatment must attain a minimum level of severity if it is to succeed, relative to the individual circumstances of each case.[111] Humiliation can, in some instances, qualify (*Hurtado v Switzerland* (1994)).[112] As a means of intimidating, offensive remarks are often successful at achieving humiliation.[113] Such remarks are usually, although not necessarily, linked to discrimination against minority groups based on disability or ethnicity. The importance of Art 3 in this respect in a prison setting has been made abundantly clear by the intimidation of black prisoners which HMCIP encountered at HMP Wandsworth, and which the recent assessment by the Race Equality Advisor found at HMP Brixton in relation to both staff and prisoners, where, of the latter, it was recorded that 'Some allegations were of offensive remarks plainly intended to humiliate.'[114] Whilst strip-searching, intimate searches and compulsory urine sampling have all been considered by the European Court not to constitute inhuman or degrading treatment,[115] handcuffing prisoners en route to and from court may contravene Art 3.[116] Equally, as recorded in the first edition of this publication, actions which are such that they could 'destroy the personality and cause severe mental and physical suffering' have been considered actionable by Strasbourg.[117]

---

110 HMCIP Inspection Report on HMP Dorchester (28 January 2000).

111 *Costello-Roberts v UK* (1993) Series A/247-C, p 59 at 30; and *Ireland v UK* (1978) Series A/25.

112 Quoted by R English in *Analysis of the Convention and the Human Rights Act 1998* (One Crown Row, Human Rights Interactive).

113 In *Ireland v UK* (1978) 2 EHRR 25 the Court held inhuman treatment to be that which deliberately causes severe mental or physical suffering, whereas degrading treatment is treatment which arouses in its victims feelings of fear, anguish and inferiority capable of humiliating or debasing them.

114 See R Ford 'Wandsworth is nasty and racist', and O Wright 'Way of fear is still the rule, say inmates' *The Times*, 18 December 1999. See also Race Equality Advisor, HMPS *Assessment of Race Relations at HMP Brixton* (RESPOND, June 2000).

115 *McFeeley v UK* Application No 8317/78, and *AB v Switzerland* Application No 20872/92. However, with regard to urine sampling during drug testing, the European Commission Chambers has brought to the attention of the UK Government a case concerning the taking of urine samples from a prisoner within the sight of prison officers: *Beaver, Henry and Hines v UK* Application No 33269/96.

116 As claimed by the Magistrates' Court Service Inspectorate, who also stated that keeping prisoners in an enclosed secure dock resembling a cage might be seen to be degrading. In the light of this the Lord Chancellor's Department has issued a new design guide for secure docks. See F Gibb 'Handcuffs breach human rights' *The Times*, 13 June 2000.

117 Quoting from *X v UK* (1981) 21 DR 99: Livingstone and Owen (n 103 above), p 107.

6.3.3   Article 6: Right to a fair and public trial within a reasonable time

Access to justice, and fairness of the trial meting out that justice, are both imperative under Art 6. Martin Narey, DG of HMPS, has already acknowledged on record that one of the areas in which the Service may be open to challenge is in respect of discipline and punishments behind prison walls. Speaking of the Human Rights Act 1998 in September 2000, he is quoted as stating that the Service might be 'vulnerable in the area of adjudication and additional days [punishment for breaches of prison discipline]. If we have to change things, fine'.[118] In the same month, HMPS issued PSI 61/2000[119] providing guidance on the implications of the 1998 Act on the conduct of adjudications and the imposition of punishments. The PSI makes clear that the Service does not consider that the current disciplinary arrangements contravene either Arts 5 or 6. In its terms:

> 'The protections of Article 6 relate to proceedings which determine "civil rights and obligations or ... any criminal charge". Our view is that prison discipline proceedings do not determine civil rights or obligations or criminal charges. They are conducted for the purpose of ensuring good order and discipline is maintained in prisons; any punishment imposed is a disciplinary punishment imposed for that purpose.'[120]

It is made clear that domestic law (confirmed by European Court case-law) has distinguished these proceedings from criminal proceedings in respect of the procedural standards necessary for fairness, that they are not adversarial, and that the decision is not resolving a dispute between two parties, but is instead reaching an administrative public law decision.[121]

A number of cases have challenged procedure in HMPS adjudications in the domestic courts, and it is worth considering comments made within these, to seek an idea of how the courts view their status. When adjudications were undertaken by prison boards of visitors, a number of challenges were mounted, and mounted successfully. While the fact that adjudications are no longer undertaken in this way is to be welcomed, it is arguable that successful challenges were more likely under the old system. That is to say that once the adjudication process passed to the hands of governors and controllers of prison establishments, adjudications came to be seen much more as administrative functions in the day-to-day running of prisons (rather than meting out 'justice'), and thus something in which the courts were more reluctant to interfere.

---

118   F Gibb and R Ford 'Prison chiefs are in the front line' *The Times*, 12 September 2000.
119   'Prison Discipline and the European Convention on Human Rights (ECHR): Guidance on Use of Additional Days' (28 September 2000), expiry date 3 October 2001.
120   Ibid, para 4.
121   Although the HMPS *Prison Disciplinary Manual* makes clear that 'adjudications are not simply administrative matters but are quasi-judicial affairs'.

Proportionate punishment

In that PSI 61/2000 warns that there could, in theory, be a challenge, this is premised upon the issue of punishments being proportionate to the conduct involved.[122] To this end the PSI directs that:

'It is therefore very important that governors do not impose punishments which are disproportionate to what is necessary, taking account of all the circumstances of the case, to achieve their aim, namely to act as a deterrent to that prisoner and others in order to ensure good order and discipline in the prison.'[123]

Governors are directed to the key question of 'whether the punishment is justified, and whether it is proportionate in the sense that a sledgehammer is not being used to crack a nut'.[124] Where additional days are imposed, because no available alternative punishment is appropriate, the PSI suggests that: 'it should be extremely rare for punishments of more than 28 days to be made'.[125] This stance is suggestive of sensitivity to argument presented at the Queen's Bench Division in *R v Governor of HMP Full Sutton ex parte Brown* that:

'where fundamental human rights are in issue, the range of responses open to a reasonable decision-maker will be narrowed. In other words, the margin of appreciation in a human rights context will be much lower than it might be in other contexts.'[126]

The situation would appear to be that, provided punishments of additional days do not exceed the figure deemed by the European Court to amount to severe punishment, there can be no argument to suggest that the prisoner faces a serious criminal charge and, as such, must thereby attract the entitlement to a first instance court which meets the requirements of Art 6 (including legal representation). The case of *Engel and Others v The Netherlands*[127] established the test to determine whether proceedings were criminal in nature as having regard to classification of the offence under domestic law, the nature of the offence and the severity of the penalty. In sum:

'The third element has proved a bar to disciplinary proceedings being considered determinative of criminal charges. Generally only the penalty of imprisonment will bring proceedings within the criminal test of Article 6. Even then a short period of detention (two days) may not suffice to invoke Article 6 protection.'[128]

As it stands currently, only a proportion of those prisoners subjected to disciplinary proceedings – those with which the adjudicating governor exercises the discretion to refer matters to the police – will ostensibly fall under the protection of Art 6. The question remains whether, in serious cases, if the

---

122 As the PSI points out, under the old remission system, a disciplinary charge leading to 18 months' loss of remission was treated by the European Court as a criminal charge to which the Convention applied, by virtue of the severity of the punishment.

123 'Prison Discipline and the European Convention on Human Rights (ECHR): Guidance on Use of Additional Days' (n 119 above), para 7.

124 Ibid, para 12.

125 Ibid, para 15.

126 (Unreported) 30 November 1999, counsel for the appellant, Ms F Krause, relying on the case of *R v Ministry of Defence ex parte Smith* [1996] QB 517.

127 1 EHRR 647.

128 S Enright and R Richter 'It's law but not as we know it' (2000) 150 NLJ 954.

matter is not referred to the police by an adjudicator, the fairness of an alternative mode of dealing under the normal disciplinary procedures could attract the requirements of Art 6, merely because of the 'potential' seriousness of the charge. However, *R v The Controller of HMYOI Doncaster ex parte Gaskin*,[129] discussed below, suggests that this is unlikely. The other alternative would be for HMPS to develop two modes of prison adjudication.

However, the heralding of the Human Rights Act 1998 as a 'living instrument' should itself be sufficient motivation to continue to challenge what are indeed, in the words of HMPS, 'quasi-judicial proceedings',[130] which, *in the prison context*, mete out what are, to a serving prisoner, *severe punishments*. One may need to be a serving prisoner to fully appreciate this fact, but fact it remains nonetheless.[131] If the first stage of the three-stage 'Engel test' is overcome, there is then ample European case-law in respect of courts martial to challenge the impartiality and fairness of the proceedings.[132] The first edition of this book elaborated upon these, and suggested that it was perhaps the sentiment rather than the facts of the case of *Findlay v UK* which would be of most value, in that *Findlay*[133] itself was limited to its own court martial facts. Suggested as a much stronger parallel was a commanding officer's power of summary dealing, a domestic disciplinary procedure underpinned by statute, where procedure parallels the role of the governor in prison adjudications. The case of *Hood v UK*[134] was elaborated upon with regard to the issues raised under Arts 5 and 6.

Access to justice
On the issue of access to justice in the prison disciplinary setting, HMPS has work to do. Matters such as access to information, opportunity to prepare a case and procedural disadvantage, are important considerations. The 1999/2000 Annual Report of the Prisons Ombudsman recorded that adjudications formed the largest category of all complaints to his office, 22% of all complaints and 42% of investigations, and the only category in which the number of eligible complaints was greater than ineligible.[135] He records that 'the main ground on which I recommended a quosh is that the adjudicator has failed to inquire sufficiently into the prisoner's defence'. Not least then, standards need to be met to ensure that certain prisoners are not at a procedural disadvantage and

---

129 CO/1621/99 (23 April 1999), QB; and (26 May 1999), CA.
130 HMPS *Prison Disciplinary Manual* (n 121 above).
131 There are over 100,000 disciplinary hearings per year. In 1997 there were 107,632 findings of guilt; 2,200 were referred to area managers for review and, of these 2,200, 666 were quashed and 97 punishments mitigated. Over the last year, complaints about adjudications made up 42% of the Prisons Ombudsman enquiries.
132 *Findlay v UK* (1997) 24 EHRR 221; *Hood v UK; Cable and Others v UK* (1999) *The Times*, March 11; *Smith and Ford v UK* Application Nos 37475/97 and 39036/97 (29 September 1999); *Moore and Gordon v UK* Application Nos 36529/97 and 37393/97 (29 September 1999); *Stephen Jordan v UK* (2001) 31 EHRR 6.
133 (1997) 24 EHRR 221.
134 (1999) 29 EHRR 365.
135 Complaints were upheld in 69 cases and recommendations made to the DG in 25 cases. See *Prisons Ombudsman's Annual Report 1999–2000* Cm 4730 (2000).

therefore denied a fair hearing. Pertinent here is whether tapes, a reader, or possibly additional time, has been afforded to a dyslexic, whether the visually or aurally impaired have been offered readers, sign-readers, a hearing loop, Braille, etc, and whether foreign prisoners have been given materials in translation and have the services of an appropriate and qualified interpreter.[136] Such issues are fundamental to facilitating prisoners' rights, something which the Foreign and Commonwealth Office has confirmed is a government concern when looking at the rights and access to justice which other countries offer. Referring to populations with high illiteracy rates and poor legal knowledge, it has recorded:

'Victims of abuse may remain ignorant that their rights have been violated and of the opportunities for redress which are available to them under the law ... Rights protected in law are meaningless unless people know they have them and unless they are fully understood by those responsible for enforcing the law.'[137]

With a UK prison population in which literacy is a major concern, and little material is available in translation, the possibility of a large proportion of prisoners holding such 'meaningless' rights is a real possibility.[138] It is a particularly important consideration having regard to the fact that in only a very few cases are prisoners allowed to be legally represented, a decision taken at the governor's discretion; which discretion is exercised after taking into account the set of criteria outlined in *R v Secretary of State for the Home Department ex parte Tarrant*.[139] With regard to the *Tarrant* criteria giving consideration to the capacity of a particular prisoner to present his own case, this was defined narrowly in *Carroll and Another's Application*[140] seeking judicial review after findings of guilt in disciplinary hearings at which they were refused legal representation. In that case O'Donnell LJ stated:

'I can only conceive of the one case where the discretion might be exercised and that is one of those set out by Webster J, where a prisoner was mentally subnormal

---

136 On 30 June 1999 there were 5,388 foreign nationals within the prison population, of which 493 were women and, of the 947 recorded as being in detention under the powers of Sch 2 or Sch 3 to the Immigration Act 1971, 511 were being held in prison establishments. See R Harris 'Foreign Prisoners' in M Leech and D Cheney *The Prisons Handbook 2001* (Waterside Press).

137 'Rights and Justice', *Foreign and Commonwealth Office Annual Report 1999*.

138 A screening test of prisoners in 1998 revealed: 52% at or below level 1 in reading; 73% at or below level 1 in writing; 69% at or below level 1 in numeracy, with level 1 giving access to only 4% of jobs. Jack Straw MP, Home Secretary 'Making prisons work better' in M Leech and D Cheney *The Prisons Handbook 2000* (Waterside Press, 1999), p 408.

139 [1984] 1 All ER 799. These include charge seriousness, the potential of any points of law arising, capacity of the prisoner to prepare his or her case, fairness, anticipated procedural difficulties and need for speed. In 1998 only 22 requests were granted out of 122,907 adjudications: see H Arnott and N Rensten 'Prison Disciplinary System' in M Leech and D Cheney *The Prisons Handbook 2001* (Waterside Press).

140 [1987] NI 6, [1987] 10 NLJB 23, CA.

and where a Governor considered that by reason of that mental subnormality he might have difficulty presenting his own case.'[141]

The issue of legal representation at adjudications was more recently challenged in *R v Controller of HMYOI Doncaster ex parte Gaskin*.[142] The applicant was charged with assault and the matter referred to the police but, as the victim would not co-operate with the police, the matter fell to be dealt with by the controller in a disciplinary adjudication. Having considered the *Tarrant* criteria, the controller was not prepared to allow the applicant to be legally represented. Counsel for the applicant stressed the vulnerability of the applicant, aged 18, and 'relied upon art 6 of the European Convention on Human Rights and what he calls the unfairness of a system which patently offends against the principle of the equality of arms'. At the renewed application seeking permission for judicial review, counsel for the applicant submitted that:

> 'the Controller of this Young Offenders Institute – indeed I think he would say those in charge of the prison system generally – has fettered his discretion by allowing legal representation in so small number of cases that they should be dismissed as *de minimis*. In essence he submits that the system has set its face against allowing inmates to be legally represented.'[143]

On the matter of Art 6, Jonathan Parker J held that:

> 'As regards the Strasbourg jurisprudence Mr Wise has referred to *Campbell and Fell* (1984) 7 EHRR 165, *Benham* 22 EHRR 293 and *Findlay* 24 EHRR 221. I content myself with the observation that in my view the Convention jurisprudence by no means establishes an inflexible rule that in every prison adjudication rights of legal representation should be accorded, nor even a looser rule that it should generally be accorded.'[144]

Considering the context of the internal system of adjudication for offences against prison discipline, the court stated what needed to be borne in mind was the fact that matters fell largely at the lower end of the scale of gravity and added:

> 'One would only expect a very small proportion of these cases to be handled with the assistance of legal representation for the prisoner. Indeed there may be very good reason in the public interest why there is not a higher proportion of cases where legal representation is allowed.'[145]

Arguably, the spectre of 'public interest' would again seem to be the shield from which challenges by prisoners in such instances will be deflected.

---

141 [1987] NI 6, [1987] 10 NLJB 23, CA, per O'Donnell LJ, p 6.
142 CO/1621/99 (23 April 1999), QB.
143 *R v Controller of HMYOI Doncaster ex parte Gaskin* (unreported) 26 May 1999, CA.
144 Ibid.
145 Ibid.

6.3.4 Articles 8 and 12: Right to respect for private and family life, home and correspondence, and right to marry and found a family

A host of areas of a prisoner's life abound under this heading, where:

> 'The state is under a negative obligation not to interfere with privacy rights, but in addition Strasbourg case law has also extended Article 8 to impose a positive duty to take measures to prevent private parties from interfering with these rights.'[146]

Personal correspondence and visits issues, disclosure of information,[147] cell searches and surveillance, distance from home and the effect of transfers, inter-prison visits and proximity and access of child and parent, balance of the rights of children with those of a parent to family life, conjugal visits and artificial insemination are all covered by Art 8. A number of these have already been voiced before the Courts in Strasbourg, and many have been challenged before the domestic courts. English argues that Art 8 is the most open-ended of the rights, partly because 'neither the Commission nor the Court have attempted any comprehensive definition of Article 8 interests, adapting them to meet changing times'.[148] As such, Art 8 offers undiscovered grounds of challenge.[149]

When the Council of Europe Committee for the Prevention of Torture visited the UK, its report on the visit, submitted to the Government, made clear a fundamental issue relevant to Art 8, namely:

> 'It is very important for prisoners to be able to maintain good contact with the outside world. Above all, they must be given the opportunity to safeguard their relations with their family and friends, and especially with their spouse or partner and their children. The continuation of such relations can be of critical importance for all concerned, particularly in the context of a prisoner's social rehabilitation. The guiding principle should be to promote contact with the outside world; any restrictions on such contacts should be based exclusively on security concerns of an appreciable nature or considerations linked to available resources.'[150]

---

146 R English *Analysis of The Convention and the Human Rights Act 1998* (One Crown Row, Human Rights Interactive).

147 Although in many instances concerning prisoners (certainly in disclosure to agencies within the criminal justice framework) it is likely that any breach regarding serving prisoners will be argued to be justified in the circumstances, eg in respect of security, public interest, child protection measures, etc.

148 R English *Analysis of The Convention and the Human Rights Act 1998* (One Crown Row, Human Rights Interactive).

149 Gay and lesbian relationships have not, to date, fallen within the Strasbourg view of the scope of family life. That said, since the first edition of this book, HMPS Assisted Prison Visits Unit has acknowledged same-sex couples within its ambit. The position of transsexuals, invariably incarcerated within a prison which accords with their birth-sex, as opposed to their assumed and lived gender identity, remains largely in a vacuum with regard to their needs and rights. See *Kerkhoven and Hinke v The Netherlands* Application No 15666/89 (1992).

150 *Report to the UK Government on the visit to the UK and the Isle of Man carried out by the European Committee for the Prevention of Torture and Inhuman or Degrading Treatment or Punishment from 8 to 17 September 1997* (Strasbourg, 13 January 2000).

Parents and children

The Council of Europe Committee for the Prevention of Torture has also raised as a concern the particular issue of the number of women in prison who are primary carers, and the fact that imprisonment may adversely affect the welfare of those in their care. Not least of the dependants to whom it gives consideration are children, and the difficult issue of whether babies and young children should remain with their mothers in prison and, if so, for how long.[151] Its recommendations include community equivalent ante-natal and post-natal care, specialist supervision of children in custodial settings in a 'child-centred' environment with opportunity to experience ordinary life outside prison walls, and facilitated child minding shared with family members outside the prison. At present, the small number of only 16 women's prisons (with only five holding remanded prisoners and three with open conditions) in the context of a growing women's prison population, means that most women are held at a considerable distance from their homes. Currently there are only four mother and baby units (MBUs) with a capacity for 64 children.[152] HMPS has made considerable steps forward in the last year since the establishment of a women's estate with the creation, in December 1999, of the post of Operational Manager for Women's Prisons. Recommendations have also been acted upon, and continue to be considered, following research into MBUs,[153] and these are likely to have borne in mind any potential challenge under the Human Rights Act 1998. Indeed, para 10.3.3 of the *Report of a Review of Principles, Policies and Procedures on Mothers and Babies/Children in Prisons*, records that 'Prison Service policy will reflect . . . Article 8, save where it is necessary to restrict the prisoner's right for a legitimate reason, such as good order and discipline, or the safety of others including babies'. That this is indeed so is confirmed by argument raised in *R v Governor of HMP Holloway ex parte L*[154] in December 1999. The case concerned an application for judicial review of a decision of a prison governor

---

151 See *10th General Report on the CPT's Activities* (Council of Europe Committee for the Prevention of Torture and Inhuman or Degrading Treatment or Punishment, Strasbourg, 18 August 2000); and also Recommendation 1469 (2000) of the Parliamentary Assembly of the Council of Europe on the subject of mothers and babies in prison.

152 In April 2000, HMPS announced the building of three prisons for women, and the conversion of three male prisons into premises for women. See R Ford 'Six more prisons to be provided for women' *The Times*, 5 April 2000. The same article recorded that there were 3,349 women prisoners, a population which had increased by 3% in the 10 months to the end of March 2000, compared with a rise of 0.3% over the same period in the male prison population. It is estimated that by 2007 the female prison population may be 5,000: see P White and C Cullen 'Projections of long term trends in the prison population to 2007' Home Office Research, Development and Statistics Directorate (10 February 2000). It is estimated that 55% of women prisoners have at least 1 child under 16: see *The Government's strategy for women offenders* (Home Office, 2000).

153 *Report of a Review of Principles, Policies and Procedures on Mothers and Babies/Children in Prison* (HMPS, 1999); The Management of Mother and Baby Units and the Application Process PSO 4801 (2000). It is worthy of note that the report *Human Rights* by the Foreign and Commonwealth Office (2000) makes mention under the heading 'Rights of Women' to addressing the issues of 'support for caring – mothers and carers matter'. Both the Women's Unit and the Listening to Women consultation exercise suggested a distinct interest in representing the needs of women per se.

154 (Unreported) 21 December 1999.

to refuse the applicant a place in an MBU, upholding the decision of an MBU admissions board. The board took into account in reaching its decision that the child protection plan, formulated by the local social services, could not be delivered in the prison. It was acknowledged that had it not been for this social services recommendation there would have been concerns, but that the prison may have been able to implement a high-monitored individualised compact in order for the applicant to join the MBU. The case makes clear that:

> 'under the prison rules, there is no absolute right to be placed in the mother and baby unit. Under the rules the Secretary of State has a discretion, if he thinks fit, to permit a woman prisoner to have her baby with her in prison, and the rules provide that special attention should be paid to the maintenance of such relationships insofar as they are desirable in the best interests of both the prisoner and his or her family. The Form 86A also mentions art 8 of the European Convention on Human Rights dealing with everyone's right to respect for his or her private and family life, and also draws attention to the United Nations Convention on the Rights of the Child, which makes it clear that in any legal proceedings dealing with children the best interests of the child shall be the primary consideration.'[155]

That said, there remains the question of whether there should be provision for father and baby units (there are none at present) in cases where the imprisoned father is the primary carer. It is an interesting area to consider when, in the issue of artificial insemination (explored below), policy applies equally to both male and female prisoners. Indeed, one of the criteria in deciding upon discretionary action allowing artificial insemination relies on the length of time for which the child might be expected to be *without a father or mother*.

Artificial insemination and conjugal visits

Perhaps the most contentious of the areas falling within Art 8 is that of conjugal visits and artificial insemination (AI). The relevant legislation is Rule 4 of the Prison Rules 1999, which reads, under the heading 'Outside Contacts':

> '(1) Special attention shall be paid to the maintenance of such relationships between a prisoner and his family as are desirable in the best interests of both.
>
> (2) A prisoner shall be encouraged and assisted to establish and maintain such relations with persons and agencies outside prison as may, in the opinion of the governor, best promote the interests of his family and his own social rehabilitation.'

The issue of AI was recently addressed in front of the domestic courts in *R v Secretary of State for the Home Department ex parte Mellor*[156] wherein the applicant challenged the decision of the Secretary of State for the Home Department refusing permission for him to inseminate his wife artificially. Mr Mellor contended that: his fundamental right to provide semen for AI of his wife (to found a family) had not been taken away expressly or by necessary implication; his exercise of that right posed no threat to prison security, good order, or discipline; and there was no pressing social or other need justifying interference with that right.

---

155 (Unreported) 21 December 1999, per Sullivan J, p 3.
156 [2000] 2 FLR 951, QBD.

The court heard that facilities for AI to prisoners are made only in exceptional circumstances[157] (applicable equally to male and female prisoners). The reasons for this approach were:

> '(a) it is an explicit consequence of imprisonment that prisoners should not have the opportunity to beget children whilst serving their sentences, until they come to the stage where they are allowed to take leave on temporary licence; (b) serious and justified public concern would be likely if prisoners continued to have the opportunity to conceive children while serving sentences; (c) that whilst many children are brought up successfully by single parents, the evidence suggests that children do better when they can stay in close contact with both parents. The creation of what would inevitably be one parent families because one partner was serving a sentence of imprisonment seems likely to be disadvantageous to society as a whole, as well as not being in the interests of the welfare of the child.'[158]

Paternalistic and social concerns raised here could, arguably, be seen as being at odds with, and undermining, arguments underlying decisions which are taken, on a regular basis, refusing to allow women prisoners to keep their children with them in prison (currently the only parent who is able to). Equally interesting is the fact that the case takes into account that the marriage of prisoners is seen as no way harmful to the public interest, and indeed that 'Marriage may, on the contrary, be a stabilising and rehabilitative influence'.[159] By extension of the arguments outlined, clearly parenthood, strangely in that it arguably adds a more uniquely dependent relationship, would not. The definitive 'line' would appear to be that entailing both sex and procreation, albeit that the latter is not considered a problem if forming part of temporary release even though the prisoner remains under sentence, and may so do for many years.

Counsel for the respondents in *Mellor* relied upon the fact that whereas Art 8 requires the State to respect existing family life, it does not afford a right to

---

157 General considerations applying in exercise of discretion are: '(a) whether the provision of AI facilities is the only means by which conception is likely to occur; (b) whether the prisoner's expected date of release is neither so near that delay would not be excessive nor so distant that he or she would be unable to assume the responsibilities of a parent; (c) whether both parties want the procedure and the medical authorities both inside and outside the prison are satisfied that the couple are medically fit to proceed with AI; (d) whether the couple were in a well-established and stable relationship before imprisonment which is likely to subsist after the prisoner's release; (e) whether there is evidence to suggest that the couple's domestic circumstances and the arrangements for the welfare of the child are satisfactory, including the length of time for which the child might be expected to be without a father or mother; (f) whether, having regard to the prisoner's history and antecedents and other relevant factors, there is evidence to suggest that it would be in the public interest to provide AI facilities in this particular case': *R v Secretary of State for the Home Department ex parte Mellor* [2000] 2 FLR 951, QBD.

158 Ibid: Mr N Sanderson, in affidavit dated 1 November 1999, sworn in the proceedings on behalf of the Secretary of State.

159 Ibid, para 27; reference to *Hamer v UK* (1979) 4 EHRR 139 at 142–143, paras 67–71.

create a family by conception of a child.[160] In sum, the Mellors were at a disadvantage having married whilst he was in prison, in which instance the State could not be held obliged to facilitate the conception of a child.[161] In the final event, the court held that Mr Mellor did not have a basic right to AI facilities, rather that he sought a 'privilege or a benefit' of access to AI, and that he was not entitled, as of right, to the co-operation and assistance of the Secretary of State to achieve artificial conception. The policy of the Secretary of State in this case was held not to be irrational, and that the public interest issues given regard to in formulating policy were neither inappropriate, irrelevant or immaterial. What remain arguable in the decision are such statements as:

> 'the need to maintain the deterrent effect of imprisonment and public confidence in the system of criminal justice, would be very likely to qualify as a sufficiently "pressing need" to justify the interference with such a right which necessarily results from a refusal of the prisoner's request by the Secretary of State.'[162]

In the *Mellor* case, both Arts 8 and 12 were considered to be pertinent. The issues of AI and conjugal visits were also debated. In respect to the latter, attention was drawn to the case of *ELH v UK*[163] where the court considered whether refusal by the Secretary of State of conjugal visits to a prisoner and spouse constituted a breach of Arts 8 and 12. The decision of the European Commission was that:

> 'the Commission recalls its case-law to the effect that, although the refusal of such visits constitutes an interference with the right to respect for one's family life under Article 8 of the Convention, for the present time it must be regarded as justified for the prevention of disorder or crime under the second paragraph of that provision. Moreover, according to the same case-law, an interference with family life justified under Article 8 para 2 of the Convention cannot at the same time constitute a violation of Article 12 ([*GS, RS v UK*] No 17142/90, Dec. 10.7.91, unpublished).'[164]

It would seem to be the case that the issue of conjugal visits, in the present climate, would undoubtedly fall at the first hurdle of prison 'order and discipline' and attend upon security measures. More 'alive' as an issue is surely the case of AI.

---

160 Relying upon D J Harris, M O'Boyle and C Warbrick, *Law of the European Convention on Human Rights* (Butterworths, 1995), p 313, where it is stated: 'It should be noted at the outset that the obligation on the state is to respect family life: it does not allow persons to claim a right to establish family life, eg by marrying or having the opportunity to have children, nor a general right to establish family life in a particular jurisdiction. However, the right to respect to one's family life may involve the recognition by the state of the reality of family life already established (*R v Secretary of State for the Home Department ex parte Mellor* [2000] 2 FLR 951, para (37))'.

161 Indeed the court gave much consideration to the arguments of the Secretary of State that 'Mr and Mrs Mellor's relationship had not been tested in normal conditions, and that its durability is thus uncertain': ibid, para 55(iv).

162 Ibid, para 52. On the case, see also C Urquhart and F Gibb 'Prisoner's plea on insemination' *The Times*, 30 June 2000; F Gibb 'Jailed killer seeks right to father child' *The Times*, 19 June 2000; and 'Prisoner has no right to artificial insemination' *The Times*, 5 September 2000.

163 (1997) 91A DR 61.

164 *ELH v UK* (1997) 91A DR 61; as quoted in *R v Secretary of State for the Home Department ex parte Mellor* [2000] 2 FLR 951, QBD.

Correspondence

The matter of the sanctity of prisoners' legal correspondence, and whether procedures for search envisaged by r 41(1) of the Prison Rules 1999 apply to prisoners' cells (in addition to the prisoner himself), was argued in the 1999 application for judicial review in the case of *Daly*.[165] The complaint was that, even in random cell searches, legally privileged correspondence was not completely excluded from the search, even if, as was stated, such correspondence was 'flicked through' without staff reading contents. Rule 41(1) states that: 'Every prisoner shall be searched when taken into custody by an officer, on his reception into a prison and subsequently as the governor thinks necessary or as the Secretary of State may direct'. This was held to include cell searches, even though subparas (2) and (3) of Rule 41 are worded in respect of searches of the person.[166] The case raised by *Daly* was focused on the policy of cell searches involving the searching of prisoners' legally privileged correspondence during absence from cell. The object of the proceedings was to seek to provide a vehicle for appealing the decision in *Main*[167] to either the House of Lords or the European Court. In both *R v Secretary of State for the Home Department ex parte Leech*[168] and *Campbell v UK*[169] it was held that correspondence between prisoner and legal adviser was of a special category, because of the presumption of propriety from the identity of parties to the correspondence. Why then should such presumption not apply to the same documents stored in a prisoner's cell.[170] In *Daly*, the argument was polarised between whether r 41(1) applied to a prisoner's cell as well as to a prisoner himself. The Human Rights Act 1998 provides a vehicle for challenge in respect of whether cell searches infringe a fundamental human right to confidential correspondence with legal advisers. Despite the fact that the issue of correspondence has already successfully exercised the European courts, it is clear that it is an area in which problems remain. The Prisons Ombudsman recorded his concern in his 1999/2000 Annual Report that letters from solicitors were being opened in error and stated:

> 'prisons must follow Prison Rules. They are not justified in opening correspondence which appears to be from legal advisors or the courts simply because it is not packaged in the recommended way. Very regrettably, some of my own correspondence has also been improperly opened.'[171]

---

165 *R v Secretary of State for the Home Department ex parte Daly* [1999] COD 388, CA.

166 Rule 41(2) and (3) state that '(2) A prisoner shall be searched in as seemly a manner as is consistent with discovering anything concealed. (3) No prisoner shall be stripped and searched in the sight of another prisoner, or in the sight of a person of the opposite sex'.

167 The case of *Main* was heard with *Simms and O'Brien*: see *R v Home Secretary ex parte Simms* [1999] QB 349, and also earlier proceedings [1998] 2 All ER 491.

168 [1994] QB 198, [1993] 4 All ER 539.

169 (1992) 15 EHRR 137.

170 Sir John Woodcock, CBE, QPM *Report of the Enquiry into the escape of six prisoners from the special security unit at Whitemoor prison, Cambridgeshire, on Friday 9 September 1994*, Cm 2741 (1994) – a prisoner should not be present during a search of his or her cell accommodation.

171 *Prisons Ombudsman's Annual Report 1999–2000*, Cm 4730 (2000).

Transfer of prisoners

The wider issue of transfer of prisoners generally, to an establishment near their family, may be tested under the Human Rights Act 1998. The case of *Wakefield v UK*[172] concerned a prisoner who was refused transfer from a prison in England to one in Scotland in order to facilitate visits by his fiancée. The European Court held that the relationship fell within 'private life' and that the right to respect for the private life of prisoners included maintenance of contact with the outside world, in order to facilitate their reintegration into society. The Court held that the refusal of a transfer was an interference with the right to respect for private life. As the prison population grows larger, not least in women's prisons, the proximity to home and family life of all prisoners becomes not only more a matter of imperative, but indeed a matter of right.

6.3.5 Article 9: Right to religious freedom

As a whole, HMPS has made a recent concerted effort to safeguard religious freedoms behind prison walls. Only in the last year has it appointed a Muslim Prison Advisor, Maqsood Ahmed, thereby reflecting its acknowledgement of the second highest religious adherence amongst those incarcerated in the UK. Prison Service Order 4550, issued on 30 October 2000, advised governors of the establishment of religious consultative services (RCSs) for some main non-Christian and Mormon religions, which are independent organisations working with HMPS in an advisory capacity on matters of religious provision.[173]

Issues which fall under the heading of Art 9 include hours allocated to religious ministers, particularly visiting ministers of non-Christian faiths, facilities for non-Christian prisoners such as prayer rooms, the affect of regime requirements on matters of religious observance, respecting religious beliefs in medical treatment, religious iconography and artefacts necessary for worship allowed in-cell, provision of required religious literature, and provision of religious diets and holidays.

There is a central impetus within HMPS to embrace religious attachment;[174] however, inconsistency in the facilities afforded to prisoners actually to 'worship' in the manner in which their religion demands are fertile areas for challenge. Indeed, not all prisons yet have a multi-faith provision, with 8% of prisons having no multi-faith accommodation at all, and, of those with multi-faith rooms, 18% of visiting ministers disapprove of the accommodation provided.[175] There is equal room for challenge on behalf of prisoners as

---

172   D 15817/89 (1 October 1990).
173   PSO 4550 'Chapter 3 of the Religion Manual' (30 October 2000).
174   Responsibility for religion in prisons is shared between the Chaplaincy and Prisoner Administration Group, both of whom work in consultation with the Advisory Group on Religion.
175   Prison Service Race Relations Group *Ninth Annual Report to the Prison Service Management Board* (2000).

members of faiths which HMPS has yet to accept as religions, including Scientology[176] and a specific strand of Rastafarianism.

There is argument to suggest that HMPS has not met all the goals necessary to facilitate adherence for members of all faiths and, in the light of the Human Rights Act 1998, HMPS may be more circumspect.

6.3.6   Article 14: Prohibition of discrimination in the enjoyment of rights

Article 14 must attend upon any of the Convention articles, being put forward in respect of breach of one of the rights. Matters of religion, race, gender, sexual orientation and disability are all sources of potential challenge. Some of these issues have already been discussed in this chapter under individual rights, for example the matter of father and baby units and issues surrounding procedural disadvantage in adjudication settings for disabled or foreign prisoners.

Women

In Europe the Committee on the Elimination of Discrimination Against Women has voiced concern on a number of issues relating to women and the UK criminal justice system, which it feels worthy of attention. These include the criminalisation of minor infringements indicative of women's poverty, which have led to the large number of women in prison, the stereotypical work and training many are afforded within prison,[177] the inadequate rehabilitative programmes for women prisoners[178] and the fact that they are more likely than the male prison population to be held far from their families.[179] One issue that may be raised under Art 14, attending upon Arts 8 and 12, is that of artificial insemination (AI), discussed earlier in relation to male prisoners. Research by Walker and Worrall on the women's lifer population has explored the issue of losses associated with indeterminate sentencing and how it is bound up with motherhood. They have raised the question of discrimination in respect of women prisoners who may wish to seek AI being 'prevented without any

---

176   Accepted as a belief under Art 9 in *X and Church of Scientology v Sweden* Application No 7805/77, (1979) 16 DR 68, as recorded by R English *Analysis of the Convention and the Human Rights Act 1998* (One Crown Row, Human Rights Interactive).

177   A key target for HMPS in 1999 was to increase the employability of women prisoners on release, and surveys of women prisoners were conducted during 1998 and 1999. Findings included limited work opportunities in prison, work experience which was considered too menial and unskilled to be of use after their release, little integration of work and training, and very few women (16%) having access to recognised vocational training. See B Hamlyn *Women Prisoners: a survey of their work and training experiences in custody and release* Research Findings No 122 (Home Office Research, Development and Statistics Directorate, 2000).

178   The first national pilot of the female sex offender programme began at HMP Styal in January 2000.

179   Concluding observations of the Committee on the Elimination of Discrimination Against Women: United Kingdom of Great Britain and Northern Ireland A/54/38, paras 278–318 (1 July 1999).

challenge or even discussion'.[180] It would be difficult, however, to sustain such a challenge given the attendant difficulties. The concerted input which HMPS is currently putting into the women's estate is admirable and, as commented upon earlier in this chapter, Human Rights Act 1998 considerations have been voiced. Indeed, it is perhaps a fact that the women's estate, being created with the Act as a contemporary issue, may well fare better long term in human rights records than that of the male, where piecemeal changes must be made to an existing structure. As Stewart of the Women's Policy Group has stated:

> 'We have been given a real "window of opportunity" to make a difference – to develop a better understanding of the needs of women; to provide regimes that will be better equipped to meet these needs; and also to build a culture and ethos in the women's estate as a whole that will support them.'[181]

That said, two points must be made. The first is that the specific acknowledgement of women within the penal system has been a long time coming, and were it not for its creation, human rights challenges by women prisoners would arguably have abounded. Secondly, the fact that the women's estate is embryonic should not lead to a complacency and thus blindness to the fact that discrimination may still exist, and that challenges under the Act are warranted.

Disability
The human rights of persons with disabilities have been supported by the UK Government abroad, most recently in the UK co-sponsored resolution in Geneva.[182] With regard to disabled prisoners in the UK, however,[183] HMPS has a very long way to go indeed in order to offer a regime which is not impoverished, merely because the prisoner is disabled. The only grounds on which a service provider can justify less favourable treatment of a disabled person (or failure to make adjustments) are within five categories, including that such treatment is necessary to protect health and safety or that the disabled person is unable to give informed consent.[184] Prison Service Order 2855 records:

> 'In accordance with the Statement of Purpose and the commitment to equality of opportunity, the Prison Service will ensure that prisoners with either physical,

---

180 S Walker and A Worrall 'Life as a Woman: the gendered pains of indeterminate imprisonment' *Prison Service Journal* No 132 (November 2000), pp 27, 31.
181 C Stewart 'Responding to the needs of women prisoners' *Prison Service Journal* No 132 (November 2000), p 41.
182 A resolution at the 56th Commission on Human Rights in Geneva inviting the High Commissioner for Human Rights, in co-operation with the Special Rapporteur on Disability, to examine measures to strengthen the protection and monitoring of the human rights of persons with disabilities. See *Human Rights, Foreign and Commonwealth Office Annual Report 2000*, Cm 4774 (July 2000), p 82.
183 There are currently circa 212 disabled prisoners within the prison system. Of those, 81 are wheelchair bound, with only 56 of those 81 having wheelchair access to cells.
184 Disability Rights Task Force on Civil Rights for Disabled People *Exclusion to Inclusion* (December 1999), p 116.

sensory or mental disabilities are able, as far as is practicable, to participate equally in prison life.'[185]

A whole host of day-to-day activities must be rethought to meet the need of including disabled prisoners in the comprehensive right of access to a full prison regime, including being able to climb stairs or understand written or spoken instructions. Not least of these adjustments include ensuring access to areas and facilities (cell, library, healthcare, food servery, etc), transport inter-prison and from prison to court, and the provision of particular innovations to ensure they are not disadvantaged in respect of such matters as visits, or indeed adjudications. This may require introduction of an auxiliary aid or service (for example, a 'big button' telephone), or alteration of the physical fabric of premises, which will enable disabled prisoners to use existing services (for example, the prison shop or library). Barriers must be overcome. It is worthy of note that learning difficulties such as dyslexia (which may severely affect a prisoner in accessing written materials for adjudications), tinnitus, severe agoraphobia, schizophrenia or depression, diabetes, and severe disfigurements, are all covered by the Disability Discrimination Act 1995. It is clear that a 'cavalier' attitude to what counts as a 'disability' may give rise to a challenge of discrimination, attendant upon a breach of another article. In a similar way that inappropriate language with minority racial and ethnic groups may be regarded as discriminatory, there are also words and phrases which must be avoided in referring to disabled prisoners. HMPS must also monitor efforts by the Disability Rights Task Force on Civil Rights for Disabled People, whose recommendations include extending the definition of disability, in order to ensure that it is conversant with those prisoners who fall within the ambit of 'disabled'.[186] As the Disability Rights Task Force makes clear, the duty upon service providers, such as, in this instance, HMPS, is 'a continuing and

---

185   'Management of Prisoners with Physical, Sensory or Mental Disabilities'. See also PSI 87/1999 of the same title. HMPS must: take reasonable steps to provide auxiliary aids or services if this would make it easier for disabled prisoners or visitors to make use of services; be prepared, as far as possible, to provide appropriate interpretation services for the purpose of necessary communication with prisoners who have a hearing impairment; keep a record, which needs to be reviewed, about the communication and mobility needs of all disabled prisoners; take positive steps to ensure that disabled prisoners have access to education facilities and programmes and that their communication needs are met; take full responsibility to ensure that disabled prisoners have access to the full range of employment opportunities available; take reasonable steps to ensure that disabled prisoners have access to physical education facilities; make the library service available to all prisoners and arrange access to large print or talking books for those prisoners who have a visual disability and sub-titled, or sign language interpreted videos for deaf prisoners; make reasonable adjustments, where attendance at particular courses is necessary, for the successful completion of sentence, to allow prisoners with disabilities to participate; make arrangements for disabled prisoners serving a long sentence to progress through the categories in the usual manner and to transfer to an establishment of the appropriate category within a reasonable time; ensure that information necessary for the discharge process is made available to the Probation Service; ensure that the process of adjudications does not discriminate against disabled prisoners; and ensure that disabled prisoners are able to receive their legal entitlement of visits.

186   See report by the Disability Rights Task Force on Civil Rights for Disabled People *Exclusion to Inclusion* (December 1999).

evolving duty; it is dependent for its enforcement on individual disabled people making claims against service providers'.[187] The Human Rights Act 1998 will ensure that such claims are heard.

Race and ethnicity

The issue of racial and ethnic discrimination was made a particular focus by the European Commission in June 2000, with a Council of Ministers agreement on a cross-Europe directive condemning discrimination and prohibiting it in the areas of employment, education, social security, healthcare and access to goods and services. The directive provides a minimum level of protection against racial discrimination, common to all Member States, and ensures that victims will have a right of redress through each State designating a body for the promotion of equal treatment to provide assistance to victims in pursuing their complaints.[188] On the European stage the Home Office has asserted its commitment to racial equality in prisons both to the Committee for the Elimination of Racial Discrimination[189] and the Human Rights Committee.[190] In the latter report the Prison Service stated that it was committed to a programme of work to reduce gaps between policy and practice, including making available appropriate products for ethnic minority groups at prison shops.

In the UK the outcome of the Stephen Lawrence Inquiry catapulted, into the public domain, the issue of institutionalised racism. When the report of the enquiry was published, the Home Secretary 'accepted the Inquiry's definition of institutional racism and said that any long established, white dominated organisation was liable to have procedures, practices and a culture that tend to exclude or to disadvantage non-white people'.[191] In his *First Annual Report on Progress* since publication of the Inquiry, the Home Secretary announced that 'The Government has gone beyond the recommendation in the Stephen Lawrence Inquiry Report and has announced that all public services are to be brought within the scope of the Race Relations Act 1976'.[192] HMPS appointed its first Race Equality Advisor in September 1999 and, 1 month later, changed the Prison Rules 1999 to include, within offences against discipline, incidents that are racially motivated. Prior to this the existing Prison Rules (and indeed staff Code of Discipline, which was also changed at this time) had no provision at all specifically recognising a racial element. Direct and indirect discrimi-

---

187   See report by the Disability Rights Task Force on Civil Rights for Disabled People *Exclusion to Inclusion* (December 1999), p 114.

188   European Commission Press Release 'Commission welcomes speedy accord on race discrimination rules' (Brussels, 6 June 2000).

189   Reports submitted by States parties under Art 9 of the Convention, Committee on the Elimination of Racial Discrimination CERD/C/338/Add 12 (Part I) (25 April 2000).

190   Consideration of Reports submitted by the States parties under Art 40 of the Covenant, Human Rights Committee CCPR/C/UK/99/5 (11 April 2000).

191   *Stephen Lawrence Inquiry, Home Secretary's Action Plan: First Annual Report on Progress, 2000.*

192   Ibid, recommendation 11, para 1, p 8. The Race Relations (Amendment) Bill was published on 3 December 1999 and places a positive statutory duty on public authorities to promote racial equality. The extension of the Race Relations Act 1976 to all public services was a proposal in July 1999 in the Commission for Racial Equality's Third Review of the Act.

nation and victimisation is now covered. The definition of 'racist incident' which was recommended in the report of the Stephen Lawrence Inquiry, was circulated throughout the Prison Service.[193] In May 2000 the DG, Martin Narey, announced new procedures for reporting racist incidents, whilst speaking at the National Association for the Care and Rehabilitation of Offenders (NACRO) Race and Prisons Conference and commenting upon its race and prisons report. He acknowledged that prisoners from ethnic groups found the existing complaints system difficult to use and that a new complaints system was being piloted in five establishments, with the new complaint form including a specific question about any possible racial element.[194]

However, in the last year it has become more than clear that challenges of discrimination in a number of areas, on racial grounds, are not unlikely within the prison setting. Even the Prison Ombudsman commented in his Annual Report for 1999/2000 that he has found: 'numerous ... entries in prisoners' history sheets that have not reflected well on the authors or the Service for which they work'.[195] Considerable publicity has surrounded findings at both HMP Wandsworth[196] and HMP Brixton.[197] In respect of HMP Brixton, an inquiry began on 9 May 2000 to assess race relations at the prison, headed by the Race Equality Advisor, with findings published in June. Racial discrimination was found to take the form of victimisation, bullying, harassment, racial stereotyping, intimidation and inappropriate use of language, directly attending upon rights such as freedom from inhuman and degrading treatment and punishment, right to a fair trial and to liberty and security of the person. With regard to Art 6, evidence was found of a regime known as 'reflections', used disproportionately against prisoners from minority ethnic groups, which consisted of basic grade staff meting out punishments (such as loss of association) without any official or legal standing.[198] It is worthy of note that the same investigation discovered a sexist culture mitigating against female staff at the prison. Of the findings of the report the DG, Martin Narey, stated, 'I have already acknowledged that the Service is not only institutionally racist, but that pockets of blatant racism still exist. Brixton may be a bad example but it is not alone'.[199] This being so, the Human Rights Act 1998 will not only present an avenue for challenges, but perhaps also lead to a change in practices and the

---

193 See Prison Service Press Release 'Racism to be targeted by change to Prison Rules' (28 October 1999); and Prison Service Press Release 'Prison Service disowns racism' (21 September 1999).

194 Speech by Martin Narey at the NACRO Conference, 9 May 2000. See Prison Service Press Release 'Prison Service announces new measures to improve reporting of racist incidents', with appended DG speech (9 May 2000).

195 *Prisons Ombudsman's Annual Report 1999–2000*, Cm 4730 (2000).

196 See O Wright 'Way of fear is still the rule, say inmates' and R Ford 'Wandsworth is nasty and racist' *The Times*, 18 December 1999.

197 R Ford 'Jail boss moves after inspection' *The Times*, 4 July 2000; and R Ford 'Race row prison faces private take-over' *The Times*, 6 July 2000.

198 Race Equality Advisor 'Assessment of Race Relations at HMP Brixton' (RESPOND, June 2000). The 'reflections' regime was stopped immediately and is now the subject of an internal investigation.

199 Prison Service Press Release, 'Prison Service recognises magnitude of poor race relations' (31 October 2000).

'prison culture' referred to in the introduction to this chapter, by virtue of its deterrent effect.

Sexual orientation

The future of sexual orientation is uncertain. Earlier discussion of the articles embodied in the Human Rights Act 1998 has touched upon such matters as provision of condoms for practising homosexuals. Beyond this there remains the issue of transsexuals, and those prisoners who have undergone sexual body alteration, and the fact that despite gender re-assignment intervention, they remain held in prison establishments which accord with their birth-sex. As a Council of Europe report has suggested:

> 'It is very evident from the available information that full legal recognition of the transsexual in his/her new gender identity is for him/her not only an existential need and essential for social acceptance, but also means full respect for her/him as an individual, a citizen with the same human rights as any other person with the same gender identity.'[200]

Could the sexual classification currently practised by HMPS be held to be 'inhuman and degrading treatment'? In addition, could the refusal of treatment to a transgendered inmate be challenged under the Human Rights Act 1998?[201] What also of the visiting rights of those prisoners who have undertaken a change of sex identity?[202]

6.4 CONCLUSION

> 'The system of justice which has put a person in prison cannot end at the prison doors. It must accompany the prisoner into the prison, his cell, and to all aspects of his life in prison.'[203]

This chapter has not exhausted all the potential avenues in which a prisoner might seek recourse under the Human Rights Act 1998, nor did it set out to do so. Indeed, the very evolving nature of the human rights field makes it virtually impossible, in any one moment, to try to encapsulate what cannot be encapsulated – that is, the organic field envisaged by the 'living instrument' that the Act is claimed to be. What has been undertaken here is an overview of how the courts, both European and domestic, have considered claims made by prisoners in respect of what they consider to be their inalienable rights – based upon their humanity. From these decisions, limited though they may be,

---

200 XXIIIrd Colloquy on European Law proceedings *Transsexualism, medicine and law*, Vrije Universiteit Amsterdam, 14–16 April 1993 (Council of Europe Publishing, 1995), p 228.
201 In *Marty Phillips v Michigan Department of Corrections* 731 F Supp 792, 798 (WD Mich 1990) refusal to provide a transgendered inmate with 2.5 mg/day of premarin constituted cruel and unusual punishment because transsexualism is not voluntarily assumed and is not merely a matter of sexual preference. See *Transsexualism, medicine and law* (n 200 above), p 201.
202 Ibid, p 225.
203 A Coyle 'Co-operation with Central and Eastern Europe' in *12th Conference of Directors of Prison Administration* Strasbourg, 26–28 November 1997, European Committee on Crime Problems (Council of Europe Publishing, 1999), pp 129, 130.

conclusions have been sought. Decisions exist in many areas pertaining to prisoners, and yet they have not even begun to exhaust possible avenues. One reason for this is that we have never been, as a society, oriented to looking at our lives through a 'rights focus'.

Arguably, the opportunity the Human Rights Act 1998 poses for prisoners to exercise their right to be 'part' of society is to be welcomed. As the introduction to this chapter made clear, the majority of those behind prison walls, whether or not they are lifers, will return to the community. It is therefore only right that they should not be marginalised in the human rights arena simply because they are behind brick walls. Prisoners are sentenced 'in our name' and they remain behind prison walls on that basis. We therefore bear a responsibility for how they are treated 'in our name'.

The majority of people do not give a thought to those behind prison bars, unless they feel (largely by media prompting) that prisoners are getting a 'soft deal' in comparison to themselves. Prisoners afford the public a benchmark from which to complain about their own treatment by Government. At least the 'resentment response' means that the general public can consider prisoners as equals, if only in the context of asserting that they are benefiting more than the free majority. Perhaps, with the absorption of the Human Rights Act 1998, the general public will be more attuned to 'rights' in their everyday life and consider more the plight of prisoners. That said, the Act must, and indeed will, require a different stance to be taken (indeed a *volte-face* in many instances) by HMPS which, regardless of public opinion, can be challenged in court for its failures.

At the Annual Conference of the Prison Governors' Association on 28 March 1999, the President stated:

> 'I call upon the Government to provide prisoners, not with luxury, but with basic decent conditions; to commit the country to the planned elimination of these squalid conditions for good. While the hopelessness and depression of prison life continues, the role of this Association must be to . . . stand up for the people in our care, your individual care and my individual care; to stand up for people who do not have a voice of their own.'[204]

The Human Rights Act 1998 may assist in giving prisoners that voice.

---

204   Christopher Scott OBE, President PGA, Chairman's Annual Address, PGA 2000 Annual Conference, 28 March 2000.

APPENDIX

Human Rights Act 1998

(1998 c 42)

ARRANGEMENT OF SECTIONS

An Act to give further effect to rights and freedoms guaranteed under the European Convention on Human Rights; to make provision with respect to holders of certain judicial offices who become judges of the European Court of Human Rights; and for connected purposes.

[9th November 1998]

Introduction

1   The Convention Rights

(1)   In this Act, 'the Convention rights' means the rights and fundamental freedoms set out in—

  (a) Articles 2 to 12 and 14 of the Convention,
  (b) Articles 1 to 3 of the First Protocol, and
  (c) Articles 1 and 2 of the Sixth Protocol,

as read with Articles 16 to 18 of the Convention.

(2)   Those Articles are to have effect for the purposes of this Act subject to any designated derogation or reservation (as to which see sections 14 and 15).

(3)   The Articles are set out in Schedule 1.

(4)   The Secretary of State may by order make such amendments to this Act as he considers appropriate to reflect the effect, in relation to the United Kingdom, of a protocol.

(5)   In subsection (4) 'protocol' means a protocol to the Convention—

  (a) which the United Kingdom has ratified; or
  (b) which the United Kingdom has signed with a view to ratification.

(6)   No amendment may be made by an order under subsection (4) so as to come into force before the protocol concerned is in force in relation to the United Kingdom.

2   Interpretation of Convention rights

(1)   A court or tribunal determining a question which has arisen in connection with a Convention right must take into account any—

(a) judgment, decision, declaration or advisory opinion of the European Court of Human Rights,
(b) opinion of the Commission given in a report adopted under Article 31 of the Convention,
(c) decision of the Commission in connection with Article 26 or 27(2) of the Convention, or
(d) decision of the Committee of Ministers taken under Article 46 of the Convention,

whenever made or given, so far as, in the opinion of the court or tribunal, it is relevant to the proceedings in which that question has arisen.

(2)   Evidence of any judgment, decision, declaration or opinion of which account may have to be taken under this section is to be given in proceedings before any court or tribunal in such manner as may be provided by rules.

(3)   In this section 'rules' means rules of court or, in the case of proceedings before a tribunal, rules made for the purposes of this section—

(a) by the Lord Chancellor or the Secretary of State, in relation to proceedings outside Scotland;
(b) by the Secretary of State, in relation to proceedings in Scotland; or
(c) by a Northern Ireland department, in relation to proceedings before a Tribunal in Northern Ireland—
   (i)   which deals with transferred matters; and
   (ii) for which no rules made under paragraph (a) are in force.

Legislation

3   Interpretation of legislation

(1)   So far as it is possible to do so, primary legislation and subordinate legislation must be read and given effect in a way which is compatible with the Convention rights.

(2)   This section—

(a) applies to primary legislation and subordinate legislation whenever enacted;
(b) does not affect the validity, continuing operation or enforcement of any incompatible primary legislation; and
(c) does not affect the validity, continuing operation or enforcement of any incompatible subordinate legislation if (disregarding any possibility of revocation) primary legislation prevents removal of the incompatibility.

4   Declaration of incompatibility

(1)   Subsection (2) applies in any proceedings in which a court determines whether a provision of primary legislation is compatible with a Convention right.

(2)   If the court is satisfied that the provision is incompatible with a Convention right, it may make a declaration of that incompatibility.

(3)   Subsection (4) applies in any proceedings in which a court determines whether a provision of subordinate legislation, made in the exercise of a power conferred by primary legislation, is compatible with a Convention right.

(4)   If the court is satisfied—

   (a) that the provision is incompatible with a Convention right, and
   (b) that (disregarding any possibility of revocation) the primary legislation concerned prevents removal of the incompatibility,

it may make a declaration of that incompatibility.

(5)   In this section 'court' means—

   (a) the House of Lords;
   (b) the Judicial Committee of the Privy Council;
   (c) the Courts-Martial Appeal Court;
   (d) in Scotland, the High Court of Justiciary sitting otherwise than as a trial court or the Court of Session;
   (e) in England and Wales or Northern Ireland, the High Court or the Court of Appeal.

(6)   A declaration under this section ('a declaration of incompatibility')—

   (a) does not affect the validity, continuing operation or enforcement of the provision in respect of which it is given; and
   (b) is not binding on the parties to the proceedings in which it is made.

5   Right of Crown to intervene

(1)   Where a court is considering whether to make a declaration of incompatibility, the Crown is entitled to notice in accordance with rules of court.

(2)   In any case to which subsection (1) applies—

   (a) a Minister of the Crown (or a person nominated by him),
   (b) a member of the Scottish Executive,
   (c) a Northern Ireland Minister,
   (d) a Northern Ireland department,

is entitled, on giving notice in accordance with rules of court, to be joined as a party to the proceedings.

(3)   Notice under subsection (2) may be given at any time during the proceedings.

(4)   A person who has been made a party to criminal proceedings (other than in Scotland) as the result of a notice under subsection (2) may, with leave, appeal to the House of Lords against any declaration of incompatibility made in the proceedings.

(5)   In subsection (4)—

'criminal proceedings' includes all proceedings before the Courts-Martial Appeal Court; and
'leave' means leave granted by the court making the declaration of incompatibility or by the House of Lords.

Public authorities

6   Acts of public authorities

(1)   It is unlawful for a public authority to act in a way which is incompatible with a Convention right.

(2)   Subsection (1) does not apply to an act if—

(a) as the result of one or more provisions of primary legislation, the authority could not have acted differently; or

(b) in the case of one or more provisions of, or made under, primary legislation which cannot be read or given effect in a way which is compatible with the Convention rights, the authority was acting so as to give effect to or enforce those provisions.

(3)   In this section, 'public authority' includes—

(a) a court or tribunal, and

(b) any person certain of whose functions are functions of a public nature,

but does not include either House of Parliament or a person exercising functions in connection with proceedings in Parliament.

(4)   In subsection (3) 'Parliament' does not include the House of Lords in its judicial capacity.

(5)   In relation to a particular act, a person is not a public authority by virtue only of subsection (3)(b) if the nature of the act is private.

(6)   'An act' includes a failure to act but does not include a failure to—

(a) introduce in, or lay before, Parliament a proposal for legislation; or

(b) make any primary legislation or remedial order.

7   Proceedings

(1)   A person who claims that a public authority has acted (or proposes to act) in a way which is made unlawful by section 6(1) may—

(a) bring proceedings against the authority under this Act in the appropriate court or tribunal, or

(b) rely on the Convention right or rights concerned in any legal proceedings,

but only if he is (or would be) a victim of the unlawful act.

(2)   In subsection (1)(a) 'appropriate court or tribunal' means such court or tribunal as may be determined in accordance with rules; and proceedings against an authority include a counterclaim or similar proceeding.

(3)   If the proceedings are brought on an application for judicial review, the applicant is to be taken to have a sufficient interest in relation to the unlawful act only if he is, or would be, a victim of that act.

(4)   If the proceedings are made by way of a petition for judicial review in Scotland, the applicant shall be taken to have title and interest to sue in relation to the unlawful act only if he is, or would be, a victim of that act.

(5)   Proceedings under subsection (1)(a) must be brought before the end of—

(a) the period of one year beginning with the date on which the act complained of took place; or

(b) such longer period as the court or tribunal considers equitable having regard to all the circumstances,

but that is subject to any rule imposing a stricter time limit in relation to the procedure in question.

(6)   In subsection (1)(b) 'legal proceedings' includes—

(a) proceedings brought by or at the instigation of a public authority; and

(b) an appeal against the decision of a court or tribunal.

(7)   For the purposes of this section, a person is a victim of an unlawful act only if he would be a victim for the purposes of Article 34 of the Convention if proceedings were brought in the European Court of Human Rights in respect of that act.

(8)   Nothing in this Act creates a criminal offence.

(9)   In this section 'rules' means—

(a) in relation to proceedings before a court or tribunal outside Scotland, rules made by the Lord Chancellor or the Secretary of State for the purposes of this section or rules of court,

(b) in relation to proceedings before a court or tribunal in Scotland, rules made by the Secretary of State for those purposes,

(c) in relation to proceedings before a tribunal in Northern Ireland—
     (i)   which deals with transferred matters; and
     (ii) for which no rules made under paragraph (a) are in force,
     rules made by a Northern Ireland department for those purposes,

and includes provision made by order under section 1 of the Courts and Legal Services Act 1990.

(10)   In making rules regard must be had to section 9.

(11)   The Minister who has power to make rules in relation to a particular tribunal may, to the extent he considers it necessary to ensure that the tribunal can provide an appropriate remedy in relation to an act (or proposed act) of a public authority which is (or would be) unlawful as a result of section 6(1), by order add to—

(a) the relief or remedies which the tribunal may grant; or

(b) the grounds on which it may grant any of them.

(12)   An order made under subsection (13) may contain such incidental, supplemental, consequential or transitional provision as the Minister making it considers appropriate.

(13)   'The Minister' includes the Northern Ireland department concerned.

8 Judicial remedies

(1)   In relation to any act (or proposed act) of a public authority which the court finds is (or would be) unlawful, it may grant such relief or remedy, or make such order, within its powers as it considers just and appropriate.

(2)   But damages may be awarded only by a court which has power to award damages, or to order the payment of compensation, in civil proceedings.

(3)   No award of damages is to be made unless, taking account of all the circumstances of the case, including—

(a) any other relief or remedy granted, or order made, in relation to the act in question (by that or any other court), and

(b) the consequences of any decision (of that or any other court) in respect of that act, the court is satisfied that the award is necessary to afford just satisfaction to the person in whose favour it is made.

(4)   In determining—

(a) whether to award damages, or
(b) the amount of an award,

the court must take into account the principles applied by the European Court of Human Rights in relation to the award of compensation under Article 41 of the Convention.

(5)   A public authority against which damages are awarded is to be treated—

(a) in Scotland, for the purposes of section 3 of the Law Reform (Miscellaneous Provisions) (Scotland) Act 1940 as if the award were made in an action of damages in which the authority has been found liable in respect of loss or damage to the person to whom the award is made;
(b) for the purposes of the Civil Liability (Contribution) Act 1978 as liable in respect of damage suffered by the person to whom the award is made.

(6)   In this section—

'court' includes a tribunal;
'damages' means damages for an unlawful act of a public authority; and
'unlawful' means unlawful under section 6(1).

9   Judicial acts

(1)   Proceedings under section 7(1)(a) in respect of a judicial act may be brought only—

(a) by exercising a right of appeal;
(b) on an application (in Scotland a petition) for judicial review; or
(c) in such other forum as may be prescribed by rules.

(2)   That does not affect any rule of law which prevents a court from being the subject of judicial review.

(3)   In proceedings under this Act in respect of a judicial act done in good faith, damages may not be awarded otherwise than to compensate a person to the extent required by Article 5(5) of the Convention.

(4)   An award of damages permitted by subsection (3) is to be made against the Crown; but no award may be made unless the appropriate person, if not a party to the proceedings, is joined.

(5)   In this section—

'appropriate person' means the Minister responsible for the court concerned, or a person or government department nominated by him;
'court' includes a tribunal;
'judge' includes a member of a tribunal, a justice of the peace and a clerk or other officer entitled to exercise the jurisdiction of a court;
'judicial act' means a judicial act of a court and includes an act done on the instructions, or on behalf, of a judge; and
'rules' has the same meaning as in section 7(11).

Remedial action

10   Power to take remedial action

(1)   This section applies if—

   (a)   a provision of legislation has been declared under section 4 to be incompatible with a Convention right and, if an appeal lies—

      (i)   all persons who may appeal have stated in writing that they do not intend to do so;

      (ii)   the time for bringing an appeal has expired and no appeal has been brought within that time; or

      (iii)   an appeal brought within that time has been determined or abandoned; or

   (b)   it appears to a Minister of the Crown or Her Majesty in Council that, having regard to a finding of the European Court of Human Rights made after the coming into force of this section in proceedings against the United Kingdom, a provision of legislation is incompatible with an obligation of the United Kingdom arising from the Convention.

(2)   If a Minister of the Crown considers that there are compelling reasons for proceeding under this section, he may by order make such amendments to the legislation as he considers necessary to remove the incompatibility.

(3)   If, in the case of subordinate legislation, a Minister of the Crown considers—

   (a)   that it is necessary to amend the primary legislation under which the subordinate legislation in question was made, in order to enable the incompatibility to be removed, and

   (b)   that there are compelling reasons for proceeding under this section,

he may by order make such amendments to the primary legislation as he considers necessary.

(4)   This section also applies where the provision in question is in subordinate legislation and has been quashed, or declared invalid, by reason of incompatibility with a Convention right and the Minister proposes to proceed under paragraph 2(b) of Schedule 2.

(5)   If the legislation is an Order in Council, the power conferred by subsection (2) or (3) is exercisable by Her Majesty in Council.

(6)   In this section 'legislation' does not include a Measure of the Church Assembly or of the General Synod of the Church of England.

(7)   Schedule 2 makes further provision about remedial orders.

Other rights and proceedings

11   Safeguard for existing human rights

A person's reliance on a Convention right does not restrict—

   (a)   any other right or freedom conferred on him by or under any law having effect in any part of the United Kingdom; or

   (b)   his right to make any claim or bring any proceedings which he could make or bring apart from sections 7 to 9.

12 Freedom of expression

(1) This section applies if a court is considering whether to grant any relief which, if granted, might affect the exercise of the Convention right to freedom of expression.

(2) If the person against whom the application for relief is made ('the respondent') is neither present nor represented, no such relief is to be granted unless the court is satisfied—

(a) that the applicant has taken all practicable steps to notify the respondent; or
(b) that there are compelling reasons why the respondent should not be notified.

(3) No such relief is to be granted so as to restrain publication before trial unless the court is satisfied that the applicant is likely to establish that publication should not be allowed.

(4) The court must have particular regard to the importance of the Convention right to freedom of expression and, where the proceedings relate to material which the respondent claims, or which appears to the court, to be journalistic, literary or artistic material (or to conduct connected with such material), to—

(a) the extent to which—
   (i) the material has, or is about to, become available to the public; or
   (ii) it is, or would be, in the public interest for the material to be published;
(b) any relevant privacy code.

(5) In this section—

'court' includes a tribunal; and
'relief' includes any remedy or order (other than in criminal proceedings).

13 Freedom of thought, conscience and religion

(1) If a court's determination of any question arising under this Act might affect the exercise by a religious organisation (itself or its members collectively) of the Convention right to freedom of thought, conscience and religion, it must have particular regard to the importance of that right.

(2) In this section 'court' includes a tribunal.

Derogations and reservations

14 Derogations

(1) In this Act, 'designated derogation' means—

(a) the United Kingdom's derogation from Article 5(3) of the Convention; and
(b) any derogation by the United Kingdom from an Article of the Convention, or of any protocol to the Convention, which is designated for the purposes of this Act in an order made by the Secretary of State.

(2) The derogation referred to in subsection (1)(a) is set out in Part I of Schedule 3.

(3) If a designated derogation is amended or replaced it ceases to be a designated derogation.

(4)   But subsection (3) does not prevent the Secretary of State from exercising his power under subsection (1)(b) to make a fresh designation order in respect of the Article concerned.

(5)   The Secretary of State must by order make such amendments to Schedule 3 as he considers appropriate to reflect—

  (a) any designation order; or
  (b) the effect of subsection (3).

(6)   A designation order may be made in anticipation of the making by the United Kingdom of a proposed derogation.

15   Reservations

(1)   In this Act, 'designated reservation' means—

  (a) the United Kingdom's reservation to Article 2 of the First Protocol to the Convention; and
  (b) any other reservation by the United Kingdom to an Article of the Convention, or of any protocol to the Convention, which is designated for the purposes of this Act in an order made by the Secretary of State.

(2)   The text of the reservation referred to in subsection (1)(a) is set out in Part II of Schedule 3.

(3)   If a designated reservation is withdrawn wholly or in part it ceases to be a designated reservation.

(4)   But subsection (3) does not prevent the Secretary of State from exercising his power under subsection (1)(b) to make a fresh designation order in respect of the Article concerned.

(5)   The Secretary of State must by order make such amendments to this Act as he considers appropriate to reflect—

  (a) any designation order; or
  (b) the effect of subsection (3).

16   Period for which designated derogations have effect

(1)   If it has not already been withdrawn by the United Kingdom, a designated derogation ceases to have effect for the purposes of this Act—

  (a) in the case of the derogation referred to in section 14(1)(a), at the end of the period of five years beginning with the date on which section 1(2) came into force;
  (b) in the case of any other derogation, at the end of the period of five years beginning with the date on which the order designating it was made.

(2)   At any time before the period—

  (a) fixed by subsection (1)(a) or (b), or
  (b) extended by an order under this subsection,

comes to an end, the Secretary of State may by order extend it by a further period of five years.

(3) An order under section 14(1)(b) ceases to have effect at the end of the period for consideration, unless a resolution has been passed by each House approving the order.

(4) Subsection (3) does not affect—

(a) anything done in reliance on the order; or
(b) the power to make a fresh order under section 14(1)(b).

(5) In subsection (3) 'period for consideration' means the period of forty days beginning with the day on which the order was made.

(6) In calculating the period for consideration, no account is to be taken of any time during which—

(a) Parliament is dissolved or prorogued; or
(b) both Houses are adjourned for more than four days.

(7) If a designated derogation is withdrawn by the United Kingdom, the Secretary of State must by order make such amendments to this Act as he considers are required to reflect that withdrawal.

17 Periodic review of designated reservations

(1) The appropriate Minister must review the designated reservation referred to in section 15(1)(a)—

(a) before the end of the period of five years beginning with the date on which section 1(2) came into force; and
(b) if that designation is still in force, before the end of the period of five years beginning with the date on which the last report relating to it was laid under subsection (3).

(2) The appropriate Minister must review each of the other designated reservations (if any)—

(a) before the end of the period of five years beginning with the date on which the order designating the reservation first came into force; and
(b) if the designation is still in force, before the end of the period of five years beginning with the date on which the last report relating to it was laid under subsection (3).

(3) The Minister conducting a review under this section must prepare a report on the result of the review and lay a copy of it before each House of Parliament.

Judges of the European Court of Human Rights

18 Appointment to European Court of Human Rights

(1) In this section 'judicial office' means the office of—

(a) Lord Justice of Appeal, Justice of the High Court or Circuit judge, in England and Wales;
(b) judge of the Court of Session or sheriff, in Scotland;
(c) Lord Justice of Appeal, judge of the High Court or county court judge, in Northern Ireland.

(2) The holder of a judicial office may become a judge of the European Court of Human Rights ('the Court') without being required to relinquish his office.

(3)   But he is not required to perform the duties of his judicial office while he is a judge of the Court.

(4)   In respect of any period during which he is a judge of the Court—

  (a) a Lord Justice of Appeal or Justice of the High Court is not to count as a judge of the relevant court for the purposes of section 2(1) or 4(1) of the Supreme Court Act 1981 (maximum number of judges) nor as a judge of the Supreme Court for the purposes of section 12(1) to (6) of that Act (salaries etc);
  (b) a judge of the Court of Session is not to count as a judge of that court for the purposes of section 1(1) of the Court of Session Act 1988 (maximum number of judges) or of section 9(1)(c) of the Administration of Justice Act 1973 ('the 1973 Act') (salaries etc);
  (c) a Lord Justice of Appeal or a judge of the High Court in Northern Ireland is not to count as a judge of the relevant court for the purposes of section 2(1) or 3(1) of the Judicature (Northern Ireland) Act 1978 (maximum number of judges) nor as a judge of the Supreme Court of Northern Ireland for the purposes of section 9(1)(d) of the 1973 Act (salaries etc);
  (d) a Circuit judge is not to count as such for the purposes of section 18 of the Courts Act 1971 (salaries etc);
  (e) a sheriff is not to count as such for the purposes of section 14 of the Sheriff Courts (Scotland) Act 1907 (salaries etc);
  (f) a county court judge of Northern Ireland is not to count as such for the purposes of section 106 of the County Courts Act (Northern Ireland) 1959 (salaries etc).

(5)   If a sheriff principal is appointed a judge of the Court, section 11(1) of the Sheriff Courts (Scotland) Act 1971 (temporary appointment of sheriff principal) applies, while he holds that appointment, as if his office is vacant.

(6)   Schedule 3 makes provision about judicial pensions in relation to the holder of a judicial office who serves as a judge of the Court.

(7)   The Lord Chancellor or the Secretary of State may by order make such transitional provision (including, in particular, provision for a temporary increase in the maximum number of judges) as he considers appropriate in relation to any holder of a judicial office who has completed his service as a judge of the Court.

Parliamentary procedure

19   Statements of compatibility

(1)   A Minister of the Crown in charge of a Bill in either House of Parliament must, before Second Reading of the Bill—

  (a) make a statement to the effect that in his view the provisions of the Bill are compatible with the Convention rights ('a statement of compatibility'); or
  (b) make a statement to the effect that although he is unable to make a statement of compatibility the government nevertheless wishes the House to proceed with the Bill.

(2)   The statement must be in writing and be published in such manner as the Minister making it considers appropriate.

Supplemental

20   Orders etc under this Act

(1)   Any power of a Minister of the Crown to make an order under this Act is exercisable by statutory instrument.

(2)   The power of the Lord Chancellor or the Secretary of State to make rules (other than rules of court) under section 2(3) or 7(9) is exercisable by statutory instrument.

(3)   Any statutory instrument made under section 14, 15 or 16(7) must be laid before Parliament.

(4)   No order may be made by the Lord Chancellor or the Secretary of State under section 1(4), 7(13) or 16(2) unless a draft of the order has been laid before, and approved by, each House of Parliament.

(5)   Any statutory instrument made under section 18(7) or Schedule 4, or to which subsection (2) applies, shall be subject to annulment in pursuance of a resolution of either House of Parliament.

(6)   The power of a Northern Ireland department to make—

    (a) rules under section 2(3)(c) or 7(9)(c), or
    (b) an order under section 7(11),

is exercisable by statutory rule for the purposes of the Statutory Rules (Northern Ireland) Order 1979.

(7)   Any rules made under section 2(3)(c) or 7(9)(c) shall be subject to negative resolution; and section 41(6) of the Interpretation Act (Northern Ireland) 1954 (meaning of 'subject to negative resolution') shall apply as if the power to make the rules were conferred by an Act of the Northern Ireland Assembly.

(8)   No order may be made by a Northern Ireland department under section 7(11) unless a draft of the order has been laid before, and approved by, the Northern Ireland Assembly.

21   Interpretation, etc

(1)   In this Act—

'amend' includes repeal and apply (with or without modifications);
'the appropriate Minister' means the Minister of the Crown having charge of the appropriate authorised government department (within the meaning of the Crown Proceedings Act 1947);
'the Commission' means the European Commission of Human Rights;
'the Convention' means the Convention for the Protection of Human Rights and Fundamental Freedoms, agreed by the Council of Europe at Rome on 4th November 1950 as it has effect for the time being in relation to the United Kingdom;
'declaration of incompatibility' means a declaration under section 4;
'Minister of the Crown' has the same meaning as in the Ministers of the Crown Act 1975;
'Northern Ireland Minister' includes the First Minister and the deputy First Minister in Northern Ireland;
'primary legislation' means any—

    (a) public general Act;
    (b) local and personal Act;

(c) private Act;

(d) Measure of the Church Assembly;

(e) Measure of the General Synod of the Church of England;

(f) Order in Council—

    (i) made in exercise of Her Majesty's Royal Prerogative;

    (ii) made under section 38(1)(a) of the Northern Ireland Constitution Act 1973 or the corresponding provision of the Northern Ireland Act 1998; or

    (iii) amending an Act of a kind mentioned in paragraph (a), (b) or (c);

and includes an order or other instrument made under primary legislation (otherwise than by the National Assembly for Wales, a member of the Scottish Executive, a Northern Ireland Minister or a Northern Ireland department) to the extent to which it operates to bring one or more provisions of that legislation into force or amends any primary legislation;

'the First Protocol' means the protocol to the Convention agreed at Paris on 20th March 1952;

'the Sixth Protocol' means the protocol to the Convention agreed at Strasbourg on 28th April 1983;

'the Eleventh Protocol' means the protocol to the Convention (restructuring the control machinery established by the Convention) agreed at Strasbourg on 11th May 1994;

'remedial order' means an order under section 10;

'subordinate legislation' means any—

(a) Order in Council other than one—

    (i) made in exercise of Her Majesty's Royal Prerogative;

    (ii) made under section 38(1)(a) of the Northern Ireland Constitution Act 1973 or the corresponding provision of the Northern Ireland Act 1998; or

    (iii) amending an Act of a kind mentioned in the definition of primary legislation;

(b) Act of the Scottish Parliament;

(c) Act of the Parliament of Northern Ireland;

(d) Measure of the Assembly established under section 1 of the Northern Ireland Assembly Act 1973;

(e) Act of the Northern Ireland Assembly;

(f) order, rules, regulations, scheme, warrant, byelaw or other instrument made under primary legislation (except to the extent to which it operates to bring one or more provisions of that legislation into force or amends any primary legislation);

(g) order, rules, regulations, scheme, warrant, byelaw or other instrument made under legislation mentioned in paragraph (b), (c), (d) or (e) or made under an Order in Council applying only to Northern Ireland;

(h) order, rules, regulations, scheme, warrant, byelaw or other instrument made by a member of the Scotish Executive, a Northern Ireland Minister or a Northern Ireland department in exercise of prerogative or other executive functions of Her Majesty which are exercisable by such a person on behalf of Her Majesty;

'transferred matters' has the same meaning as in the Northern Ireland Act 1998; and 'tribunal' means any tribunal in which legal proceedings may be brought.

(2)   The references in paragraphs (b) and (c) of section 2(1) to Articles are to Articles of the Convention as they had effect immediately before the coming into force of the Eleventh Protocol.

(3)   The reference in paragraph (d) of section 2(1) to Article 46 includes a reference to Articles 32 and 54 of the Convention as they had effect immediately before the coming into force of the Eleventh Protocol.

(4)   The references in section 2(1) to a report or decision of the Commission or a decision of the Committee of Ministers include references to a report or decision made as provided by paragraphs 3, 4 and 6 of Article 5 of the Eleventh Protocol (transitional provisions).

(5)   Any liability under the Army Act 1955, the Air Force Act 1955 or the Naval Discipline Act 1957 to suffer death for an offence is replaced by a liability to imprisonment for life or any less punishment authorised by those Acts; and those Acts shall accordingly have effect with the necessary modifications.

22   Short title, commencement, application and extent

(1)   This Act may be cited as the Human Rights Act 1998.

(2)   Sections 18 and 20 and this section come into force on the passing of this Act.

(3)   The other provisions of this Act come into force on such day as the Secretary of State may by order appoint; and different days may be appointed for different purposes.

(4)   Paragraph (b) of subsection (1) of section 7 applies to proceedings brought by or at the instigation of a public authority whenever the act in question took place; but otherwise that subsection does not apply to an act taking place before the coming into force of that section.

(5)   This Act binds the Crown.

(6)   This Act extends to Northern Ireland.

(7)   Section 21(5), so far as it relates to any provision contained in the Army Act 1955, the Air Force Act 1955 or the Naval Discipline Act 1957, extends to any place to which that provision extends.

SCHEDULES

SCHEDULE 1

THE ARTICLES

PART I

THE CONVENTION

Rights and Freedoms

Article 2

Right to life

1.   Everyone's right to life shall be protected by law. No one shall be deprived of his life intentionally save in the execution of a sentence of a court following his conviction of a crime for which this penalty is provided by law.

2.   Deprivation of life shall not be regarded as inflicted in contravention of this Article when it results from the use of force which is no more than absolutely necessary:

(a) in defence of any person from unlawful violence;
(b) in order to effect a lawful arrest or to prevent the escape of a person lawfully detained;
(c) in action lawfully taken for the purpose of quelling a riot or insurrection.

Article 3

Prohibition of torture

No one shall be subjected to torture or to inhuman or degrading treatment or punishment.

Article 4

Prohibition of slavery and forced labour

1.   No one shall be held in slavery or servitude.

2.   No one shall be required to perform forced or compulsory labour.

3.   For the purpose of this Article the term 'forced or compulsory labour' shall not include:

(a) any work required to be done in the ordinary course of detention imposed according to the provisions of Article 5 of this Convention or during conditional release from such detention;
(b) any service of a military character or, in case of conscientious objectors in countries where they are recognised, service exacted instead of compulsory military service;
(c) any service exacted in case of an emergency or calamity threatening the life or well-being of the community;

(d) any work or service which forms part of normal civic obligations.

Article 5

Right to liberty and security

1. Everyone has the right to liberty and security of person. No one shall be deprived of his liberty save in the following cases and in accordance with a procedure prescribed by law:

(a) the lawful detention of a person after conviction by a competent court;

(b) the lawful arrest or detention of a person for non-compliance with the lawful order of a court or in order to secure the fulfilment of any obligation prescribed by law;

(c) the lawful arrest or detention of a person effected for the purpose of bringing him before the competent legal authority on reasonable suspicion of having committed an offence or when it is reasonably considered necessary to prevent his committing an offence or fleeing after having done so;

(d) the detention of a minor by lawful order for the purpose of educational supervision or his lawful detention for the purpose of bringing him before the competent legal authority;

(e) the lawful detention of persons for the prevention of the spreading of infectious diseases, of persons of unsound mind, alcoholics or drug addicts or vagrants;

(f) the lawful arrest or detention of a person to prevent his effecting an unauthorised entry into the country or of a person against whom action is being taken with a view to deportation or extradition.

2. Everyone who is arrested shall be informed promptly, in a language which he understands, of the reasons for his arrest and of any charge against him.

3. Everyone arrested or detained in accordance with the provisions of paragraph 1(c) of this Article shall be brought promptly before a judge or other officer authorised by law to exercise judicial power and shall be entitled to trial within a reasonable time or to release pending trial. Release may be conditioned by guarantees to appear for trial.

4. Everyone who is deprived of his liberty by arrest or detention shall be entitled to take proceedings by which the lawfulness of his detention shall be decided speedily by a court and his release ordered if the detention is not lawful.

5. Everyone who has been the victim of arrest or detention in contravention of the provisions of this Article shall have an enforceable right to compensation.

Article 6

Right to a fair trial

1. In the determination of his civil rights and obligations or of any criminal charge against him, everyone is entitled to a fair and public hearing within a reasonable time by an independent and impartial tribunal established by law. Judgment shall be pronounced publicly but the press and public may be excluded from all or part of the trial in the interest of morals, public order or national security in a democratic society, where the interests of juveniles or the protection of the private life of the parties so require, or to the extent strictly necessary in the opinion of the court in special circumstances where publicity would prejudice the interests of justice.

2.   Everyone charged with a criminal offence shall be presumed innocent until proved guilty according to law.

3.   Everyone charged with a criminal offence has the following minimum rights:

(a)   to be informed promptly, in a language which he understands and in detail, of the nature and cause of the accusation against him;
(b)   to have adequate time and facilities for the preparation of his defence;
(c)   to defend himself in person or through legal assistance of his own choosing or, if he has not sufficient means to pay for legal assistance, to be given it free when the interests of justice so require;
(d)   to examine or have examined witnesses against him and to obtain the attendance and examination of witnesses on his behalf under the same conditions as witnesses against him;
(e)   to have the free assistance of an interpreter if he cannot understand or speak the language used in court.

Article 7

No punishment without law

1.   No one shall be held guilty of any criminal offence on account of any act or omission which did not constitute a criminal offence under national or international law at the time when it was committed. Nor shall a heavier penalty be imposed than the one that was applicable at the time the criminal offence was committed.

2.   This Article shall not prejudice the trial and punishment of any person for any act or omission which, at the time when it was committed, was criminal according to the general principles of law recognised by civilised nations.

Article 8

Right to respect for private and family life

1.   Everyone has the right to respect for his private and family life, his home and his correspondence.

2.   There shall be no interference by a public authority with the exercise of this right except such as is in accordance with the law and is necessary in a democratic society in the interests of national security, public safety or the economic well-being of the country, for the prevention of disorder or crime, for the protection of health or morals, or for the protection of the rights and freedoms of others.

Article 9

Freedom of thought, conscience and religion

1.   Everyone has the right to freedom of thought, conscience and religion; this right includes freedom to change his religion or belief and freedom, either alone or in community with others and in public or private, to manifest his religion or belief, in worship, teaching, practice and observance.

2.   Freedom to manifest one's religion or beliefs shall be subject only to such limitations as are prescribed by law and are necessary in a democratic society in the interests of public safety, for the protection of public order, health or morals, or for the protection of the rights and freedoms of others.

Article 10

Freedom of expression

1. Everyone has the right to freedom of expression. This right shall include freedom to hold opinions and to receive and impart information and ideas without interference by public authority and regardless of frontiers. This Article shall not prevent States from requiring the licensing of broadcasting, television or cinema enterprises.

2. The exercise of these freedoms, since it carries with it duties and responsibilities, may be subject to such formalities, conditions, restrictions or penalties as are prescribed by law and are necessary in a democratic society, in the interests of national security, territorial integrity or public safety, for the prevention of disorder or crime, for the protection of health or morals, for the protection of the reputation or rights of others, for preventing the disclosure of information received in confidence, or for maintaining the authority and impartiality of the judiciary.

Article 11

Freedom of assembly and association

1. Everyone has the right to freedom of peaceful assembly and to freedom of association with others, including the right to form and to join trade unions for the protection of his interests.

2. No restrictions shall be placed on the exercise of these rights other than such as are prescribed by law and are necessary in a democratic society in the interests of national security or public safety, for the prevention of disorder or crime, for the protection of health or morals or for the protection of the rights and freedoms of others. This Article shall not prevent the imposition of lawful restrictions on the exercise of these rights by members of the armed forces, of the police or of the administration of the State.

Article 12

Right to marry

Men and women of marriageable age have the right to marry and to found a family, according to the national laws governing the exercise of this right.

Article 14

Prohibition of discrimination

The enjoyment of the rights and freedoms set forth in this Convention shall be secured without discrimination on any ground such as sex, race, colour, language, religion, political or other opinion, national or social origin, association with a national minority, property, birth or other status.

Article 16

Restrictions on political activity of aliens

Nothing in Articles 10, 11 and 14 shall be regarded as preventing the High Contracting Parties from imposing restrictions on the political activity of aliens.

Article 17

Prohibition of abuse of rights

Nothing in this Convention may be interpreted as implying for any State, group or person any right to engage in any activity or perform any act aimed at the destruction of any of the rights and freedoms set forth herein or at their limitation to a greater extent than is provided for in the Convention.

Article 18

Limitation on use of restrictions on rights

The restrictions permitted under this Convention to the said rights and freedoms shall not be applied for any purpose other than those for which they have been prescribed.

PART II

THE FIRST PROTOCOL

Article 1

Protection of property

Every natural or legal person is entitled to the peaceful enjoyment of his possessions. No one shall be deprived of his possessions except in the public interest and subject to the conditions provided for by law and by the general principles of international law.

The preceding provisions shall not, however, in any way impair the right of a State to enforce such laws as it deems necessary to control the use of property in accordance with the general interest or to secure the payment of taxes or other contributions or penalties.

Article 2

Right to education

No person shall be denied the right to education. In the exercise of any functions which it assumes in relation to education and to teaching, the State shall respect the right of parents to ensure such education and teaching in conformity with their own religious and philosophical convictions.

Article 3

Right to free elections

The High Contracting Parties undertake to hold free elections at reasonable intervals by secret ballot, under conditions which will ensure the free expression of the opinion of the people in the choice of the legislature.

PART III

THE SIXTH PROTOCOL

Article 1

Abolition of the death penalty

The death penalty shall be abolished. No one shall be condemned to such penalty or executed.

Article 2

Death penalty in time of war

A State may make provisions in its law for the death penalty in respect of acts committed in time of war or of imminent threat of war; such penalty shall be applied only in the instances laid down in the law and in accordance with its provisions. The State shall communicate to the Secretary of the Council of Europe the relevant provisions of that law.

SCHEDULE 2

REMEDIAL ORDERS

Orders

1.—(1)   A remedial order may—

(a) contain such incidental, supplemental, consequential or transitional provision as the person making it considers appropriate;
(b) be made so as to have effect from a date earlier than that on which it is made;
(c) make provision for the delegation of specific functions;
(d) make different provision for different cases.

(2)   The power conferred by sub-paragraph (1)(a) includes—

(a) power to amend primary legislation (including primary legislation other than that which contains the incompatible provision); and
(b) power to amend or revoke subordinate legislation (including subordinate legislation other than that which contains the incompatible provision).

(3)   A remedial order may be made so as to have the same extent as the legislation which it affects.

(4)   No person is to be guilty of an offence solely as a result of the retrospective effect of a remedial order.

Procedure

2.   No remedial order may be made unless—

(a) a draft of the order has been approved by a resolution of each House of Parliament made after the end of the period of 60 days beginning with the day on which the draft was laid; or
(b) it is declared in the order that it appears to the person making it that, because of the urgency of the matter, it is necessary to make the order without a draft being so approved.

Orders laid in draft

3.—(1)   No draft may be laid under paragraph 2(a) unless—

(a) the person proposing to make the order has laid before Parliament a document which contains a draft of the proposed order and the required information; and
(b) the period of 60 days, beginning with the day on which the document required by this sub-paragraph was laid, has ended.

(2)   If representations have been made during that period, the draft laid under paragraph 2(a) must be accompanied by a statement containing—

(a) a summary of the representations; and
(b) if, as a result of the representations, the proposed order has been changed, details of the changes.

Urgent cases

4.—(1)   If a remedial order ('the original order') is made without being approved in draft, the person making it must lay it before Parliament, accompanied by the required information, after it is made.

(2) If representations have been made during the period of 60 days beginning with the day on which the original order was made, the person making it must (after the end of that period) lay before Parliament a statement containing—

(a) a summary of the representations; and
(b) if, as a result of the representations, he considers it appropriate to make changes to the original order, details of the changes.

(3)   If sub-paragraph (2)(b) applies, the person making the statement must—

(a) make a further remedial order replacing the original order; and
(b) lay the replacement order before Parliament.

(4)   If, at the end of the period of 120 days beginning with the day on which the original order was made, a resolution has not been passed by each House approving the original or replacement order, the order ceases to have effect (but without that affecting anything previously done under either order or the power to make a fresh remedial order).

Definitions

5.   In this Schedule—

'representations' means representations about a remedial order (or proposed remedial order) made to the person making (or proposing to make) it and includes any relevant Parliamentary report or resolution; and
'required information' means—

(a) an explanation of the incompatibility which the order (or proposed order) seeks to remove, including particulars of the relevant declaration, finding or order; and
(b) a statement of the reasons for proceeding under section 10 and for making an order in those terms.

Calculating periods

6. In calculating any period for the purposes of this Schedule, no account is to be taken of any time during which—

(a) Parliament is dissolved or prorogued; or
(b) both Houses are adjourned for more than four days.

SCHEDULE 3

DEROGATION AND RESERVATION

PART I

DEROGATION

The 1988 notification

The United Kingdom Permanent Representative to the Council of Europe presents his compliments to the Secretary General of the Council, and has the honour to convey the following information in order to ensure compliance with the obligations of Her Majesty's Government in the United Kingdom under Article 15(3) of the Convention for the Protection of Human Rights and Fundamental Freedoms signed at Rome on 4 November 1950.

There have been in the United Kingdom in recent years campaigns of organised terrorism connected with the affairs of Northern Ireland which have manifested themselves in activities which have included repeated murder, attempted murder, maiming, intimidation and violent civil disturbance and in bombing and fire raising which have resulted in death, injury and widespread destruction of property. As a result, a public emergency within the meaning of Article 15(1) of the Convention exists in the United Kingdom.

The Government found it necessary in 1974 to introduce and since then, in cases concerning persons reasonably suspected of involvement in terrorism connected with the affairs of Northern Ireland, or of certain offences under the legislation, who have been detained for 48 hours, to exercise powers enabling further detention without charge, for periods of up to five days, on the authority of the Secretary of State. These powers are at present to be found in Section 12 of the Prevention of Terrorism (Temporary Provisions) Act 1984, Article 9 of the Prevention of Terrorism (Supplemental Temporary Provisions) Order 1984 and Article 10 of the Prevention of Terrorism (Supplemental Temporary Provisions) (Northern Ireland) Order 1984.

Section 12 of the Prevention of Terrorism (Temporary Provisions) Act 1984 provides for a person whom a constable has arrested on reasonable grounds of suspecting him to be guilty of an offence under Section 1, 9 or 10 of the Act, or to be or to have been involved in terrorism connected with the affairs of Northern Ireland, to be detained in right of the arrest for up to 48 hours and thereafter, where the Secretary of State extends the detention period, for up to a further five days. Section 12 substantially re-enacted Section 12 of the Prevention of Terrorism (Temporary Provisions) Act 1976 which, in turn, substantially re-enacted Section 7 of the Prevention of Terrorism (Temporary Provisions) Act 1974.

Article 10 of the Prevention of Terrorism (Supplemental Temporary Provisions) (Northern Ireland) Order 1984 (SI 1984/417) and Article 9 of the Prevention of

Terrorism (Supplemental Temporary Provisions) Order 1984 (SI 1984/418) were both made under Sections 13 and 14 of and Schedule 3 to the 1984 Act and substantially re-enacted powers of detention in Orders made under the 1974 and 1976 Acts. A person who is being examined under Article 4 of either Order on his arrival in, or on seeking to leave, Northern Ireland or Great Britain for the purpose of determining whether he is or has been involved in terrorism connected with the affairs of Northern Ireland, or whether there are grounds for suspecting that he has committed an offence under Section 9 of the 1984 Act, may be detained under Article 4 or 10, as appropriate, pending the conclusion of his examination. The period of this examination may exceed 12 hours if an examining officer has reasonable grounds for suspecting him to be or to have been involved in acts of terrorism connected with the affairs of Northern Ireland.

Where such a person is detained under the said Article 9 or 10 he may be detained for up to 48 hours on the authority of an examining officer and thereafter, where the Secretary of State extends the detention period, for up to a further five days.

In its judgment of 29 November 1988 in the Case of *Brogan and Others*, the European Court of Human Rights held that there had been a violation of Article 5(3) in respect of each of the applicants, all of whom had been detained under Section 12 of the 1984 Act. The Court held that even the shortest of the four periods of detention concerned, namely four days and six hours, fell outside the constraints as to time permitted by the first part of Article 5(3). In addition, the Court held that there had been a violation of Article 5(3) in the case of each applicant.

Following this judgment, the Secretary of State for the Home Department informed Parliament on 6 December 1988 that, against the background of the terrorist campaign, and the over-riding need to bring terrorists to justice, the Government did not believe that the maximum period of detention should be reduced. He informed Parliament that the Government were examining the matter with a view to responding to the judgment. On 22 December 1988, the Secretary of State further informed Parliament that it remained the Government's wish, if it could be achieved, to find a judicial process under which extended detention might be reviewed and where appropriate authorised by a judge or other judicial officer. But a further period of reflection and consultation was necessary before the Government could bring forward a firm and final view.

Since the judgment of 29 November as well as previously, the Government have found it necessary to continue to exercise, in relation to terrorism connected with the affairs of Northern Ireland, the powers described above enabling further detention without charge for periods of up to 5 days, on the authority of the Secretary of State, to the extent strictly required by the exigencies of the situation to enable necessary enquiries and investigations properly to be completed in order to decide whether criminal proceedings should be instituted. To the extent that the exercise of these powers may be inconsistent with the obligations imposed by the Convention the Government has availed itself of the right of derogation conferred by Article 15(1) of the Convention and will continue to do so until further notice.

Dated 23 December 1988.

The 1989 notification

The United Kingdom Permanent Representative to the Council of Europe presents his compliments to the Secretary General of the Council, and has the honour to convey the following information.

In his communication to the Secretary General of 23 December 1988, reference was made to the introduction and exercise of certain powers under section 12 of the Prevention of Terrorism (Temporary Provisions) Act 1984, Article 9 of the Prevention of Terrorism (Supplemental Temporary Provisions) Order 1984 and Article 10 of the Prevention of Terrorism (Supplemental Temporary Provisions) (Northern Ireland) Order 1984.

These provisions have been replaced by section 14 of and paragraph 6 of Schedule 5 to the Prevention of Terrorism (Temporary Provisions) Act 1989, which make comparable provision. They came into force on 22 March 1989. A copy of these provisions is enclosed.

The United Kingdom Permanent Representative avails himself of this opportunity to renew to the Secretary General the assurance of his highest consideration.

23 March 1989.

PART II

RESERVATION

At the time of signing the present (First) Protocol, I declare that, in view of certain provisions of the Education Acts in the United Kingdom, the principle affirmed in the second sentence of Article 2 is accepted by the United Kingdom only so far as it is compatible with the provision of efficient instruction and training, and the avoidance of unreasonable public expenditure.

Dated 20 March 1952. Made by the United Kingdom Permanent Representative to the Council of Europe.

SCHEDULE 4

JUDICIAL PENSIONS

Duty to make orders about pensions

1.—(1) The appropriate Minister must by order make provision with respect to pensions payable to or in respect of any holder of a judicial office who serves as an ECHR judge.

(2) A pensions order must include such provision as the Minister making it considers is necessary to secure that—

  (a) an ECHR judge who was, immediately before his appointment as an ECHR judge, a member of a judicial pension scheme is entitled to remain as a member of that scheme;
  (b) the terms on which he remains a member of the scheme are those which would have been applicable had he not been appointed as an ECHR judge; and
  (c) entitlement to benefits payable in accordance with the scheme continues to be determined as if, while serving as an ECHR judge, his salary was that which would (but for section 18(4)) have been payable to him in respect of his continuing service as the holder of his judicial office.

Contributions

2.   A pensions order may, in particular, make provision—

(a)   for any contributions which are payable by a person who remains a member of a scheme as a result of the order, and which would otherwise be payable by deduction from his salary, to be made otherwise than by deduction from his salary as an ECHR judge; and

(b)   for such contributions to be collected in such manner as may be determined by the administrators of the scheme.

Amendments of other enactments

3.   A pensions order may amend any provision of, or made under, a pensions Act in such manner and to such extent as the Minister making the order considers necessary or expedient to ensure the proper administration of any scheme to which it relates.

Definitions

4.   In this Schedule—

'appropriate Minister' means—

(a)   in relation to any judicial office whose jurisdiction is exercisable exclusively in relation to Scotland, the Secretary of State; and

(b)   otherwise, the Lord Chancellor;

'ECHR judge' means the holder of a judicial office who is serving as a judge of the Court; 'judicial pension scheme' means a scheme established by and in accordance with a pensions Act; 'pensions Act' means—

(a)   the County Courts Act (Northern Ireland) 1959;

(b)   the Sheriffs' Pensions (Scotland) Act 1961;

(c)   the Judicial Pensions Act 1981; or

(d)   the Judicial Pensions and Retirement Act 1993; and

'pensions order' means an order made under paragraph 1.

INDEX

References are to paragraph numbers.